Religion, Politics and Society in Britain 1066–1272

Religion, Politics and Society in Britain

Series editor: Keith Robbins

The Conversion of Britain: Religion, Politics and Society in Britain, 600–800
Barbara Yorke

The Age of Reformation: The Tudor and Stewart Realms, 1485–1603
Alec Ryrie

The Post-Reformation: Religion, Politics and Society in Britain, 1603–1714
John Spurr

Eighteenth-Century Britain: Religion and Politics, 1714–1815
Nigel Yates

Providence and Empire: Religion, Politics and Society in the United Kingdom, 1815–1914
Stewart Brown

Religion and Society in Twentieth-Century Britain
Callum G. Brown

Religion, Politics and Society in Britain 1066–1272

Henry Mayr-Harting

Longman
is an imprint of

Harlow, England • London • New York • Boston • San Francisco • Toronto
Sydney • Tokyo • Singapore • Hong Kong • Seoul • Taipei • New Delhi
Cape Town • Madrid • Mexico City • Amsterdam • Munich • Paris • Milan

PEARSON EDUCATION LIMITED

Edinburgh Gate
Harlow CM20 2JE
United Kingdom
Tel: +44 (0)1279 623623
Fax: +44 (0)1279 431059
Website: www.pearsoned.co.uk

First edition published in Great Britain in 2011

Pearson Education is not responsible for the content of third party internet sites.

ISBN: 978-0-582-41413-6

British Library Cataloguing in Publication Data
A CIP catalogue record for this book can be obtained from the British Library

Library of Congress Cataloging in Publication Data
Mayr-Harting, Henry.
  Religion, politics, and society in Britain, 1066–1272 / Henry Mayr-Harting. – 1st ed.
    p. cm. – (Religion, politics, and society in Britain)
  Includes bibliographical references (p.   ) and index.
  ISBN 978-0-582-41413-6 (pbk.)
    1. Great Britain–Church history–1066–1485.   2. Christianity and politics–Great
Britain–History–To 1500.   I. Title.
  BR746.M39 2011
  274.2'04–dc22
                                                                        2010052008

10 9 8 7 6 5 4 3 2 1
15 14 13 12 11

Set by 35 in 10/13.5pt Sabon
Printed and bound in Malaysia (CTP-VP)

To Felix and Loredana
Ursula and Robin

Contents

Series Editor's Preface   x

Acknowledgements   xii

Abbreviations   xiv

Introduction   xv

1   Church and Economy in the Long
Twelfth Century   1

2   The Church and the Norman Conquest   22

The Gregorian Reform 22
Lanfranc 28
Gervase 37

3   Henry I and His Religion   45

Religion and friendship 45
The Investiture Contest in England 49
The primacy dispute between Canterbury and York 56
Henry I, Melbourne church and Athelwold of Carlisle 65
Conclusion 72

4   The Conflict between Henry II and Thomas Becket   74

Introduction 74
The first year of Becket as Archbishop 75
What the breach might have been about, but was not 76
The breach: Canterbury rights 80
Clash of personalities 85
Dramatic gesturing 86
Becket's 'conversion' 87
Why did Becket's death create a sensation? 89
Becket and theology 91

5   Parishes and Parish Priests   95

Parish religion and the 'higher culture' 95
The legal reforms of Henry II and parish priests 103
  What was *novel disseisin*? 104
  When did *novel disseisin* as a civil action come in? 105
  What had the parish clergy to do with all this? 108
Parish churches 112
The rise of clericalism 119
Cathedrals and parish religion 124

6   The Monastic Century 1066–1216   130

Introduction 130
The black monks 133
  Liturgy and ritual 133
  Material interests 136
  Black-monk shrines 137
  Shrines and their communities 142
  Kings and black-monk shrines 146
The Cistercians 148
  Cistercian economy and religion 148
  The Cistercians and political life 155
  The founding of Beaulieu Abbey (Hampshire) 162
The Augustinian Canons 166
  Llanthony and Nostell 168
  The *Bridlington Dialogue* and Bridlington Priory 169
  St Frideswide's Priory, Oxford 176
  Henry I and the Augustinian Canons 179
Women's religious houses 179

7   Archbishop Hubert Walter and St Hugh of Lincoln:
        Church and King in the Late Twelfth Century   183

Hubert Walter 186
St Hugh, Bishop of Lincoln (1186–1200) 193
Conclusion 203

8   Intellectual Life and Culture and How They Related
        to Politics in the Twelfth and Early Thirteenth
        Century   205

Science and the Exchequer under Henry I 205
The writing of history and Stephen's reign 210
The beginnings of legal study at Oxford in the reign of
  Henry II 216
The theologisation of society 221

9   The Early English Franciscans   229

Poverty 229
Poverty and learning 233
Poverty and learning in England 236
Confession 240
Learning and politics 247

10 Changes and Continuities under Henry III   259

Pope, king and church 259
Parish clergy revisited 266
Monasteries 273

Notes   280
Select Bibliography   325
Index   339

Series Editor's Preface

No understanding of British history is possible without grappling with the relationship between religion, politics and society. How that should be done, however, is another matter. Historians of religion, who have frequently thought of themselves as ecclesiastical historians, have had one set of preoccupations. Political historians have had another. They have acknowledged, however, that both religion and politics can only be understood, in any given period, in a social context. This series makes the interplay between religion, politics and society its preoccupation. Even so, it does not assume that what is entailed by religion and politics remains the same throughout, to be considered as a constant in separate volumes merely because of the passage of time.

In its completed form the series will have probed the nature of these links from c. 600 to the present day and offered a perspective, over such a long period, that has not before been attempted in a systematic fashion. There is, however, no straitjacket that requires individual authors to adhere to a common understanding of what such an undertaking involves. Even if there could be a general agreement about concepts, that is to say about what religion is or how politics can be identified, the social context of such categorisations is not static. The spheres notionally allocated to the one or to the other alter with the circumstances. Sometimes it might appear that they cannot be separated. Sometimes it might appear that they sharply conflict. Each period under review will have its defining characteristics in this regard.

It is the Christian religion, in its manifold institutional manifestations, with which authors are overwhelmingly concerned since it is with conversion that the series begins. It ends, however, with a volume in which Christianity exists alongside other world religions but in a society frequently perceived to be secular. Yet, what de-Christianisation is taken to be depends upon what Christianisation has been taken to be. There is, therefore, a relationship between topics that are tackled in the first volume, and those considered in the last, which might at first seem unlikely. In between, of course, are the 'Christian Centuries' which, despite their label, are no less full of 'boundary disputes', both before and after the Reformation. The perspective of the series, additionally, is broadly pan-insular. The Britain of 600 is plainly not the Britain of the early twenty-first century. However, the current political structures of Britain–Ireland have arguably owed as much to religion as to politics. Christendom has been inherently ambiguous.

It would be surprising if readers, not to mention authors, understood the totality of the picture that is presented in the same way. What is common, however, is a realisation that the narrative of religion, politics and society in Britain is not a simple tale that points in a single direction but rather one of enduring and by no means exhausted complexity.

Keith Robbins

Acknowledgements

It may seem surprising to some that after publishing two books on the tenth-century Ottonians, their art, religious culture and intellectual world, I should, as if suddenly, produce a book on religion in Britain from 1066 to 1272. But it is not sudden at all. My doctoral thesis was on the Bishops of Chichester and their documents in the twelfth century. Since the 1960s, therefore, the Carolingians and Ottonians on the one hand and twelfth-century British (more particularly English) history on the other have been two parallel and absorbing strands in my studies and teaching. For many years in Oxford I gave undergraduate lecture courses on English History 1066–1215 generally, or on Religion, Politics and Society in England for the same period, and these lectures have formed a part-basis of the present book.

While this book was in preparation I received a British Academy grant, which I acknowledge with gratitude, to have a part-time Research Assistant for six months. That was Timothy Crafter. Tim was marvellous. He understood perfectly what I needed and helped me a great deal with the bibliography and with sorting out some knotty problems. His influence would have been more apparent had so much of it not been preventative – warning me against certain lines of argument and forestalling my gaffes (any which remain are entirely my responsibility). It was always stimulating to talk with him.

In an important sense my help has lain in all those historians whose publications I have used and cited, as well as some others whom I have not cited but who have influenced me. Amongst others to whom I am indebted I wish to mention above all Christopher Brooke, who has been a guiding spirit to me since I was a lecturer in his department at the University of Liverpool in the 1960s; and also to Hugh Doherty, the late Valerie Flint, David Howlett, John Maddicott, Stella Panayotova, Richard Sharpe, and Nicholas Vincent. None of these is responsible for any defects or errors.

I owe a large debt of gratitude to my wife, Caroline, for much general support and encouragement, and in particular for typing the list of abbreviations and the select bibliography. I am also grateful for the help and kindness I have received from Keith Robbins, most astute and sympathetic of General Editors, and from Mari Shullaw and Josie O'Donoghue at Pearson and latterly from Kathy Auger.

For some of the illustrations I am indebted to the photographic skills of friends; for the two of Iffley church to Roger Ainsworth, and for that of Melbourne church to Sarah Railton. I thank the vicars/rectors of both churches for their permission to use these photographs in my book. For permission to reproduce the illustration from the St Albans Psalter I am grateful to the Dombibliothek of Hildesheim, and for help to its Director, Jochen Bepler. I am grateful to David Sansom for the map of the region of Bridlington.

Publisher's Acknowledgements

We are grateful to the following for permission to reproduce copyright material:

Plate 1 © Holmes Garden Photos/Alamy; Plate 2 © The Print Collector/ Alamy; Plates 3 and 4 courtesy of Roger Ainsworth; Plate 5 courtesy of Dombibliothek Hildesheim; Plate 6 courtesy of Sarah Railton; Plate 7 © Cotswolds Photo Library/Alamy; Plate 8 by Richard Chevis, by permission of the Bishop of Chichester.

Map on page 171 by David Sansom.

Abbreviations

CCCM = Corpus Christianorum Continuatio Mediaevalis (Brepols, Turnhout)

C and S = *Councils and Synods with other documents relating to the English Church*, II, Part I, 1205–1265, eds F.M. Powicke and C.R. Cheney (1964)

CS = Camden Series (Royal Historical Society)

EEA = English Episcopal Acta (British Academy Series): EEA 1, ed. David Smith; EEA 4, ed. David Smith; EEA 9, ed. Nicholas Vincent; EEA 10 ed. Frances Ramsey; EEA 18, ed. B.R. Kemp; EEA 20, ed. Marie Lovatt; EEA 24, ed. M.G. Snape; EEA 26, ed. D.P. Johnson

EETS = Early English Text Society

EHD = *English Historical Documents* (1042–1189, ed. D.C. Douglas, 1953; 1189–1327, ed. Harry Rothwell, 1975)

EHR = *English Historical Review*

EYC = *Early Yorkshire Charters*, eds W. Farrer and C.T. Clay (12 vols, 1914–65)

JEH = *Journal of Ecclesiastical History*

MTB = *Materials for the History of Thomas Becket*, 6 vols, ed. J. Craigie Robertson, RS 67 (1875–83)

MV = *Magna Vita S. Hugonis, The Life of St Hugh of Lincoln*, eds Decima Douie and Hugh Farmer (2 vols, 1961, 1962)

ODNB = *Oxford Dictionary of National Biography* (2004)

PRS = Pipe Roll Society

RS = Rolls Series (HM Stationery Office)

TRHS = *Transactions of the Royal Historical Society*

VCH = Victoria County History

Introduction

The period of British history covered by this volume is an important, almost dramatic one, in terms of the interaction of religion, politics and society. First of all there was the Gregorian Reform of the Papacy in the later eleventh century, which revolutionised the concept of how the clergy and the laity related to each other and began the effective governmental domination of the church by the papacy in the medieval West. Not one chapter of this book can shake itself free of this revolution in European history.

Next, during the period, two radically innovative forms of the Christian religion were developed, one by the Cistercians of the twelfth century, the other by the Friars of the thirteenth. When Ralph Haget, Abbot of the Cistercian monastery of Fountains in the 1190s, said of his inner vision, or experience of the Trinity while he chanted two verses of the Psalm, *Confitemini Domino*, that 'from that moment no misfortune, no sadness has ever come to me which could not be mitigated by the remembrance of that vision, and such a confidence and hope was poured into my soul by this showing, that I could never after doubt of my salvation', he was saying something that an eighteenth-century Methodist might well have been able to repeat, but which I doubt could have been said by anyone in so personal a way before 1050 or 1100. The Cistercians of course accepted papal and episcopal authority, but there was an implicit challenge from them, in giving such weight to inner spiritual experience, against all external ecclesiastical authority, and even against some of the effects of the Gregorian Reform itself. And in their truly Protestant sense of personal calling can be seen a response to the older Benedictine monasteries becoming filled, under demographic pressure, with conscript armies of sometimes unwilling or unsuitable recruits. Despite this the twelfth century was also a period of exceptional vibrancy for many traditional Benedictine monasteries, and for the regular canons. Where the Friars are concerned, one may see their espousal of poverty, particularly with the Franciscans, and their espousal of learning, as a reaction to the build-up of wealth by many ecclesiastical institutions including Cistercian, and to the fact that mere logic-choppers in the academic world were starting to be big earners. They moved, welcomed, into the University of Paris, where their abhorrences had already been articulated by the school of moral theologians under Peter the Chanter in the last decades of the twelfth century.

Our period was also one of many arresting personalities: amongst kings in relation to religion at least David I of Scotland; amongst political bishops Lanfranc, Thomas Becket, and Hubert Walter of Canterbury, Thurstan of York, St Hugh and Robert Grosseteste of Lincoln, and Richard of Wych of Chichester; amongst spiritual leaders St Anselm, Ailred of Rievaulx and Haymo of Faversham; amongst potent holy persons or recluses Christina of Markyate, Wulfric of Haselbury and Godric of Finchale; amongst outstanding writers William of Malmesbury, John of Salisbury, Jocelin of Brakelond, and the author of the *Song of Lewes*; amongst exceptional scholars/scientists Adelard of Bath, Alexander Nequam, Robert Grosseteste, and Richard Rufus of Cornwall; and amongst laymen in relation to religion Simon de Montfort and others. These are not people with medieval quirks which make them inaccessible to the understanding of us moderns. They are human beings, who can speak to us from their own situations as directly as human beings of stature can from any age.

I do not hesitate to call the people I have named Christian humanists, in the sense that their religious values were also human values, supported (where relevant) by what we would call humane learning. This may prompt the reader to ask where in my book has that well-known phenomenon, 'The Twelfth-Century Renaissance', got to. My answer is that it is everywhere, but I do not use the label in a litanising way.

What is this book about? In today's culture everyone has to have a 'story'. My story is not a narrative of political events or ecclesiastical politics. Narrative histories can be highly illuminating in the hands of historians like David Carpenter. But often they seem to me to lack explanatory force as to change and continuity. On one occasion a review of a collection of analytical papers centred on Richard I's reign, which I was asked to write for a national Sunday broadsheet, was rejected on the grounds that I had not 'told the story'. What story was that? No doubt they wanted a rousing narrative about the life and deeds of Richard the Lionheart, spiced up with a few disparaging remarks about the author (whom in actual fact I admire). On the other hand, I do not entirely go along with the flight from politics, which one may note sometimes among historians. Robert Bartlett's *England under the Norman and Angevin*

Kings, indeed relatively devoid of politics, represents an outstanding achievement, which I have constantly drawn on. In general, however, to feed the widespread and rather manufactured disillusionment with politics and politicians, by giving the impression that politics does not matter, can be a dangerous game for a historian to play. When I gave the lectures to students, which are partly the basis for this book, those students were facing examination questions that were in my opinion *too* political on balance. So I used to say that my lectures might help them to take a broader view of what politics was, thus bringing relevantly into their answers social, cultural and religious perspectives.

Hence Keith Robbins's invitation to contribute to his series, *Religion, Politics and Society* was very welcome to me, because I felt that the purpose of his series and my approach were ideally suited to each other.

What, then, is my 'story'? It is a story first and foremost about how a constantly changing religious culture impacted in various ways on politics and political culture. The phrase 'political culture' is itself one of contested meaning nowadays. I mean it in the most neutral and untheoretical possible sense of how power relations and patronage actually worked, and how people thought about these. One cannot of course mean anything with absolute neutrality. There will be those who say, quite rightly, that to study the impact of religious culture on political culture is in itself anything but a neutral approach to the examination of power relations. So perhaps I should agree that I have my own not entirely neutral vantage point, like anyone else, but that I have tried not to allow my perception of what the political culture is to be distorted by it.

But my story has at least two different levels to it. It is also about the impact of religious culture on society as a whole, as the title of the series suggests to be appropriate. When one is talking about religion as an ingredient in the sense of community within the shires and hundreds and villages or parishes, however, one is still talking about politics. For as I have been constantly at pains to argue (this is not an assumption or a premise) there is a continuum in the political culture between 'higher' politics (kings, barons, bishops, etc.) and the politics of the localities.

At this point the reader may wish to raise a question: is it possible to study the impact of a religious culture on a political culture and a society without also by reverse, studying the impact of the society and its political culture on the religious culture? It is emphatically not possible, and in this book the reader will see it constantly happening beginning with the opening chapter, where an attempt is made to show the impact on the church and religion of the agrarian and commercial expansion of the twelfth century. Further on, to give just two examples, neither the shrines of black-monk monasteries nor the religious/economic character of Cistercian monasteries are explicable without considering the needs of a society of burgeoning wealth. Nor are the friars of the thirteenth century explicable without the already developing urbanisation of Britain. Moreover it is impossible to suppose that the massive attempt to Christianise the parishes could have occurred without having a profound effect on the Christianity which made this effort, e.g. in the educational standards of the clergy, and in the heightened sense of the authority with which they felt themselves to be invested.

We must also take into account the whole nature of politics in our period, so utterly different from our own. When we talk about politics, in modern times we are thinking of capital cities with rulers or political bodies, where bureaucracies are primarily located, and where political events and speeches principally happen. Twelfth-century Britain was not at all like this, and it was only beginning to happen in England in the thirteenth century. For most of our period the English kings were itinerant, moving in England and in their French dominions from one royal centre to another. Royal ministers or administrators were mostly clerics. Bishops and many abbots were important secular as well as spiritual lords. When, like Richard I on crusade, kings were away from their kingdom, power readily fell into the hands of grandee churchmen like Hubert Walter, Archbishop of Canterbury. There was no lay bureaucracy as such. The whole image of kingship was largely constructed by churchmen. There were no humanists who were not Christian humanists. So religion and politics were intertwined, each suffused with the other, in a way impossible from the sixteenth century onwards. All this means that we are far from being able to distinguish religious culture and political culture as two separate forces impacting on each other. They are too much mingled with each other for that.

The reader will see that I have often been concerned with the history of the other countries of Britain besides England. But I cannot deny that this is a distinctly Anglo-centric book, at least as to the rest of Britain. That is not only because I know more about England and better understand it. It is also because I have conceived the whole study in such a way that the English sources for it are immeasurably more abundant than those for any other parts of Britain.

There may be readers who feel that my treatment of some important themes has been inadequate. Why, for instance, have I not said more about religion and national identity? On this particular theme I have said some things of relevance in relation to Wales and Scotland, and even to England when writing of the thirteenth-century Robert Grosseteste. However, I am not sure how much religion as such had to do with national identity in the Britain of my period. Religion is not necessarily an important element in the rise of a national identity. Rees Davies brilliantly showed how much English domination in this period had to do with the rise of national identity in Wales, Scotland and Ireland. But religion, or even ecclesiastical politics, played little part in his analysis. John Gillingham, in his *The English in the Twelfth Century*, has shown that there was a resurgence of English national identity in the mid-twelfth century, in which clerics, with their literary interests, played no small part. But as he himself says, quoting Diana Greenway on the archdeacon, Henry of Huntingdon, these were clerics 'passionately concerned with the history of secular power' (p. 141). It would be a mistake to think of religion as being the force in the articulation of national identity in twelfth- and thirteenth-century Britain that Catholicism was in twentieth-century Poland, Orthodoxy has been in Russia, or Hinduism is to some Indian nationalists. For more on this, and on the significance of the *Ecclesia Anglicana* in the twelfth century, see pp. 184–5.

All the same, to those who think that I should have said more about this or any other theme, I quote the words of a friend of mine when I observed to him that in a very fine book of his there was nothing about X, naming what I thought an important topic. He replied disarmingly, 'I didn't think it necessary to write about X, while there were people like you around to do so!'

CHAPTER 1

Church and Economy in the Long Twelfth Century

The ideas of both *the* church and *the* economy are in an important sense anachronistic for this period. The concepts of the universal church and of the English church (not the British church) were of course there in the background, but in the foreground what generally mattered most to people were their own individual churches – the church of Christ Church Canterbury, the church of St Augustine's Canterbury, the church of Bath, the church of Wells, the parish church of Kirklevington, etc. So when I talk about the church, I am usually talking about observable trends or tendencies or mentalities within the churches. Again, for this period it would be absurd to think of an entity called the economy of a country which anybody could perceive as a whole, let alone try to manage. But that does not make it nonsense to observe some widespread economic trends or developments occurring in various parts of the country, not least within the churches, which because of the preservation of their records often give us our best evidence of such developments.

There can be no doubt that the long twelfth century, say from the Norman Conquest of 1066 to Magna Carta of 1215, saw a great rise in population and economic prosperity.[1] Within Britain the evidence for this is by far the clearest in England. How do we know about population in twelfth-century England? We do not have censuses; they started only in 1801. We do not have parish registers, which have enabled the Cambridge Institute of Demography to make great strides forward in the study of their subject; they started only in the sixteenth century. For twelfth-century demography we are not in a world of accurate quantitative measurement. Nonetheless we have strong if impressionistic indications that population was rising, of which nobody doubts the validity. They relate partly to evident pressures on land – the assarting (forest clearance for cultivation) and draining of lands, or the demand for peasant tenancies; partly to the large numbers of new towns being established and established ones being enlarged; and partly to the ease with which the new religious orders, like the Cistercians, Augustinians and Gilbertines, could recruit not only many monks and nuns but also thousands of lay brothers to act as their labour force.[2] This rise in population carried on continuously throughout the thirteenth century, and here we get a new kind of evidence for it, new because it comes from a type of manorial account which landlords only began to keep in the thirteenth century, but evidence of pressure on land entirely congruent with that of the twelfth century. This evidence is the writs of entry, showing that landlords could continue to charge peasants a high price when they entered on a land tenancy.[3]

A neat example of the importance of assarts comes from Peterborough Abbey. The abbey nearly went broke as a result of the Norman Conquest and the Norman abbots using its lands to reward their followers, military and otherwise. It was saved in the twelfth century by the new wealth acquired from assarting on its lands in Northamptonshire. This process was already well under way by 1143 when King Stephen granted Peterborough freedom from secular impositions for its assarts there.[4] None of it, however, would have been any good to the abbey if it could not find tenants for its new holdings.

The Cambridge demographic research has shown that, on its evidence, the key factor in demographic growth is nuptiality, namely the age at which people get married. The younger they tend to marry, the greater the rise in population. We have no evidence for this factor in the twelfth century. On the Cambridge showing, however, the growth in the means to feed and care for people once they are born cannot be taken as revealing the cause of population growth, but it can be seen as a response to and stimulated by it. In the pages of the *Economic History Review* during the 1950s, two fine social and economic historians had a debate about the estates of Glastonbury Abbey, Somerset. Reginald Lennard said that by 1189 20 Glastonbury manors had peasants occupying some of its demesnes, i.e. lands which would otherwise have been directly administered by the abbey and from which it would directly draw all the profits. M.M. Postan replied that this was only since the previous Glastonbury estates survey of 1171, and that therefore there were far more of such peasant holdings than Lennard had thought.[5] Both of them saw this only from the point of view of the landlord, Postan thus taking the gloomier view of the Glastonbury Abbey economy. But the situation was obviously good for peasants who wanted to feed their families. So was all the assarting and draining of lands in Lincolnshire at the same time, as H.E. Hallam showed; to a great extent, he wrote, this was 'a small man's enterprise'.[6] In fact it is now argued that in many twelfth-century villages the pattern and conditions of peasant tenancies did not evolve gradually but were created at a stroke, with an implication that peasants had at least some bargaining power on their side.[7] In this connection, one cannot help observing that in the accounts of miracles of healing collected at saints' shrines, of which more later and which are so revealing of social ills, there is very little evidence of anything like malnutrition. At his Canterbury shrine, Thomas Becket was far more likely to have to cure you of insomnia or constipation, typical ills not of economic misery but of rising economic opportunities![8]

One may question whether the spread of peasant holdings on to the demesnes of landlords was such a bad business for landlords either. In the expanding economy of the twelfth century landlords needed labour to meet new consumer demand, whether in the form of labour services due from the tenancies or of money in the form of rents to pay for labour. In the twelfth century landlords often did not try to maximise their profits either by direct management of much of their estates or by drawing up written accounts for their manors.[9] Why this was so is a complex question, but it was so. Perhaps they felt well enough off as it was. Only towards the end of the twelfth century did this seriously begin to change, partly because landlords started to feel the pinch of increasing royal taxation. The point to make here is that while landlords were extensively leasing out, lesser men could profit mightily from the situation. For example, the Abbey of Bury St Edmunds had long leased out its manor of Tilney (Norfolk) for £5 a year. Five pounds represented the annual income of a comfortably off parish priest or the annual salary that a Spanish professor of mathematics would be paid by the king for teaching in the school of Northampton.[10] Around 1190 Abbot Samson of Bury decided to take Tilney back into his own direct administration. The first year he made a profit of £25 out of it, and in the second, not quite so good year, £20.[11] Somebody – it might have been a knightly man or an enterprising merchant or peasant, but in any case somebody too unimportant to be named in the historical record – must have been making a fortune out of that lease.

The estates of Glastonbury Abbey have already been mentioned. Going back to Somerset, the biography of an anchorite, or recluse, Wulfric, who lived next to the church in the village of Haselbury Plucknett during the second quarter of the twelfth century, gives us an interesting economic setting. Haselbury was situated in one of the richest parts of Somerset both in agrarian and pastoral terms already in the time of Domesday Book

(1086), and during the twelfth century marshes were being drained on the nearby River Yeo. In the Life of Wulfric new fisheries on this river are also mentioned. Wulfric himself had a full-time 'boy' as a servant, he could call on the services of a scribe, and he accumulated sheep, cows and lots of gold, silver and precious clothes, probably by no means all of it other people's.[12] Even an ascetic could flourish materially in a prospering community!

The great expansion of towns is predicated on the rising profitability of agriculture. As Susan Reynolds has said – and she applies this even to sea-ports which engaged in long-distance trade – 'what provided the basis of most towns' livelihood was not the cake of overseas commerce but the bread and butter of distribution and marketing for the surrounding region'.[13] Between 1066 and 1215 something over 100 new towns were successfully established in England.[14] A good example of these is Banbury in North Oxfordshire, founded by Bishop Alexander of Lincoln in the 1140s primarily to act as a market for the surpluses of the more southerly estates of his bishopric. The town was laid out in a planned way with burgage tenures on either side of the main street.[15] Burgage tenures usually involved no labour services but only payment of a money rent, parts or the whole of them could be sub-let, and they allowed of unusually free sale or purchase. Hence such tenures were much in demand not only by merchants, bakers and the like, but also by religious houses and country barons and knights, because they were an exceptionally fluid form of investment. It goes without saying, however, that they were in demand only so far as the market was a success.

Of towns which had been Saxon *burhs*, many were only on the threshold of their true development at the time of the Norman Conquest. With Oxford, for example, the initial boost probably came with William the Conqueror's putting its castle into the hands of Robert d'Oilly. Some destruction of Saxon houses was almost certainly the initial result of the building or enlargement of this castle, but thereafter the greater security which it afforded surely stimulated Oxford's market, trade and industry. The clearest sign of its twelfth-century growth in prosperity is the large number of stone churches whose existence is attested within a radius of a few hundred yards of its centre, Carfax. These churches are too early to be explained by the rise of the university; the very earliest evidence of scholars in any numbers comes from the 1170s. Another sign is the establishment of Jewish money-dealers in the town from no later than about 1140, with a Jewish quarter in existence by 1180. We meet the Oxford Jews, several of whom we can name, including one Moses the Liberal apparently a patron of learning and supporter of scholars, first of all in the records of the royal Exchequer a propos of their financial dealings with Henry II's government. Some remarkable documents survive, however, recording loans by Jews to Oxford citizens of the 1180s and 1190s.[16] The first specialised Oxford guild was in existence by the 1160s – a guild of shoemakers.[17] Some of the tired old oxen who crossed the ford probably failed to make it much further!

Bristol is another town, originally also an Anglo-Saxon *burh*, whose rising prosperity can be charted by the number of its Norman churches. They included Earl Robert of Gloucester's foundation of the Benedictine priory of St James (Robert a natural son of Henry I), and, more important, the Abbey of St Augustine, a house of Augustinian canons founded by Robert Fitz Harding, a wealthy Norman supporter of Henry I's daughter Matilda against Stephen, and of her son Henry II. Thus Bristol rose on the Angevin cause. Once again, a fine early Norman castle had much to do with its rise. During the twelfth century the import of wine and wood and the export of (Cotswold) wool became big business at the port of Bristol.[18] But every conurbation needs a secure food supply. London, for instance, besides its vital agragrian hinterland, particularly in Kent, received a regular supply of pickled herrings from Yarmouth.[19] When Henry II's expedition of 1171 sailed to Ireland (to cut a baron, one of the Clares called Strongbow, down to size), the king's fleet was provisioned with huge quantities of grain, raised quickly in Somerset by his sheriff in that shire.[20] We are catching a glimpse here of how and from where the city itself was normally fed. Like Oxford, Bristol had a flourishing Jewish community in the twelfth and thirteenth centuries; Moses the Liberal, mentioned above, had migrated from Bristol to Oxford before 1177.[21]

Both Oxford and Bristol became cathedral cities only in the 1540s under Henry VIII, both episcopal seats being created out of the two distinguished houses of Augustinian canons which had been dissolved as such in the Dissolution of the Monasteries, St Frideswide's at Oxford, and St Augustine's at Bristol. Unlike Oxford, Bristol did not become a notable centre of learning until modern times. Yet strangely enough, the university in Oxford probably owed its rise in part at least to the town's commercial *decline* in the thirteenth century. For its food and its trade, Oxford had depended very much on the navigation of the River Thames. It was at the point on the Thames, also, where the road from Southampton to Northampton, much used by the kings in their journeys, crossed the river. Oxford reached its commercial apogee in the late twelfth century. Thereafter the Thames got clogged up with fish weirs and navigation suffered. A clause of Magna Carta (1215, cl. 33) complains about it – a clause very likely inserted as a result of Oxford pressure, but probably without avail. So the merchants moved out, leaving a lot of cheap run-down property, ideal for scholars to move into.[22]

For comparison with Bristol and Oxford we may move up to York. Donald Nicholl gives a lively picture of York around 1114, when Thurstan became its Archbishop. He writes of the contribution of the Jews to the life of the city. They came as money-lenders who could advance York's commercial enterprises, but they could and did also help Christian scholars with their study of the Hebrew Bible. For example, a Yorkshire boy studied Hebrew with them for three years, and copied out 40 psalms in Hebrew script, whose calligraphy was much admired by the Jews themselves. That was Maurice who later became Prior of Kirkham, a house of Augustinian Canons in Yorkshire. Having written of the Scandinavian and Norman elements in the city, and of the establishment after the Norman Conquest of important monastic communities there Nicholl continues[22a]:

It can be seen that the community of some eight or nine thousand souls at York which now had Thurstan as its pastor embraced a variety of races and cultures such as few modern communities of a similar size could equal . . . Around the cathedral centred the life of the archbishop's familia and his canons, the intellectuals, the music master and the master of the schools; around the mint dwelt the goldsmiths and metal-workers; along the wharves traders berthed their ships from the East Riding, from Ireland and Germany and the shores about the North Sea.

One of the most revealing signs, or indeed consequences, for English religious life, of rising economic prosperity in the twelfth century, is the large number of recluses. There have always been hermits, anchorites and reclusive holy persons, male and female, in the Christian religion and not only in the Christian religion. But they appear to be extraordinarily numerous in twelfth-century England. When the Cistercian abbot, John of Ford, was writing his Life of Wulfric of Haselbury in the 1180s, some thirty years after that Somerset anchorite had died, he uncovered a whole network of recluses in South Somerset and Dorset who had known him (this way of life was a good recipe for longevity!), including several women – Matilda of Wareham, Odolina of Crewkerne and Aldida of Sturminster Newton. Much earlier, c. 1115–20, when the celebrated Christina of Markyate was looking to establish herself in a hermitage, she ran into a whole network of male and female recluses in Eastern England. The pipe rolls (the royal Exchequer accounts) show that in 1162–63 Henry II was paying out sums of money in various parts of the country to support at least six recluses. This year is not chosen quite at random, for it was the first year that the king's redoubtable clerical opponent, Thomas Becket, was Archbishop of Canterbury. In 1169 when Nigel, Bishop of Ely and Royal Treasurer, died, and the revenues of the bishopric of Ely fell into the king's hands, and its accounts are recorded in the pipe roll, we see again that the bishop had been supporting half a dozen more such individuals.[23] The evidence goes on and on. The famous ones, like Wulfric of Haselbury or Christina of Markyate, were famous because *lives* of them were written. There was, however, perhaps an element of chance in who was written up or even in whose *lives* have survived (at least four manuscripts of the Life of Wulfric have survived, but only one for Christina of Markyate and that by a lucky chance). We should not assume that all the others were lesser in way of life or influence.

One might have imagined that the life of a recluse might have seemed the ideal route out of poverty into an existence which may have been ascetic but was certainly not poor. But where we know anything the very reverse was the case. Christina of Markyate's background was that of the well-to-do Anglo-Danish upper class of Huntingdon, and she became a recluse to escape a marriage to an eligible Huntingdon bachelor.[24] Wulfric of Haselbury was born into a modest English family in Compton Martin, on the other side of Somerset from Haselbury Plucknett, but he became a parish priest at a period when the material possibilities for that profession were rising, and as a priest he followed the hounds and hunted with falcons while, 'amidst the captives of worldly vanity, he awaited the moment of his calling' (i.e. his conversion to a truly religious way of life).[25] Matilda of Wareham had made a living as a cushion- or quilt-maker before she became a recluse.[26] Godric of Finchale (Co. Durham) had started as a small pedlar in the villages of East Anglia and became a top merchant, building his fortune on long-distance trading journeys to Denmark, Flanders and Scotland (suggesting that towns like Aberdeen, St Andrews and Dundee, growing in the twelfth century, were being drawn into the English urban boom) before throwing it all in to establish himself as a hermit on the banks of the River Wear.[27] His *Life* was written by Reginald, a monk of Durham. Robert of Knaresborough in Yorkshire (ob. 1218) came from an upper-class family in York, of which his brother became mayor, while his mother was a York money-lender.[28] The latter is a striking example of how twelfth-century women could make careers for themselves, especially in towns; perhaps her opportunity came after the 1190 pogrom of Jews at York, or perhaps she was a member of the rival economic establishment that was part responsible for it.

None of this ought really to surprise us. Any materially expanding, upwardly mobile society generates people who become disgusted with the rat race and want to opt out of the competition for money, status (Godric was said little by little to have been able to keep the company of city merchants),[29] and husbands. Peter Brown, explaining the background from which the Holy Men of Late Antiquity in the East Mediterranean arose, has pointed out that these men were not oppressed peasants. Their malaise was more subtle. 'Late Roman Egypt was a land of vigorous villages where tensions sprang quite as much from the disruptive effects of new wealth and new opportunities as from the immemorial depredations of the tax-collector.'[30] One may even say something similar of Galilee in the first century AD. Nobody could suppose that Peter gave up everything to follow Jesus because his fishing business was doing badly, when it was employing staff, when there were salt pans on the shores of Lake Galilee, and when new markets for preserved fish were opening up because of the Roman occupation of Palestine, and indeed across the Roman Empire.[31]

It will already have become abundantly clear that the church was a beneficiary on a large scale of the expanding wealth of twelfth-century England. At the time of the Norman Conquest and of Domesday Book (1086) there were many hugely wealthy churches whose endowments often went back centuries, and hugely wealthy churchmen. All the same, the twelfth-century church saw something akin to an economic miracle if we think of the development of cathedrals with their organisation of dean, precentor, treasurer and schoolmaster/chancellor, and prebends (i.e. lands or churches allocated to the support of each canon); of the impositions on abbeys to help finance the royal government; of the establishment of archdeaconries as officials in every diocese; of the vast increase in the numbers of parish churches and their endowments; of the new orders of monks or canons and nuns, and the new hospitals and schools which were endowed; of the innumerable and often spectacular cathedrals, abbeys and parish churches which were built. Much of the wealth to do all this was the wealth of the churches, or the bishops, themselves; but much of it was lay wealth. We shall be returning to all this when we come to cathedrals and monasteries and parish churches, and their impact on societies.

The church was not only a beneficiary of expanding wealth in the twelfth century; it was also a creator of it. First of all in *attitudes*. Do changes in attitudes affect economic realities or do economic changes affect attitudes? Probably it is both ways round. Whatever the case, sentiment (to use the language of the stockbrokers), sentiment about humankind, became more optimistic from around 1100. The most obvious sign of it is that the devil, who had cramped people's style (including economic style) and caused pessimism about the possibilities of human nature, started to get driven out of human affairs, and not abolished of course, but pushed down into hell. The great breakthrough here came with the *Cur Deus Homo* of St Anselm, written in the 1090s after he had become archbishop of Canterbury. *Why had God become Man?* Not everyone found Anselm's answer to this question satisfactory, but in one important point he laid down a marker. God had not become man in order that, in this death, Christ could 'buy' the devil out of his rights over human beings, rights created by sin, because, Anselm maintained, the devil had never had any rightful dominion over men and women.[32] Incidentally, many of Anselm's own trusted correspondents were women. A little later, in the 1120s, a group of English Benedictine abbots whom we shall come to in a later chapter, were very keen to press for the idea and the liturgical celebration of the Immaculate Conception of Mary, the idea that Mary as the mother of God had been preserved from original sin at the moment of conception.[33] This notion that a human being could in principle be sinless was strongly opposed by monks of the Cistercian order, who saw themselves as in many ways rivals of the traditional Benedictines. But as we shall also see later, the Cistercians themselves had in other respects very optimistic ideas about the moral and material improvability of the human condition.

As the twelfth century went on, phenomena which had previously been regarded as demonic, such as ghostly apparitions, came to be regarded as in a sort of natural category, namely of marvels. Of course in visions of hell or the after life, such as the Vision of Thurkill, the devil still held sway in his own dominion.[34] But stories of revenants, or generally troubled and guilt-ridden persons appearing in the world from the afterlife, for instance, were increasingly absorbed into concepts of the natural world. Walter Map, in his *Courtiers' Trifles* (early 1180s), an entertaining book full of legends, wonders and gossip – 'a rough inventory of the mental furniture of a learned and witty twelfth-century clerk', as Christopher Brooke calls it[35] – describes a *prodigium* which makes the point. A knight of Northumberland had a visitation from his long dead father, who wanted to be absolved by a priest from his sin of withholding tithes. The knight at first thought it was the devil, but he was mistaken.[36]

During the twelfth century, disease itself – and this had an important bearing on life expectancy and material well-being – came to be seen increasingly as having natural rather than diabolical causes. Revenants, or apparitions of the walking dead, which were widely thought to spread disease, are again a case in point. Robert Bartlett has said that the explanation of that phenomenon had to be made in some way to fit Christian tenets; and referring to the *History of English Affairs*, written by the Yorkshire Augustinian Canon, William of Newburgh, in the 1190s, he adds:

William of Newburgh manages a neat combination of Christian metaphysics and naturalism by describing the reanimation of the corpses as 'the work of Satan' but by attributing the spread of disease to the contaminated air that the corpses created. Indeed, describing a case at Berwick, he writes that 'the simpler folk feared that they might be attacked and beaten by the lifeless monster, while the more thoughtful were concerned that the air might be infected and corrupted from the wanderings of the plague-bringing corpse, with subsequent sickness and death'.[37]

One may note here the assumption that the more educated you were, the more likely you were to explain disease in a natural or positivist way.

Another interesting example of the natural explanation of disease is found in Walter Daniel's *Life of Ailred of Rievaulx*, written not long after Ailred's death in 1167. Walter Daniel was not the greatest brain nor the least neurotic psyche in twelfth-century Britain, but he was an educated man and he was interested in medicine. He tells an extraordinary tale about how Ailred encountered a man who had swallowed a little frog in his drinking water which had grown inside him, eaten away his entrails, and made him look a horrifying figure with drawn face, bloodshot eyes, and dimmed pupils. Now kings are powerless to eject frogs from their bellies (says Walter with his rare capacity to hit some irrelevant nail on the head), but Ailred, 'dismounting from his horse', inserted two fingers into the man's mouth, uttered a prayer (the nearest we get to any implication of the miraculous), and lo and behold, the frog climbed onto his fingers and departed. Then out came a lot of horrible pus and glutinous humours and the man was cured.[38] 'A likely story', one might say; but a story driven by the natural.

The practical interest in health and health care taken by the church, though also by the lay aristocracy, is a notable feature of the twelfth century. At the time of the Norman Conquest a distinguished doctor, Baldwin, who came from Chartres, was Abbot of Bury St Edmunds.[39] An even more famous doctor, Faritius, a Tuscan from Arezzo, became Abbot of Abingdon under Henry I, the king believing that he was often curable only by Faritius's antidotes. The queen also trusted him above all other doctors. It was said that he would have been elected Archbishop of Canterbury in 1114 had it not been thought inappropriate that one who

spent so much time examining women's urine should occupy that position.[40] Later on Henry I had another remarkable foreigner, the Spanish Jew
Petrus Alphonsi, as his personal physician.

Under this king many hospitals were established at English towns –
London, Colchester, Norwich, Newcastle, Barnstaple and others.[41] True,
twelfth-century hospitals had much broader charitable purposes than
simply to care for the sick, as is illustrated by the foundation of St
Bartholomew's Smithfield, which made special provision for children
whose mothers had died in childbirth.[42] Others were established to receive
pilgrims. But there is much evidence that a primary concern of hospitals
was to look after the sick. True again, many hospitals were founded as
leper hospitals, with the idea of isolating lepers. Henry I's own queen,
Matilda, founded the leper hospital of St Giles, Holborn.[43] The twelfth
century developed this zeal for identifying and isolating minorities, such as
heretics, Jews and lepers,[44] rather in the way that the scholastics of that
century were developing the method of breaking down a question into its
subdivisions and then examining each of these separately. However, in
the case of lepers, this still meant care for the sick, for once founded their
hospitals were continually enlarged and protected, and by none more
assiduously than churchmen. Roger of Pont l'Evêque, Archbishop of York,
who was not everyone's favourite in his time and who actually had a reputation for meanness,[45] issued a string of documents during his episcopate
(1154–81) for the protection of St Peter's/St Leonard's Hospital York and
for the enlargement of its resources.[46] Admittedly the latter was mostly to
be done with other people's money, but at least it showed his concern. In
the 1180s Bishop Seffrid II of Chichester granted from his own resources
to St Mary's Hospital for eight 'lepers' outside the gate of Chichester eight
woollen tunics each Christmas, eight linen tunics at Easter and a bacon or
ham at Christmas (pig-farming was altogether fairly big business in
twelfth-century England).[47] When the Third Lateran Council of 1179
ordered that where possible, 'lepers' should live a common life with their
own church and cemetery,[48] it was ordering something that was already
being done on a wide scale, but here Bishop Seffrid was building on it
perhaps under its immediate impact. One may wonder how good people
were at diagnosing leprosy as distinct from other forms of external illness
(just as church courts often lumped all kinds of confused people with real
heretics). But there are strong grounds for thinking that leprosy could be
and generally was distinguished from other skin illnesses. It remains the
case on the other hand that many hospitals were for the sick generally.
St Mary's Hospital, Chichester, for instance, was explicitly stated to be for

lepers, whereas the York hospital was stated to be for receiving the poor and curing the sick.[49]

Pursuing further the subject of health care, so obviously an important aspect of explaining twelfth-century material well-being, this century saw growing numbers of men described in the documentary sources as *medicus*, or doctor, so much so that it has been seen as the first age of the English medical profession. We should not get over-excited about this. Sometimes the term could have meant little more than a village healer. Even when it indicated some practical knowledge of surgery or medical text books, the person in question was not necessarily a full-time doctor, any more than the person called in a royal record of 1199 Master William the Poet necessarily spent his time doing nothing but writing poetry (particularly if he were the William of Blois who was to become Bishop of Lincoln in 1203!).[50] Nonetheless when every salutary caution has been borne in mind, we do appear to have the embryonic beginnings of a medical profession in England during the second half of the twelfth century. Talbot and Hammond listed 98 doctors for this half century, and that number could almost certainly be at least doubled by an exhaustive scouring of the sources.[51] Most of the 98 seem to be men of substance (three in Oxford), some are known to have owned medical books, and 31 are given the title of master (*magister*), which was not always recorded when it might have been. A *magister* was a person of education and trained intellect, whose medicine, even if secondary in his professional life, was unlikely to have been mere folk healing. In addition we now know that knowledge of medicine as taught at the famous medical school of Salerno in South Italy was starting to reach England before 1200.[52] Its reception shows a more positivist approach to the subject.

When later on we speak of people's search for healing at the saints' shrines at churches, we shall of course be talking about supernatural rather than scientific medicine. It is important to remember that the search for supernatural or 'folk' healing, which if it causes people to feel healed is in itself conducive to better health in society, did not collapse in face of a more positivist approach to medicine, any more than Lourdes has collapsed because of modern medicine. Twelfth-century men and women could move fluidly between the two kinds, treating one as now an alternative, now as an extension, of the other.[53] They felt that within the area of health care, their possibilities of choice (if allusion to a modern mantra can be forgiven) were being enlarged. In 1200, when the body of St Hugh of Lincoln was being carried back from London, where he had died, to Lincoln, it rested one night at Biggleswade (Beds), where in the evening a man broke his arm in the crush around the bier. He was in great pain and was told that if he could hang on, in the morning his arm could be set by doctors – not a bad indication of the availability of practical medicine at the time. However in the night he received a healing vision from the saintly bishop himself.[54]

One of the marks of economic growth in the twelfth century was the development of specialised production. We have already mentioned shoes at Oxford, to which we could add that there were two goldsmiths among the leading 63 citizens there in 1191.[55] In York the market for cutlery gave rise to specialised production there.[56] It even seems that there was a commercialised market for devotional objets d'art. A sculptor and painter came to Godric of Finchale because he could not sell his work at St Cuthbert's fair in Durham. Godric prophesied good sales for him – after the poor man had given him a golden cross, a rather steep consultant's fee one might think – and it worked.[57] Miracle or no, this story suggests that by the later twelfth century art was more a matter of the market and less an exclusive matter for patron and artist than one might think. Similarly, toys could be bought commercially. When Gilbert of Sempringham thought that his followers needed cheering up, while they were in London to answer charges of the king's justices (1160s), he bought them some spinning tops.[58] The fact that the recluse, Matilda of Wareham, could earn a living making cushions or quilts again points to an increase in profitable specialised production.

The churches played an important role in stimulating specialised production and the development of specialised skills. When the bishopric of Chichester with its revenues, and its financial commitments too, fell into the king's hands in 1169, its accounts show that one mark a year (two-thirds of a pound) was being paid to a glazier for the upkeep of the cathedral glass.[59] One mark a year would have been a significant proportion of a craftsman's annual wage. Although we sometimes think of monks devotedly labouring in their cloisters to produce their manuscripts, the rich abbey of St Albans already in the first half of the century was employing professional scribes – not monks nor necessarily clergy at all – for this purpose.[60] At the same time Westminster Abbey, who felt that they had many rights and properties which they lacked the documentary evidence to prove, were employing skilled professional forgers to make good the deficiency.[61] At Norwich Cathedral Priory, when the dubious and anti-semitic cult of 'Little' St William got going in the second half of the century, the boy saint always wanted candles in gratitude for cures at this shrine. He gave nasty dreams to people who failed to give them.[62]

His shrine helped to pay the Norwich electricity bill, so to speak; and it also gave the city's chandlers profitable business.[63]

A most intriguing possible example of economic specialisation is presented to us by Farne Island off the coast of Northumberland. In the twelfth century the powerful Durham Cathedral Priory were keen to monasticise and take under their control the previous sites of hermitages such as Godric's at Finchale or that on the Farne Islands. One motive for this may have been to establish centres where their monks who were so disposed could live a more contemplative life than was possible in the bustling Cathedral Priory itself, where moreover the liturgical schedule was a heavy one. But another motive was undoubtedly economic. During the time of Bartholomew as hermit on Farne Island, this clearly had to do with its eider ducks, which were stringently guarded by the Durham monks. Bartholomew was a Durham monk who arrived on the island 1149–53 and died there in 1193. This is what his *Life*, written by Geoffrey of Coldingham, another monk of Durham, had to say about the eider ducks:

For ages this island has offered an abode to certain birds, whose name and type has persisted miraculously. In the nesting season they gather there. They soon obtain the grace of such tameness from the holiness of the place, or rather from those who have sanctified the place by their way of life [i.e. the hermits who live or have lived there under Durham sponsorship], that they do not abhor being seen or being in contact with humans. They love quiet, and yet are not disturbed by noise. Nests are prepared everywhere far from the inhabitants. No one presumes to harm them or to touch their eggs without permission. The brethren [i.e. there were presumably other hermits besides Bartholomew] serve some of these eggs to themselves or their visitors. The birds are not troubled by their use as food. They seek food in the sea with their males. Their chicks, as soon as they are hatched, follow on, their mothers going ahead, and having once entered their native waters do not return to their nests. Their mothers also, forgetting the soft bed which had been theirs, recover their pristine rapport with the sea.[64]

Now given that we know of the existence of such a person as a cushion- or quilt-maker in twelfth-century England (i.e. Matilda of Wareham) it seems clear that the real economic interest of Durham here was not the eiders' eggs but their soft beds, that is eider down. An eider duck produces at least twice as much down as is necessary to accommodate her eggs and herself, and she will willingly step aside to allow a human being to take half of it. Thus harmony with nature and profitable business may be satisfactorily combined.

It would be a mistake to see specialisation in the twelfth century only in terms of production of consumer goods, and not also of professional skills, as the case of scribes and glaziers already imply. If the century may be called the first age of the medical profession, it was also the first age of the engineering profession. The reason was advances in warfare. Twelfth-century warfare was not primarily a matter of open battles, but of castle-building and siege warfare. The Italians took the lead here. If the crusaders needed to besiege a fortress out in Palestine, the Genoese could lay on a siege for them in all its aspects – mercenaries, siege engines, siege platforms, ships from which operations could be conducted. In the 1150s, the Holy Roman/German Emperor, Frederick Barbarossa, depended on Italian engineers for his military efforts to master the cities of Northern Italy, as the cities of Northern Italy did to resist him.[65] In Britain, where castle warfare was of paramount importance, a leaf was taken out of the Italian book. Engineers were employed to do clever things (*ad facienda ingenia*), particularly ballistic clever things, in attacks on castles, as well as to destroy enemy castles. When Henry II in 1176 ordered baronial castles to be destroyed, the royal justices who went into East Anglia, for instance, to supervise such demolitions took a qualified and well-paid engineer, an Englishman called Ailnoth, with them.[66] This was the age when the crossbowmen, the arblasters or *arbalistarii*, vital both in besieging and in resisting sieges,[67] came into their own. For example, in the 1150s a crossbowman called Walter had a landed holding of some significance in Suffolk, while in the 1140s another called Odo appears quite high up in a witness list to a document of Bishop William of Norwich.[68] A number of crossbowmen may originally have come from Wales, always a source of supply for skilled soldiers in the twelfth century.

By 1200 a whole class of knightly men, and probably also a little below knightly level, had come to be seen as professional administrators. They were used as such by Richard I's government, headed by his chief minister who was also Archbishop of Canterbury, Hubert Walter (we shall return to him later). Men of this middling level of society, or many of them, rose to be useful as professionals, in large part at least because they were needed as jurors in numbers all over England to execute Henry II's legal reforms and new legal processes. Thus under Hubert Walter there were to be three knights in each shire to be keepers of the pleas of the crown (i.e. to assess and keep a record of any action, event or death, from which the king might be owed money). This was the origin of the coroner's office.[69] Under a royal edict of 1195 for the pursuit of criminals, all men above the age of 15 were to be drafted into a sort of communal police force for keeping the king's peace, and supervising this draft were knights appointed (*milites assignati*) to the task.[70] When in 1198 the king's government proposed a new carucage or land tax, a knight in each shire, accompanied by a clerk to keep a record, was to assess the value of the land to be taxed.[71] It is very likely that similar men to these (and one has to remember how mobile English society was and how easily men could rise into this knightly class by wealth and ability) were employed by the great landholders and the great churches to administer and do the accounting for their estates and manors when they began to shift markedly from leasing to direct management around 1200.[72] Was, for instance, the obviously efficient leaseholder of Tilney left unemployed when Abbot Samson of Bury St Edmunds took this manor back into the abbey's direct management? One may doubt it.

Professional surveys – of estates and assets – were a developing feature of Henry II's government. The royal example spread. In 1185, just when emphasis on direct management of their estates by great landholders was coming to be in vogue, the Order of Templars held an inquest of their lands, widely scattered in England, and of their donors. The record survives. The Templars were a crusading order and a military mainstay of the Christian crusading state in Palestine. They held lands throughout the West to enable them to perform their function. The mid-1180s was a critical time for them because of the threat of the Muslim, Saladin. In fact the Latin Kingdom of Jerusalem fell to Saladin after the Battle of Hattin (1187). Hence the Templars needed help and needed to know what their assets and who their friends and donors were. The administrative centre of the Templars in England was the Old Temple, Holborn, London, but they also had regional administrative units, or preceptories; and it was clearly the preceptors, professional estates stewards who were themselves Knights Templars and came largely from middling or knightly families, who conducted the 1185 survey.[73] The survey may sound dryly tenurial, but in fact, whether one is interested in blacksmiths or goldsmiths, doctors or bakers, piglets or cart-horses, boon works or labour services, it is riveting.

Where did the greatest development of professionalism and professional elitism occur in twelfth-century English society? Undoubtedly amongst the clergy. But that must await a later chapter when we consider the parish clergy.

The accumulation of wealth and the development of organisation had some good results for social and spiritual welfare. Many parish churches were endowed and there was a great expansion of schools (under church control), even in places like Dunstable and Huntingdon. There were also some less good results, most of all the frenetic careerism to which it led.

There had of course always been careerism in the church, and it was not necessarily for the worse. Pope Gregory the Great in his *Pastoral Care* of the 590s had contrasted laudable ambition, where the motive to do a good job for one's neighbour's sake outstripped the love of prestige, with laudable lack of ambition or desire to lead a secluded and contemplative life. But two things made careerism show its less attractive face rather often. One was indeed the love of prestige, particularly as bishops were normally appointed by the king's influence except in Stephen's reign when Archbishop Theobald of Canterbury often had the leading voice,[74] and hence to be appointed a bishop was to prove that one had arrived politically. Walter Map in his satirical *Courtiers' Trifles* wrote of how he could not control his own household, who would side with guests outstaying their welcome, so putting himself to great expense, and saying to him, 'don't be too anxious; trust in the Lord; it is common talk that they will make you a bishop!'[75] Walter had indeed no need to be anxious financially. He was canon and prebendary in two cathedrals; in 1196–97 he received the plum archdeaconry of Oxford. But he died still only an archdeacon in 1209 or 1210.[76]

The other thing which made careerism show its less attractive side, notwithstanding that there had always been careerists in the church, was that wealth and organisation had greatly expanded the opportunities for it. Now there were not only bishoprics, and in the monastic world abbacies and priorships, but also cathedral dignities (deanships, precentorships, chancellorships, etc.) and prebends, canonries in collegiate churches, and perhaps above all archdeaconries. The pattern of cathedral dignities and prebends (i.e. individual shares in the endowments for the canons) developed in England after the Norman Conquest and in some cathedrals only after 1100.[77] Archdeacons, hardly known in England before 1066, were a feature of the church introduced after the Norman Conquest, seemingly from Normandy by Archbishop Lanfranc of Canterbury. By about 1100 most archdeacons were territorial, i.e. they were Archdeacon of Bedford, or Archdeacon of Wiltshire or Archdeacon of Oxford.[78] In the enforcement of church discipline over clergy and laity they were the bishops' right-hand officers, and not infrequently their nephews. And they generally became very rich. When the learned and clever John of Salisbury wrote his satirical moralising work on politics, the *Policraticus* in the 1150s, he made an overblown attack on ambition, writ large in church and secular affairs, and on its sister vice of avarice. Quite a lot of what he wrote was clearly targeted on archdeacons.[79] Then in 1164–66 he wrote to his old friend Nicholas of Sigillo, formerly a royal clerk, who had talked down archdeacons, congratulating him on now becoming Archdeacon of Huntingdon by appointment of the Bishop of Lincoln. His letter was witty, and expresses what was to become a well-worn question: can an archdeacon be saved?

'I seem to remember', he began, 'that there was a race of men known in the Church of God by the title of archdeacons, for whom you used to lament, my discerning friend, that every road to salvation was closed. They love gifts, you used to say, and follow after rewards. They are inclined to outrage, rejoice in false accusation, turn the sins of the people into food and drink, live by plunder so that a host is not safe with his guest. The most eminent of them preach the Law of God but do it not. Such and such like qualities your pious compassion used to bewail in the most wretched state of the men. Your friends, and all good men, must thank God and the Bishop of Lincoln, who have opened your eyes and revealed to you a path by which this race of men can not merely obtain salvation, but add to it the loftier aureole, etc., etc. It is the Lord's doing; it is He who has opened the blindness of your eyes, laid bare the truth, and made you change your baleful view on the case of archdeacons.'[80]

The new archdeacon is much more likely to have enjoyed than been embarrassed by this letter from one of the wits of the twelfth century.

The last word in this chapter concerns the recluse, Christina of Markyate, and her relationship with Abbot Geoffrey of St Albans (1119–46). It is relevant to a chapter on economic aspects of the church, because Abbot Geoffrey is an example of how expanding prosperity, refined administration and economic specialisation, and of course the advances of law, legalism and law courts which went with them, were already, in the first half of the twelfth century, affecting the conduct of, and the concept of how to be, a good churchman. Christina was born into upper-class Huntingdon c. 1096–98, from which she fled around 1115 into a life of celibacy to avoid an arranged marriage, and after quite an Aeneid, she finally settled into her hermitage at Markyate (Herts), a few miles north of St Albans Abbey and under its sponsorship.[81] The *Life of Christina of Markyate* was written by an anonymous monk of St Albans in the 1150s, soon after her death. At times this work verges on the prurient, and the impressions it gives are not always accurate, for instance in exaggerating the permanency of the rift between Christina and her parents. But if one takes it for what it is, the life of a female hermit as seen from the point of view of a great abbey, it is a work of great historical value. Christina's friendship with Abbot Geoffrey began in the mid-1120s.

Abbot Geoffrey came from Maine, a county to the south of Normandy and effectively a part of it. He was appointed to be schoolmaster of St Albans, but he did not come quickly enough (he did not come *tempestive*, as the St Albans Chronicle says), so that by the time he arrived the post had gone to someone else, and he had to be content with the lesser (but still desirable) schoolmastership of nearby Dunstable. The shock waves of frenetic careerism even reached down to schoolmasterships. But St Albans must have retained a high opinion of him, for they were willing to lend him some valuable copes (a nice example of the importance of ecclesiastical embroidery to black-monk ritualism) in order to put on a school play about St Catherine (a nice example of St Albans' interest in religious drama, of which we know from other sources). The night after the play his house burned down, and the copes were destroyed. Having nothing with which to compensate the abbey except his own person, he offered himself as a monk.[82]

The friendship between Christina and Geoffrey became a close one, vividly described in the *Life*. As a mystic, Christina perceived Geoffrey's wrong actions in the community of monks and reproached him for them. She had visions of him when his visits were about to occur. He always came to consult her and seek her blessing before he embarked on a journey. As head of a large business corporation, i.e. the abbey, he was a tenant-in-chief of the king and thus necessarily involved in royal politics. Before one of his journeys to court, it is he who came out with one of the classic statements of how untrustworthy King Stephen was, when he said to Christina, 'I am going to court, but of my return I know nothing.'[83] Of course such a friendship was impossible 'without the malicious wagging of many tongues'.[84] The anonymous monk adamantly denied that the gossip had any foundation, and this is eminently believable for the author does not evade Christina's sexual temptations and fantasies when they were at issue. There was, for instance, a cleric of standing for whom she had conceived a passion (probably c. 1123) and who 'behaved in so scandalous a manner that I cannot make it known, lest I pollute the wax by writing it, or the air by saying it'! But, he adds with a fascinating piece of psychology, only one thing brought her respite; in the actual presence of this cleric, her passion abated. 'In his absence she used to be so inwardly inflamed that she thought that the clothes which clung to her body might be set on fire.'[85] The whole narrative is already an example of what Caroline Walker Bynum, writing about later medieval religion, has called the new freedom to face up to the body, the new concern to give full significance to flesh – to matter, body and sensual response.[86] It is because of the openness of a narrative like this that the denial of a sexual element in the friendship of Christina and Geoffrey seems entirely believable.

Geoffrey was a good, hard-working abbot. He organised the finances of the abbey; he rebuilt the shrine of St Alban, but also distributed part of the abbey's wealth to the poor and founded the Hospital of St Julien outside the town on the London road; he believed that a monastery prayed on its belly and assigned specific cheeses to the kitchen; he drew up new regulations for the infirmary.[87] He is emphatically not an example of how wealth may corrupt the higher clergy. No, the point that has to be made about him is a quite different one. Geoffrey's whole spiritual life and vision and inspiration are represented as being based on the prophetic powers and prayer of Christina. 'Their affection was mutual', says the Life, 'but different according to their modes of holiness. He supported her materially; she commended him to God more earnestly in her prayers.'[88] That was the division of labour between them. There is a graphic illustration of this in the now well-known initial letter to Psalm 105 of the St Albans Psalter, showing Christina praying to Christ for a group of monks standing behind her, headed apparently by Abbot Geoffrey [see Plate 5].[89] When we look back at the great bishops and abbots of the tenth century, things are very different. These were the great *Adelsheilige*, nobleman saints like Ethelwold of Winchester, Dunstan of Canterbury and Oswald of Worcester. They ran their own spiritual engines and their external works were a manifestation, or an extension, of their inner driving force. They did not administer; they ruled. And they ruled with sometimes spectacular manipulation of supernatural power. Here in twelfth-century Markyate/St Albans, however, we have the split between spiritual power and ecclesiastical authority.

A similar theme had already been struck when Anselm became Archbishop of Canterbury in 1093. When he wanted to resist his appointment, on the grounds that he had shunned worldly affairs since he became a monk and did not wish to become entangled in business now, the bishops, who had been royal chaplains almost to a man before they became bishops, said to him in effect, 'You pray to God for us, and we shall look after your worldly affairs for you'.[90] One hears echoes of this theme – you be the spiritual one; we'll take care of external affairs – down the twelfth century. For example, some time just before 1150 the Augustinian Canons of Lanthony got agitated about challenges to their rights in Prestbury church (Glos). The Canons who leaned to the contemplative side of their order, had at the time just lost their great patron, Robert of Bethune, Bishop of Hereford (1130–48) and previously their prior. They appealed to a friend of Bishop Robert, Bishop Hilary of Chichester (1147–69), for help. Hilary wrote back a brisk letter (he was a canon lawyer rather than a theologian), ending:

We exhort you not to be easily moved by such things but always to be intent on the divine service to which you are bound. For we and other friends of your late father, as has been given to us from above [almost as if this division of labour were of supernatural origin!] will be vigilant for you and will direct your worldly affairs (negotia), which were entrusted to us, freely as if they were our own.[91]

Hilary often ended his letters and documents with the work *valete*, farewell. This one he unusually and rather pointedly ends, 'Farewell and pray for us'!

Although it does not strictly belong to the subject matter of this chapter, it would seem false to avoid the question of how significant was the fact that the relationship between Geoffrey and Christina was that between a man and a woman. On the one hand there are grounds for believing that it was not sexual; on the other hand it did not pass without giving some scandal at the time. Perhaps Henrietta Leyser has struck the right note in setting it in the context of twelfth-century devotional fashions which stressed special relationships between holy women and Christ.[92] In the case of Geoffrey and Christina it would be absurd to deny that gender played any role, but as Leyser's point implies, twelfth-century religion was increasingly stressing inner spiritual experience as against external ritual, even amongst the most ritualistic of monasteries like St Albans. Men as priests were the only external mediators between God and humankind. But where interiority rises and the more validity attaches to inner human religious experience, the less relevant does gender become. The most striking feature of the story of Christina of Markyate as told in her *Life* is the high value placed by a community of men on the religious or prophetic experiences of a woman.

CHAPTER 2

The Church and the Norman Conquest

The Gregorian Reform

To understand the church and politics in the time of the Norman Conquest, and indeed for the whole of our period, it is necessary first to consider what was happening in Rome during the second half of the eleventh century. When Colin Morris wrote his masterly book on the Western church from 1050 to 1250, he appositely entitled it *The Papal Monarchy*. There is less escape from the papacy in those two centuries than in any other period of church history, before or after them. The reason was the Gregorian Reform, named after Pope Gregory VII (1073–85). This reform aimed to release the whole clerical order from the power and influence of secular authority, particularly in appointments to churches; to purify that order and remove it from the world, particularly as regards paying seculars for ecclesiastical positions (simony) and as regards forbidding the clergy to be married; to place the papacy firmly at the head of the whole clerical order; and to assert the superiority of that order, the *sacerdotium*, over secular power, the *regnum*. For Gregory VII, the least cleric in minor orders was superior to an emperor.

This reform, as we describe it, did not start only with the pontificate of Gregory VII. The German Emperors had high notions about the religious standards of the clergy, and the pope who really started the blitz on simony and clerical marriage was a Lotharingian, i.e. from the Empire at that time, namely Leo IX. From the start, the reforming popes were under pressure to respond to the urban masses in towns of rising prosperity, e.g. Milan. These urbanites resented the unspiritual and materialistic lives of their clergy, and the way that money could buy from rulers and aristocrats plum ecclesiastical positions in church institutions which had only too tight a stranglehold on the economic life of their towns. Townsmen felt that they could have their own understanding of the New Testament, and doubted the validity of sacraments administered by priests whose lives they often regarded as sordid. The popes were nothing loath, pressure or no pressure, to side with such people against their bishops, monks and canons.[1] Although, however, the Gregorian Reform started before Gregory was pope, it was this pope who gave it the impetus which makes the whole movement rightly carry his name.

Hildebrand, who took the name Gregory when he became pope, was brought up and educated in Rome itself. He was born probably about 1015, became Archdeacon of Rome in his mid-forties and pope in his late fifties. He stood some 163 cm or 5 ft 4½ in tall, was strongly built, and in his skull type was Mediterranean rather than Germanic.[2] He must have had a great deal of personal presence,[3] and the voice in his letters comes through as one of unmistakable masterfulness. There is no doubt that he was motivated by strong religious zeal and pastoral concern. He celebrated Mass daily, he had the 'gift of tears' at prayer, and his letters often concluded with prayers concerning the goodness of God's creation or the saving blood of Jesus.[4] One of Gregory's contemporaries called him 'Holy Satan', which nicely hits off his religious zeal, his ruthlessness and divisiveness, and his demonic energy. To Gregory, all clerical marriage was a breach of chastity, however respectable it might often have appeared to priests themselves and their congregations. But his programme of clerical chastity was not only about prohibition. He encouraged non-monastic clergy to live a communal life of prayer and worship, according to the newly propagated canons' Rule of Augustine of Hippo.[5] There was a pastoral point here. Lay people should be able to respect the clergy who ministered to them by seeing their religious way of life, a life where monastic, contemplative and liturgical prayer was practised in so far as it was compatible with their pastoral duties.

But it does not fit the evidence to say that religious zeal and moral reform, zeal to extirpate clerical marriage and simony, was all there was to it. In 1075, when Bishop Otto of Constance, having tried once, refused to obey Gregory's order to promulgate again in his diocese the papal prohibition of clerical marriage, the pope declared him deposed and released his subjects from their obedience to him. Was this really the way to make clerical 'chastity' stick? If clerical 'chastity' had been Gregory's primary concern, would it really have made sense to release from their obedience to their bishop the very South German clergy whose aggressive uxoriousness had made Bishop Otto's task impossible? Again, in late 1074 – so even earlier in his pontificate, Gregory lent a ready ear to a cleric/canon of Toul who was complaining that Bishop Pibo of Toul was a simoniac and had a wife/mistress. This cleric obviously had a personal grievance, but even in the act of commissioning Archbishop Udo of Trier to enquire into these charges, which were subsequently found to be groundless, Gregory implicitly condemned Pibo by referring to him as the 'so-called bishop of Toul'.[6] Was it really the way to extirpate simony to assume the guilt of a bishop who would subsequently be declared innocent? Desire for moral reform, no doubt; but was there not an equal desire in both these cases to put bishops firmly in their place (not least by supporting their underlings against them), a place which was under papal authority? Certainly in the case of Pibo of Toul, Udo of Trier thought so.[7]

The French Catholic historian, Augustin Fliche, writing his *La Reforme Gregorienne* in the 1920s, saw Gregory as first impressed by the need for moral reform of church and clergy, and only in the second place coming to see a need for the strong assertion of papal authority in order to combat abuses. A decade later Gerd Tellenbach published a book whose argument was the exact opposite of Fliche's: that every aspect of Gregorian moral reform was already embedded in the imperial system, but whereas in the imperial ideology the emperor was the leader of the Christian society and the pope played second fiddle to him, now with the Gregorian Reform the whole orb was tipped upside down to place the pope on top. To anyone who knows the German/(Holy) Roman Empire of the tenth and eleventh centuries (as Fliche apparently did not), with its largely sacred purposes and its many bishops venerated as saints, it is difficult not to agree with Tellenbach. It is difficult to think otherwise than that it was not moral reform that was the achievement of the Gregorian papacy but a revolution in the concept of 'the right order of the world'.[8] Many years ago Henry Chadwick published a famous paper about the early church, entitled *The Circle and the Ellipse*. He saw two models of the church. One was that of a circle, with Jerusalem at its centre and all the churches united to it as if by spokes from the rim. The other was of an ellipse, where all the churches were indeed united, but by a line which formed an ellipse, rather than a circular line from which all the churches could be related to one central point.[9] The bishops of the Empire in the tenth and eleventh centuries, while accepting papal primacy as a matter of course, tended to be 'elliptical' in their normal attitudes to the universal church. Gregory VII was absolutely 'circular'. Rome was the centre of Christendom.

Gregory made much of the principle of obedience within the church, and he quoted his great namesake as pope, Pope Gregory I (the Great 590-604), to justify his emphasis. But there was an important difference between the two. For Gregory the Great obedience was a monastic principle about how the will should be orientated; for Gregory VII it was a hierarchical principle about the obedience owed to one's rightful superiors in the ecclesiastical hierarchy.[10] This was the principle by which Gregory VII sought to wrest bishops from the control of the secular power, especially of the Emperor. Let me put in different words what I have been saying in the last few paragraphs. Allied to the religious and moral zeal of the Gregorian Reform there developed a revolutionary new concept of how the world should be structured based on rationality and logical order; and law and justice were fundamental to rationality and logical order. Alexander Murray, in the pivotal fifth chapter of his book, *Reason and Society in the Middle Ages*, shows how reason, as against magic or ritual, made great advances across the eleventh and twelfth centuries. Of course ritual and magic remained just as reason and logic were not absent from the world before 1050. We are talking of a change in the balance, a change in *characteristic* mentalities. *Why* this change came about lies beyond the scope of our present discussion. One may suspect it to be an amalgam of logical studies in the rising cathedral schools of northern France and legal studies in the city schools of northern Italy. We shall encounter both when we come to Lanfranc of Canterbury shortly. It may seem unlikely to propose that there could have been such a dramatic change in mentality in so short a time as is suggested. The idea of the technological panacea of the first half of the nineteenth century, however, is a parallel case, not in physical/material results but in a drastic change of mentality.

In the so-called Dark Ages, when law codes were compiled and issued, although the individual laws in them were not necessarily inapplicable to actual legal procedures, their primary purpose as codes was to symbolise the status of the law-giver as a political authority. They belonged in that world of ritual and symbol which we have mentioned. The one obvious exception to this is the ninth-century collection of canon law, the Pseudo-Isidore or False Decretals, but in general the observation is valid. Under Archbishop Heribert of Cologne (999–1021), for instance, a compilation of canon law was copied, beautifully written in two columns, the manuscript in large format and looking absolutely pristine, scarcely a mark in the margins, apparently unused, and on the first folio are written the words in handsome capitals, LIBER HERIBERTI ARCHIEPISCOPI, the Book of Archbishop Heribert. This book was an icon, or an image of power and authority.[11]

The same is not untrue of the canon law collections made for the papacy under Gregory VII. The clear lay-out of the books of Anselm of

Lucca's compilation is an example. Books 1 and 2, with 89 and 82 texts respectively, deal with the primacy and sovereignty of the papacy. Books 3, 4 and 5 deal with the privileges and material rights of its churches. Only with Book 6 do we come to bishops, and mainly about their election. Books 7 and 8 are about the lesser clergy, Book 9 about the sacraments, Book 10 about marriage.[12] Symbolism indeed; but what is symbolised is hierarchy, or the right order of the world as it should actually work. Under Gregory himself there was a huge effort to ransack the Lateran archives in Rome for papal letters and new evidences of the legal exercise of papal authority, evidences which went into the collection of Anselm of Lucca and other collections.[13] It was rather like the ransacking of the records in the Tower of London in the early years of James I's reign when the king was making his 'impositions'.

Gregory intended canon law to be rigorously applied. In dark-age Christendom everyone accepted the papal primacy, but now this became primacy with jurisdictional teeth. What Gregory effected for the first time was that Rome should become the *jurisdictional* centre of (anyhow) Western Christendom.[14] The papal curia was born, the papacy as a law court, a court of first instance and of appeal. Initially Gregory did it by sending out legates who travelled widely, in the case of Gerald of Ostia to France, Germany, Spain and Denmark in 1074, and amongst other things generated legal business destined to be dealt with in Rome, the pope complaining if he did not receive reports quickly enough. Papal legates had been sent out before Gregory became pope, but not seriously before he became Archdeacon of Rome and the dominant influence behind the papacy c. 1059.[15] During the twelfth century the whole business of legal appeals to Rome mounted astonishingly. St Bernard complained of it in 1147; amidst the clamour of lawsuits, he thought, the popes were losing sight of their spiritual life.[16] The system of legates was even sooner found to have its drawbacks. The power given to legates made the issue of who became legates potentially explosive. Archbishop Manasses of Rheims began his archiepiscopate in the mid-1070s as a friend to Gregory and his reforming ideals. But then Gregory gave Hugh de Die, Archbishop of Lyon, and the one archbishop he got on with, the legateship for France. That gave Hugh the power to visit and exercise jurisdiction within Manasses's metropolitan province of Rheims, which naturally led to a split between Gregory and Manasses.[17]

An emphasis on law and its actual application is written all over Gregory VII's letters. To Archbishop Siegfried of Mainz, troubled in 1074 that the Bishops of Prague and Olmütz were not willing to accept his metropolitan/archiepiscopal authority, Gregory wrote:

You have transferred this affair from our judgement to the tribunal of your personal opinion. We invite you, brother, to peruse with us the sacred canons. There you will find that apostolic decisions cannot be reversed by any patriarch or primate.[18]

To Archbishop Anno of Cologne in 1075, he wrote concerning his orders about clerical celibacy: 'these orders are not our invention, but we proclaim them on the decrees of the ancient fathers'. He went on to write that a council should be called where canon law should be expounded for the benefit of those guilty of incelibacy.[19]

Gregory did not much like archbishops. With their primatial claims, often built up over centuries, he saw them as only too often obstacles to the advance of reform and papal authority. That was the basis of Lanfranc's trouble with him. Archbishop Liemar of Bremen wrote in exasperation that Gregory ordered bishops around as if they were bailiffs on his estates.[20]

Besides religious/moral zeal and the establishment of 'right order' in the world, there is one further element in the Gregorian Reform which ought to be mentioned: a determination to press the rights and prestige of the Church of Rome as far as possible, and in this particular case that was a long way. The Roman church had long claimed to be the mother of all churches. Whatever their church, it was a basic instinct of all churchmen in the Middle Ages to fight like tigers for the rights, privileges and possessions of their churches. We shall see it later when we come to Thomas Becket and Canterbury. Gregory's alleged last words are famous: 'I have loved justice and hated iniquity, therefore I die in exile.' Gregory died in Salerno and if one asks what was so awful about dying in Salerno (*pace* Cowdrey and his more positive interpretation),[21] one can only answer that Salerno was not Rome.

When Gregory wrote to Bishop Hermann of Metz arguing that he could depose the Emperor Henry IV if he wanted or needed, he maintained that one reason was the sanctity of popes compared with kings: 'Very few kings of saintly life can be found out of an innumerable multitude, while in one single chair of successive bishops – the Roman – nearly one hundred are counted amongst the holiest of men.' The same point is made even more strongly in the *Dictatus Papae* (1075), which some have thought to be the chapter titles for a very papalist collection of canon law, others to be a definition of 'emergency powers in the Roman see to enable it to take action for the reform of the church'.[22] Clause 28 says, 'a duly ordained pope is undoubtedly made a saint by the merits of St Peter'. Extravagant language, some may think; but as one looked back over the 150 or so popes up to Gregory's time, about 100 of them were indeed venerated as saints.[23] Under one guise, the Gregorian Reform could be viewed as the greatest of the many, many struggles in the Middle Ages for the rights and prestige of one see.

The reader may feel that this is a very long introduction on the Gregorian Reform for a chapter purporting to be about the Norman Conquest. But William the Conqueror's invasion of England received the explicit blessing of Pope Alexander II, at whose elbow by now stood the influential Archdeacon Hildebrand of Rome. The papacy had already found Normandy and its Duke receptive to reforming ideals. And then, everything said later on about the imposition of logical order, the advance of clericalism and of the order of Augustinian Canons, papalism and resistance to it, the development of canon law, and papal legateships, flows more or less directly from the Gregorian Reform.

From here on this chapter will be in the nature of a diptych, however disparate in size its two panels, the larger panel representing religion and politics as a macrocosm, the smaller as a microcosm; the larger religion and politics from top down, the smaller from bottom up; the larger representing a well-known figure, namely Lanfranc, Archbishop of Canterbury, the smaller a character little heard of called Gervase.

Lanfranc

Unlike his successor in the archbishopric of Canterbury, Saint Anselm, Lanfranc is not an easy man for us to know personally. Margaret Gibson ended her distinguished book on him with a neat fantasy. In national politics, she wrote, he was a pragmatist; at home in the abbeys of Bec and then Canterbury, he was resplendent in the praises of his monks; but 'we ourselves see him walking away through the cloister – with his hood up'.[24] He was born probably about 1010 in North Italy. That means that he would have been nearly fifty when Hildebrand became Archdeacon of Rome and over sixty when he became pope. Somewhere in North Italy he studied the liberal arts, including logic, which had a large influence on his later thinking; and wherever he studied law, he was during his younger years a notable practising lawyer in the important law courts of Pavia. He experienced a religious conversion, a second conversion as it is sometimes called in the case of those already Christian, and became a monk at the still new and ascetic abbey of Bec in Normandy about 1042, rising to be Prior only three years later. He attracted many pupils to Bec, not all of them necessarily monks, because of the breadth of his teaching. This was at the time when Duke William of Normandy was controlling reforming synods. In 1063 Duke William made him Abbot of Caen, and in 1070, after William had become also King of England, Archbishop of Canterbury in succession to the simoniac Englishman, Stigand. He accepted both these appointments with the greatest reluctance.

Thus, in point of age Lanfranc was a man of the pre-Gregorian church. But in his monastic/religious zeal, his power of logical reasoning, and the centrality of law to his ecclesiastic outlook, he was very much a churchman of the Gregorian age. The very likeness of Gregory VII and Lanfranc to each other was a significant ingredient in the tensions between them. Lanfranc played a large role in the friendly relationship of Duke William to the early Gregorian papacy,[25] while on the one occasion when there was a rift between them and the duke ordered Lanfranc into exile, it was immediately healed by Lanfranc's sense of humour. 'If you want me to be able to carry out your command', he is reported to have said, 'get me a better horse!'[26] Of course there was no more talk of exile after that.

Lanfranc was an archbishop to the core, just the kind of archbishop most suspect to Pope Gregory VII. Archbishops generally had no small idea of their rights and privileges, and all Lanfranc's undoubted pastoral commitment did not detract from his interest in the place of an archbishop in the order and structure of the church. Small wonder! For perhaps the first great *archbishop*, as such, in the Western church was his seventh-century predecessor at Canterbury, Archbishop Theodore, and it had all built up from there.[27] But the first great problem to hit Lanfranc when he became archbishop was the 'primacy dispute' between Canterbury and York and whether Thomas of Bayeux, the newly appointed Archbishop of York, should be subject to the authority of Lanfranc as Primate of all Britain. Thomas's argument – and like all archbishops he was egged on by the partisan clergy of his church – was that precedence between the two archbishops should go by seniority, and he had been appointed a few months before Lanfranc. To make matters worse, while Stigand had been Archbishop of Canterbury, Canterbury had suffered various depredations of its rights by York, especially the usurpation of the archbishop's right to consecrate the king. But Lanfranc had a trump card in his hand. A bishop had to be consecrated according to law by three bishops, but at that time York only had one suffragan bishop, Durham, in its metropolitan province. So Thomas had to wait until Lanfranc was consecrated, to be consecrated by Lanfranc with other bishops – at Canterbury (Christmas Day, 1070).

There were wheels within wheels in all this. Thomas had sat at Lanfranc's feet at Bec as one of his pupils and there was probably a great deal of personal respect between the two of them. On the other hand he was a protégé of Bishop Odo of Bayeux, the king's half-brother and no friend to Lanfranc. The Abbey of St Stephen's, Caen, where Lanfranc was abbot for seven years and which was in Odo's own diocese, enjoyed certain rights against the bishop; while again it was against Odo of Bayeux as Earl of Kent that Lanfranc secured the restoration of Canterbury lands at the Trial of Penenden Heath (?1072).[28] Moreover, important as monasticism was in the religion of eleventh-century Normandy, as exemplified by Bec and Lanfranc but not only by them, it also had some very important clerical families whose role was honourable and constructive, and one of these families was that of Thomas of Bayeux himself. He was Treasurer of Bayeux Cathedral; his brother, Samson, became Bishop of Worcester (1096–1112); Samson's son, another Thomas, followed his brother at one remove in being Archbishop of York (1108–1114). As can be seen, this, as well as other Norman clerical families, remained a force well into Henry I's reign.[29] So in this primacy dispute of the 1070s there were ambivalences caused by old loyalties and old rivalries.

Although Lanfranc had neither precedent nor documentary evidence on his side in seeking to extract an oath of obedience from York, crucially he was on a winning wicket with William the Conqueror. At first the Conqueror was inclined to favour the York case of seniority, for it was his idea that all his tenants-in-chief (and that included all important landholding churchmen) should owe their first loyalty directly to him, and there was a divide-and-rule element in his thinking about this issue, as there would be with Henry I. But Lanfranc won him over with an irresistible argument, which stressed that the unity of the English Church, indeed of the British Church, under Canterbury was a necessary condition for the unity of the kingdom under the Conqueror. We have the argument from Hugh the Chantor, a canon of York and a source extremely hostile to Lanfranc, but it is so likely an argument for Lanfranc to have put, that we may take it as that put by Lanfranc. Lanfranc is reported to have said:

that it was expedient for the union and solidarity of the kingdom that all Britain should be subject to one primate; it might otherwise happen, in the king's time or that of one of his successors, that some one of the Danes, Norwegians or Scots, who used to sail up to York in their attacks on the realm, might be made king by the Archbishop of York and the fickle and treacherous Yorkshiremen, and the kingdom disturbed and divided.[30]

Lanfranc was perhaps reminding the king here that if an Archbishop of York could consecrate him (when the job ought to have been done by Canterbury), he could consecrate someone else. Perhaps, too, the reference to the fickle Yorkshiremen reminded the king of his difficulties to get through Yorkshire to York only the previous year, 1069, when the northern risings against him had already shown that it was vital for him to hold that city.

Once persuaded, William bludgeoned Thomas into submission. When the latter resisted, the king lost his temper, said he would hate him for ever, and threatened that none of Thomas's near kinsmen should stay in England or Normandy (a threat that mattered very much to Thomas given what we have just said about his clerical family) unless he made his profession personally to Lanfranc. At last Thomas came to Canterbury for consecration. When Lanfranc put to him the customary question, 'wilt thou be subject to the holy church of Canterbury, and to me and my successors?' he paused momentarily, and in tears, he answered with a sigh, 'I will be subject to thee as long as thou livest, but not to thy successors, unless the pope shall so judge.'[31]

After this, the two archbishops travelled to Rome together to put their cases, a sign of their personal amity as are later exchanges of letters between them; and Pope Alexander II, less of a centraliser than Gregory VII would be, referred the case back to the judgement of the bishops and abbots of the whole kingdom. It was thrashed out at two assemblies held at Winchester and Windsor in 1072. Although Thomas was by then prepared to promise obedience unconditionally to Lanfranc and his successors, and with a public oath, Lanfranc, 'out of love for the king' waived the oath, and accepted only a written profession.[32] That shows that William I still wanted to hold a balance between the two archbishops, and Lanfranc's concession was enough to keep the door open for a dispute that would run on and on. The other major compromise of 1072 was that while the Archbishop of York renounced any claim to jurisdiction over the three bishoprics of Lincoln, Worcester and Lichfield (now in 1072 Chester), Lanfranc conceded that not only Durham but also the whole of Scotland should be under York. That was an obvious dent in Lanfranc's claim to be Primate of Britain. Not as large a dent in practice, however, as in theory; for William I failed to master Scotland militarily, while in terms of personal influence, Canterbury's at this time was in fact greater than York's.[33]

Lanfranc appears strictly to have held to the 1072 agreement over Scotland. Soon afterwards he readily co-operated with Archbishop Thomas in the latter's consecration of Bishop Ralph of the Orkneys (1073–1100), ordering the bishops of Chester and Worcester to go and make up the necessary numbers of consecrating bishops.[34] Later, when Queen Margaret of Scotland, whose daughter Matilda would marry Henry I, asked him to send some Canterbury monks to help start her foundation of Holy Trinity Abbey, Dunfermline, he sent three monks, but far from using this as an occasion to insinuate Canterbury influence into Scotland, he asked for them back as soon as possible because they could ill be spared from Canterbury! For a moment in this letter the curtain is pulled up from behind Lanfranc the great churchman/lawyer, and we catch a glimpse of a humane person and a monk of modesty and humility:

You, who are born of a royal line, brought up as befits a queen and nobly wedded to a noble king (Malcolm), are choosing me as your father – a low-grade foreigner steeped in sin – and you ask me to accept you as your spiritual daughter. I am not what you think me to be; but may I be so because you think it. Do not continue under a misapprehension, but pray for me that I may be a father fit to pray to God for you and to be heard on your account.[35]

Dented Lanfranc's claims to an all-British primacy may have been by Scotland, but they were kept alive by his being asked in 1074 to consecrate Patrick, a monk of Worcester, as bishop of Dublin. Since Pope Gregory VII commended this consecration as an opportunity to bring Irish marital customs in line with canon law, and in this Lanfranc concurred with him, it must have seemed to Lanfranc as yet another example, corresponding to his own, of the pastoral role of monasticism in the churches of the British Isles. Again, just as in the Canterbury and York dispute of 1070 Lanfranc's position dovetailed perfectly with the king's on the necessary unity of the kingdom of the English, so now Lanfranc's claim to be Primate of Britain, embodied in Patrick's profession of obedience to him, neatly corresponded to William's own claim to be *Rex Britanniae*.[36]

In all these matters one has to remember the very positive ideology of kingship and secular power which Lanfranc displayed while he was still writing in Normandy before he became archbishop, particularly in his commentaries on the Pauline epistles. Perhaps this is another way in which one could call him a pre-Gregorian man. To Lanfranc, secular rulers were the guarantors of peace and morality. Their authority must be upheld. In a passage ringing with Augustine's *City of God*, Book 19, he wrote (on 1 Timothy, 2, 1–2):

In the peace of princes are preserved the quiet and good estate of
churches; for in wars and discords their tranquillity is shattered, religion
grows cold, deference is destroyed, and where deference is destroyed
chastity of living is violated.[37]

To Lanfranc, rationality was embodied in a chain of command, and
especially in law. Late in his archepiscopate, for instance, he wrote a characteristic letter to Bishop Maurice of London (1086–1107), ordering him
as Maurice's metropolitan to sort out a dispute at Barking Abbey between
the abbess and the prioress. The abbess is to give directions, which are to
be obeyed so long as they are reasonable, or a better translation, in confor-
mity with reason, and which do not conflict with canon law. 'Order the
abbess to be an abbess and the prioress to be a prioress', he wrote.[38] Very
different he was from one of the great English bishops of the tenth century,
Ethelwold of Winchester, for example. Ethelwold ruled by ritual and
magic, terror and charisma, the generous flashing around of gold. He
was a Holy Man Bishop, an *Adelsheilige* or nobleman saint.[39] Lanfranc's
parentage and original social status are virtually unknown, and in any
case he would have regarded all that as irrelevant. He was the new type of
classless, law-centred churchman. Very Gregorian!

But Lanfranc's archiepiscopal philosophy, shared by later archbishops
of Canterbury, not least Thomas Becket, was almost bound to mean trouble
with the papacy over its claims to supremacy. While Alexander II remained
pope, he was entirely supportive of Lanfranc in the primacy dispute, even
conceding to him in effect a standing papal legation which enabled him
to settle disputes as if they had been settled in the pope's own presence,
i.e. without his having to keep visiting Rome.[40] But the chill wind of papal
centralism had already begun to blow from Hildebrand before he became
pope. In 1072, when he was still Archdeacon of Rome, he responded tersely
to a request from Lanfranc that his recently established, or re-established,
powers as primate should be embodied in a papal privilege, by saying that
to receive such a privilege it was necessary to come in person to Rome.[41]
Thereafter as pope, Gregory kept insisting that Lanfranc should visit
Rome to receive from him his pallium, the symbol of his metropolitan or
archiepiscopal authority. This is an example of the way Gregory sought to
concentrate jurisdiction on Rome itself. His policy was to write fair words
to William ('you are the jewel of princes', etc.),[42] because while he was
embroiled with the Emperor Henry IV he could not afford to make
enemies of other secular rulers, and harsh words to Lanfranc.

Lanfranc was well up to countering this kind of thing. He wrote back (1080) with coolness and irony:

*I cannot myself understand that either personal absence or the great
distance separating us can have the least bearing on this question.
My mind submits to your commands in all respects and in all matters
according to canon law. Were I ever able to speak with you in person,
I should demonstrate that my devotion for you had increased, whereas
you (if it may be said with respect) have declined somewhat from your
original cordiality.*[43]

One may see from this letter that Lanfranc in no way denied papal primacy; but he wanted the archbishop's office in practice not to suffer erosion. Nonetheless it is hard not to see him in the long run on a losing wicket via à vis the papacy. He compiled his own collection of canon law, the *Collectio Lanfranci*, based mainly on the Pseudo-Isidore or 'False Decretals' which was a ninth-century compilation with heavy emphasis on papal powers. He cannot have failed to notice this fact. But Z.N. Brooke, who identified Lanfranc's own copy of this collection in a manuscript now at Trinity College, Cambridge, showed how Lanfranc himself (almost certainly) had gone through this manuscript writing reference marks in the margins in the form of a small a, all of them in red ink, and the great majority of them referring to the powers of metropolitans, or archbishops. Brooke then went on to illustrate the entirely practical purpose of these reference marks with a letter of Lanfranc to Bishop Herfast of Thetford.[44] The rich abbey of Bury St Edmunds had appealed to the pope against Herfast for harassing it. Herfast, it appears had sought to augment the meagre resources of his bishopric by locating his see at Bury St Edmunds and appropriating its properties. The idea of a cathedral monastery was no anomaly in England at this time, what with Canterbury itself, Winchester, Worcester, and from the 1080s Durham; and exactly what Herfast sought to do in the 1070s would be done by Bishop John of Wells with respect to Bath Abbey in 1090.[45]

Lanfranc turned round and wrote to Herfast, without a word about the papacy, telling him to read Scripture and master the decrees of the Roman pontiffs and the canons of councils. There he would discover that of which he was ignorant. Then follows a string of canonical citations, not referring to papal authority at all, but all of them having to do with the powers and duties and authority of metropolitan bishops within their province. Every one of the passages cited in Lanfranc's letter has a red 'a' beside it in the margin, and the effect is heightened, as Brooke showed, by the fact that the order in which they are cited in the letter is exactly that of the order in which they come in Lanfranc's collection.[46] There have been scholars in recent years who have pointed out that a number of passages relating to metropolitan authority have not got 'a's in the margin of Lanfranc's manuscript and they have thus doubted whether Lanfranc had quite the single-minded, metropolitan/archiepiscopal purpose in studying his canon law collection. But a careful study of the manuscript itself largely dispels these doubts. The passages where 'a's are missing are mainly in the texts of councils, especially the Visigothic councils, where archiepiscopal authority had been heavily stressed, texts in which every conciliar canon is clearly rubricated with the subject matter of the particular canon. In these texts it was easy to find canons relating to metropolitan authority. Where the 'a's occur is on pages with great blocks of unrubricated, unparagraphed texts, in which it was anything but easy to find what one was looking for by merely scanning the page.[47] Lanfranc's practicality extended to not scattering 'a's, as if in a paper chase for future historians, where a's were not necessary.

One of the reasons why it was said that Lanfranc was on a losing wicket in his deployment of texts from his own canon law collection was that not only did he go against its whole papalist grain, but that also two could play at the game of citing canonical texts in support of a particular ecclesiastical position. It was played against him in the last year of his life in 1088 by William of St Calais, Bishop of Durham, out of Lanfranc's own *Collectio Canonum*. William of St Calais joined Odo of Bayeux's rebellion against William II, or at least detached himself from the king, in 1088, and was brought to trial at a Great Council at Salisbury in November. Lanfranc insisted that the bishop was being judged as one who held a great fief of the king. Bishop William, on the other hand, claimed that as a bishop he could only be judged according to canon law, and he declared that he was appealing to Rome. A dispute on such a subject, involving Lanfranc (as himself a great tenant-in-chief of the king) on the secular side, was naturally an explosive *cause célèbre*. An account of the bishop's trial survives, written from a Durham viewpoint, in dramatic language, and virulently hostile to Lanfranc.[48] Historians are not agreed about whether or not this account is strictly contemporary with the event, or is rather from the first half of the twelfth century, but either way it can hardly be a fiction constructed as a later academic exercise. Once again Lanfranc must have felt ambivalences. He might support the rightful secular authority and he might not be able to swallow the Bishop of Durham's papalism, but the bishop was also a devout monk who had read Bede's *Ecclesiastical*

History and *Life of St Cuthbert* and had brought monks to Durham under the inspiration of northern monasticism in the seventh century as described by Bede.[49]

Bishop William of Durham also had his authorised copy of Lanfranc's collection of canon law; it has been identified as a manuscript now at Peterhouse, Cambridge. He too made little reference marks in the margins, or at least somebody in Durham made them around the time of his trial. They mark passages, among others, about a bishop's right to appeal to Rome, not to be tried while despoiled of his possessions, to be tried (when tried) with the participation of other bishops of his province. Bishop William is said to have raised all these points against Lanfranc, according to the report of his trial.[50]

One last observation about both Bishop William and Archbishop Lanfranc. William was forced into exile in Normandy from 1089 to 1093, when St Anselm became Archbishop of Canterbury. When he returned to Durham he brought with him a remarkable collection of books for the cathedral/monastery.[51] They included a giant bible, with superbly ornamented initial letters for the beginning of each book, set in oceans of beautifully written text. It can still be seen in the Durham Cathedral Treasury. Such eleventh-century bibles, focusing on the text with fine art rather than swamping it with illustrations, are veritable symbols of the Gregorian Reform, because they symbolically highlight the responsibility of the church and in particular the papacy to expound the meaning of Scripture and to be a fount of orthodoxy.[52] William's devotion to the papacy seems more than something which he adopted in 1088 for the political needs of the moment. It was under William, also, that the majestic cathedral, which still stands today, was begun. It had obviously been planned initially to have a flat wooden ceiling like that of the Norman church of Ely. But very early on that plan was changed in favour of having a much more impressive stone ribbed vault [see Plate 1]. What I am about to say obviously has an element of the subjective about it. We have to remember that when William turned his cathedral into a Benedictine monastery, and Walcher before him who had tried to turn it into a house of regular canons – and these transformations themselves accorded with the Gregorian pastoral ideal – they clearly trampled on some local aristocratic interests and thus made enemies.[53] Walcher's murder is an indication of that. So, as with his giant Bible, I believe this vaulting was a statement of ideals, ideals of episcopal majesty and of cathedral monasticism.

As for Lanfranc, he gave up formal teaching of the liberal arts when he was at Bec, in favour of scripture and theology. He became a famous biblical scholar and theologian. But in his influential commentaries on St Paul's epistles, he continued to use the discipline of logic in order to elucidate Paul's thinking.[54] Again in his treatise on the Real Presence of Christ in the Eucharist, the upshot of his debate with the clever Berengar of Tours who appeared to deny a corporeal presence in favour of one more symbolist or memorialist, Lanfranc used the logical works of Boethius with the Aristotelian logic embedded in them. Against Berengar he distinguished the principal from the secondary essences of things, conceiving a world divided into substance and accidents, *genera* or genus and species. Lanfranc the scholar saw a logical/rational order of creation, and that was surely not a separate compartment of his life from Lanfranc the archbishop who strove for logical/rational order in the church.[55] Moreover, the Lanfranc who stressed the real presence of Christ in the Eucharistic was necessarily stressing the consecrating power of the priesthood, and that was why the priesthood should be considered superior to the laity from secular rulers downward. Here was Lanfranc the Gregorian!

Gervase

We have the story of Gervase as it was told by the Abbey of Ely; very few stories of not particularly well-known lay people at this period – the late eleventh century – reach us from themselves rather than from their social and, generally, ecclesiastical superiors. So in the first place we are being transported now from an archbishop's world to a monastery's. That is not such a big jump as might at first appear, for compared to the West as a whole, monasticism had had an exceptionally high place in English religion. An arresting example of this is that England had a type of institution unknown on the Continent, the monastic cathedral. In 1066 there were three monastic cathedrals – Canterbury itself, Winchester and Worcester. Lanfranc, himself a monk, not only kept that, but also strengthened it. Lawyer-like, he compiled a book of *Monastic Constitutions*, or customs, which he handed down in an authoritarian way in the first instance to Prior Henry of Canterbury, another monk of Bec.[56] The prior in these institutions was the equivalent to the dean of a cathedral of secular canons, the monastery being equivalent to the chapter (and the bishop the equivalent to the abbot). Writing some twenty years ago about Aethelwold, the great tenth-century Bishop of Winchester, Patrick Wormald made a telling contrast between Winchester and Magdeburg at that time. The Abbey of St Maurice Magdeburg, was one of the great monasteries of the German empire, but when in 968 Otto I elevated Magdeburg into the seat of an archbishopric, nobody dreamt of keeping it as a monastic cathedral like Winchester. The monks were packed off to the outskirts of the city, minus most of their endowments, and Magdeburg became a cathedral of secular canons.[57] In the 1080s, the probable decade of Gervase's story, Ely was not yet the seat of a bishop, though it would become one in 1109, but it was an ancient and prestigious church, founded by St Aethelfryth (or St Etheldreda) in the seventh century, and, according to Domesday Book the abbey was one of the three richest landholders in Cambridgeshire, the other two being Count Alan of Richmond, the Breton, and a Norman baron of the second order called Picot, Picot of Cambridgeshire as Domesday Book calls him.

When Norman monks began to be appointed to English abbacies as they fell vacant after the Conquest, they varied very much in their attitudes towards their monasteries. Some treated them as the acquisitions of conquest, like Norman secular barons taking over their landed acquisitions. Thus the monks of Abingdon would complain that Ethelelm, a monk of Jumièges, had alienated many of their lands to his relatives, and a similar complaint was made of Turold at Peterborough.[58] The monks of Glastonbury presumably detected the attitude of a conqueror in Thurstan of Caen, though there the *casus belli* was the style of chant, the monks wanting to keep their old chants as against those of Bec which Thurstan wanted to foist on them. One should note, incidentally, that even in the case of a Norman abbot with an unsavoury reputation, this shows his concern for the order of monastic life in itself. However, the dénouement at Glastonbury was a terrible one. In a fit of uncontrollable anger, Thurstan set his knights onto the monks. Three of them were killed and many more injured in their own church where they tried to take refuge.[59] One may see from this what part of the problem was. Like secular barons abbeys owed contingents of knights for when the king called out his army or for local purposes, and in the early years after the Conquest they had often not yet been enfeoffed with lands and were boarded within the monastery. That was not a recipe for monastic peace. The saintly Bishop Wulfstan II of Worcester, in effect abbot of the cathedral monastery there, would eat with his knights and, in an attempt to moderate their drinking, would occasionally sip from a very small cup to show good manners and fellowship.[60] It may even be that Ethelelm of Abingdon, despite later being complained of, was trying to do his abbey a good turn by getting the knights out of the abbey and onto their own lands.[61]

Whatever the case elsewhere, however, neither of the first two Norman abbots of Ely showed the slightest disposition to treat their abbey as if it was a Norman conquest, rather than as their having the charge of a religious institution and a community of monks, and both were warmly approved of by the twelfth-century chronicler of the abbey in the *Liber Eliensis*. When Theodwine was appointed, by the king c. 1073–75 he refused to accept the position until the king restored everything he had taken from the abbey's treasury.[62] That was a lot, because Cambridgeshire had seen heroic opposition to the Norman Conquest, let by Hereward the Wake, in which Ely had been a storm centre. Theodwine, like Ethelelm of Abingdon, had been a monk of Jumièges. Simeon, abbot 1082–93, was the brother of Bishop Walkelin of Winchester, – so another clerical (or monastic) family – from Rouen. He blotted his copybook initially with the community by accepting his abbatial blessing from the Bishop of Lincoln against the custom of the church. That was quickly overlooked, however, because of his kindness and pure way of life, his starting the rebuilding of the abbey church, his securing restitution of the abbey's lands and rights from William the Conqueror, and his alert protection of the abbey from all predators (as we are about to see).[63]

We should divest ourselves of one idea in particular: that there was racial tension between Normans and English after the Conquest. There never was. This was a later construct imposed on the Norman Conquest by the half-English, half-Norman William of Malmesbury, writing in the 1120s.[64] He was widely read and influential, but what he imposed was a class distinction of his day between those who by then spoke French and held positions of responsibility, and those who spoke only English and held none. When English writers earlier wrote against Normans, it was because such Normans were seen as bullies and predators, not because they were Normans. Ann Williams has pointed out that by 1086 many socially modest people called Frenchmen (*francigenae*) are mentioned in Domesday Book. These Frenchmen could scarcely have been settled amongst the rural population had there been racial tension between English and Normans.[65] True many Norman barons used their English acquisitions to help endow their family monasteries back in Normandy. Count Robert of Mortain, half-brother of William I and a baron of the first order, and his son William, built up Grestain Abbey in this way, to give an example.[66] That was only natural because to them Normandy was their homeland. The Anglo-Norman kingdom was no mere political fiction; the Channel united a whole aristocracy which now straddled it. At the same time the Norman kings and aristocracy were active in causing the restitution of lands wrongly taken from monasteries, and Norman barons played a part in building up at least some monasteries in England.[67] Moreover there were fruitful exchanges of personnel between English and Norman monasteries after, as before, the Norman Conquest. Ely itself had a monk of Bec amongst its number at the time in question, perhaps to help impart some of the best of Bec ways, and even its chants, for before the Norman Conquest, Ely was famous for its music and for its religious devotion.[68]

The story of Gervase and his death is undoubtedly the story of a heart attack (the only heart attack I know of which can be ascribed to the circumstances of the Norman Conquest). It comes in the *Liber Eliensis* immediately after the description in the book of the wrongs inflicted on Ely by the Norman baron, Picot:

Picot (sheriff of Cambridgeshire) had officials, authors of deceit, who followed him in his crooked exactions, but God scattered them in the pride of their heart. One of these, Gervase by name, was replete with malice and ignorant of good. He was a craftsman of anger, an inventor of crime, a confuser of right and wrong, whose master, the said Picot, entrusted to him as more faithful in depravity than all the rest, the business of his whole sheriffdom. He greatly harassed the men of St Etheldreda and attacked her possessions by every means and with a heavy hand as if he had taken up a crusade against her. Whoever was oppressed by him for whatever cause, and called upon the name of the saint in order to try and make him act in this way less often, such a man he imprisoned or fined or called frequently to the courts or attacked cruelly. The abbot took ill the daily complaints of his men and ordered the community to sing the seven penitential psalms before the holy virgin's tomb to beg mercy from her. The abbot himself was promptly summoned to court, a day and place being fixed for the hearing of a dispute. The Brethren were hard at prayer and the abbot was on his way when he heard that the bullying barrator had come to a wretched end.

This is how it all happened. The night before the abbot was due to arrive for the lawsuit, St Etheldreda, dressed as an abbess with a pastoral staff, accompanied by her two sisters, stood over him (Gervase) angrily and rebuked him in a terrifying voice as follows: 'Are you not the man who so often troubles my men, whose patron I am, holding me in contempt, and never desists from disturbing my church? Take this for your reward so that others may learn through you not to disturb a family of Christ'. With that she took the staff which she was carrying and pushed its point heavily on the place of his heart as if to pierce him through. Then her sisters Saint Withburga and Saint Sexburga, who had come with her, attacked him with the hard points of their staffs. His fearful groans and

*horrible cries aroused the whole household, as he said in the hearing of
all, 'my lady have pity, my lady have pity'. On hearing this the servants
came rushing to inquire of the cause of his pain. There was a resounding
noise around him as he lay there, and he said to them, 'did you not see
how St Etheldreda as she was leaving transfixed me in the breast with
the point of her staff, as did her sisters? And again the pain returns,
I am dying as it pierces me anew.' With that he expired.*

*After this had happened the abbot was met on the journey, told the
news and returned, and the story spread about the region. It caused fear
of the saint throughout the neighbourhood, and for a long time no baron,
judge, official or representative of any power dared to snatch at the
possessions of Ely, since the holy virgin protected her possessions
everywhere in manly style.*[69]

The abbot in question could have been Theodwine in the early to mid-
1070s, or more likely Simeon. Domesday Book shows that within twenty
years of the Norman Conquest, Picot, besides being sheriff of the shire,
had indeed become a large-scale landholder in Cambridgeshire. Within
the manors which Picot held in that shire, however, numerous men are
described as holding land of the Abbot of Ely or of being his sokemen (i.e.
being obliged to attend the abbot's law court, which one way or another
brought in money for the abbot). Often these tenants of the abbey were
able to sell their land at will; sometimes they were not. But in the former
case it is always stated that the soke, i.e. the duty to attend the abbot's
court, remains with the abbot. Thus, on Picot's own estates there were
many opportunities for him to trouble 'the men of St Aethelthryth', namely
of Ely Abbey, and to summon them to his own court, illegally from the
abbey's point of view.

The point of view that we are getting in this narrative is of course Ely's;
there is no corresponding statement representing how Picot looked at it all.
Picot was probably uncomprehending of a situation where landlordship
and jurisdiction did not go together, for in eleventh-century France generally, with the rise of the *seigneurie banale* they were inseparable. Perhaps
more to the point is the real possibility that the men who were obliged to
attend the abbey's court would themselves rather have attended Picot's.
Barons were not necessarily harsher or more rapacious than monasteries in
their jurisdiction. Perhaps some at least of those whom the abbey regarded
as being 'troubled' by Picot were in fact complicit in his doings. Perhaps
not everyone shared Ely's hatred of Picot. However, this was not enough
to save Gervase from his fate.

Gervase, the egregious official of Picot, does not appear in Domesday Book. The likeliest reason for this is that his death had already occurred before its compilation in 1086. For many of Picot's tenants are mentioned in Domesday Book, some only generally as 'men' or 'knights', but others by name; and it is unlikely that so important an official and protégé as Gervase was would not have been a tenant and appeared by name were he still alive in 1086. His death probably occurred, therefore, between 1082, the earliest date of Abbot Simeon, and 1086. In his death scene, the words spoken by St Etheldreda must be an imaginative or fictitious invention. Historians of ancient and medieval times commonly put speeches considered to be appropriate into the mouths of the *dramatis personae* of history. But despite the partisan and bombastic language of the Ely chronicler, there seems no reason to doubt the historical veracity of the other concrete details, including the reported words of Gervase.

Stress is known to be a major contributory cause of heart attacks, and it is possible to see quite clearly the pressures that Gervase was under when his death occurred. And seeing these gives us an idea of how the Norman Conquest worked on the ground, at least in Cambridgeshire when a powerful religious institution and a rapacious baron faced each other at close quarters.

The problem about Picot for Ely, perhaps for the whole of Cambridgeshire, was how to restrain him. It was almost useless to look to the king. William the Conqueror is viewed as the strong king *par excellence* by those who deal in categories of strong and weak kings; but his strength, apart from validating restitutions of lands, was strictly circumscribed. John Gillingham has written on how the Conqueror had established his baron, Ilbert de Lacy, in the Honour of Pontefract in order to hold the 'Aire Gap' between the Pennines and the River Ouse, dominated by the castle of Pontefract, for him, so that he could always cross the River Aire and reach York. William had been held up fighting at the Aire for three weeks when he tried to reach York in 1069, and it had been a crisis for him. Provided Ilbert de Lacy did that job for him, it would seem that the king gave him a free hand in the region.[70] Much the same might be said of Picot in Cambridgeshire. Cambridgeshire had been another area of serious rebellion and crisis for the Conqueror in the early years after 1066, to emphasise what has already been said. If Picot kept Cambridgeshire quiet for the Conqueror, it seems that for the rest he could do pretty much as he liked.

For the Ely monks there was only one other alternative: recourse to their saint and foundress, Etheldreda, whose body lay in an antique marble sarcophagus, raised since the tenth century to a high level in the vicinity of the altar.[71] It is a commonplace to say that in our period the supernatural presence of a saint was felt most powerfully where his or her bodily remains lay. The ritual of appealing to a saint by the monks' prostrating themselves before the tomb and singing the seven penitential psalms was a well-known one in eleventh-century French monasteries. In its most extreme form it actually involved the 'humiliation' of a saint by bringing the tomb or feretory down from a high-placed shrine and putting it on the floor, as if monks and saint were debasing themselves together in penance. It was a frank complaint against a saint supposed to protect his or her monastery from the wrath of God and the attacks of man.[72] It is possible that such a ritual of humiliation lay behind what the *Liber Eliensis* (composed 1131–74) describes here, but that with the advance of legal rationality in England, it was becoming unfashionable to go too deeply into ritualistic magic.

What was the point of the solemnities surrounding all these prostrations and chantings of the seven penitential psalms? It was too much to hope that they could impress the brazen Picots of the world, but they were undoubtedly designed to, and did, impress large sectors of public opinion in a region.[73] Moving over to France once more, it is possible to see how in the region of Conques Abbey in the Massif Centrale, the shrine of St Faith became in the eleventh century the focus of opposition to the unbridled rapacity of the Counts of Rouergue and the castellans of their region. It was a rallying point, although people needed little rallying, for the Counts' actions hit monks and peasants alike.[74] Anyone who knows the awesome tenth-century statue of St Faith, at Conques to this day, with the saint seated erect and hieratic, eyes staring straight ahead, covered with gold sheeting and encrusted with gems, will appreciate how above all it was intended to inspire terror, especially terror in those who attacked the rights and property of her monastery. So it was at Ely, where there were richly made statues of Etheldreda and her sisters Withburga and Sexburga. In the case of Ely one may see that Norman abbots and English monks were entirely at one in having recourse to their English saint in order to resist the despoliations of a Norman baron. There was no question of any conflict along Norman/English lines as such.

By now it must be quite clear what the pressures on Gervase were. On the one hand, as a dependant of Picot he was obliged to enforce the will and further the interests of an ambitious, unscrupulous and strong-willed Norman baron. On the other hand he had to bear the brunt of the growing public hatred and disapproval in Cambridgeshire, orchestrated without a doubt by Ely around the figure of St Etheldreda, in that region. One may see Gervase as not merely the predator of the Ely propaganda, but also as a victim of the Norman Conquest and its ensuing social tensions, unable to stand the strain of being between the hammer of Picot and the anvil of Ely. One is almost tempted to say that the saint chose a soft target.

There is a lot more to be said about the Norman Conquest between the heights of Lanfranc and the low life of Gervase. Some of it will come into later chapters, but much of it will be omitted altogether. For this book has to cover two centuries, and I shall often prefer to move, as in this chapter, by giving characteristic impressions rather than by trying to compress everything into a comprehensive survey which will give readers indigestion!

CHAPTER 3

Henry I and His Religion

Religion and friendship

The reigns of the first two Henrys (1100–35, 1154–89), father and grandson, occupy between them 70 years of the twelfth century. It is not easy to size up the character of Henry I, partly because he was an evasive man who would not have wanted to be sized up. Here is the rather ironic, double-edged appraisal of Sir Richard Southern:

Despite the more favourable opinion of his contemporaries, Henry's personality makes a more unpleasing impression than that of Rufus. He was equally licentious, and avaricious; and in his early years at least, until he developed a pronounced strain of piety, his aims were equally secular. But he had more craft and policy; more capacity to wait, to present a good face to the world, and to advance step by step towards his goal. He was a man of great political sagacity and formidable resolution. As a younger son he had learned to be content with small advantages when greater ones were not to be had; but he had not lost the capacity for large designs or for rapid action when need arose. He was too much of a politician ever to outrage religious feelings as Rufus did, but his smooth words concealed a purpose very little different from that of Rufus.[1]

The idea that Henry only developed a strain of piety later on, of which Martin Brett's reference to 'that spiritual panic which seems to have beset Henry in his later years' is a variant,[2] arises mainly from Henry's appointment of two saintly Augustinian canons to bishoprics, against the run of play, in his later years. These were Robert of Bethune at Hereford in 1130 and Athelwold at Carlisle in 1133. Of the former Henry is reported to have said that he wished there to be at least one good root in the church after his days.[3] But is it not entirely fair to imply that his piety is only a late development in Henry. Orderic Vitalis tells of a visit he made to his own monastery of St Evroult (Normandy) in 1113, before he had any particular reason for panic. He sat for a long time in the monks' cloister, considering carefully the regularity of their monastic life and praising them for it. The next day he came into their chapter-house and humbly asked to be admitted to their fraternity. Orderic tells one this immediately after reporting the appointment by the king of two ideal bishops to Norman sees in the two previous years, Geoffrey as Archbishop of Rouen (1111) and Audoen as Bishop of Evreux (1112). Of both he says that they were eloquent, learned, and of sound teaching.[4] In England Roger of Salisbury is generally taken to be the typical Henrician bishop, an astute and sometimes harsh businessman who headed the Exchequer, and who is said to have originally recommended himself as a Norman priest to Henry by the speed with which he could say Mass. But Roger cared about learning and education too. The canons of Salisbury in his time as bishop were making a gigantic effort to build up a great library of theological, patristic, and religious manuscripts (this was their 'twelfth-century Renaissance'). And Teresa Webber, who has demonstrated all this, thinks that Roger with his continental contacts may well have helped them to secure exemplars for copying at Salisbury. Certain it was that early on he took the initiative, using his acquaintance with Hildebert, Bishop of Le Mans, to get a suitable schoolmaster for his cathedral. Hildebert sent Guy of Étampes, precentor of his own cathedral, telling Roger that 'in him you will find many masters'.[5]

Henry certainly had many sins – cruelty, sexual promiscuity, avarice, amongst them.[6] But to think that a man cannot be genuinely religious because he has many sins and vices is a very Protestant notion of religion. This notion has, however, coloured interpretation of some of Henry's religious traits. For example, stress is sometimes placed, in his especially favouring the Augustinian Canons, on their houses being relatively cheap to found and so (for an avaricious man) a cheap way of gaining the kudos of religious patronage.[7] A section of a later chapter devoted to the Augustinian Canons. Here I only say that whatever degree of truth there is in this, it overlooks the enthusiasm of his queen, Matilda, daughter of the saintly Queen Margaret of Scotland, for the Canons, and the fact that religious reformers themselves saw them as a way forward around 1100, in providing a combination of the pastoral and contemplative lives.[8] In 1121, after Matilda had died, Henry ordered a light to burn at his wife's tomb in Westminster Abbey, in perpetuity.[9]

After the enumeration of all Henry I's defects of character, it may seem paradoxical to say that the cultivation of friendship was a marked feature of his operating politically. This does not necessarily mean that he liked personally every one who was drawn into his friendship circle. Friendship in the twelfth century should be conceived at the political level as a mode of operation to express or achieve common purposes and interests. It should be set in a classical literary culture of friendship, with Cicero at its centre, to ennoble what might otherwise seem base and mercenary.[10] Because of the idealistic classical setting, historians like to use the Latin work for friendship, *amicitia*, to describe this feature of the political culture. Nonetheless there are, if not always, often grounds to think that, with Henry, political mode and personal feelings coincided.

William of Malmesbury wrote that Henry was tenacious in his hatreds and in his friendships.[11] William was not here writing with hostile intent; indeed it was part of an admiring encomium about the king's keeping law and order. But in actual fact Henry showed a remarkable willingness to be reconciled to his enemies (with a few necessary exceptions such as William Clito, his nephew and challenger), and 'to receive them kindly into his friendship', as Orderic wrote.[12] William of Warenne, for instance, disappointed of a marriage with one of Henry I's relations between 1101–03, joined Robert Duke of Normandy, i.e. he rebelled against Henry, but became reconciled with him and fought on his side at the Battle of Tinchebrai (1106) where Henry defeated his elder brother and reunited the Anglo-Norman kingdom as one entity. In 1110 Henry gave him the castle of Saint-Saens, just three miles up the river Varenne from the Warenne castle of Bellencombre. Twenty-five years later William was at the king's death-bed.[13] Another telling little illustration of *amicitia* as Henry I's normal mode is in the Abingdon Chronicle. During a vacancy in the abbacy of Abingdon, Simon the king's dispenser went to the king in Normandy to argue, face to face, his right to the church of Marcham and land there, held by the abbey. Simon easily persuaded the king of this, says the Chronicle ruefully, since there was no opposing party present to resist.[14] One legal historian has cited this to show how ad hoc the righting of legal wrongs was under Henry I, for which regularised legal procedures would be advanced under Henry II later. This totally misses a psychological point, however, that the *normal* expectation of anyone visiting Henry I's court would be a friendly reception.

Nothing illustrates Henry I's *amicitia* at work better than his dealings with the Welsh, as the late Sir Rees Davies brilliantly showed. Henry did not engage in campaigns of conquest, unlike Edward I later:

*Welsh princelings were invited or summoned – the distinction was
academic – to court. Such visits were in part social and doubtless flattered
the ego of the guests, as they were plied with gifts, pensions, feasts and
other signs of attention. But the king also gradually bound them in a
nexus of obligation, patronage and reward. He cajoled them with gifts
(as he did Iorwerth ap Bleddyn of Powys in 1102); he flattered them with
attention and honours (as in his promise to Owain ap Cadwgan of Powys
in 1114 to make him a knight); he enticed them with the prospect of
exalting them over and above their kinsmen.*[15]

Indeed, fostering their friendship with himself was far from incompatible
with setting Welsh grandees at each others' throats. A contemporary Welsh
chronicler was in awe at Henry I's cunning and the Welsh fear of him. The
king gave certain favoured English barons a stake in the Norman settlement of Wales, e.g. Gilbert FitzRichard of Clare a lordship in Ceredigion.
He managed at one and the same time, therefore, to forward his friendship
with his own magnates and with the Welsh on whom they intruded.

It looks, although this cannot be proved, as if Henry were doing something very similar with the Welsh church to what he was doing with the
Welsh princes, namely holding opposing forces or persons in balance by
the mediating influence of his friendship on both sides. His reign was a
decisive period in the development of Welsh diocesan structure, as well as
in the subjugation of the Welsh episcopate to the metropolitan authority of
Canterbury. Within this development, the clash between the two principal
bishops in Wales, Urban of Llandaff and Bernard of St David's, about the
territorial extent of their dioceses helped to bring about the delineation
of Welsh dioceses altogether. The fact that Bernard of St David's had been
a chaplain of Henry I's queen, Matilda, the frequency of his attendances at
court after he became bishop in 1115, and his closeness to Roger of Salisbury,
all made him manifestly a member of Henry's friendship circle. Urban of
Llandaff was perhaps not quite so close a friend of Henry I as was Bernard
of St David's, but he clearly was a friend. A familiar figure at court, his
settlement with Robert Earl of Gloucester, the king's natural son, over their
respective rights in Glamorgan was made in Henry I's presence at Woodstock. This is, incidentally, a good illustration of how dependent on royal
power churchmen in the post-Gregorian age could be in maintaining their
material position vis à vis secular magnates. Eventually, but only after a
long tussle and more as a result of papal than royal decisions, Llandaff lost
out to St David's in its territorial claims. But it was not much longer before
St David's lost out to Canterbury in claiming that it was the metropolitan
see of Wales and therefore ought not to be subject to Canterbury.[16]

It was not against Urban's friendship with Henry that he should appeal to the pope about his territory, and Henry did nothing to discourage his appeals. This was unlike the rival claims to metropolitan status of Canterbury and York, where Henry had not only a certain interest to play divide-and-rule but also an interest to restrict appeals to the pope. In Wales, however, his interest in divide-and-rule positively meant encouraging Urban's appeals to Rome. For whereas York's claim to independent metropolitan status might in some circumstances facilitate the King of England's political control over Scotland (through York), a similar claim by St David's (based partly on its strength vis à vis Llandaff) could only weaken such control in Wales. Scotland might reasonably be thought of, from an English perspective, as subject to either York or Canterbury; but Wales could only be meaningfully thought of as subject to Canterbury. Thus, while Bernard of St David's was a friend of the king, Urban of Llandaff could also help him by emphasising, in his appeals to Rome about his territory, his subjection to Canterbury against Bernard's metropolitan claims over Wales as Bishop of St David's.

All this is to speak as if the whole history of the Welsh church in Henry's time boiled down to a tale of ecclesiastical/political antics. It did not do so at all. Both the churches of St David's and Llandaff in this period developed their cultural personalities in writings about their history and traditions, their customs and their saints. However polemically motivated this cultural build-up was, its net result was to enrich the whole Welsh church. Moreover, the appeals of Urban of Llandaff to the papacy helped to bring Wales into the mainstream of Western Christendom, and complaints by the cosmopolitan Gerald of Wales later in the century of the backwardness of the clergy in his archdeaconry of Brecon, paradoxically further illustrate this development.[17]

The Investiture Contest in England

The Investiture Contest was about whether a king ought rightly to invest a bishop, when he entered on his office, with his staff (and from the mid-eleventh century his ring). After all, the king may have been secular lord of a bishop, but staff and ring were symbols of his spiritual functions. Thus royal investiture was symbolically making a great claim for a king's power over bishops, which implicitly challenged papal authority over them. The reader may be surprised that only now, rather than under Gregory VII or William I, is this important subject mentioned. The fact is, however, that it was only after St Anselm, in exile as Archbishop of Canterbury, heard Pope Urban II pronounce the decrees against investiture at a Council of

Rome in 1099, that it became an issue in England. Anselm had not raised a murmur against it in his early years as archbishop. From 1099 it became for him an issue of obedience to papal command,[18] and thus an issue which faced Henry I from the beginning of his reign. Henry was initially taken aback by this, but never did his genius for delay show to better advantage. His skill yielded for him, eventually in 1107, a settlement with the papacy and Anselm highly advantageous to himself.

It is important to appreciate that in the German empire of the tenth and early eleventh centuries, where investiture passed virtually unchallenged, the ruler did not personify the state (under some notion of what the state was) in his investiture of bishops, but the Vicar of Christ.[19] There is a story about the Emperor Henry III (1039–56) that when a certain abbot did not want to be invested by the Emperor with his pastoral staff, Henry put it into the hand of a statue of Christ and said to the abbot, 'Go and receive your staff at the hand of the King Almighty.' To the Emperor, one was the same as the other.[20] Such was the notion of the sacrality of kingship, such the nature of the theocracy with king/emperor at its head. His investiture must be seen as flowing from his function in the church of Christ, from his divine commission in the whole of Christian society. Investiture was only one ritual act in a succession of such acts – inthronisation, bishops' presence at crown-wearings or church consecrations with the ruler in attendance – which initiated a bishop into his position.[21] In that age when public ceremonial and ritual were far more important in ruler image-making and expression of policy than were speeches or writings or art, it goes without saying that massive significance attached to the symbolism of investiture. At that time symbolism was itself *Realpolitik*.

But the significance of symbols can easily change according to intellectual, social and political changes going on around them. Once the papal reformers, in changes described in Chapter 2, started to assert the superiority of spiritual rule over secular rule, indeed started to see rule (and bishoprics) in those divided terms as spiritual *or* secular, then and only then was investiture attacked as contrary to the freedom of the church and as a symbol of a lay rule over the church which the reformers detested. The attack on investiture was the product of a new, and legalistic, differentiation between royal and priestly power.[22] All the same, important as symbolism was, investiture was not the substance of the great struggle between *regnum* and *sacerdotium*, kingship and priesthood, for mastery of the world. Hence, while Gregory VII issued decrees against investiture in 1075, and more stringently in 1080, he did not insist on them when he judged lay rulers to be generally in tune with reforming ideals. The prime example of that was William the Conqueror.[23]

Paradoxically, the very isolation of investiture from the cosmic issue of *regnum/sacerdotium* as a whole,[24] enabled it to bear within itself the seeds of compromise about the cosmic issue. Once it came to be viewed as a single act, in a juristic sense, isolated from the whole series of symbolic transactions which had previously been the ensemble of making a bishop, that great race of compromisers – the lawyers – could get to work compromising. Ivo of Chartres, one of the most famous canon lawyers of the whole Middle Ages, was the first to show what the Carlyles called 'the mediating tendency'.[25] In 1096–97 he wrote to Hugh, Archbishop of Lyon, about Daimbert, Archbishop of Sens, who was alleged to have accepted investiture from the King of France. Even if he had done this, wrote Ivo, it was not a transgression against religion. The popes themselves recognised the rights of kings to make a concession of the bishopric because of all the ecclesiastical properties obtained through royal munificence; and in what form the concession was made – by word of mouth or by staff – mattered little, since kings thereby did not intend to give anything spiritual. (The Emperor Henry III would not have agreed with this half a century earlier.) Prohibition of royal investiture was not a provision of the eternal law, but only of the popes. What made it illegal was the fact that they had prohibited it. If anyone thought that there was anything sacramental about the giving and receiving of the pastoral staff, it was he who was a heretic.[26] Hugh the Chantor, himself a person of judgement, thought Ivo's the sensible view on investitures.[27]

Ivo of Chartres was perhaps the first of those liberal North European churchmen – we saw several of their like in the Second Vatican Council – who had a moderating effect on bitter ecclesiastical disputes by being able to differentiate between what was essential and what was not. But, although he would have been happy to see lay investiture go, because he was also not unhappy to see it stay the future did not lie with his approach. Too many churchmen had become repelled by lay investiture. Nearer the mark than Ivo, so far as the English compromise of 1107 was concerned, was Hugh of Fleury in his *Treatise on Royal Power and Sacerdotal Dignity* (1102–05). The king, Hugh thought, could confer on a cleric the honour of a bishopric, but not by investiture of ring and staff. These were spiritual symbols which a bishop ought to receive at his consecration from his archbishop. Like Ivo, Hugh showed the spirit of compromise, but *his* idea of compromise was closer to what happened in 1107, whereby the king gave up investiture but was allowed to receive the homage of bishops before their consecration.[28] (Hugh's treatise was actually dedicated to Henry I.) Essentially the distinction between the spiritual significance of investiture and the royal right of *concessio* is present both in Hugh and in 1107.

Of course, there were those, 'old-fashioned men' as Southern called them, to whom these distinctions between the spiritual and secular aspects of a bishopric would have been meaningless, who saw a bishopric as 'a single indivisible whole, comprising lands and authority, sacramental power and territorial rights'.[29] But by the last years of the eleventh century the days of such old fashioned men were already numbered. As we saw, Archbishop Lanfranc, a great canon lawyer himself, based his prosecution of Bishop William of Durham in 1088 on the distinction between his bishopric as such, and his barony which he held as bishop and for which he was answerable to the king.[30] The integrity of the bishopric in its spiritual and material aspects was already broken in many minds by 1100. How bishops managed their double lives would constitute their greatest political problem for a very long time to come, as we shall see from the contrast between Archbishop Hubert Walter and Hugh of Lincoln in a later chapter.

When in August 1100 William Rufus died in a hunting accident in the New Forest, Henry I hurried to England and seized the kingship, forestalling his elder brother Duke Robert of Normandy, who had just returned from the First Crusade. Thereafter the primary objective of his 35-year reign was to reunite England and Normandy under his one rule, and, after the Battle of Tinchebrai in 1106 had brought this about, to keep them united against the claims to Normandy of pro-Robert barons and against those of Robert's son, William Clito; and after Clito's death to try to ensure the succession of his daughter, Matilda, to both England and Normandy (his son William having been drowned in the Disaster of the White Ship, 1120). For as we have already explained, with so many barons holding lands on either side of the Channel and at this time feeling themselves to be more Norman than English, no ruler of England who did not also rule Normandy could survive; the loyalties of his barons would be too divided to allow for it.

One of the first things Henry did as king was to invite the exiled Archbishop of Canterbury, Anselm, back to England. It was a pressing invitation, born partly of the guilty knowledge that in his haste Henry had been crowned by the ready-to-hand Maurice, Bishop of London, thereby breaching an important Canterbury right to perform the coronation. When Anselm returned he at once took Henry by surprise. Having encountered the papal decrees against investiture and paying homage to a lay ruler for a bishopric, Anselm refused to pay homage to Henry or to accept those whom the king had invested. But as a shock-absorber Henry had unusual gifts. He played for time. He had to tide himself over a period when an invasion of England by Duke Robert was imminent. Indeed one may wonder why Anselm did not support Robert against Henry. But as Southern wrote, one can only suppose that Anselm 'preferred an effective ruler, however unpleasant, to an ineffective one, however recommended by his personal qualities'.[31] In 1101/02, the crisis surmounted, Henry insisted on compliance, and Anselm went into exile and had his lands sequestered.

From 1102 to 1107, when the English compromise over investitures was finally agreed, the story is one of negotiations. These negotiations were for the most part between king and pope (Pascal II) directly, for Anselm held sacred the principle of obedience to the papal decrees of 1099. In this he was more papalist than the pope. He was never part of the 'mediating tendency' which influenced both pope and king in these years. Anselm was no lawyer, and as Southern, again, has written, 'this admission of the possibility of compromise is the first sign that the period of the Hildebrandine Reform is coming to an end and is being replaced by the age of lawyers and administrators, differing in their briefs, but in their methods understanding each other very well'.[32] Actually the mediating tendency also shows something else: how significant the political influence of thinkers and tract-writers could be by around 1100.

It is easy to show what Henry I gained from the Compromise of 1107. By giving up investiture he lost what it is tempting to see by then as a mere empty shell of symbolism. By retaining the homage of bishops before their consecration, he held on in full to the substance of power in bishop-making. Immediately the Compromise was concluded, four bishops who had been waiting in the wings for this to happen were consecrated, staunch royal chaplains to a man – William Warelwast to Exeter, Reinhelm to Hereford, William Giffard to Winchester, and greatest of all, Roger to Salisbury. As bishops these were very important in keeping Henry I's government going, Roger for instance as head of the newly established Exchequer. Several more royal chaplains would follow as bishops during the reign, up to its last years, and the same story would be repeated under Henry II, most of all when a string of royal chaplains would be appointed to bishoprics after Henry's putting down of the great rebellion of 1173–74. This view of Henry's gain by the Compromise of 1107 was put forward forcefully by Hugh the Chantor, a contemporary of Henry, saying:

He did at length give up investitures because of the prohibition and
anathema of the Roman church, a concession which cost him little or
nothing – a little perhaps of his royal dignity, but nothing of his power
to enthrone anyone he pleased.[33]

Hugh should have known, for the Church of York owed his hero, Archbishop Thurstan, a royal chaplain, to Henry's appointment in 1114.

One has to be careful, however, not to exaggerate how much the king gained, at least morally speaking, from the Compromise of 1107. Christopher Brooke has made an important point in saying that the surrender of the old symbol (of investiture with the spiritual insignia of staff and ring) 'was a powerful reminder that bishops were not simply royal nominees'.[34] However close to the royal government many of them might be, the most important aspect of their power, through consecration, was God-given. To see how powerfully this was felt, we need only consider the reaction to Archbishop Thomas Becket's murder in 1170. Henry I himself did not appoint only royal chaplains during the rest of his reign. He appointed the learned Gilbert, called 'the Universal' because he was thought to know everything, to the bishopric of London in 1128 and he tried to appoint the learned Robert Pullen to a bishopric. Moreover, late in his reign he appointed two bishops of saintly character, Robert of Bethune to Hereford (1130) and Athelwold, the Augustinian Canon, to Carlisle (1133).[35] Nor were royal servants necessarily mere hard-bitten secularists. Roger of Salisbury, as we have said, was involved in the scholarly and educational efforts of his cathedral, and Thurstan had wide-ranging spiritual and pastoral objectives at York.

In fact, given the victory for the king of the Compromise of 1107, the wonder of the rest of the twelfth century is how decent the general standard of the episcopate was. There were of course factors keeping it up – the constant conciliar legislation from papal, metropolitan, and papal legatine councils which *set* standards; the rise in the social and educational level of parish priests, as we shall see later; the efforts, often unpopular, of support teams of archdeacons to discipline the clergy and laity, and to improve the participation of the latter in church life; the development of groups of intelligent and educated clerks in bishops' households, well versed in developing law and legal procedures, who came to form the dynamic of diocesan administration and could ensure the smooth running of a diocese, even if the bishop were negligent or demented (for bishops did not usually retire in those days). There were naturally exceptions, like Hugh Nonant, described by John Gillingham as 'John's chief propagandist and, in his spare time, Bishop of Coventry'.[36] But as a whole even the curialist bishops were attentive to their pastoral duties and not disedifying in their lives.

And, to continue the story of bishop-making into the twelfth century as a whole, the twelfth century was far from being composed only of curialist bishops. Royal power over the church did not operate evenly throughout the century, and when it was strong, kings did not always want curialists. Henry I, for instance, exercised considerable influence in the election of the Augustinian Canon, William of Corbeil, as Archbishop of Canterbury in 1123.[37] At a time when the monastic cathedral of Canterbury wanted another monk but when most of the bishops had turned against having yet more monks as bishops, William should not be seen only as a compromise candidate as between monastic and secular clergy, but also as positively expressing Henry I's devotion to the order of Augustinian Canons. Late in Stephen's reign and early in Henry II's, Archbishop Theobald, again a monk of Bec, was able to develop his metropolitan position as Archbishop of Canterbury, to exercise considerable influence over episcopal elections, and that led to serious theologians and pastors like Gilbert Foliot (the later opponent of Becket) and Bartholomew coming in at Hereford and Exeter, to name but two. The secret here was not so much royal weakness as the great access of moral authority to Theobald, who everyone could see sought to hold the unity of the English Church in a divided kingdom, 'to preserve the rights of his see and to work for better order and peace in the land'.[38]

The reader may have been wondering where the right of the clergy and people of a see to elect freely their preferred candidate had got to in all this. It was not negated by the Compromise of 1107, nor was it incompatible in itself with the duty of a newly elected bishop to pay homage to the king before consecration. There must often have been occasions when this right became a virtual dead letter in face of the king's will. The writ of Henry II to the electors at Winchester in 1174, ordering them to hold a free election to the bishopric and to elect the arch-curialist Richard of Ilchester, who was duly elected, is notorious.[39] However, one need not imagine a conflict of interests between king (or archbishop) and clergy and people to be the norm. One of the reasons why the church of York were pleased to get Thurstan as their archbishop in 1114, apart from his being learned, witty and charming, was precisely because he was a curialist and could keep them in good standing with the king and with his many other contacts. Again, in December 1148 Robert de Chesney, who had been Archdeacon of Leicester, was elected Bishop of Lincoln. For the next 18 years he would be the model of a pastoral bishop. A letter from Gilbert Foliot, recently made

Bishop of Hereford, to Pope Eugenius III, speaks of Robert as elected by the clergy and people of the diocese before an assembly of bishops in London, including Archbishop Theobald and Gilbert himself. There is no doubt that Robert was enthusiastically received at Lincoln when he returned there in January 1149. But an endorsement to Robert's written profession of obedience to the Archbishop of Canterbury, dated 19 December 1148, shows that the election took place in the Westminster Chapter House, in the presence of King Stephen and Queen Matilda;[40] and Henry of Huntingdon, a fellow archdeacon of Robert in the Lincoln diocese, speaks of his being elected with 'the very joyful approval of *king*, clergy, and people'.[41]

It may seem as if we have been straying rather far from Henry I and his religion in recent paragraphs. But considering what an important staging post the Compromise of 1107 was for the political, ecclesiastical and religious history of England during the rest of the twelfth century, I hope this straying will not have seemed unjustified.

The primacy dispute between Canterbury and York

The primacy dispute was a *cause célèbre* of ecclesiastical politics, necessarily involving the king, which reached its climax under Henry I, though it rumbled on afterwards. Everybody recognised at this time that the Archbishop of Canterbury was of superior dignity to the Archbishop of York. But was York under the *authority* of Canterbury, as the church of Canterbury claimed, citing Anglo-Saxon custom? Did the Archbishop of York, before he was consecrated, owe a profession of obedience to the Archbishop of Canterbury as Primate of Britain? Or had he an independent primacy, an independent metropolitan status, as the church of York maintained, citing the arrangements made by Pope Gregory the Great as recorded in Bede's *Ecclesiastical History* for the two metropolitan sees of London (read as Canterbury from Augustine's time on) and York; and citing also the lack of any provision in canon law for one metropolitan, or archbishop, to be subordinate to the authority of another? As already said (p. 31), the way Lanfranc and Thomas I of York resolved their differences over the latter's profession of obedience left the way open for much argument later. Under Henry I it became a long-running issue which drew in both king and a succession of popes, until it was in practice resolved by Archbishop Thurstan's consecration by the pope in 1119 while avoiding taking a profession of obedience to the Archbishop of Canterbury. After that there never was further talk of professions of obedience, although that by no means meant the end of tensions between the two sees.

All this may seem like inward-looking ecclesiastical pedantry to us, but as historians we have to recognise that it mattered hugely to people at the time and we have to ask why. It is not hard to see *how much* it mattered. Hugh the Chantor, having just said how wise as well as learned Gerard of York was, tells us that at the Council of Westminster in 1102,

when the monks had prepared a seat higher than any others for their archbishop (i.e. of Canterbury), Gerard felt himself insulted, and calling down the hatred of God on whoever had vulgarly made this preparation, kicked over the seat and would not sit down until a seat was made as high as the other archbishop's, wishing to show plainly that he owed him no subjection.[42]

Earlier, in 1093, when Archbishop Thomas I of York was ready, wearing his pontifical vestments, to consecrate St Anselm, a petition was made that the archbishop should consecrate Anselm as Primate of all Britain, whereupon Thomas went back into the vestry, took off his vestments and refused to proceed. Anselm himself and Walkelin, Bishop of Winchester, had to follow him into the vestry, go down on their knees and say appeasing words to the archbishop. The archbishop, mollified, put on his vestments again, went back to the altar, and the word 'primate' having been erased from the petition, amended to Anselm's consecration as metropolitan of Canterbury, consecrated him.[43] The same attitude constantly surfaced in the twelfth century. Later in the century, Walter de Lucy, Abbot of Battle in Sussex, would say that he would rather resign his abbacy than lose one jot or tittle of his abbey's rights.[44]

The passions aroused by the rights and privileges and possessions of particular episcopal and monastic churches in the Middle Ages were so elemental, so in the foreground of every picture of the church, so apparently a priori a factor in ecclesiastical politics, that we medieval historians sometimes take them for granted and do not see the need to answer to non-medievalists *why* it was so. The question is indeed not easy to answer, but it is important not to think that the phenomenon is unknown in our own time. We have only to think of football clubs. Anyone who lives in the environment of a collegiate university can observe pale reflections of it. Many discussions between college representatives at such a university can be virtually unintelligible until one realises that they are not about the commonwealth of learning or even about the good of the university but about college interest as perceived by individual representatives.

Distinguished men and women are often elected to be heads of such colleges who have never previously put a foot inside them but are soon fighting like tigers for the rights and interests of their new college. In medieval churches, unlike in modern colleges, the lives of the monks or resident canons, celibates in the first case and supposedly so in the second, were totally tied up with their churches, churches with their much cherished, living, and often age-old traditions. One can see this in the whole attitude of Orderic Vitalis towards St Evroult.[45] As a historian he was to St Evroult in Normandy (though himself from Shrewsbury), something akin to what Hugh the Chantor was to York and Eadmer to Canterbury. Perhaps above all, in the case of monastic churches and of monastic cathedrals like Canterbury, Winchester and Durham, was the importance of their patron saint in his or her shrine (Dunstan, Alphege and others at Canterbury; Swithun at Winchester; Cuthbert at Durham).[46] The rights and possessions of Durham, for example, were the rights and possessions of St Cuthbert; if the monks of the cathedral priory of Durham failed to champion these, Cuthbert might not protect them. If they had fought loyally for him and he did not honour the *quid pro quo* by protecting them, they had the right to expostulate with him, as the monks of Ely did with their patron saint, Etheldreda (see pp. 42–4). Modern colleges do not usually have a force in their communities, or a focus of loyalty, to compare with St Cuthbert at Durham. On the other hand, behind their Heads, modern colleges, like medieval cathedrals and monasteries, have groups of Fellows as the latter had monks or canons, who egg them on, and criticise them savagely if they culpably fail their societies in championing their interests.

Under Henry I we are considering the primacy dispute when it hotted up in 1114 with the election of Ralph, previously monk of Bec and then Bishop of Rochester, as Archbishop of Canterbury, and four months later Thurstan as Archbishop of York. An important difference between 1070, when Lanfranc and Thomas were battling it out, and 1114, was that in 1070 the two archbishops stood practically on their own, whereas by 1114 things had so developed at Canterbury and York that Ralph and Thurstan had behind them substantial and highly articulate communities, seconds at the ringside, both supporting and pressurising them with their explosive *ésprit de corps*.[47]

Henry I's objectives in the whole matter were twofold: to support the primacy of Canterbury over York for the sake of the political unity of England (like his father, William I), and to ensure by all means that the issue was not submitted to the judgement of the pope, so preserving royal jurisdiction over the church. It should not be deduced from his sometimes seeming to change sides that he did not much care about the whole business. In order to achieve the second and to him vital aim of keeping it out of the papal court, he had sometimes to offer hope to York that they might be favoured by him, so that they would not go all out for judgement from a papacy which always favoured them. In any case this was the kind of game at which Henry was a consummate master.[48] The papacy's consistent support of York in their not submitting to Canterbury (the reasons for which we shall come to in a moment) also made Henry anxious generally to keep papal legates out of England; and the more he kept them out, the more they would support York if they got in, and thus the more anxious still he was to keep them out.[49] Since papal legates of the Gregorian Reform always wanted to insist on one of the main planks of reform, clerical celibacy, one tactic of the king for keeping them out was to back up internal legislation against clerical marriage himself. (This being so, Henry of Huntingdon's idea, that Henry only did this so that he could charge clergy money for licences to keep their wives against canon law, could not have had more behind it than occasional apparent anecdotal evidence.)[50]

The primacy dispute took a new and dramatic turn from 1114 to 1119. In 1109, after Anselm's death, Thomas II of York took a profession of obedience to a non-existent Archbishop of Canterbury before being consecrated by the Bishop of London and others. He did it on the king's insistence and Hugh the Chantor opined that Thomas would never have acted so weakly had he not been over-weight and flabby.[51] Thereafter Henry waited until after the death of Thomas II to fill the archbishopric of Canterbury, so that (according to arguments being used forty years earlier) Canterbury's case for primacy would not be prejudiced by their archbishop's having to be consecrated by an Archbishop of York. This seems as much Henry's motive for keeping the archbishopric of Canterbury vacant as avaricious desire to draw the revenues of the archbishopric for the five-year vacancy (1109–14) in the archbishopric of Canterbury.[52] Archbishop Thomas died on 24 February 1114. Ralph, already a consecrated bishop, was translated from Rochester to Canterbury on 26 April 1114. And Thurstan, a royal clerk of high standing and unimpeachable way of life, was elected Archbishop of York on 16 August 1114. But Thurstan was not consecrated a bishop until 19 October 1119, because he consistently refused to made a profession of obedience to the Archbishop of Canterbury, his rightful consecrator, before being consecrated. Here we come to another factor which complicated Henry I's approach to the whole issue. Whatever Henry, in supporting Canterbury's case, thought of Archbishop Ralph personally, he always regarded Thurstan as a personal friend of his.

With Henry – and he was not uncharacteristic of his time in this – personal friendship could easily cut across 'policy'. Never did Henry's proverbial loyalty and friendship show to more striking effect than in his dealings with his policy opponent, Thurstan.

The historian is fortunate in having a first-hand, knowledgeable, and highly partisan account of the years 1114 to 1119 from each side: Eadmer's *Historia Novorum* from Canterbury, and Hugh the Chantor's *History of the Church of York*. Both are 'gloves-off' accounts by two men each himself deeply involved in the efforts of his church, and each only with eyes for the defects of their opponents. Of the two, however, Hugh the Chantor had the more powerful mind and incisive judgement. And one cannot help feeling that the same went for their respective principals, for Archbishop Ralph and his Canterbury advisers were floored by every *coup de main* of Thurstan.

I promised earlier to say why York was consistently favoured by the papacy. One reason was that York's main argument was that the 'constitution' of Pope Gregory the Great, five centuries back as recorded by Bede, knew nothing of the obedience or subordination of one primate to the other, as between York and London (soon to become Canterbury). That argument, based on an ancient papal ruling, was accepted by the early twelfth-century popes, more than was the Canterbury argument based mainly on English precedent. In a stiff letter of Pope Pascal II to the Archbishop of Canterbury (1117), Gregory's words are cited, the pope adding, 'although you hold the first place, he (the Archbishop of York) is neither a suffragan of your church nor owes you any obedience'.[53] But there was another not less powerful reason, and that was Thurstan's friendship with each pope in the period 1114–19, and with John of Gaeta, a powerful cardinal in the papal curia under Pascal II before he became Pope Gelasius II, and with many other members of the Curia – and indeed with practically anyone who mattered in North-West Europe. His friendships on the Continent were much enhanced by the long periods of exile from his see while he remained unconsecrated. In a great age of self-conscious, renaissance-like friendship, Thurstan was one of the great friends. One of his many attractions to the canons of York when he was elected archbishop, apart from his alert and ebullient personality, was his numerous friendships made with the great barons of the North, David of Scotland and others, while he was at court.[54]

It is impossible and unnecessary here to give a blow by blow account of the whole story of the primacy dispute in its crucial five years. I cannot detail, within the scope of this chapter, the poor handling of the

Canterbury cause by Archbishop Ralph, his maladroit letters to the popes and his poor intelligence compared to York's about where the popes actually were. But one or two highlights may be mentioned which help to illustrate the general character of ecclesiastical politics and Henry I's approach to it.

In 1116 an impasse was reached between Thurstan on the one side, and the king and Archbishop of Canterbury on the other, with Thurstan's continuing to refuse the profession of obedience to Canterbury to the detriment of his church, and, as a serious churchman, feeling increasingly conscience-stricken at his drawing the revenues of his archbishopric while being unable to perform episcopal functions because of his lack of consecration. In this impasse he took everyone by surprise. He resigned the archbishopric. This was very awkward for the king, with an important friend whom he had been trying to keep on board. At first no one believed it. But the great Count Robert of Meulan said, 'if I know my man, he will be in earnest'. Everyone who knew him, says Hugh the Chantor, was devastated by his action. He himself, however, 'gave no sign of sadness, but was his usual delightful and amusing self, as if nothing contrary had happened to him'.[55] That was the kind of thing which made Thurstan irresistible to Henry I. It is a perfect illustration of how much personality mattered in such politics.

Eadmer wrote of Thurstan's renunciation in a mean spirit, saying that although he promised the king and archbishop that he would never reclaim the archbishopric for himself, after only a matter of days he started to miss the old respect paid to him, and his honours, and to regret what he had done, and tried to get his archbishopric back, still without having to make a profession to Canterbury.[56] Whatever the truth of this – and it need not have been all fiction – it was Henry himself who made it clear that he still wanted Thurstan as Archbishop of York, who still supported Thurstan personally, and who, when Archbishop Ralph wanted someone else to be appointed at York, refused to accept that the archbishopric was vacant.[57] This was a typical self-contradiction of Henry, a self-contradiction between policy and friendship.

Thurstan was reinstated as Archbishop-Elect in February 1118, but he was consecrated as a bishop only on 19 October 1119 by Pope Calixtus II, the day before the pope opened the Council of Rheims. Henry I had tried to extract a promise from Thurstan that he would not be consecrated by the pope without his permission, and the king had been led to believe by his special envoy to the papacy, William Warelwast, Bishop of Exeter, that Thurstan would abide by this. Relying on this, the king had allowed both

Thurstan and the Archbishop of Canterbury, who had of course also been summoned, to attend the Council. But amongst the churchmen gathered at Rheims were large numbers of Thurstan's friends, and the pressures on him to be consecrated there were enormous. The pope consecrated Thurstan in Rheims cathedral in the presence of many archbishops, bishops, and abbots.[58] Thurstan thus finally escaped having to make a profession of obedience to Canterbury before consecration (and refused to made one afterwards). Only the Archdeacon of Canterbury was present to speak up for the rights of the church of Canterbury, and he, it seems, did not go down well with 'the Romans'. The Archbishop of Canterbury himself, albeit summoned, was not present, delayed (so the Canterburians claimed) by illness. Though as Thurstan wittily observed, no amount of illness would have detained him had he thought that he could by any means have obtained a profession of obedience.[59]

Henry reacted in the only way he possibly could. He refused to let Thurstan back into England and took over the temporalities of his see. Even a friendly meeting with the pope in November 1119 could not change his behaviour; that would have involved too immediate a loss of face for the king, though who knows how it might have helped below the surface to start a rapprochement. For it is dropped quite suddenly into Hugh's narrative, as it is albeit less pointedly into other contemporary narratives, that Henry and Calixtus were quite closely related to each other![60] They were second cousins once removed. At their meeting, the king is reported to have said, 'My lord pope and father, I cannot lawfully do what you ask by receiving the Archbishop of York, because I have given my word that he shall not enter the realm of England with my leave, unless he makes his profession personally to Archbishop Ralph.' Whereupon the pope replied, 'Sweetest son [surely the only time Henry I was so addressed by anyone!], in the name of St Peter whose vicar I am though unworthy, I absolve you from this promise!'[61]

For the time Henry stood firm. But once again it is hard to avoid the impression that he still regarded Thurstan as his friend, and vice versa.[62] The particularly striking point about Thurstan's behaviour, after his victory of receiving consecration as a bishop without having to make a profession to Canterbury before it, was that he went to the ends of the earth to save Henry's face. The greatest example of many is that he refused the papal legateship over England which the pope offered him in 1120. 'He prostrated himself at the pope's feet, beseeching him not to enjoin on him a duty which would expose him permanently to the wrath which the king now felt against his person.'[63] This certainly would have been a humiliating setback for Henry, who, when William of Corbeil became Archbishop of Canterbury in 1123, secured a standing legateship for him, thereby seeking to avoid that the primacy should have constantly to be batted between England and the papacy.[64] (For though the issue of the profession of obedience was ended in York's favour in 1119–21, there were other issues of privilege and symbolism which remained.) In this refusal, Thurstan seemed to save not only Henry's face but also the pope's, by exaggerating the king's wrath to give his excuse greater force. If only Thomas Becket had shown a similar ability and disposition to save the face of his king, how different the story of his conflict with Henry II might have been!

When Thurstan finally got back to his see as a consecrated bishop, he devoted himself with energy and imagination to his pastorate. At the political level, however, there was one more twist to the primacy issue, namely his effort to bring the Scottish bishops under his jurisdiction. We noted in the previous chapter that one of Lanfranc's concessions after Archbishop Thomas of York had professed obedience to him was that the whole of Scotland should be under York (though what that could mean if York was under Canterbury is not quite clear). Lanfranc honoured that concession, and once again Pope Calixtus II backed Thurstan, particularly as regarding his authority over Bishop John of Glasgow. But a very different spirit obtained in the Canterbury of 1119–20, smarting from Thurstan's victory over them in escaping the profession of obedience. In 1120 Canterbury, with the support of King Alexander I of Scotland, Henry I's brother-in-law, and of John of Glasgow, got their own candidate into the bishopric of St Andrews, which, if anywhere, might be deemed the primatial see of Scotland. This backfired badly onto Canterbury. The trouble was that the candidate was none other than Eadmer, their own monk, and he proved to be hopeless. It soon became clear that, far from fighting for the independence of his new see, Eadmer saw his role at St Andrews as helping to secure the primacy of all Britain for Canterbury. That was not what King Alexander had in mind. Eadmer, a man of spirituality no doubt, lacked the steel to face opposition, and by the spring of 1121 he was back in Canterbury having relinquished his bishopric.[65]

Only in January 1124, when Eadmer died, was another bishop appointed to St Andrews, and that was Robert Prior of Nostell, a house of Augustinian Canons in Yorkshire. This must have been by the influence of both King Alexander and Thurstan. Both were devotees of the Augustinians and what their religion and pastorate could achieve. Alexander had already in 1120 established a colony of them from Nostell at Scone in Gowrie, the great Scottish royal centre, while Thurstan had given Nostell a central part to play in his cathedral and diocese.[66] When Robert was finally consecrated in 1127 by Thurstan, Thurstan required no oath of obedience from him, probably as Donald Nicholl has said, because of the personal regard that existed between the two men. Here, if anywhere in twelfth-century Britain, was personal friendship given the primacy over law and legal obligation. As Nicholl again has written, 'Robert of Nostell's promotion to St Andrew's only became comprehensible against a background of personal contact between Scotland and York.'[67] Robert remained Bishop of St Andrew's until his death in 1150.

It is vital to the appreciation of all English/Scottish relations at this time that although one can locate a territorial border between the two kingdoms, *political* geography cut across this border. We cannot simply say that in Cumberland and Westmorland, Northumberland or Durham the King of England held sway whereas north of these the King of Scotland did so. Of course there was an English royal administration which stretched to the border, with royal officials, like Odard of Bamburgh, Sheriff of Northumberland (though Odard also saw himself as holding an aristocratic lordship in the North).[68] For certain purposes, e.g. justice or accounting for the profits of the silver mines near Carlisle, this administration was important. But in other respects it could be seen as only 'a thin veneer over northern society'.[69] The borderland between England and Scotland was a region of great lordships, where ties of aristocratic kinship often linked lordships on each side of the border, where patronage of the kings generally counted for more than direct royal jurisdiction bounded by specific boundaries, and where loyalties might be owed to both kings at the same time.[70] For example, between Galloway and Carlisle Robert de Brus was established; he owed great estates to Henry I, but was always a close associate of David of Scotland.[71] Ranulph de Meschin, kinsman of Henry I and one of the great lords of the North, and a friend of Thurstan from long before the latter's appointment to York, held a 'frontier lordship' in which Henry I's writ probably did not run.[72] But insofar as he held the lordship of Carlisle until 1120/21, he was holding a lordship on which the kings of Scotland had strong claims. Thus the peace of the borderlands, which Henry undoubtedly established, depended on what might be called a *modus vivendi* between the kings,[73] or equally a friendship, and even shared purposes such as the advancement of religion through the Augustinian Canons.

An ecclesiastical example of cross-border allegiances was the bishopric of Glasgow. Revived by David as Earl (before he became king), the first bishop, Michael, was a Cumbrian who functioned in the diocese of York while Thurstan was as yet unconsecrated. Michael's successor, John, 'one of the outstanding prelates of medieval Scotland' (Barrow), did not accept that he owed obedience to the Archbishop of York, as Thurstan claimed; nor did the Scottish kings Alexander and his younger brother, David.[74] The friendship of David and Thurstan survived this tension; Thurstan had a gift for friendships which overrode political tensions, as had the kings with whom he dealt. However, Thurstan again had the backing of the papacy, so that it went hard for David and Bishop John when they supported the anti-pope Anacletus II (a mistake easily made!) rather than Innocent II in the papal schism of 1130. John retired to the monastery of Tiron for some years. As a cardinal, Innocent II had always been one of the great supporters of the new orders, like the Cistercians and Augustinian Canons, in the curia, so he naturally had Thurstan's backing. As to Henry I he was fortunately and early brought round to Innocent's side by St Bernard's advocacy. The great Cistercian Abbot of Clairvaux wrote to Henry saying:

What are you afraid of? Do you fear to incur sin by obeying Innocent? Think how many other sins you must answer to God for! Leave this one to me. This sin is on me![75]

It may seem as if we have devoted disproportionate space to Thurstan, but I am unapologetic. First his appeals to the papacy were a vital element in increasing papal influence over the churches in Britain, as were Urban of Llandaff's. Second, his friendship with Henry, as a senior churchman, gave characteristic colour to ecclesiastical politics in his time. Third, Thurstan was pre-eminent in setting a high standard of pastorate within his own diocese, as we shall see in more detail in a later chapter.

Henry I, Melbourne church, and Athelwold of Carlisle

As with Gervase and Ely in the last chapter, Melbourne church in Derbyshire and how Bishop Athelwold was (and was not) connected to it, is a useful microcosm of Henry I, his relationships and his religion.[76]

According to Richard Gem, a great authority on English Romanesque architecture, Melbourne has some features which would take its origins back to before c. 1125.[77] As Melbourne was a royal manor whose church was only given by Henry I to Athelwold when he became Bishop of Carlisle in 1133, Melbourne church must be considered *in conception* a royal church rather than an episcopal church. That is important because there has been an argument that with the Scots on the rampage in Cumberland later in the 1130s, Athelwold could develop Melbourne as a sort of episcopal church for himself, in dignified seclusion away from the turmoil. I follow Richard Gem in regarding Melbourne as a royal church. Two important features which both bring Melbourne close to the German imperial ambit of architecture, for all that we call it a Norman church, are the large triforium gallery at the west end and the two-storeyed chancel.

When one walks into Melbourne church one is deeply impressed by its powerful architecture, but one gasps when one sees it all from the west gallery [see Plate 6]. It is easily the grandest outlook on the church from anywhere, the only viewpoint from which one can grasp it as a whole, with its rhythm of columns and arches, its aisles and galleried walkways, its upper and lower chancels. It speaks of the presence of the ruler, as the royal loggias in German rococo churches do, even when he or she is absent. The two-level chancel puts one in mind of the similar feature at Schwarzrheindorf near Bonn, a mid-twelfth-century chapel of the archbishop of Cologne.

It is always an important question about a building what was supposed to happen inside it, and that is not easy to answer in the case of Melbourne church in the twelfth century (only from the late Middle Ages do we know that it acted as a parish church), although a strong case has been made that it had a community of Augustinian Canons.[78] But another important question often superimposes itself on the first question: what is its architecture meant to symbolise? The World Trade Center in New York, for instance, was much more than the sum total of its office space. To those who designed it, with its twin towers, it perhaps signified something like the thumbs up for capitalism. Another example is the John Rylands Library in Manchester. At a time in the late nineteenth century when many libraries were being built in classical styles, this building, to house a collection of *religious* books, was built in the Gothic style. Its entrance hall, the size of a small Gothic cathedral, had no books in it whatsoever. Waste of space? Not at all! Rather a sort of setting to celebrate symbolically the marriage of learning and divine wisdom, and to compose the minds of those who enter for study. What we can say is that whatever went on inside it Melbourne was conceived as a royal church and a symbol of royal power. And to those who protest, 'But what about the glory of God?', I reply, 'Yes indeed! To few kings, however, have the glory of God and the majesty of kingship been mutually exclusive propositions.' Moreover everyone familiar with Norman architecture will understand how often even parish churches were built not only as a great pastoral effort (which they certainly were), but also to symbolise the means and power of the local aristocracy who were their patrons.

Henry I was himself by no means impervious to religious ritual and symbolism. He was present at the dedication of the new choir of Canterbury Cathedral in 1130, a resplendent occasion. When the monks chanted the versicle 'awesome is this place; truly this is the house of God and the gate of heaven', Henry beholding the new choir at that moment ablaze with lights, was moved to swear with his royal oath, 'by the death of God', that truly the sanctuary was awesome.[79] The chroniclers say that Henry gave up the ceremony of solemn crown-wearings at the Great Councils of the realm. Among other reasons it has been argued, because the festivities were too expensive. But he wore his crown on politically important or sensitive occasions as an affirmation of his link to divinity through his kingship. Most of all he wore it at Pentecost 1109 when the envoys of the Emperor Henry V came to London to seek his daughter in marriage. This was the most splendid court he held, it was said, and everyone was impressed by the Emperor's envoys, their massive physique and magnificent apparel.[80] To become the father-in-law of the Holy Roman Emperor, besides being a diplomatic coup, represented a huge access of sacrality to the kingly *persona*. At one time, as only the third son of a king, Henry looked as if he would have to be content with a mere money fief. He paid an enormous dowry for Matilda.

However much Henry might have to economise on real-life crown-wearings, he was probably interested in this kind of thing in theory. A manuscript from Bury St Edmunds, an abbey under royal patronage, shows St Edmund, a ninth-century King of East Anglia, being crowned by angels, and crowned with an imperial type crown, a diadem with *pendilia*, like the Byzantine imperial crowns.[81] The manuscript is dated to about 1125, just in the time that Melbourne church was begun. It seems likely that about this time, Henry I obtained for his treasury an imperial crown, doubtless obtained from the Empire *via* the king's daughter, wife of the Emperor Henry V.[82] Now here is a striking fact. Karl Leyser showed that, again, around 1125, preparations were being made for Matilda and Henry V, the latter Henry's son-in-law, to succeed to his English kingdom and to the Duchy of Normandy.[83] This was after Henry I had lost his only legitimate heir, William, in 1120 with the disaster of the White Ship. The preparations all came to nothing because Henry V died in 1125. But from all this it is clear why, around the time that Melbourne church was begun, the idea of projecting not only a royal image but even an imperial image of himself could not have left Henry I cold.

The reader might well be asking some questions abut all this. If Henry was a strong king, good at raising money, why did he need symbolism? And if he needed it at all, why could he have possibly needed it at Melbourne? And in any case, did other people take the least notice of it? I'm not one of those who derides the concept of the Strong King in the Middle Ages, just because Sellars and Yeatman espoused it in irony. But there is a sort of Pauline paradox about strong kings; they were also weak kings because they made so many enemies. Henry I may well not have thought himself a strong king so much as a very vulnerable one. A well-informed contemporary writer tells us that he went round in constant fear of some awful disaster or attack; and the French abbot, Suger, who admired Henry's mode of government, gives a similar picture. The king, he said, was so frightened of attempts on his life that he changed the location of his bed every night![84] Henry may have raised a lot of money, but he *needed* much more money than his predecessors. William the Conqueror had ruled a united English/Norman lordship. Henry, even when he did so, faced constant challenge to his rule in Normandy, and if he couldn't keep a grip on Normandy that would be the end of his grip on England. Because many Norman barons who owed him homage in England also held lands in Normandy which they regarded as their homeland. So lose out in Normandy and of course he loses loyalty in England. Keeping a grip on Normandy was fabulously expensive. It was expensive in diplomacy, like marrying his daughter to an emperor to get the latter's support against the King of France, who loved to fish in troubled Norman waters. The dowry that he had to pay for his daughter and then recoup from the country, has been reasonably posited as the occasion for the establishment of the Exchequer.[85] But it wasn't only diplomacy that was expensive. Even the best diplomats sometimes have to go to war. Henry, under Norman exigencies, developed a crack troop of household knights to form the core element of his battles and sieges.[86] Such people knew their price in the world of rising professional chivalry. Besides one could not mulch the rich at will. John later thought one could and Magna Carta was the resultant backfire on him. If a king didn't want more rebellion on his hands than he could cope with, nice judgement was required about whom payments could be exacted from and whom they could not.

Money was not the only trouble. It is sometimes said that Henry developed a whole class of loyal officials in the shires, particularly sheriffs and chamberlains, who owed everything to him and would do his bidding in the functions of government. But actually many of these men were very dangerous. I recently heard Tom Bisson, a distinguished Harvard Professor, say of the early twelfth century that officials were not *only* officials but were also men in search of lordship. They could rarely be treated as mere curialist creatures.[87]

The reason why I dwell on the weaknesses in the very structure of Henry's rule is because the symbolist projection of a ruler's image is often not a triumphalist expression of real strength, but a desperate response to weakness.

So why might Henry have needed royal symbolism particularly at Melbourne? First of all Melbourne occupies what was then a vital strategic point in the country. The River Trent is the classic divider between north and south England, and that Melbourne was related to an important crossing of the Trent is shown by the early causeway built to link it to such a crossing at Swarkestone. This crossing is at an ideal place to join up a journey from the South or South East to the North West. Henry I is known to have visited Cumberland only once in his thirty-five year reign, in 1122 when he established the Augustinian Priory of Carlisle and paid for the town's castle and walls. But he attached great importance to keeping a grip on it because it was an economically thriving region and not least because around this time silver mines had been discovered near Carlisle.[88] In 1122 he appointed as Prior of Carlisle Athelwold, whom he would in 1133 raise to be Bishop of Carlisle and to whom in the same year he would give his church at Melbourne.[89] So one should not think of Melbourne as a secluded place where the bishop of Carlisle could find a peaceful retreat from the Scottish raids into Cumberland, but as a strategic lynch-pin between Henry's principal area of travel in the South (when he was in England and not in Normandy) and the North West which he was determined to hold for the English monarchy and where there were powerful lordships under his patronage.[90]

As is implicit in all this, Henry's kingship was itinerant. He did not have one capital on which a bureaucracy was based, a bureaucracy which could be relied on to effect the rulers' will in the provinces. He had local government officials, but as has been said, these could not be relied upon to act as pure bureaucrats. It was still necessary to have a strong face-to-face element in politics; the ruler had to show his face. Now although King John would later emphasise the geographical importance of Melbourne by visiting his manor there on several occasions, there is no evidence that Henry I ever visited it. It was very much at the edge of his usual English itinerary. So what was the point of having a symbolically royal or imperial church to which the king never, or practically never, came? The question may be turned round the other way. When could his symbolical presence be more useful than when he himself was generally absent? One may think this magnificent church an expensive form of symbolism *in absentia*. It would indeed have needed a master mason. Such people, generally anonymous at this time, would not have come cheaply. But otherwise, there was a quarry of Staffordshire Millstone Grit, of which the church was built, within the parish. A quarry to hand was always real but inexpensive power. And as to labour, at least for carting the stone, a manor had its own labour services to draw on: Melbourne had 20 villeins and 6 bordars already by 1086, according to Domesday Book.

On my third question, whether anyone was the least impressed by such symbolism, there is frankly no way of knowing, although we shall see indications (see below p. 107) that under Henry II the projection of kingship seems to have had some effect in the Midlands. The most important effect of such symbolic projections, however, propaganda as it might be called today, is the effect it has on those who put it out, the access of self-confidence that it may give to rulers and their courtiers, and the sense given to themselves of an exalted and justifying framework to their actions, however base these often continue to look to others. With regard to Melbourne church, I am not speaking here only of the king. When Henry I gave Athelwold the church (keeping the manor) in 1133, an obvious commission went with it – to hold this vital spot for the king; not to hold it militarily, for he can have been in no position to do that, but to hold it as a focus of loyalty. That was in addition to his chief commission, as Bishop of Carlisle, to be a bastion of loyalty to the king in North-West England, which Henry rarely reached in person. Athelwold had long been a trusted friend, indeed the confessor, of Henry I. We shall have poor imaginations if we cannot perceive the courage and uplift which he derived for these commissions from being given and advancing such a building.

Now some further words about Athelwold himself, who was intimately associated with the early history of Melbourne church, and probably with at least some of the later stages of its building. With none was Henry I's friendship more important than that with David, King of Scotland (1124–53). This friendship was of great consequence for Athelwold. David, younger than Henry, was his brother-in-law, i.e. the brother of Henry's wife, Matilda, and he had been brought up at the court first of William Rufus, and then of Henry himself. David named his own son after Henry. Through Henry, David had important lordships in England. One of the lesser of these was in Cholsey, Berkshire, some miles up the River Thames from Reading, where Henry expected him to defend the rights of his new foundation of Reading Abbey,[91] a job similar to what he expected Athelwold to do in Melbourne. In a fine paper on David of Scotland, Geoffrey Barrow has followed up an account of this political friendship by writing:

There may even have been something like affection between David and Henry I, despite the gulf – to our eyes a yawning gulf – between Henry's meanness, rapacity, perfunctory piety and insatiable sexual appetites, and David's generosity, consuming religious devotion, and puritanical chastity.[92]

A vital point *for us* is that one result of this friendship was that David allowed the Scots' claims to Cumberland and Carlisle to remain dormant while Henry lived. Their friendship, and these dormant claims to Cumberland and Carlisle, is the context into which Athelwold's appointment to be bishop of Carlisle and the grant of Melbourne church fits. Athelwold was an Augustinian canon, who was both Prior of Carlisle Priory from 1122 and Prior of the Augustinian house at Nostell in Yorkshire, the house from which he originally came, by at latest 1124. So, incidentally, he was used to distant commuting before 1133! Pluralism should not always be regarded as an abuse rather than a way of supervising important religious work on more than one front. It should be noted that against the general run of curialist bishops, Athelwold was one of two Augustinian canons of some spirituality whom Henry I appointed to bishoprics late in his reign, the other being Robert of Bethune at Hereford. Obviously Henry was a friend of Nostell Priory as well as of Athelwold before 1122. But so was David, and in 1124 another canon of Nostell, Robert, became bishop of St Andrews, as we said earlier. So by 1133 there was a friendship network of many years standing which bound Henry I, Athelwold, Nostell Priory in Yorkshire and David of Scotland together.

It was all a different story after Henry's death in 1135 and the story is worth continuing for a few years more, because it highlights the similarity of David of Scotland's friendship with Bishop Athelwold to Henry I's. In 1136/37 David revolted against Stephen and the assaults of this considerable ruler on Cumberland started in order to reclaim his rights, as he saw them.

How did this affect Athelwold as bishop of Carlisle? Not nearly as much as some historians of Melbourne have maintained, who thought that Athelwold had to prepare himself for a long exile and that was what Melbourne was about. It is true that he felt unable to detach himself from Stephen in Stephen's early years because of his more southerly interests, and that he witnessed several of Stephen's documents in this time. Hence David was forced to expel him from Carlisle in 1136. But we know from John of Hexham that already in September 1138, the papal legate to Britain, Cardinal Alberic of Ostia took Athelwold with him to meet David and got him restored to the Scottish king's favour and to his bishopric of Carlisle.[93] By the treaty of 1139 between Stephen and David, the lordship over Carlisle was ceded to David and that was definitively the end of Athelwold's troubles in Cumberland. So it was only for two years that Athelwold had to think about settling elsewhere, for instance in Melbourne, and even in those two years I doubt that he had to think about it very hard. For the way I read all this is as follows: David never really wanted to lose his friend Athelwold, and having forced him out of Carlisle, he wanted him back. But it was impossible for him to reverse his action without loss of face, unless, in doing what he wanted to do anyhow he could be seen to be responding to some powerful external impulse, like the face-to-face request of a visiting papal legate. If that is right, Athelwold will all along have known that he had never really lost the friendship, the *amicitia*, of the constant David. And this is further proved by the fact that, to judge by Athelwold's witnessing of David's royal documents from 1141 onwards, he clearly became a regular member of the Scottish court in the 1140s, living in harmony with his episcopal neighbour, John of Glasgow. [94]

Conclusion

How what has been said in this last section of the chapter relates to its earlier sections, on Henry I's political mode of friendship, should be obvious. But it may seem here as if what has been said about the importance of royal symbolism goes against what was said earlier about Henry's willingness to abandon the symbolism of royal investiture of bishops with ring and staff. But actually the opposite seems more true. We used the phrase earlier of investiture as something which might by 1107 seem the empty shell of symbolism. One may doubt, however, whether it looked that way to Henry, else why should he have engaged in tough and lengthy negotiations before relinquishing it. And if he took a low estimate of the symbolism of investiture, 'a powerful reminder that bishops were not simply royal nominees' (Christopher Brooke again), might he not have seemed to underestimate the symbolism of his own anointing and crowning, a powerful reminder that *his* power derived its legitimacy from God?

A final word on friendship. There have been several students of medieval friendship in recent years, and one of the most notable of them is Julian Haseldine. He has shown how the self-conscious and literary cultivation of friendship as a cultural mode was important in the twelfth century, strikingly beginning in Henry I's period, not least as a factor moderating the conflicts which arose between religious orders old and new.[95] That has obvious resonances in the literate Henry I, and the way friendship moderated the conflicting aims of himself and others.

On a broader cultural front, David Knowles in his 1941 paper 'The Humanism of the Twelfth Century', showed, particularly through Abelard, Héloise and Ailred of Rievaulx, but bringing in others too, that the period c. 1120–60 was a high point for vivid self-expression and intense emotional sensibilities (including friendship), underpinned by knowledge of the Latin classics of antiquity.[96] It is not surprising that Ailred of Rievaulx, who fell in love with Cicero's *De Amicitia* when he was a boy, should have spent some of his early manhood at the court of King David of Scotland, before he converted to the Cistercian way of life. Knowles saw a change and a 'declension' from all this between 1150 and 1200.[97] He did not say why he thought it happened, but he implied that the rise of law, administration and scholasticism had something to do with it. For he wrote, 'the great figures of the early thirteenth century, whether thinkers or administrators, are all but inarticulate when not in their schools or chanceries'.[98]

It may be subjective to say it, but there is a quality about friendship where Henry I is concerned which is hard to find repeated later in the twelfth century. Politically the advance of legal process, government administration and professionalisation had probably made it unrepeatable. Henry II and Thomas Becket were boon companions when the latter was Chancellor. But the story of their soured relationship after Becket became Archbishop suggests that they could never have had the kind of friendship that Henry I had with Thurstan or David. Perhaps Henry II and Hugh of Lincoln come closer, but that is again different in various ways. Henry I's *amicitia*, or friendship, is a political/cultural/religious phenomenon rather particular to the first half of the twelfth century.

CHAPTER 4

The Conflict between Henry II and Thomas Becket

Introduction

In this chapter I am going to discuss the conflict by making points about it rather than by offering a narrative of it, although I hope the outline of events will be clear from my discussion. I should like to think that it will be possible for readers to read and understand this chapter without necessarily having the story already fixed in their heads. None of the best narratives is without much excellent scholarly and critical discussion, but for those who would like to read an account of Becket written in chronological order, I recommend one or more of the books by Anne Duggan, Frank Barlow or David Knowles in my bibliography.

It may seem rather sensationalist to devote a whole chapter to the fireworks of this conflict in the 1160s, particularly when it is so difficult to disentangle principles from personal issues, and material interests from spiritual objectives. If one asks whose fault it was that the conflict was drawn out for so many years, as Anne Duggan has said, 'answers depend on how the situation is read'.[1] How differently the situation can be read is revealed by the writings of two very recent authors: Duggan herself, favourable but not uncritically so to Becket; and Donald Matthew unfavourable but not blind to Henry II's faults. The 1160s were radically untypical of the relations between king and church in twelfth-century England, which were generally those of a *modus vivendi*, if perhaps compromise and peace were more on the king's terms than those of the church, even in Stephen's reign. But a crisis can shed light on ordinary conditions; it can show up where the most inflammable elements of a structure are.

Thomas Becket was born in London probably in 1120. He was thus some twelve years older than Henry II, whose boon companion he became as soon as Henry became king in 1154 and made Thomas his Chancellor. He was the son of a Norman merchant who had settled in London. He was not, therefore, a person of social consequence, and he had come into the court through the household of Archbishop Theobald. His neglect of the archbishop once he 'graduated' from his *familia*, which pained Theobald and contributed to his sense of isolation,[2] was not totally out of character. He was tall and dark, not particularly well educated, and he rose on his wits and force of personality. He became Archbishop of Canterbury on the Sunday after Pentecost in June 1162, aged perhaps 42.

The first year of Becket as Archbishop

The breach between the king and Becket did not occur until about July 1163; there is evidence that the first year of Becket's archiepiscopate was predominantly amicable. He himself, looking back from 1169, considered that he had been on good terms with Henry at the time of the Council of Tours (May 1163).[3] Another piece of evidence, from Reginald of Durham's *Life of Godric of Finchale*, the Wearside hermit, shows that there was no immediate breach between king and archbishop. Godric sent a message to Becket by a monk of Westminster who visited him saying that he should hold firmly to his course although he would be exiled. The monk was amazed 'because St Thomas at that time had been recently made archbishop and according to the opinions of men still had the good will of the king, although the king's mind – God being the sole witness – was already corrupted'.[4] There is hindsight here; the prophecies of holy men often represent insights into the first stirrings of actual trouble. But what this is evidence of, from a source with no axe to grind on the point, is that it took time before an open breach occurred.

It is sometimes argued, against the view that there was no immediate breach, that Becket's refusal to continue as royal Chancellor after becoming archbishop and receiving his pallium at once caused his relations with the king to plummet. True it was normal in the twelfth century for the Chancellor to become a bishop and normal when he did so to resign so comparatively trifling an office. But Henry had higher hopes for the Chancellorship, based on the model of Rainald Dassel who was both Archbishop of Cologne and Imperial Chancellor under the Emperor Frederick Barbarossa. His idea clearly was that in his dual role, the chancellorship greatly elevated in it, Becket would somehow control the British churches in the royal interest. Henry was disappointed when instead Becket, high-mindedly conceiving such secular concerns to be incompatible with his new spiritual office, returned the seal and insignia of the chancellorship to Henry abroad. Ralph of Diceto (Diss) has a highly coloured account, in retrospect, of how when Thomas went down to Southampton in January 1163 to greet the king on his return to England after a four-and-a-half year absence, 'he was admitted to the kiss of peace but not into the fullness of grace as the king publicly demonstrated to all who were present, by the manner in which he turned his face away from the archbishop'.[5] Herbert of Bosham, however, has the two riding off together from the meeting, chatting amicably.[6] While William FitzStephen, who was in the best position to know, represents Becket's initial loss of the king's goodwill as something more gradual and does not single out the chancellorship for special mention.[7]

What the breach might have been about, but was not

If there was no open breach for at least a year, that gives us an opportunity to see what the conflict was *not* about, though it might have been, or to look at what Becket did not challenge in that first year. That will in turn help us to see what the conflict *was* about.

First of all, it is difficult to see that, from the start anyhow, papal jurisdiction in England was a front-line issue. Z.N. Brooke, in his masterpiece *The English Church and the Papacy from the Conquest to the Reign of John*, saw the history of his period as the rivalry of two masters, king and pope, for the primary obedience of the English church. At first William the Conqueror put up a barrier against papal jurisdiction, which was most decisively breached by Becket who fought for papal authority. Of course, as Brooke himself recognised, this over-simplified Becket's role in his scheme, since the many appeals of for example Thurstan of York and Urban of Llandaff under Henry I, and the willingness of Archbishop Theobald, Gilbert Foliot and others to act as papal judge-delegates in England under Stephen and early Henry II, had already advanced papal authority before Becket's time. But Becket – such would be my argument – did very little to advance it further.

In March 1163 the legal dispute between the Bishop of Lincoln and the Abbey of St Albans about St Albans' claim to be free of the jurisdiction of its diocesan, the Bishop of Lincoln, came to a head. St Albans made its claim on the grounds that it was an ancient royal foundation, so the royal dignity was involved, and Henry II had insisted on hearing the case himself at Westminster. The abbey had appealed to Rome, and in 1162 the Bishops of Norwich and Chichester were commissioned by the pope to hear the case in England as papal judges-delegate. They had already cited the Prior of St Albans to appear before them. When he arrived at Westminster, with a barrow load of documents and some of his monks to handle them, and found himself before the full *curia regis*, he asked the king whether, if he proved his case there, he need plead again before the papal judges-delegate. The king at that point consulted with some of his leading counsellors, particularly be it noted Archbishop Thomas. Did the archbishop say to the king, 'You cannot suppress the papal jurisdiction just like that!' Clearly not, for the king then said that what the abbot (sic) said was consonant with reason: 'for it would not do honour to our majesty if a lawsuit once decided in our palace, were to await another sentence in the lord pope's court'.[8] In other words Becket on this occasion allowed the papal jurisdiction to be suppressed. This is all the more striking as under late Stephen and certainly in the early years of Henry II there is abundant evidence of a clamp-down by the king on papal jurisdiction,[9] so that by 1163 any churchman who behaved as Becket did at Westminster would not fail to be aware of his being complicit in that clamp-down.

Again, probably some time later in 1163, Becket ignored papal jurisdiction when, as metropolitan, he gave judgment in a lawsuit involving money between two clerics, against Hubert, a clergyman at St Paul's Cathedral, although before judgment had been given Hubert had appealed to the pope. None other than Becket's future opponent, Gilbert Foliot, Bishop of London, wrote to him to ask him to relax his sentence.[10] Subsequently, of course, after he went into exile late in 1164, Becket presented himself to the papal court as the sole friend of Rome in England. It was his only way to be restored to his archbishopric. But as Donald Matthew has said of this, given that Henry II himself through Gilbert Foliot was appealing to the papacy, 'although his case has been widely accepted, at the time its absurdity would have been manifest to everyone, not least the curia itself'.[11]

Thus Becket can hardly be called a champion of papal jurisdiction in England during his first year as archbishop.

Henry II had his 'customs', defining his relations with the church, set out in writing in the Constitutions of Clarendon which he presented to Becket and the bishops at the Council of Clarendon in January 1164. Why he wanted to set them down in writing when he exercised them all already in practice is a question to which we shall come shortly. By Clause 4 he in effect restricted appeals to the papacy without the king's permission.

Another important clause concerned the patronage of churches. If controversy arose about this, it ought to be heard and settled in the king's court.[12]
Patronage of a church meant the right to appoint the priest. To present a
man to a church meant that, king or bishop or monastery or lay aristocrat,
the patron had the disposal of a salary for one of his clerks, particularly if the
latter could put in a vicar, still draw a profit, and do some other job for
the patron. Henry II clearly exercised jurisdiction over such lawsuits before
1164. For instance, some time probably in the first half of 1163, he ordered
Bishop Robert de Chesney of Lincoln, by a writ, to let the Cluniac Priory
of Castle Acre (Norfolk) have the churches of Long Sutton and Lutton
(Northants) because they had twice proved their right to them in his synod
against the sons of William the Chaplain of Sutton. He then added in a
well-known type of phrase of royal writs in that period: 'unless you do this
Archbishop Thomas of Canterbury will do it'.[13] Here the king by his inter-
vention in effect asserted his jurisdiction over lawsuits about churches,
if only to force the church to implement its own decisions. Moreover he
expected Becket to co-operate in the exercise of his jurisdiction. One might
wonder whether he was mentioned here precisely because the king did not
trust him and wanted to force his hand. But I am informed by an expert in
royal writs of Henry II that this is too clever by half and that such a clause
should be read as trusting the person named. So again on patronage of
churches, Becket did not challenge the king in his first year as archbishop.

Perhaps the most vexed question in the conflict, while it lasted, was
criminous clerks. By whom should clergymen accused of crimes be tried?
By whom punished? The background to this has been seen as the two
developing systems of law, church or canon law and royal law, and their
courts and justice. There were bound to be overlaps and clashes of jurisdiction. The Constitutions of Clarendon in 1164 can be seen as an attempt
to identify and define such overlaps to the king's advantage. This is what
Clause 3 of the Constitutions said: if there is an accusation against a cleric
he should be summoned to the royal court; there in the royal court it
should be decided whether he should answer for it in the royal court or the
ecclesiastical court; if in the latter, the king's justice should send someone
along to see how the matter was dealt with there; and if the cleric confessed
or was convicted, the church thereafter should not protect him (i.e. he
should be degraded from his clerical orders and handed over to be punished
in the royal court).[14] Obviously this gave the initiative all along the line to
the secular courts, and Henry II had good reason to want ecclesiastical
criminal justice tightened up, for there seems to have been widespread
feeling that it was too lenient and also corrupt. William FitzStephen, one of

Becket's biographers, himself tells of how, some years before 1164, in 1158, the wife of a burgess of Scarborough was falsely accused of adultery and summoned to clear herself at the rural dean's court, and how her husband paid substantial sums of money to the archdeacon and rural dean to have her treated gently.[15] More generally, from the earliest years of Henry II's reign, the king was trying to clear up after the 'Anarchy' of Stephen's reign, sending out justices into the shires, preventing unjust dispossessions of property, chasing those who were fugitives from justice, etc. One cannot doubt that a major motive for Clause 3 of the Constitutions was that Henry genuinely did not wish to see the treatment of criminous clerks as an ugly gap in his criminal justice system.

The striking point for Becket in Clause 3 of the Constitutions was the very last phrase, whose effect was to hand the cleric over for punishment to the secular courts. Degradation from clerical orders was in itself a heavy punishment; it involved not only loss of face, but also quite often loss of livelihood. Becket argued that if a cleric was then handed over to secular punishment, that was double punishment, and his famous adage was, 'not even God punishes twice for the same offence'.[16] But it looks as if the royal government had been assuming a right to punish criminous clerks, and that under Becket's nose. For in the Pipe Roll (the Exchequer account) of September/October 1162, under Buckinghamshire and Bedfordshire, the royal sheriff is shown as paying out 62 shillings and 11 pence, a hefty sum, for custody of a priest and his brother who killed a man and his wife.[17] The king's government might of course just have been holding this priest until he could be tried in the church courts, but it looks like another sign of Henry II's government directing and controlling ecclesiastical jurisdiction.

If I argue that Becket did not challenge royal restriction of the pope's appellate jurisdiction or *de facto* royal jurisdiction over patronage of churches (advowsons) or royal punishment of criminous clerks, before late 1163 or 1164, and thus that such issues were not the initial cause of the conflict, nobody should conclude that I think them unimportant. They were genuinely *potential* causes of conflict between church and secular power. The point about all of them, however, is that as they worked out in practice they were all susceptible to compromise, and compromise over them was the normal state of affairs in the twelfth century. On appeals to Rome, there was a large expansion of these and of appointment of papal judges-delegate in England in the decades after Becket's martyrdom, but it was generally recognised, including by the most canonistically minded of bishops, that where the king had an interest in a lawsuit it should be determined in his presence.[18] On advowsons, provided both parties in a dispute agreed to keep it in the church courts, it remained there; it required one party or the other to take out a royal writ to remove it to the secular courts.[19] On criminous clerks, many historians have argued that Henry II was, even according to canon law, on better ground than was Becket. But that is not correct. The canon law stated that when a cleric was degraded, *curiae tradatur* (i.e. he was to be handed over to the secular court). The word *tradatur*, however, is in the subjunctive and can therefore mean in Latin either he shall be handed over, or he *may* be handed over. And if he may be handed over, who was to decide whether he should be handed over. Surely, according to canon law, the church.[20] And that is normally how it worked out in practice after 1170, as Christopher Cheney showed more than seventy years ago.[21]

The breach: Canterbury rights

So what did start the conflict? Or rather, perhaps, what was the *casus belli*? What caused the open breach between king and archbishop? It is not always noticed that William FitzStephen, at that time Becket's secretary, or the *dictator* (draughter of documents) in his chancery as he calls himself, a sensibly judging man who was in the best position of anyone to know, gives us a direct and explicit answer to this question. As we have said, FitzStephen sees the general withdrawal of his goodwill by Henry as a gradual process, due to the backbiting of Becket's enemies at court and the withdrawal of Becket's service to him. But then there comes his account of a dramatic breach.

'This was the first cause of (Henry's) hatred of the archbishop', FitzStephen begins. He goes on to narrate how Becket sought to recover the castle of Tonbridge alienated from Canterbury by Roger de Clare; but Roger refused, maintaining that he only owed homage to the king for it. Earl Roger was related to almost all the nobles of England and he had a sister who was the most beautiful woman in the kingdom whom the king had at some time desired. Again, the Archbishop had given the church of Eynesford (Kent) to a cleric called Lawrence, but the lord of the vill, William of Eynesford, expelled Lawrence's men and so the Archbishop excommunicated him. The king wrote to Becket requiring him to absolve William. The archbishop replied that it was not for the king to give orders about who should be excommunicated and who absolved. The king maintained that it was against his royal dignity that any tenant–in–chief or official of his should be excommunicated without his permission (this was indeed re-stated in Clause 7 of the Constitutions of Clarendon). Finally to mollify the king who was now incandescent with rage and would not speak to him except through intermediaries, Becket absolved William. FitzStephen finished his narrative, leaving no doubt that this being 'the first cause of hatred' applied to both the Tonbridge and Eynesford cases, by reporting that the king said of Becket at Windsor, 'now I have no more love for him' or 'now he is no longer in my favour' (nunc ei inde gratiam non habeo).[22] And every subsequent event in Becket's life shows that Henry meant it.

Becket cannot have been unaware of how inflammatory the king would find his behaviour in all this. In 1159 Robert of Valoines and the Abbot of St Albans were in a dispute about rights over a wood at Northaw (Herts), and Pope Adrian IV (the one English pope who himself came from St Albans!) ordered Archbishop Theobald and Bishop Hilary of Chichester as papal judges-delegate to excommunicate Robert if he were contumacious. But the bishops, knowing that King Henry had forbidden all bishops to excommunicate any of his barons, were afraid to do this.[23] The *Gesta Abbatum* of St Albans is based on a reliable contemporary chronicle at this time,[24] and it shows that the king's attitude to excommunication of his barons was well known while Becket was still Chancellor.

So what caused Becket, who had allowed so much to pass unchallenged, to behave so provocatively over Roger de Clare and William of Eynesford now? It was obviously because now the rights of the church of Canterbury were at stake. Or rather the rights of the Archbishopric of Canterbury, for the non-monastic archbishop and the monks of Christ Church Cathedral Priory had in some respects different perceptions of what the rights of Canterbury were. The rights of Canterbury would remain a major part of the story for the rest of Becket's life. Becket would countenance no reconciliation with Henry when in exile until every jot and tittle of his Canterbury rights had been restored. In 1169, when he solemnly issued a list of excommunications, after naming a few political opponents, he gets down to a long list of people who constitute a roll call of baronial, knightly and scarcely knightly Kentishmen. Robert de Broc was one of them and he had built a house at Canterbury with timber taken from the Archbishop's woods.[25] Others of these men must have been making hay with the Archbishop's rights in Kent while the sun of his absence shone.

David Knowles, in his fine character study of Thomas Becket, wrote:

As the struggle wore on, the precise object for which the archbishop fought had changed its appearance to his eyes. At the beginning it had been the forensic rights of the church and the clerical order [we have seen that this needs modifying]; then it had become at Clarendon the freedom of the English Church as part of the universal Church in its relations with Rome [this too]; finally it had broadened into a defence of the rights of God as against Caesar. There is no question that Thomas's conception of the issue deepened and became more spiritualised, and that his attitude acquired thereby a dignity and strength which it had lacked before.[26]

There is no need to deny that this deepening occurred, and it certainly was what Becket himself thought, but it is equally clear that Becket never lost his focus on championing his Canterbury rights. If ever Henry spoke the infamous words 'who will rid me of this turbulent priest', which set his four knights off on their fateful mission, they were occasioned by Becket's excommunication of Roger, Archbishop of York and the bishops of London and Salisbury for their coronation of Henry's son, the Younger Henry, in the absence of Becket, thereby denying the right of the Archbishop of Canterbury to crown a King of England. Almost Becket's last words were, 'To God and blessed Mary, St Denis, and St Alphege I commend myself and my Church.'[27] One can understand his invoking St Denis, patron saint of France where he had been in exile for so many years. But St Alphege? Would he be one of the first members of the heavenly kingdom whom one would normally call to mind when confronted by four murderous knights about to kill one? Alphege, however, was an early eleventh-century Archbishop of Canterbury, pelted to death with ox bones by drunken Danes for defending the material possessions of the Church of Canterbury. And he was deemed a martyr for that.

It is instructive to compare Becket's attitude to the possessions and privileges of Canterbury with that of Anselm, on whom he consciously modelled himself. Southern rightly saw this same attitude as one of the principles which Anselm clung to through thick and thin during his archiepiscopate. During Anselm's time as archbishop three main issues concerning papal authority arose in England. First, the recognition of a rightful pope in a schism. Anselm had already recognised Urban II as the rightful pope before he became archbishop; William Rufus had not, and hence the conflict between king and archbishop in 1095. Second, Anselm's insistence, in obedience to the papacy, on the decrees against lay investiture of bishops. This brought him into conflict with Henry I. But third, the question of whether papal legates had the right to enter England brought him into conflict with Pope Paschal II and had him seeking the help of Henry I, because he claimed a standing papal legation in England as a Canterbury right.[28]

From the moment Henry declared that he had no more love of or favour for Becket, the nature of the conflict totally changed. From then on Henry, peeved by the contempt shown to him by his creature who would have been nothing without him, was out to destroy Becket personally. He raised the question of criminous clerks in the way and at the time he did, at the Council of Westminster in October 1163, to divide the episcopate behind Becket. When he found that they were united on the issue at the Council of Clarendon in January 1164 he promptly dropped it. Criminous clerks as an issue only caused difficulty for four months of the twelfth century. Then at the Council of Clarendon he produced the Constitutions of Clarendon, the 'customs' of the king as exercised by his grandfather, Henry I. As I have said some of the Constitutions were genuinely problematical. But why when Henry II was exercising them already should he want to set them down in writing? Surely one does not go into somebody's office, thump the table, and demand some right or other, when one is exercising it quietly already. Obviously he put them in writing in order to discomfort Becket and cause his leadership to be challenged. He succeeded, albeit in an unexpected way. Then Henry, as Becket's feudal lord, summoned him to answer charges at the Council of Northampton (October 1164). As one charge receded, another was raised. They could all be described were it relevant to present purposes. But it is not. It was almost a case of any stick with which to beat a dog. Finally Becket slipped away from Northampton under a perceived threat of physical danger and fled across the Channel. Thus when the bishops who were the king's supporters kept trying to reassure the exiled Becket that the king's intentions were entirely pacific and that he wanted nothing more than reconciliation, they were being decidedly disingenuous.[29] From October 1163 to October 1164 Henry II entirely dictated the terms of the conflict, and in that crucial year at least, it is useless to call Becket obstinate. What can be said of him, however, is that he lacked the social *savoir-faire* or relaxation to respond in any but the uptight way which would never cut ice with a bully like Henry. In his incapacity to relax, Becket perhaps showed something of the psychology of one of those frenetic careerists of whom I wrote in the first chapter.

Why did it take so long as six years while Becket was in exile to reach even the semblance of a reconciliation? Why, when Pope Alexander III himself was desperate for a compromise (because on the one hand he did not want to drive Henry II into alliance with the schismatic Emperor Frederick Barbarossa, but on the other hand he could not be seen to detach himself from Becket), did not reconciliation happen sooner? Why, when Gilbert Foliot, Becket's leading opponent amongst the English bishops, thought compromise with the king was possible, could Becket not think so? Until Becket's exile, Foliot had been more papalist than Becket, but he also put forward a theory that one must distinguish between the temporal possessions of a bishopric which were held from the earthly king and its spiritual possessions which were subject only to the heavenly king. Ought that not to have been an acceptable basis of compromise?[30] Foliot was a serious and by 1164 experienced churchman, of great learning and high moral character.

If we try to answer this question we must first make a purely logistical point. With Becket in France, and constant appeal being made to the papal court in Rome by both sides (the king became as much a papalist as any-one!), the dispute became a slow-motion performance. But there are more important answers to give. Foliot was more a lawyer than a theologian (thought not negligible as a theologian), with a special expertise in Roman Law, whereas on Becket's side theologians rather than lawyers were uppermost.[31] And as was said in the previous chapter, lawyers always had a much stronger instinct for compromise than had theologians. Again, insofar as Canterbury rights remained central to Becket's stand, one could observe that it was easier for a Bishop of London than for an Archbishop of Canterbury to compromise Canterbury rights! Some may doubt whether Canterbury rights did indeed figure so large in the dispute, for the churchmen who wrote to Becket from England wrote mainly about his stand on the 'customs', i.e. having first got the other bishops to accept the Constitutions of Clarendon and then, conscience stricken, done a *volte face* on this. Had Becket moved on, as he himself implied, to seeing the dispute as one about the liberty of the church as a whole? Up to a point, but there is evidence that he continued, in exile, to think of the church's liberty and Canterbury rights as part and parcel of each other – and that was not an unreasonable position to hold. For in a reply to a letter from 'the English Clergy', he wrote in July 1166 of how he had been forced to place his goods, as Archbishop of Canterbury, under the protection of Rome, adding, 'wrongly do we call them his (the archbishop's) goods, since they are the goods of the poor, the patrimony of the Crucified, which were entrusted to him rather than given'.[32] This was no doubt sincerely written, but it suggests a degree of sublimation concerning Canterbury rights, brought about perhaps by nearly two years of exile; and the subsequent dispute makes it look as if Becket did not remain quite so sublime about Canterbury rights. What it principally suggests, however, is that Becket knew what people were actually saying about him on this subject.

Clash of personalities

In the drawn-out struggle, the clash of personalities should not be under-rated – Henry II angry, self-pitying, cruel and dissembling, Becket tactless and haranguing, thinking himself patient but easily prone to exasperation. Obsessed as he became about his relationship with the king, Becket never thought of saving Henry's face as Thurstan of York did with Henry I. He ignored the gentle advice of the pope and John of Salisbury not to insist on minutiae; he would not return to England until every yard of church land had been restored.[33] Nor should it be imagined that the clash of personalities was only between Henry and Becket. The voluminous correspondence generated during Becket's exile does not on the whole make pleasant reading, with so much of cross-purposes, special pleading and acrimony. But even in the midst of all this, Gilbert Foliot's notorious letter, *Multiplicem*, (1166) blaming Becket for the whole dispute, stands out for its personal nastiness. A brilliant piece of rhetoric, which nobody in Becket's circle could equal, it is a pouring out of pent-up bile and hatred, a tissue of distortions and half-truths.[34] Here we have another answer to the question, 'If Foliot could compromise with the king, why could not Becket?' Foliot was a willing accomplice to the destruction of Becket by Henry II. The hatred went back to Becket as Chancellor, his conduct and his acquiescence in the king's treatment of the church. Thus he felt about Becket's elevation to Canterbury in 1162 that he, Foliot, 'was the true leader of the English church'.[35]

What had happened in all this to the friendship which was such an ingredient in the politics of Henry I's reign? One may doubt whether there was ever true friendship between Henry and Becket, even as Chancellor, in the sense of *amicitia* held by twelfth-century writers, whatever their boon companionship might have signified. This was no coming together of equals. On more than one occasion during the conflict Henry showed his contempt for Becket's low birth. He was 'simply a creature who could be broken at any time'.[36] Contrast the blazing 'family' row that Henry and Roger of Worcester, who was not just any aristocrat but a first cousin of the king, and who was also a supporter of Becket, had near Falaise in 1170. When both had exhausted their complaints and taunts against each other, they made friends again and discussed how to make peace with Thomas.[37] But with the humourless Becket, Henry showed only pique that his creature had failed him. Although Becket, at least in his younger days was said to have had a modest and pleasant turn of speech and engaging

manners, 'no one who knew him indicates that he was warm and affectionate, (or) that he had the gift of friendship'. So wrote Frank Barlow.[38]
And Julian Haseldine has made the telling observation that during his
exile he relied for much of his support on the ready-made friendship
networks of his secretary John of Salisbury and of the famous abbot, Peter
of Celle. Becket never seems to have built up his own friendship network as
Thurstan had.[39]

Dramatic gesturing

There was quite as much theatre as rancour in this conflict. Gesture and
theatre were integral to politics at that time. Perhaps they still are. In
deadly earnest the actors may have been, but they could still act out their
roles symbolically as if in a play. The narrators understood the game-rules
as well as the actors did. Henry II was a master at the 'staging' of his
emotions. The uncertainty of when his anger would erupt and he would
break out into a rage was a deliberate game. This kind of thing was part of
'the regular repertoire of every twelfth-century king with professional
training'.[40] He knew the dramatic value of keeping people on tenter-
hooks, arriving very late for the first day of the Council of Northampton
(1164) having been out hunting with falcons.[41] He celebrated Christmas
1164, after Becket had just departed the land, at the Castle of
Berkhamstead, which he had wrested from Becket, in a sort of gesture
of high glee.[42]

Becket understood well how to play the same game of gestures and
symbols. Whereas Roger of Pont l'Eveque, Archbishop of York, had his cross
carried in front of him by his cross-bearer at the Council of Northampton,
Becket carried his own cross in. Roger was provoking Becket, who maintained that the Archbishop of York had no right to have his cross carried
before him in the southern province. Becket was provoking the king. He
maintained that he carried his cross as a symbol of peace, but to Henry it
was an aggressive gesture, the equivalent in a churchman to a layman's
carrying a weapon in the king's presence.[43] The day before he slipped out
of Northampton, namely 13 October 1164, was the feast of Edward the
Confessor. Edward had been canonised in 1161, but only in 1163, one year
before, had his feast been celebrated for the first time. All this mattered
deeply to Henry II, who in the earlier years of his reign needed every scrap
of sacrality that he could attach to his kingship; and the canonisation of
an Anglo-Saxon king was an important contribution, not only for adding
to the aura of kingship generally, but also for legitimating the rule of

the Normans and Angevins as true successors of the Angle-Saxons. But on 13 October 1164, Becket chose to celebrate not the Mass of Edward the Confessor, but a votive Mass of St Stephen, the first martyr, whose introit began with the words, 'princes also sat against me' (Psalm 119, 23).[44] This was gesture politics in the extreme. It was a snub to Henry II, and he already cast himself self-consciously in the role of a martyr.

In exile one might almost say that Becket raised his game. In late May or early June 1166 he sent a letter of admonition to the king, shorn of all but the barest address, and with apparently no salutation such as was usual, and he sent it by the hand of the Cistercian Abbot of Cercamp, which Henry thought beneath his dignity. Henry called it an impudent piece of writing from 'a certain Thomas once our Chancellor'![45] About the time that he wrote that letter Becket visited Soissons to pray at the shrine of St Drausius the patron saint of champions who were about to wage the ordeal of battle. He was about to publish the excommunications of his enemies at Vézelay (which included all those who in future would put their hands on the possessions and goods of the church of Canterbury to abuse them).[46] The dividing line between military aggression, such as he had employed on occasions as Chancellor, and religious or spiritual aggression, sometimes seems a thin one with Becket. Perhaps Henry was not so mistaken in seeing aggression in his carrying his cross at Northampton.

Becket's 'conversion'

To say that Becket played out his role in a conflict by means of public symbol and gesture is very different from saying that his whole conduct as arch-bishop was an act. This was maintained by A.L. Poole in 1951, when he sought to explain the apparently startling transition from worldly chancellor to saintly archbishop. Poole wrote:

In that rapid transition from the gay, splendidly dressed courtier who romped with the king to the proud and austere priest who mortified his flesh by abstinence and flagellation and excelled in ostentatious acts of charity and humility, one can see a great actor superbly living the parts he was called upon to play. He had an amazing versatility which enabled him to change easily from, as he once expressed it, being 'a patron of play-actors and a follower of hounds to become a shepherd of souls'.[47]

Poole's view was a slightly less sophisticated interpretation of that put forward twenty years previously (1931) by Z.N. Brooke:

(Becket) was one of those men who, exalting to the full the role they have to play . . . were actors playing a part, but unconscious actors . . . when he was appointed archbishop it needed no miraculous conversion; he pictured himself in the part at once, and he warned the king of the consequences.[48]

This view of Becket as the great actor, whether as Chancellor or as Archbishop, was highly influential at least in student circles for several decades. But it cannot now be sustained, at least in the way it was presented by Brooke and Poole. That is largely because Beryl Smalley, in a brilliant discussion, made Becket's so-called conversion when he became archbishop look much less clear-cut.[49] First, in his time as 'worldly' Chancellor, the always chaste-living Becket, if he did not aspire to sanctity himself, longed to be the friend of Holy Men. He sought to be the 'pen-friend' of Peter of Celle; Smalley wrote that to receive a letter of spiritual direction from him conferred a certificate of piety![50] Peter refused, writing that he was too humble to become the intimate of so important a person as the Chancellor. Becket successfully sought to acquire a copy of the sermons of Master Gebuin, Precentor or Chanter of Troyes, 'St Bernard without tears' as Smalley called them.[51] Becket read them, one of them about the types of constancy required for martyrdom. He came to know while he was Chancellor the saintly Archbishop of Bordeaux and popular preacher, Geoffrey of Loroux, known as Geoffrey Babion, 'the Stammerer'. Much earlier as a teacher in the school of Angers, 'he had most success with duller pupils; his stammer made him speak so slowly that they could take in what he said'. He and Becket as Chancellor together witnessed charters of Henry II when the king was in the Bordeaux region in 1156–57. Becket had a paradigm of a churchman before his eyes in Geoffrey, and one who stood up for the liberties of his church against secular government. 'He had less glitter than St Anselm, but Becket knew him personally and not only on hearsay.'[52]

The second point in which Smalley has changed historians' view of Becket's 'conversion' is by showing that it was commonly accepted that the life of a prelate (such as a bishop) should differ from that of a secular clerk, as Becket was while Chancellor. It was not something peculiar to Becket. The expectations placed on an Archbishop of Canterbury were however exceptionally high because all but one of Becket's predecessors since the Norman Conquest had been Benedictine monks of Bec in Normandy, and the exception, William of Corbeil, although not a monk, was of the religious order of Augustinian Canons and had contacts with Anselm's friends and pupils. It amounted almost to a commonplace idea, firmly grounded in the writings of Pope Gregory the Great under whom Canterbury was first established, rather than a counsel of perfection, that an Archbishop of Canterbury should have something monastic about him and should lead a life of prayer as well as of action. These were current ideas about the office, and as Smalley wrote: 'Becket's conversion was predictable, given his temperament and circumstances. The sources point to a theatrical streak in him; but it is not play-acting to take ideas seriously.'[53]

Why did Becket's death create a sensation?

The reader may have been wondering, if Becket's sights were to the degree I maintain set on Canterbury rights and were so localised, why his death created such a sensation across Europe. Of course the murder of a bishop or archbishop was always bound to produce shock waves, but why in Becket's case such a sensation as would lead to his canonisation only two-and-a-half years after his death? Various answers may be suggested to this. One was the innate distinction of his person and presence. Becket may not have been pre-eminent for his gifts of friendship, but he had a charm and magnetism that drew others to himself, and he could inspire great loyalty, as those of his clerks who stood by him for so long to the detriment of their careers show. David Knowles, in his extremely perceptive character study of Thomas Becket has this to say, commenting on Becket's lack of any literary output other than his official letters:

There are men whose personality and charm reveal themselves in every page they write or word they speak. Such were Cicero and Augustine in the old world, Anselm and Bernard in the twelfth century, Cromwell, perhaps, Abraham Lincoln, and Newman in the modern world. The charm and power of others were felt by their contemporaries; we see it in their influence and their achievements; but their surviving words are not conductors of the magnetic spark. Such in the recent past [this was written in 1949] was David Lloyd George, such was Cardinal Manning, such, perhaps, with certain reservations, was the great Napoleon, such, in the twelfth century, was Archbishop Thomas.[54]

When the tall and dark archbishop first arrived in Flanders on his exile, he had the same difficulty to preserve his incognito as the fleeing Charles II would later have, 'His commanding presence', wrote Knowles, 'his fine hands, and the air with which he gave presents of food to children convinced cottagers and innkeepers that they were entertaining one of the great.' And when he cast an appraising look at a falcon on a knight's wrist, the knight said to his friend, 'that's the Archbishop of Canterbury or his look-alike'.[55] Frank Barlow, commenting on Herbert of Bosham's famous passage about Becket after his death – 'Truly he was great always and everywhere, great in the palace, great in his priesthood, great at court, great in the church, great in his pilgrimage (or exile), great in his return, and singularly great at his journey's end' – has written, 'Herbert, looking back from afar, saw more than a sense of theatre in his actor; he was conscious of an innate and constant greatness.'[56]

Another reason why Becket's death caused such a sensation was because of his six-year exile. Becket may have made few friends for himself during this time, but he became famous all over Europe as a man with a cause. His biographers wrote of his whole life and not just of his death in a hagiographic vein, representing him in the light of Christ's Passion, of the early Christian martyrdom narratives, and not least of Abel, the first martyr of all (who had not died defending any article of faith!). That does not mean they were unreliable as to facts; it was a matter of how they interpreted them, and in that there was naturally a good deal of retrospect. But it was not all retrospect, as can be seen from Becket's own self-presentation as a sort of martyr in his celebrating Stephen the protomartyr on 13 October 1164 when it was the feast of King Edward the Confessor. Becket's contemporaries, or some of them, saw his whole struggle with Henry II as a sort of martyrdom, even had he not finally been killed – what one could call a white sort, as distinct from the red martyrdom when the martyr's blood was actually shed.[57] In this, as in so much else, they followed the writings of Pope Gregory the Great:

There are two types of martyrdom: one in the soul and another in deed as well as soul, one hidden and the other public. Holy Church is full of flowers of the elect, so that in times of peace she has lilies, and in times of persecution roses [hence white and red].[58]

With many contemporaries, however, this view of Becket's white martyrdom during his life was only retrospective, he having been found to have been wearing a hair shirt when he died. And even then there were monks of Canterbury who were not so sure. One of them was reported to have said that the archbishop ought not to be regarded as a martyr, having been slain as the reward of his own obstinacy.[59]

Becket and theology

In the final analysis, there would be something cheap in proposing that the whole Becket conflict, on Becket's side, was only about Canterbury rights. Becket could never speak just for himself, because his whole drama was acted out before an educated theological audience the like of which had not been seen in the West for many centuries. That was mainly thanks to the rising cathedral schools of Northern France and above all Paris. Peter the Chanter, whose school was probably the most distinguished theological school at Paris in the last three decades of the twelfth century, staunchly advocated the sanctity of Becket – for standing up to secular tyranny, for refusing to allow fees for sealing documents in his chancery, for opposing the handing over of clerks to the secular courts, as well as for his actual martyrdom. (Although the Chanter had to argue against those in Paris who thought that Becket's constancy was mere contumacy.)[60] Robert Courson, later Cardinal, would echo the Chanter's view. So would Stephen Langton, Becket's successor but three as Archbishop of Canterbury who probably studied under Peter before he became a Paris professor himself. Beryl Smalley has said of the discussions at Paris about the relations of *regnum* and *sacerdotium* (very much a Gregorian Reform question), rather in abeyance in previous decades, that the Becket conflict made them burst into flame again.[61] For all the miracles worked at Becket's tomb in Canterbury – and Herbert of Bosham discounted the importance of these compared with considering his way of life[62] – Becket's posthumous fame radiated across Europe quite as much from Paris as from Canterbury. This public of theologians was indeed yet another reason why his death caused such a sensation.

The three most notable bishops of English sees in Becket's time who had studied in Paris all supported him. Bartholomew of Exeter had clearly studied at Paris and appears even to have taught there in the early 1140s. The date of his most important work, the widely circulated *Penitential*, is rather a matter of guess-work, but perhaps should be dated from his time as Archdeacon of Exeter in the late 1150s or very early 1160s. It is far removed from being a tariff of penances for various sins, as earlier penitentials generally were. It is a work of moral and pastoral theology in 135 chapters. Out of cowardice Bartholomew shied away from supporting Becket against the king at the Council of Northampton, but then incurred the king's displeasure by sticking loyally to his archbishop during his exile. He was a confidant of John of Salisbury, one of Becket's closest companions in exile.[63] Robert of Melun, a distinguished Paris master, became in old age Bishop of Hereford, a position he held for just over three years between 1163 and 1167. He was considered by Becket in 1164 to be one of his supporters, albeit he got cold feet later on.[64] Roger of Worcester was the staunchest of Becket's episcopal supporters amongst the English bishops. As we have already implied, being the first cousin of the king gave him a certain *franchise*; he could get away with speaking and acting as he thought. But he was also a theologian by training. Robert of Cricklade, during the conflict Prior of St Frideswide, Oxford, had met Roger in a Paris inn and asked him with whom he was studying theology. He was studying with none other than the Master Robert of Melun who subsequently became Bishop of Hereford. 'I am very pleased', Robert of Cricklade said; 'I was afraid that that heretic [i.e. Peter Lombard] had you ensnared in his net.'[65] To be studying with Robert of Melun and to be thought to be, studying with Peter Lombard suggests that Roger was perceived as a high-flying theology student in Paris.

Roger of Worcester and Bartholomew of Exeter would come to be regarded as the most distinguished canon lawyers, who were constantly used as papal judges-delegate, in the England of the 1170s and 1180s. It was a natural progression from the more speculative world of theology to the more practical world of canon law and judicial activity, at least where theologians who became bishops were concerned. But in the early 1160s, when the two became bishops, they must still be considered primarily as theologians. Thus the most distinguished canon lawyers, like Gilbert Foliot and Hilary of Chichester, backed Henry II, which would be unexpected if one took the view that the conflict was mainly about the clash of secular and ecclesiastical jurisdictions. The theologians backed Becket, which is what one might expect if the theologians of West Europe (and even beyond) were watching it as a dramatic clash between *regnum* and *sacerdotium*, between the Church as represented by the apocalyptic Woman in the Sky and the powers of earth as represented by the dragon with seven heads and ten horns, indeed between the cosmic principles of good and evil always in strife with each other in the world, as the Cathar heretics in France and the Rhineland at this time were always emphasising.

If we now make a contrast between Becket and his predecessor Anselm, Anselm's theology was deeply rooted in his own whole mind and person. Who can doubt that his thinking in *Why God became Man (Cur Deus Homo)*, with its sense of God's presence in human affairs and written while he was Archbishop of Canterbury, informed his whole activity as archbishop, even if this is something of the Spirit which we cannot express concretely?[66] It is tempting to say that while Anselm was his own theologian,

Becket had to have his theology supplied to him by others. It was not integral to the man himself. But the temptation to make too much of this contrast should be resisted. Theology mattered to Becket. The first thing that he did when he was consecrated bishop on the Sunday after Pentecost and became truly Archbishop was not to assert a Canterbury right or an ecclesiastical jurisdictional right, nor to declare himself the pope's champion. It was to order that first Sunday after Pentecost henceforth to be kept as the Feast of the Trinity by the whole English church.[67] This shows how alive he was to liturgy, as does his celebration of the votive Mass of St Stephen on 13 October 1164. But it also shows theological awareness. Peter Lombard's *Sentences* of the 1150s, the most comprehensive work of scholastic theology up to that time, set down 'the Mystery of the Trinity' in 'Distinction' after 'Distinction' at the beginning of his work.[68] Abelard had already written majestically on this theme in the 1130s. Anonymous tracts on the Trinity were being produced galore in France during the decades of the mid-twelfth century. So did one need to have that much theological awareness to see the importance of the Trinity by 1162? Perhaps not, but Becket showed that it mattered to him by channelling a huge intellectual effort into a major religious devotion.

Something rather remarkable connects to this action of Becket. While he was in exile he commissioned a copy of Peter Lombard's Great Gloss on the Bible, drawn up in four folio volumes. The whole project was masterminded by Herbert of Bosham, a spirited clerk loyal to him throughout his exile, and his secretary and most important theological advisor. Herbert was not the scribe or the illustrator of these manuscripts, but they were set out according to his plan. Stella Panayotova has studied the volume devoted to the Psalms. What she shows is that whether or not Becket was actually a participator in the plan, and whether or not the manuscript was completed in time for Becket to use it (it probably was), it was clearly planned with his interests and needs very much in mind. It reveals that Becket wanted to use his time in exile not only writing querulous letters on ecclesiastical subjects but also improving his grasp of theology in line with the latest Parisian learning. For at the Cistercian monastery of Pontigny, the Archbishop and Herbert daily studied the Bible together. One of Herbert's own editorial contributions was to enable one to follow various groupings of psalms, like the seven penitential psalms or all the psalms beginning with alleluia. With the help of Cassiodorus's and Gilbert of Poitiers' commentaries on the psalms, he assigned a theme for each psalm which was expressed in a brief introduction, or *capitulum*, to it, and which was reinforced by small illustrations. Thus, for instance, the introductions tell us that Psalms 2, 8 and 81 are the first second and fifth psalms to discuss (by way of adumbration) the two natures, divine and human, of Christ. This is not only christological but also trinitarian theology. In such manner, Herbert helped to make the psalter at once an instrument of scholastic theology and of meditation while reciting the psalms.[69]

When Becket came back to Canterbury from his exile to an ecstatic welcome a month before he was murdered, after a peace had been patched up with Henry II, one may doubt whether he anticipated that his life would end so soon. For he brought back with him quite a library of books, which were still preserved separately at Canterbury when they were catalogued around 1300. They included the Great Gloss of Peter Lombard on the psalms and the Pauline Epistles, Peter Lombard's *Sentences*, Homilies by Gregory the Great, and many collections of sermons or treatises which would help with preaching. The collection tends towards what one might call the applied rather than the philosophical sort of theology. Augustine of Hippo is lacking in it. But it suggests that Becket intended to take his pastorate and its theological basis seriously.[70]

It is doubtful that Henry II lost much if any power over the church by the martyrdom of Becket. The end of the conflict was marked, that last gesture in the drama was played out, by Henry's very public pilgrimage to Canterbury and his penance there in 1174. But kings always seemed to gain face rather than lose it by public penitence in the earlier Middle Ages, as the Emperor Henry IV did at Canossa nearly a hundred years previously. The saddest loss of Becket's martyrdom may have been to the English church, despite its gain of a glorious and much venerated saint. For the signs were that Becket had returned from abroad with a deepened religion and a new eagerness for his pastoral role. But we shall never quite know about this; for he was soon cut off.

CHAPTER 5

Parishes and Parish Priests

Parish religion and the 'higher culture'

This chapter, contrary to what its title might suggest, is not about local history as such. Rather it raises the question how far and in what ways the parishes or villages were part of the larger political community. Religion cannot be the sole answer to that question, which is one reason why we are going to look at the legal reforms of Henry II, and why this chapter is focused on the period of that king in the second half of the twelfth century. But religion is an important part of it.

My question here is prompted above all by the American anthropologist, Robert Redfield, and his writings of the 1950s. In his book, *The Little Community*, Redfield wrote mainly about the self-contained elements in peasant communities. But he followed this up with another short book, *Peasant Society and Culture*, which was a study of how what he called the higher and lower traditions or cultures interacted with each other. They were interdependent. 'The ethics of the Old Testament arose out of tribal peoples', he wrote, 'and returned to peasant communities after they had been the subject of thought by philosophers and theologians.' In a similar way, he saw the great Sanskrit epic, the *Ramayana*, originating in the 'little' culture (as he sometimes called it), being taken over by a poet in the higher culture, and then returning in a Hindi version to Indian village life. Again he saw participation of the little culture in the great when he wrote of the shaman – priests of Yucatan villages – that their rituals and prayers 'would have their full explanation only if we knew what were the ritual and related body of thought at Chechen Itza or Coba'. He even drew a parallel between a pundit reading from the lofty but hard-to-understand *Ramayana* and an actor paraphrasing it, on the one hand, and the gospel followed by a sermon at Mass on the other hand.[1]

It would not be hard to find examples of the participation of the little culture in the great culture of the kind that Redfield wrote about, in twelfth-century England. For example, in Haselbury Plucknett, Somerset, during the first half of the twelfth century, the English priest, Osbern, who may not even have been able to speak French (his father could not), summoned to himself an English village boy called Taillefer, named after the minstrel who sang the (French and very aristocratic) *Chanson de Roland*.[2] One of the most brilliant carvings on a capital of the south door of Iffley Church near Oxford is of two mounted knights in single combat, a kind of scene very much from the aristocratic world of the *Chanson de Roland*. It may be relevant that the earliest known manuscript of the *Chanson de Roland* is thought likely to have belonged in the twelfth century to Oseney Abbey, a house of Augustinian Canons in Oxford. Of course it was probably not the villagers of Iffley who chose that particular subject for the sculpture, but it was surely unlikely to have been ordered by someone who saw no continuum whatsoever between the higher culture and parish culture.

Redfield asked how the higher culture and the little culture might become accommodated to each other.[3] This is a question akin to one that we might ask here: how different from each other, or integrated with each other, were the Christianity of the parishes and the 'higher' Christianity in twelfth-century England? Something that happened at Stanway, Gloucestershire, on 13 May 1170, the Vigil of the Ascension in the year that Thomas Becket was martyred, perhaps tells us something of how such accommodation or integration could work in twelfth-century England. The parish priest, Roger, was celebrating Mass when the large crucifix, attached firmly to the walls behind the altar, flew from its position, grazed the priest's head as it travelled, and crashed to the floor behind him. Roger went to his diocesan bishop and namesake, Bishop Roger of Worcester, with the story, and the bishop sent some of his clerks, including one Master Silvester, to enquire into the whole business. They pronounced the story to be true. Gerald of Wales, who recorded it in his *Gemma Ecclesiastica*, said that nobody knew what it portended, unless (he added significantly) it had been a portent of Becket's martyrdom later that year.[4] Bishop Roger, whose clerk Silvester was, had been one of the most notable supporters of Becket among the bishops. What Gerald said here, suggesting an interpretation of the portent, must have been the result of a conversation between him and Master Silvester, probably long after the event. For Silvester subsequently became Archdeacon of Chichester, and Gerald has another story about how a crucifix flew from its place in the Church of the Holy Cross, Chichester, and knocked an immoral deacon unconscious.[5] This story would have been especially relevant to Silvester as Archdeacon, having particular responsibility for the morals of the clergy; and he was Archdeacon in the late 1190s, at about the time Gerald was writing his *Gemma Ecclesiastica*. He seems, in fact, to have been Gerald's expert on flying crucifixes. He took them quite as seriously, representative of the 'higher' Christianity that he was, as Roger, the priest of Stanway (Glos), did. He was their interpreter. A bishop's clerk knew what an event, inexplicable in a village, portended in the wider world; an archdeacon knew when an immoral clergyman had got his come-uppance.

We are seeing in these stories about flying crucifixes an example of a much more general point: that parish Christianity as we know it was largely a construct of the higher clerical mind. Such stories, far from being a distinguishing mark of unintegrated popular religion with its superstitions, were part of the higher culture also. They were symptomatic of something in the character of twelfth-century English Christianity as a whole, namely a rising interest in portents and omens (*prodigia*). We should perhaps pause here to ask: what is the difference between portents and prodigies on the one hand, and miracles (which we shall meet a lot in the next chapter) on the other. In the twelfth century, every significant library clearly had a copy of Isidore of Seville's *Etymologies*, a hugely popular encyclopaedia (c. 635). To summarise what he says or implies, a miracle must always be a divine sign pointing to God and his action and purposes in the world, whereas a portent or prodigy may be a divine sign, but it may not be so – it may only be a curiosity of (as yet) unknown nature.[6] That is not all there was to it, because as Carl Watkins has brilliantly shown, in the twelfth century the boundaries between the supernatural and what Watkins following Alexander Murray calls 'the concept of regular nature' were constantly shifting. This shifting was fed by advances in understanding physical causes in nature, increasing interest in human psychology and indeed the arts of measurement, and the growing focus of lawyers on the natural law.[7]

In the tenth century there had been a keen sense that the whole world was, as it were, electrically charged with the supernatural, like our sense of the electric current always flowing through the underground railway, though only sometimes visible when sparks fly from the wheels of a train. By the twelfth century this sense of the immanence of the supernatural in the world was not lost but it was weakened. Nature was coming to seem less integral with the supernatural, and more – to use the phrase of Benedicta Ward – as 'an entity in itself'.[8] We shall have more to say about God and nature when we come to the Franciscan scholar, Richard Rufus, in Chapter 9.

William of Malmesbury, the learned monk and classicist, and very much a representative of the 'higher' culture in the first half of the twelfth century, is a good example of how one can distinguish an interest in portents and marvels from one in miracles, for he was interested in both. Of the former, for example, he related how at one Easter Sunday dinner King Edward the Confessor burst out laughing because he had suddenly seen a wonder, namely that the Seven Sleepers on Mount Cheilaion, who had been sleeping on their right sides for two hundred years, had just turned over onto their left sides![9] But William showed a serious devotional and theological streak in his work on the *Miracles of the Virgin*, more serious than most twelfth-century compilations of miracles which were intended to publicise the shrines of saints. The miracles, he wrote, were 'particularly useful for the souls of simple men in kindling their love for Our Lady'. Here we must remember how much the Marian doctrines of the Immaculate Conception and Assumption were being discussed in the twelfth century. As Rodney Thomson has well shown, however, little of this sort of consideration applies to William's marvels, whose workers are 'more often demonic than saintly'.[10]

To bring this relative disengagement of the natural and supernatural worlds from each other, as a feature of twelfth-century English Christianity, back to politics: it runs parallel with the idea brought about by the Gregorian Reform that there was a distinction, or a much sharper distinction than was previously held, between the spiritual and secular powers in the world.

So far we have been considering the relation of parish religion to the 'higher' religion rather in the abstract. Now we need to look at parish churches as such. The eleventh century was the century par excellence in which the parish and the parish church developed as institutions. The twelfth century saw the actual covering of the whole land with parish churches, and saw those churches come under the control of bishops. Before the eleventh century pastoral care was mainly in the hands of ancient minster churches which had communities of priests whose ministrations covered wide areas. Within these areas village or manorial or parish churches, with one priest per church, came to be founded. Originally such smaller churches were subject and owed dues to the minsters, but all that faded away, though the minsters were often left as the collegiate churches of the Middle Ages with their bodies of canons. Since the parishioners owed tithes and altar offerings to their parish churches, it must have been important from an early stage that parishes had defined boundaries both in the country and in towns, so that who or which land belonged to which parish was clear. As historians, however, we only start to get a clear view of parish boundaries from about 1200; and what we see then is that processes of considerable complexity and variety must have lain behind the development of the parish system.[11] It would be quite beyond the scope of this book to plunge into the detail of this story for the sake of it. We should, however, make two points about parish development which are of importance for how parish religion related to the wider or higher society.

The first point is how much closer than before aristocratic lordship was coming to villages in the eleventh century with the break up of huge estates in face of late Anglo-Saxon state power and the practice of dividing inheritances.[12] Whether parishes corresponded more to villages (units of settlement) or to manors (units of lordship), and how far manors more or less corresponded with villages, are complex questions to which the answer must vary from case to case. And the last question, on the relation of manors to villages, has an importance for our theme – the relation of parish religion to aristocratic religion. For particularly in Lowland Britain, with its characteristic nucleated village settlements and their open fields around them, strips in the open fields of the same village might be held by peasants subject to different lords. For example in the mid-twelfth century, the manor of Iffley was held by the minor baron, Robert of St Remy, whose principal residence it was. The manor of Cowley was held by Oseney Abbey. Iffley and Cowley were next-door villages, both of them now suburbs of Oxford. But some of the villagers of Cowley belonged to, or owed suit of court at, the manor of Iffley, and the building of Iffley church in the 1170s was very much an external expression of Robert of St Remy's lordship. In such circumstances it is easy to see how the solidarities of lord and tenants and the solidarities of village communities could cut across each other when a new parish church was built.[13]

The main point for us here, however, is that, as John Blair has written, new and tighter manorial structures:

fostered a closer link between minor royal servants and small estates, and thus contributed to a growing and broad-based class of local proprietors rooted in the communities: the original 'English country gentry'.[14]

And Blair continues:

The aristocratic urge to own a church, ubiquitous across early medieval Europe, was now focused at a much more local level.

The second point about parish development which bears on how parish religion related to the wider society is this. Historians used to lay stress almost exclusively on the *lord's* motives for founding a parish church on his lands, particularly his economic motives, since a church would bring in payments of tithes, payments for burial rights and the tax known as church-scot, etc., as well as enabling him to provide an income for a chaplain protégé of his whom he could appoint to the church. Until the mid-twelfth century, it was stressed, the church was the lord's own church, his property. But in recent decades the emphasis of historians has shifted to the impetus from *below* in the founding of parish churches; to the voluntary collaboration of the parishioners, some of them prosperous peasant farmers; to the demands being made by lay people themselves not devoid of religious motivation for the convenience of a church closer to them than a sometimes distant minster. That does not mean that the term 'proprietary church' as applied to a lord has become meaningless; only that the collaborative element and even the corporate endowment of parish churches should also be emphasised.[15] This should not be a difficult idea for us to grasp in the present day, for when we enter almost any ancient parish church, we are at once aware of a wide spectrum of aristocratic and non-aristocratic society represented in its funerary monuments. Thus the solidarities created or strengthened by a new parish church must normally have encompassed both the little and higher cultures. Put another way, there is no need to regard the creation of parish churches as yet another form of lordly oppression.

In thinking about the relation of parish religion to the higher religious culture we have to ask how fluid were the boundaries between aristocratic and peasant society as a whole. In twelfth-century England the answer would appear to be pretty fluid. Knights, it is true, were normally distinguishable socially, as people who came from recognised knightly families.[16] But economically prosperous peasants and knights must often have looked like each other, particularly in the case of the *milites mediocres*, or low-grade knights mentioned in the sources.[17] And freemen and townsmen of sufficient means were expected by the Assize of Arms (1181) to bear arms alongside knights if the king needed them locally or called out an army as Henry II seems to have done in 1174 in the North when the Scots invaded. Again, when the royal justices came into a shire to hear the pleas of the crown, as laid down by the form of proceeding in 1194, two knights from each hundred were to associate themselves with ten other knights to form the juries, 'or if knights were lacking, freemen with standing at law'.[18] This last clause is important for us, because it assumes that there was no problem about knights and freemen working together in the processes of law. Likewise, when late in Henry II's reign, Glanvill specified that the juries for the Grand Assize should consist of 12 knights and for the Assize of Novel Disseisin of 12 freemen of standing at law,[19] it is very likely that in either case there would in practice have had to be a mixture of both sorts in both kinds of jury.

One revealing anecdote in Gerald of Wales suggests how actively knights might participate in the religion of their parish churches. The saintly Hugh, Bishop of Lincoln, came once to a parish church in his diocese where at the end of Mass the priest began to recite various gospels, thereby hoping to increase his altar offerings or as we might say, the size of his collection, apparently because these were the favourite gospel passages of certain local knights. Gerald treats this as an example of the cupidity of priests, but it can also be read as the involvement of knights in their parish. The bishop remarked wittily, 'What will this priest say to-morrow who has poured out everything he knows to-day?'[20]

A factor which might at first sight seem to militate against any continuum between the 'higher' and the 'little' cultures in twelfth-century England was the language barrier between French and English vernaculars. After the Norman Conquest the difference between French and English speakers was the difference between the immigrant aristocracy and the indigenous population. But only for a short time. It soon became a purely social difference between upper and lower classes. A striking story in the Life of Wulfric of Haselbury is about how Wulfric worked a miracle whereby he enabled a dumb man to speak both English and French. The parish priest of the village, the English Brihtric, with whom Wulfric generally got along well, waxed indignant about this:

'All these years I have served you', he said to Wulfric, 'and to-day I have clearly proved that it was for nothing. To a stranger, whose tongue it would have been enough to open, you have kindly given the use of two languages, while to me, who am forced to remain dumb in the presence of the bishop and the archdeacon, you have never imparted a word of French'![21]

A parish priest forced to remain dumb in the presence of his own bishop and archdeacon! What a chasm is here revealed in the first half of the twelfth century between the French-speaking higher clergy and the English-speaking lower clergy! Of course some bishops and archdeacons, perhaps many, could bridge the divide. Gilbert Foliot, for instance, could speak in Latin (*the* clerical language), French and English. What is most poignant about Brihtric's story, however, is his own sense of inferiority and exclusion.

Where the line should be drawn in English society between French and English speakers must have been constantly moving downwards, until English started to be the fashionable aristocratic language again in the second half of the thirteenth century. Intriguingly, the line must have fallen somewhere in the social area of lesser knights and upper peasants who were most involved as parties and juries in the legal reforms of Henry II. When the Abbot of Crowland became ill during the lawsuit of the 1190s between himself and William de Roumara, Earl of Lincoln, about the Marsh between Crowland and Spalding, a jury was appointed to 'view' him, i.e. to make sure that his excuse was genuine. The Abbot complained that those who claimed to have been appointed were not of knightly rank, they were not girded with swords, and a third of them could not speak French.[22]

But the barrier was not an insuperable one. There were interpreters, and above all many English people set about learning French. The English Wulfric of Haselbury had learnt it, before becoming an ascetic recluse, as a priest in the household of a French-speaking lord, alongside other aristocratic accomplishments such as riding to hounds and falconry. Gilbert of Sempringham, the famous parish priest and founder of a monastic order in Lincolnshire, whose father was a Norman knight and whose mother was a low-born English woman, if he spoke English at home, must have learnt French when his father sent him to study in France. But Robert Bartlett has shown how even English villagers had plenty of opportunities in England to learn to speak French, albeit their accent could be criticised as 'the rough and corrupt French of the English'.[23] An English speaker with any sort of ambition had to learn French. It may occasionally look otherwise. Abbot Samson of Bury St Edmunds had a policy to keep the administration of his abbey's manors directly in his own hands, but one sole manor he put into the hands of a certain Englishman, of villein origins, whose fidelity he entirely trusted, 'because he was a good farmer, and because he spoke no French'.[24] Perhaps the Abbot thought his speaking only English made him a plain, no-nonsense person. Perhaps too he would have less opportunity to scheme against the Abbot; for English Benedictine abbots of the twelfth century could be fearful paranoiacs. But the implication of the story is that normally nobody would be promoted to the administration of a manor who could not speak French.

If, therefore, we cannot fully illustrate the continuum between the 'higher' religious culture and 'parish religion' in twelfth-century England, we can see that there *was* such a continuum. Arguments against it, like the language barrier, may modify this, but cannot nullify it.

The legal reforms of Henry II and parish priests

Until recently I never imagined that I – or anyone – would be writing about the legal reforms of Henry II and parish priests in conjunction with each other. To plunge suddenly into those legal reforms must seem like plunging into a dark forest. But if the reader will follow me for only a few pages, we shall come out into a clearing positively peopled with parish priests!

All Henry II's legal reforms were based on one simple principle – discovering the facts of a case before you convicted a criminal or before you settled a legal dispute. For this purpose juries, usually of 12 men, were appointed. They were groups of fact-finders. Basing judgments on facts was not exactly a new principle; it went back at least to the Emperor Charlemagne nearly four centuries earlier. Indeed, there is hardly anything in Henry II's legal reforms that cannot be traced back to Charlemagne. But this cardinal principle of basing judgments on facts was something of a revival in relation to the recent English past. Actually fact-finding was basic to the whole mode of Henry II's government. In 1170 he sacked many of the royal sheriffs, but not before he had made systematic enquiries into their extortions, and the extortions of barons' officials too. In 1176 and again in 1185 he set in motion enquiries into 'women in the gift of the king'. The widows and daughters of the king's tenants-in-chief could not get married without his licence, for which of course he invariably charged, unless (in John's case) he married them off to one of his low-born favourites. Either way he wanted first to know their worth in the marriage market – their lands, their heirs, their age, etc. So as an estate agent values a house before it goes on the market, Henry surveyed the facts about aristocratic women and had them valued before charging licences.[25]

We cannot here attempt a comprehensive survey of all the legal proce-dures and actions which Henry brought in, or of the writs which initiated them. Henry is generally and not wrongly credited with the creation of the English common law, which was never a code but the accumulation of writs and actions, to which additions were constantly being made. We now take just one of those actions initiated by writ, known as *novel disseisin* (n.d.) arguably the most important single legal action brought in by Henry II.[26] It was an action to remedy forcible dispossession, or disseisin, from your land. The argument was carried back only to who was in possession of the land a very few years previously – when the king last crossed to Normandy, or something like that. If it was found that you were not recently in possession but you thought it was your right, you could always take out a Writ of Right. But that was not often done; hence *novel disseisin* was important partly because although the argument was mainly about recent possession, it was usually regarded as settling the matter of right.

We are now going to consider: a) what *novel disseisin* was; b) when it came in; and c) what the parish clergy had to do with it.

What was *novel disseisin*?

Having said that n.d. was a remedy for a recent forcible dispossession, we had better give the text of the writ as in Glanville's treatise *On the Laws and Customs of England* which initiated the action:

> *The king to the sheriff, greeting. N. has complained to me that R. unjustly and without judgement has disseised him of his free tenement (landholding) in such and such a vill (village) since my last sea crossing to Normandy. . . . You are to see that the tenement is viewed by twelve free and lawful men of the neighbourhood and their names are to be written down on the back of this writ. And summon them by good summoners to be before me (on such and such a day) ready to make a recognition.*[27]

So the king receives a complaint about disseisin. Note that it is about an unjust disseisin, so a resolution of the case involves from the start not only the issue of dispossession but also of right. The king sends a written order, a writ, to his local government official in the shire, namely the shire reeve or sheriff. The sheriff must appoint a jury of free men to go and view the land in order to help them give a factual answer, or recognition, to the question, who was in possession and whether justly on the day that the king last crossed to Normandy. Then they come before the itinerant royal justices to report, or to make a 'recognition'.

For present purposes, the point to be particularly noted about the whole action is that it is a civil action, i.e. where the initiative must be taken by a private individual who deems himself to have been wronged, rather than a criminal action, i.e. where the king takes the initiative against those who have been guilty of criminal dispossessions. During the first half of his reign, Henry II, who had to mop up after the 'anarchy' of Stephen's reign, ordered frequent corrections of disseisin and punishments for those guilty of it. Such orders were part of his drives against crime, including crimes committed by clerics.[28] But *novel disseisin* was qualitatively different from such criminal drives, because it took the initiative away from the king and his travelling justices, and transferred it into the hands of a private individual, royal justice only responding to the individual's initial complaint.

Moreover – and here I am following the persuasive arguments of the legal historians Sutherland and Milsom – n.d. was an instrument put into the hands of quite small men, and from almost the beginning it was often used by such men against their lords, although there was also a more general public order purpose to it.[29] One may note that this is not an action about large estates, but typically about a piece of land in a village. Also, it is not necessary to have knights for the jury but only freemen (though knights seem not to be debarred), i.e. judgment by peers. Again, almost immediately after the form of the n.d. writ in Glanvill, there follows another, specifically to do with R having raised the level of his mill pond in a village and thus caused N to be disseised of some land by flooding.[30] People raising the level of their fish ponds or mill ponds were a major source of aggravation in the twelfth-century countryside,[31] in the latter case because they needed a good pressure of water through the mill race to turn the mill wheel. Now given how often mill rights, the rights to have peasants grind their corn at your mill – for a price – were part of the rights of a manorial lord, this form of the n.d. writ must necessarily have been used sometimes by underlings against their lords.

It may be starting to look as if this talk of setting men against their lords runs contrary to the idea of the continuum between the 'higher' and the 'little' cultures which I was considering in the previous section of this chapter. I answer not only that criminality breaks any social or cultural continuum, but also that when people go to law with each other it speaks for their living in the same world, not in separate sealed-off worlds.

When did *novel disseisin* as a civil action come in?

Now that I have described what n.d. was, when it came in is of obvious political importance. When did it suit Henry II polit-ically to put an instrument into the hands of freemen which they could potentially use against their lords? When did the action which early in Henry's reign appears only as a criminal action, become also the civil action, subject to private initiative, which one sees in Glanville's treatise (c. 1187–89) from the end of Henry's reign? There has been much argument about this, by historians who it seems to me have sometimes read the existence of Glanville's civil action into Pipe Roll references to the assize concerning disseisin when the context shows that a fine (what the twelfth century called an amercement) is referred to in a criminal case. The only sure way of knowing that Glanville's civil action has come in is when the Pipe Rolls refer to an individual paying for an assize or a writ, or particularly to have a recognition of land. Before the records of the king's courts started being preserved in the 1190s, the Pipe Rolls are normally our only source for this. And what the Pipe Rolls show is that while the idea was already present in the late 1160s and early 1170s, payments for recognitions really only took off in numbers in 1175 and especially 1176.[32] They are not at first all for small men, but the principle was there from the mid-1170s. Furthermore, although the Pipe Rolls show when recognitions took off, they cannot give the whole story, because as the king travelled, payments for writs could have been made into his private finance office, the Chamber,[33] for which no accounts survive at this time.

In a general way, we can tell that free peasants were going to law in the king's courts in the last quarter of the twelfth century because by about 1200 we are getting references in charters of peasants to their seals which confirm such charters, e.g. two small land transactions in Northamptonshire one of Henry son of Huddret and the other of Ulian son of Thurstan. Nobody had a seal who did not ever expect to have to validate his documents in a law suit.[34]

The mid-1170s was a significant and powerful period for Henry II. Early in his reign he was hugely hampered in collecting his regular revenues from royal manors, because so many of them were in the hands of powerful barons, not so much barons who had made themselves powerful in Stephen's reign (as one might imagine), as those on whom he had depended in his struggle for the kingship and whom he had to reward. These he had neither the power nor the means to confront.[35] Hence in his early years he had to make up his cash shortfall by squeezing the church and particularly the revenues of its vacant bishoprics. When in 1171 he needed to lead an expedition to Ireland, which he had already designed as a lordship or appanage for one of his sons, and where a Norman baron called Strongbow, one of the Clares, was getting too big for his boots,[36] Henry could never have afforded it were there not by then a string of bishoprics become vacant during the Becket controversy whose revenues he could still use. Then in 1173–74 came the Great Baronial Rebellion, with his son the younger Henry at its centre, a close-run thing in which the father, Henry II, finally triumphed.[37] This was a real watershed in the reign, for it made Henry much more powerful than previously vis à vis barons altogether.

In 1176 the king took various actions which can only, *in toto*, be called anti-baronial. In that year came the first judicial eyre which systematically covered the whole country with three royal judges travelling around in each of six circuits. That was not in itself an attack on baronial courts, but in spreading the tentacles of royal judicial power so effectively into the localities, its side effect was inevitably to weaken baronial authority there. Again R.A. Brown showed that Henry II's attack on baronial castles in 1176/1177 represented the largest shift of castle power from barons to king in the whole of the Angevin period.[38] This year was also the year in which par excellence Henry was extracting massive payments from barons for no other reason than to have the goodwill (not the friendship, now!) of the king, a perfect example of the arbitrary exercise of power by which Jolliffe characterised the Angevin kings.[39] So if Henry II was putting an instrument into the hands of freemen to litigate against their social superiors, the mid-1170s was a very significant time to be doing it.

And it was certainly not by accident that Henry did this. During the Great Rebellion of 1173–74 groups of peasants intervened on several occasions, seemingly out of the blue, always with devastating effect, and always on the king's side against rebel barons. We have to piece this together from various sources, but that makes the combined evidence the more telling. Earl Robert of Leicester, after landing with Flemish mercenaries in East Anglia, was defeated by the king's forces, and then his mercenaries fell into the hands of peasants (*indigenarum*), who slaughtered many of them, some by drowning them in bogs. We have this from William of Canterbury.[40] Roger de Mowbray, trying to relieve Leicester Castle, was captured by peasants (*rusticis*) in Derbyshire. We have it from the *Gesta Henrici II*.[41] From Diceto, a multitude of Lincoln men, transported by water, forced the surrender of Axholme (Lincs).[42] In 1174 the Scots, led by King William the Lion, entered the fray on the rebels' side. Henry II had an army of Yorkshiremen called out consisting of some 60 mounted barons and knights and a number of footmen (*pedestres*) who must have been freemen. The Yorkshireman, William of Newburgh, as well as Diceto (more briefly), tells the story.[43] The Scots were resting near Alnwick Castle. It was July; there was a sea mist, and when it lifted the Yorkshiremen found themselves directly in front of the Scots, and surprised them. They killed or took captive the lot including King William, a capture which incidentally put paid to any idea of an independent Scottish church for some time. If one reads William of Newburgh, his implication is that the damage to the Scots in this surprise attack was done principally by the non-nobles, including the capture of the Scottish king.[44] No wonder then that after 1174 Henry was willing to trust freemen to use the royal courts against lords!

What had the parish clergy to do with all this?

What we have described above makes clear that peasant communities were participators in the wider political community. But it seems inconceivable that this could have been so without specific links or, to use Peter Brown's language of East Mediterranean holy men of an earlier age, hinge-men.[45] Such hinge-men could be the upper, more prosperous and more legally aware peasants, for twelfth-century peasant communities were clearly layered in the way this implied. But taking all the evidence into account, the clue to who these hinge-men were seems to lie more strongly with the parish clergy, people of increasing authority and standing as the twelfth century advanced.

In March 1165, when Becket was already in exile, Bishop Arnulf of Lisieux wrote him a letter which mentions the parish clergy, or lower clergy, interestingly. Arnulf had studied the liberal arts and theology at Paris and law in Italy. He was a diplomat par excellence, an accomplished letter-writer, and a known wit.[46] He had been a papal legate in all but name on the Second Crusade in the 1140s where he was always a force for peace between the crusaders and the Byzantine Emperor, unlike his fellow bishop, Godfrey of Langres, whom Arnulf compared to the wine of Cyprus, 'sweet to taste but lethal unless diluted with water'.[47] He had been Henry's principal adviser on ecclesiastical affairs in Normandy for a long time, and he achieved the feat of having the ear of both king and pope during the Becket conflict.[48] When he wrote this letter in 1165, therefore, he was nearly 60 and a man of huge experience as well as judgement. In his letter Arnulf starts by paying Becket compliments, and then sizes up the situation in England with regard to his supporters and opponents. Among the bishops there were those who held to his cause as the cause of Christ, but there were others who 'brandished their swords' against him. 'Almost all the lower clergy (*fere omnes qui in inferioribus sunt gradibus*)', he continues, 'embrace your person sincerely with the arms of charity.'[49] Whether this observation about, in effect, the parish clergy was true or not, or how Arnulf knew it, or whether he knew it only of Kent, is almost beside the point for our present purposes. What it shows is that the astutely judging Arnulf thought of the lower clergy as a significant element in the polity.

Small wonder! When Becket rode triumphantly the 12 miles from the port of Sandwich to Canterbury on 2 December 1170 after his return from exile, the villagers on the route came out to cheer him, headed by their priests in vestments with processional crosses.[50] The fact that, as told by Herbert of Bosham, this follows a hagiographical motif, Christ's entry into

Jerusalem on Palm Sunday (the people threw garments in his path, chanting 'blessed is He who cometh in the name of the Lord'), does not necessarily mean that it didn't happen. The villagers knew the gospels too. It could be argued that as the villages on the route mainly belonged to the archbishop's Kentish manors, this story is no indicator of how peasants or parish clergy in general felt about Becket. But what remains, for our purposes, is Herbert of Bosham's concept (like Bishop Arnulf's) that parish priests were the natural mediators or 'hinge-men' between the villages and the wider community.

It would be nice if it was possible to show that the parish priests of Yorkshire played any part in the calling out of the footmen of Yorkshire to face the Scots in 1174. But it is not possible. However, 36 years earlier in 1138, when the Scots invaded the north of England prior to their defeat at the Battle of the Standard, under Walter d'Espec, as described by Ailred of Rievaulx, Archbishop Thurstan of York summoned all able-bodied men in his diocese to resist the invaders. They were to march out 'from every parish, with their priests before them bearing the cross and banners and relics of the saints'. Robert Bartlett uses this episode to illustrate the cult of saints and their relics at this time – and every parish church with a consecrated altar must have had relics.[51] I use it, once again, to reveal the parish priests as middle men, this time actually to mobilise free peasants for an army. One might think this rather early in the twelfth century for the parish priests to be given so clear and ostensible a responsibility. But one has to remember that Thurstan himself was one of the twelfth-century architects of the heightened pastoral role of the parishes and standing of their clergy.

Although we cannot tell what part, if any, the priests of Yorkshire played in the calling out of the peasant militias in 1174, we do have a rather striking testimony of the authority attributed to them during the previous twenty years. Sometime during his first decade as Archbishop of York (1154–64), Roger of Pont l'Evêque issued a document exhorting the faithful of his diocese to maintain their customary alms to the St Leonard's Hospital, York, of one thrave of corn from every plough-team. Having *exhorted* the laity, he *ordered* the priests strictly to admonish their parishioners to pay these alms, adding that if anyone made a bequest on their death to the Hospital, the priests were to order it to be paid punctiliously (*studiosius*). He issued a similar order to the priests of Holderness, with the further addition that if anyone failed to obey, the priests were to excommunicate them.[52] These orders not only gave the parish clergy considerable authority; they also assumed that the clergy already had it. Roger of Pont l'Evêque was not everyone's favourite bishop in the twelfth century. His rivalry with Becket went back to Archbishop Theobald's household, and he had a reputation for meanness. But he staunchly supported St Leonard's Hospital throughout his archiepiscopate, albeit mostly with other people's money. Given the twists and turns in the history of the York archbishopric in the previous 15 years to Roger, however, and given that these orders about the hospital were early in his pontificate, the priestly authority which we are seeing here must have had to do, to a large extent, with Archbishop Thurstan (1114–40).

Not that authority was conferred on parish priests only from above; some were quite capable of exercising their own charisma. Gilbert of Sempringham, probably around 1120 when he was in his early thirties and parish priest of the parish churches of Sempringham and Torrington (Lincolnshire), established by his knightly father, is the subject of the following story:

One of his parishioners cheated him of his tithes of produce, and what he should have put aside for the church he took home with the rest of his corn and put it into his own barn for his own future use. When the rector of the church (i.e. Gilbert) discovered this he immediately forced the peasant to throw all his corn out of his store sheaf by sheaf. A whole tenth of this which clearly belonged to him and his church, he caused to be heaped in one pile in the middle of the village, set alight and burnt, in detestation of such a crime and to inspire fear in others. For he considered it unworthy that what had been stolen furtively from God and his holy church should go to men's use. For he was a magnanimous man who set little store by loss, so long as natural justice and ecclesiastical law were preserved intact.[53]

The peasant here was evidently a prosperous peasant in a prosperous region, and it is scarcely possible to imagine such a man thinking he could get away with this if it were done right under the nose of the rector's official. The problem for him, and the advantage to Gilbert, must have been village gossip, particularly the gossip of envious neighbours, who had not sought to benefit from similar dishonesty and who possibly orchestrated the gossip. Wulfric, not the parish priest but his supporter, was a past master of the orchestration of gossip in Haselbury Plucknett.[54] To know, if not to control, the flow of gossip in a village (or town) was power indeed.

It may be thought that Gilberts of Sempringham did not grow on every tree. Not every parish priest was of knightly background and would found a religious order and become a canonised saint. True, but that argument is somewhat double-edged. Precisely because Gilbert founded an order and was later (1202) canonised a life of him was written and we have come to know about him as a parish priest. That does not give us the right to assume that we would know about any parish priest who did exercise charisma. There were growing opportunities for them to do so. The development of saints' shrines and cults at a number of great churches, especially in the 1170s, provided one such opportunity. A parish priest accompanied an epileptic peasant from the Hundred of Lothingland (Suffolk) to the shrine of St William of Norwich where the peasant was cured.[55] Even when we do not hear of many other priests actually accompanying their sick charges to shrines, it must often have been that they were agents of, or channels of communication between, the shrines and the villages, and thereby came to be associated in their parishioners' minds with the holy.

There is another remarkable case of priestly authority in respect of the exaction of tithes, reported by Walter Map. We have already touched on it in the context of ghosts and revenants (pp. 9–10). This is what Map wrote:

A knight of Northumberland was seated alone after dinner in summer, when his father who had died long before approached him clad in a foul and ragged shroud. He thought the appearance was a devil, but his father said, 'Dearest son, fear not. I am your father and bring you no ill; but call the priest and you will see why I come.' The priest was summoned and many came running to the place. Falling at his feet the ghost said, 'I am that wretch whom long since you excommunicated unnamed, with many more, for unrighteous withholding of tithes; but the common prayers of the church and the alms of the faithful have by God's grace so helped me that I am permitted to ask for absolution.' So being absolved he went, with a great train of people following, to his grave and sank into it, and it closed over him of its own accord.[56]

The priest here was obviously a parish priest, who had the right to tithes and had been attempting to exercise his authority over a knight.

To exercise authority when collecting alms for a good cause or one's own rightful tithes was obviously not always plain sailing as the above cases make clear. The need to resort to ritual public burnings of tithes withheld, or to instruments like excommunication, or the very need to be able to wave an archbishop's mandate in the faces of one's parishioners, shows that it was not. Priests must often have aroused hostility in asserting their rights, and must often have been confronted with resistance from powerful personalities and accomplished cheats. Yet the need to assert their rights or go to the wall, coupled with the dovetailing of priests' and parishioners' interests (spiritual, political and material) in many other ways, may paradoxically have been one of the biggest spurs to strengthening their authority.

We add one further case to the subject of peasant militias and priests as hinge-men to the wider community. Earl Robert of Leicester and his Flemish mercenaries in East Anglia in 1173 were mentioned earlier. Before these mercenaries were drowned in bogs, a party of them had raided the church of Gedgrave (Suffolk), thinking that there would be money and treasure inside it. They pushed past the parish priest, who tried to block their path at the door, but inside they perceived the crucifix to be bleeding, and terrified, they fled.[57] Did this kind of sacrilegious intention towards one of their churches, and this kind of contempt for the authority of one of their priests, an authority vindicated by the crucifix, perhaps act as a goad to East Anglian peasants?

Parish churches

To understand the rise in the standing of the parish clergy as a whole in twelfth-century England, we have to consider a) the economic aspects, and b) the rise in clericalism.

A huge amount of wealth – the wealth of kings, bishops, barons, knights, monasteries, and even of villagers – went into the building of parish churches and endowments for their priests in the twelfth century. The expansion of parishes was the economic miracle of the century in England. In Sussex, for example, between 1086 and 1200, the number of parish churches about doubled, and the provision for their priests must have much more than doubled. One of these churches was at Hellingly, established by the lords of Hellingly, Rikward and Ralph Brade. The building was begun in the Norman style. The church was appropriated to the Premonstratensian Canons of Otham, that is the two Brades presented them to the bishop to be instituted as the church's permanent rector, enjoying the great tithes, but saving a reasonable income from the endowments of the church on which a vicar, the priest actually ministering in the church, could live. Subsequently, however, the Bishop of Chichester, Seffrid II, felt that he needed to raise further the level of the endowment, perhaps to make sure that a vicar could be paid for. And so Nicholas, son of Ralph Brade, responded, and his charter says the following:

When Bishop Seffrid II dedicated the church of Hellingly, I endowed the same with twelve denariates of land belonging to my freehold, of which William de Meriefield is tenant, because the bishop urgently asked for an endowment, lest so excellent a work should to some extent be deprived of its right.[58]

What did it mean when a monastery became rector of a parish church? It happened very often in the twelfth century that churches were 'appropriated' to religious houses in this way. If they had founded them themselves they wanted a return for their investment. Lay founders wanted to make benefactions to monasteries in order to benefit from their prayers and enhance the social standing of their own families. If a monastery became the rector of a church it received the lion's share of its revenues, especially the great tithes (of corn). If a monastery received the patronage of a church (the right to appoint the priest, or to present the priest to the bishop for institution as came to be the correct form), it gave them the opportunity to provide a loyal legal or administrative servant or a chaplain of the monastery with a living, and probably an annual sum of money, a pension, from the income of the church as well. Glastonbury Abbey, for instance, had strings of parish churches in Somerset from which they received pensions,[59] either as patrons or because their rights as rector had been commuted for money.

If the rector himself was the resident priest and pastor, which he might often have been in the twelfth century, then he was what we would call the parish priest, and the standing of such priests in their villages clearly rose during the twelfth century. From Domesday Book (1086), according to Reginald Lennard, the impression of the evidence as a whole is that the village priest was usually reckoned to be a member of the peasant community. For instance, the priest of Wetmore (Staffordshire) had a house and a croft of inland. He looked much like the cowman who had a similar holding, and he owed labour service on one day a week.[60] But what if the rector was a monastery, or an individual who was an absentee, appointed by a king or a baron or a bishop, who drew an income while doing some more 'important' job for his patron elsewhere?[61] Who then looked after the community pastorally?

The bishops' answer to this in the twelfth century is clear. Almost all of them, even the most political, show a commendable pastoral drive here. Their policy was to ensure that if the rector was not the resident priest, a sufficiency of the endowments of the church was defined and earmarked to give a proper living and security of tenure to whoever was. This had been a principle of the canon law of the church as a whole since the First Lateran Council of 1123, if not before.[62] All over England from the mid-twelfth century, bishops came to insist that vicarages, or perpetual vicarages, as they were called, should be ordained, not least where the churches belonged to monasteries.[63] For example, in the 1150s the aristocratic Bishop Hugh de Puiset of Durham, when he confirmed to Durham Cathedral Priory, a Benedictine monastery, its eleven churches in Yorkshire, laid down (very likely as a condition for issuing his charter of confirmation) that they were all to be served by vicars, who were to be chosen by the bishop and assigned a sufficient portion to live on (and from which to be able to pay their dues to the bishop!).[64] One could cite hundreds of other twelfth-century English charters like this. It was, or came to be, the same in Wales. Bishop William of Llandaff, in a charter of 1186–91, insisted that provision must be made for vicars ministering in all of Gloucester's churches in his diocese, though at the same time the pensions of the Abbey from these churches were increased.[65]

We should not get too optimistic about how well the system of vicarages worked in practice. The Fourth Lateran Council (1215) shows that in some parts priests were left with too little to live on.[66] Archbishop Hubert Walter's Westminster Council (1200) implied the same.[67] It was not always possible to define precisely the vicar's portion at the first statement of the principle, though we know of many cases where that followed. Typically all the tithes other than of corn, the altar offerings and some part of the church land would be the vicar's.[68] Where there was no vicarage and the rector was a monastery or an absentee, and the parish was served by a chaplain without security of tenure, we do not have to think that such a chaplain was necessarily poor, or ill-educated, or ill-regarded. Moreover, there were some, perhaps many, priests with private means, who did not have to worry about vicarages. By the thirteenth century there were already absentee vicars. In general, however, there appear in the late twelfth century to have been in most parts of the country many resident parish priests sufficiently paid and well respected.

There were ordained priests who had no benefice in the twelfth century. We know of some and they were probably only the tip of the iceberg. That does not necessarily mean that there was a mass of clergy milling about who were economically in a bad way. Before being ordained a priest, a man had to show that he had means of support, i.e. that he had a 'title'.[69] In the late thirteenth century, when we have the evidence of bishops' registers, which we lack for the twelfth, we can compare the lists and numbers ordained with those who got to be presented to benefices. The disparity was huge. The numbers of those being ordained was many times greater than those who were ever instituted in rectories and vicarages. Yet as Simon Townley has said, there is little evidence at that time of the social unrest which might be expected had large numbers of clergy failed to find work (e.g. as private chaplains or chaplains in parishes).[70] In the late twelfth century there is little sign of anti-clericalism, a phenomenon usually associated more with the lesser clergy than with the laity, except for the writings of a few satirists and moralists (themselves disappointed of promotion) about the wealth of the monasteries.

Perhaps the most interesting story about an unbeneficed priest in twelfth-century England concerns Bartholomew, Bishop of Exeter (1161–84). It was recorded only in the first half of the thirteenth century, but none of its principal features in unlikely. While going around his diocese, Bartholomew stayed in a village and in the night he heard mournful voices like those of children coming from the cemetery. They were saying, 'Woe to us! Who will pray for us, and give alms and celebrate masses for our salvation?' Next morning, when the bishop summoned the village priest and others, it transpired that in the night an important man in the village had died, who had retained a priest at his own expense to say Mass every day for the dead. The bishop summoned the dead man's chaplain, gave him part of the income of the village church, and ordered him to continue with his daily Mass.[71] The two elements of particular interest in this story are the lack of any apparent friction between the parish priest and another priest in the village, and the effort of the bishop to bring the dead man's chaplain into the parish system which he attempted to control. But there must have been many more such cases where the bishop had little control.

Besides the parish clergy, rural deans could play a significant part in local pastoral care. Rural deans have been called the non-commissioned officers of the twelfth-century clergy. They were not of the higher clergy like archdeacons, but were rather specially designated parish clergy who presided over local clerical synods. Their duties have generally been seen as formal and legal or disciplinary, but that is because the surviving documentary evidence for them is mostly of that character.[72] Occasionally, however, we glimpse them acting in the more sympathetic role of healers, with the help of saints' relics. When there was a plague of livestock at Bucklebury (Berkshire), Roger, Abbot of Reading (1158–65), took the famous relic of the Hand of St James out there, and Peter, Dean of Bucklebury asked the abbot to celebrate Mass and bless the area from a high spot.[73] Again, in the district of Gloucester, when an evil spirit caused a monk and a woman to go mad, 'and tired out many nurses', the dean of the district came with the blood of Thomas Becket in a phial, and the spirit, 'unable to bear the supervention of one stronger than himself', jumped precipitously out of them.[74]

What kind of preaching, or what content of preaching, did all this effort at pastoral provision result in? We have rather little evidence for this until the thirteenth century (see below, pp. 246–7). But we do have some. We have the *Ormulum*, a collection of twenty-minute sermons on liturgical gospel readings, made by an Augustinian Canon (see below, p. 167). We know that Abbot Odo of Battle (1175–1200) composed commentaries on Scripture, some of which he preached in English to uneducated people. We have a model sermon in English from a twelfth-century collection of sermons, on the subject of faith, hope and charity, ending in hell-fire stuff about the importance of repentance in order to achieve a state of charity (thus connecting it to the practice of confession (see Chapter 9). We have from the early thirteenth century guides to preaching written by Englishmen like Alexander of Ashby, Prior of the Augustinian Canons of Canons Ashby (Northamptonshire) and Thomas of Chobham.[75] And in a text of diocesan statutes appended to Hubert Walter's Council decrees of 1200, we have an instruction that priests should teach the Our Father 'in the mother tongue'; the Creed; the *Confiteor*; faith, hope and charity; and the sacrament of confirmation.[76] Altogether, while hoping that much teaching would be based on grace and the sacraments, such as is implied by the pastoral writings of the canons of Salisbury (see below, p. 128), one may suspect that sin and repentance bulked large.

From where were parish clergy recruited? There is not the evidence to answer this question comprehensively. Many could have been intelligent boys, spotted on bishops' or barons' or cathedral or monastic estates amongst tenant families, who were educated in local schools, became chaplains in lay or ecclesiastical households, and were thus channelled into benefices if not into higher offices. Morey and Brooke have shown how many chaplains in Gilbert Foliot's household were still young men, being educated there before going on to higher study; some of them could have obtained the richer rectories in the bishop's patronage.[77] There were plenty of opportunities for able boys to learn Latin and the basics of other subjects at one of the many town schools with good teachers.[78] John of Salisbury initially learned the rudiments of Latin – and he became one of the finest Latinists of twelfth-century Europe – from a priest of Old Sarum. And as Michael Clanchy has argued, there must have been many similar opportunities for peasant boys in the parishes.[79] The fact that many lay barons and even knights were keen to have rights of advowsons to churches, i.e. the right to present a suitable clergyman to the bishop for institution in a church, suggests that they had relatives or chaplains up their sleeves to appoint.

Parish priests were by no means necessarily of peasant origin. There is a rather touching instance of this in Ralph of Caugy's grant of the church of Ellingham (Northumberland) to the cathedral priory of Durham in the 1150s, confirmed by Bishop Hugh de Puiset. The Caugys were a north-eastern baronial family. By this grant Godfrey, the present rector of Ellingham, was to retain his position for life. But when he died, Ralph of Caugy's son, another Ralph, was to succeed Godfrey as rector, because 'he will be very suitable for this' (*ad id magis fuerit idoneus*).[80] As the Venerable Bede, himself a Northumbrian, said in his *Commentary on Solomon's Temple*, worthy priests are chosen from the whole church regardless of persons (i.e. regardless of social standing).[81] No doubt the father was glad to make satisfactory provision for his son, or for one of his sons. But lay patrons in general evidently cared as much as anyone about the suitability of priests in their churches, for their families would lose face if they did not care; and that too was part of the strength and standing of parish clergy in the localities.

If one thing stands out in the surviving documents of twelfth-century English bishops, it is their determination to control the churches, and the disposal of the churches, in their diocese. This was the very stuff of the Gregorian Reform. Of the 220 surviving documents, or *acta*, of Robert de Chesney, Bishop of Lincoln (1148–66), 99 confirm grants of churches or settlements of disputes over churches.[82] Chesney has sometimes been seen as a stay-at-home bishop, albeit in the largest English diocese. Instead of being a great bishop on the political scene, not least in keeping his distance from the pyrotechnics of the Becket conflict, he worked away at the pastoral and administrative problems of his diocese, aided by a group of professional clerks which included Master Peter de Melide, Master Malger of Newark, and Master Ralph the Physician. As a picture of Chesney this is all very well, but one could match it with many other bishops who were much more politically significant, e.g. as royal courtiers, than he was.[83]

Part of the bishop's control, as we have already implied, was over who was appointed to a rectorship or a vicarage. And here there was one important obstacle to episcopal control in the twelfth century, namely married clergy with sons who treated their fathers' church benefices as hereditary. Since the Norman Conquest clerical marriage had been forbid-den in innumerable councils and while these prohibitions were largely working for the higher clergy, including cathedral canons, by the mid-twelfth century, they were not nearly so effective with the lower clergy.[84] Dynasties of priests whose benefices were passed on from father to son are legion in the twelfth century. Only from the early thirteenth century, when it became clear that marriages had to be celebrated in church, and the less formal ideas of what constituted a marriage faded, could a change be made and marriage of priests go.[85] In the twelfth century, not only were hereditary benefices a fact of life, but they were also written about with implicit approbation by members of the higher clergy. In Abbot John of Ford's Life of Wulfric of Haselbury, Osbern, the son of Brihtric who would succeed his father as parish priest, is seen while still a boy as the saint's regular altar server and runner of messages. Later, as parish priest himself he was a close friend of Wulfric; he heard his last confession and gave him the last sacrament; and after Wulfric's death he thwarted the efforts of the monks of Montacute, with considerable pluck, to take over the body.[86] Ailred of Rievaulx wrote a glowing short book about his forebears, who were hereditary priests of Hexham, and how they had restored the church and revived the cults of its relics.[87] While between 1148 and 1153 Gilbert Foliot, as Bishop of Hereford, wrote to Pope Eugenius III on behalf of the priest-son of a priest and rural dean, who had been upright and energetic in doing the business of the church. The son had been excommunicated and thus deprived of his benefice for no other reason than that it had been the church of his father. The poor man had not been making trouble; in fact he had been doing penance and fasting for long enough, Gilbert urged.[88]

The problem for bishops of hereditary benefices becomes clear from cases like this. They posed a dilemma. On the one hand, if a benefice was regarded as hereditary, the bishop's own possibility to make a suitable appointment was in principle curtailed. On the other hand, for the very reason that they were hereditary, sons were early inducted into priestly work and the liturgy, and early became devoted to their churches. They were likely to become serious priests. So often the best professionals at anything are those who follow in their fathers' footsteps. A family business often brings out the best in people. Moreover where we have the evidence the sons invariably seem to have been popular with their parishioners. Would bishops have been able to fill all the hereditary benefices were they able at a stroke to remove all their incumbents? One may doubt it. Now hereditary benefices may suggest the innerliness of village communities and may seem to work against the idea of parish religion as participator in the higher culture. But one might also argue that anything that raised the standing of parish priests in their own communities made them the better qualified to act as hinge-men between their parishes and the wider world, or between the parishes and the wider church.

The rise of clericalism

In the society in which we live today, to be called a clericalist is generally pejorative, while to be called anti-clerical is often regarded as something of a compliment. But clericalism can be thought of in different ways: as the manipulation of worldly politics and material affairs in the clerical interest; or as the ideology underpinning a new, or newly powerful élite, in European and British society;[89] or as the ideal which emphasised the sacredness of the priestly vocation, requiring priests to live up to their high calling. It may be argued that all these three ideas are different strands, inextricably woven together in the one phenomenon of clericalism. But I shall now concentrate on the third aspect, the high ideal of the priestly vocation. For if it is right to argue that the standing of the clerical order as a whole, religious and moral as well as economic standing, rose in the twelfth century, it is hard to believe that this could have happened *only* by the power politics implicit in the first two strands, without the idealism of the third.

It was mentioned briefly in the second chapter (p. 28) that clericalism flowed naturally from the Gregorian Reform. It is clear that the Gregorian Reform strove to make priestly power superior to secular power in the world, and to have the clergy to stand totally apart from it – in dress, in mores, and in holiness. But another factor also came into play. The theological controversy of the 1050s between Lanfranc and Berengar of Tours was about the Eucharist, the Sacrament of the Altar, and what it meant in logic to talk about Christ's presence therein.[90] As a result of their debate, and the general interest in the Eucharist at that time, attention naturally came to be focused on those who administered the sacrament, who brought about Christ's presence in the Eucharist, namely the priests. It was a short step from there to a fear that such a sacred order should be polluted by contact with women let alone by sexual intercourse, or that its sacral powers should be prostituted by being bought and sold with money.[91] The fear of pollution of priests through sexual intercourse can be clearly seen in a letter of St Anselm and in the very language he uses, written before he became Archbishop of Canterbury:

It can never be fitting that anyone should reverently stand where those stinking with impudent wantonness, despising the prohibition of God and the saints, serve the altars, or not so much serve them as pollute them.

Nobody thinks that what is done at the altar is to be contemned, but that those doing it are to be execrated, as people who do not respect the presence of God and the angels. They should be driven away by the detestation of men, and should cease to contaminate the sacred mysteries. It is not at all appropriate that those who have cut themselves off by their impurity should have any share in the fellowship of the altar.[92]

Behind all the talk of pollution and contamination here, one must remember that there was also a sacramental theology, which would be developed, especially at Paris, during the twelfth century. Moreover, the late eleventh and early twelfth centuries were also a period in which people's search for their vocation, not only priestly vocation, reached the proportions of a new religious phenomenon in European society, as Henrietta Leyser has vividly shown.[93] We shall return to this search for vocation when considering the Cistercians later. But it is everywhere to be seen in various ways. John of Salisbury, for instance, in the very process of criticising ambitious or tyrannical priests in his *Policraticus* (1156–59), sometimes wrongly thought of as a cynical work, implies a high ideal of the priestly calling as such.[94]

The rise of clericalism was hardly a triumphant one in twelfth-century England. The number of apparently popular married priests and sons of priests among the lower clergy suggests that fear of pollution was not everywhere rabid. But clericalism was growing. We cannot here attempt a comprehensive survey of the phenomenon; all we can do is to give a few pointers.

Let us start with bishops and their mitres. Wearing a mitre represents an obvious exaltation of a bishop's office and authority. Mitres first developed as the result of a mistranslation of the Bible, and they developed first in twelfth-century England. When Moses was said to have a horned face (*cornuta facies*, Exodus 34, 29), this was a translation into Latin by Jerome of a Hebrew word which meant a shining or glorified face. Jerome himself did not think that Moses was literally horned; his face was *glorificata*. But in Aelfric's English biblical paraphrase of the eleventh century, *cornuta* was translated as *gehyrned*, or horned.[95] And so, in English illustrations of the eleventh and twelfth centuries, Moses is shown literally wearing horns. That may seem ridiculous to us, but it was taken so seriously in the twelfth century that c. 1125 side-horned mitres came in, with the two conical points side-by-side both facing frontwards. Representations with this sort of mitre are on the seals of Bishops Alexander and Robert de Chesney of Lincoln, and very splendidly, on Thomas Becket's. They probably derive from the horned Moses. From around the mid-twelfth century, the 'horns' are turned round to be one behind the other as we know the mitre. The whole development can be followed on bishops' seals, which represent bishops' own images of themselves.[96]

Now to the lower clergy. Latin was the international language for the clergy. Canons of cathedrals, monks, and learned clerics could communicate in Latin. So could bishops, though sometimes as with their handwriting rather more shakily for lack of practice. It was of course the language of the liturgy in the whole Western church. As Robert Bartlett writes, the Latin-literate usually had the option of excluding the laity by use of their own private language.[97] There is no doubt, therefore, that Latin was both an instrument and a symbol of clericalism. But how were the parish clergy on their Latin? In most cases we cannot tell, and some (as one might expect) were clearly hopeless.[98] But we might make three points about this. First, there were many schools and schoolmasters up and down the country, as we have said, where or from whom Latin could be learnt. Second, even if priests could often not translate or construe the Latin liturgical words they spoke, the very fact of speaking them gave them a mystique, almost as if they were pronouncing magical formulae. And third, when a writer like Gerald of Wales derides the silly mistakes in Latin made by the clergy, like the priest who promised a bishop (possibly a figment of Gerald's imagination) 200 sheep, *oves*, when he meant 200 eggs, *ova*,[99] one should not overlook that people who make silly mistakes in a language have usually been grappling with it. Silly mistakes tend to indicate some, if not perfect, knowledge of a language.

Whatever their Latin was like, members of the lower clergy were clearly eager to own books, whose texts were of course in Latin, and no doubt eager for their ownership to be known. Books were expensive and gave their owners prestige. Wulfric of Haselbury copied out books, both for his own use and for the church of Haselbury Plucknett, the latter presumably in the keeping of the parish priest. He was wont to make covers of fine textiles for them, emphasising their importance and value as objects. A woman from eastern England, prompted by a dream, sent him a precious textile to make a book cover; and when he lacked suitable material for this purpose, his friend Walter, monk of Glastonbury, would help out.[100] *The Life and Miracles of St William of Norwich* have a tale about how the author of the *Miracles* himself, Thomas of Monmouth, lost a psalter (probably not finely illuminated), which someone stole and Ralph, priest of St Michael's Norwich bought for three pence; and when Ralph learned that it was stolen, he delayed to bring it back, 'whether from shame or because he was corrupted with the desire of keeping it, I know not'.[101] Three pence might have been 0.3 per cent or more of Ralph's income, perhaps the equivalent of £80 or more of an Anglican vicar's stipend today. In the early thirteenth century, Francis of Assisi was confronted by Franciscan brethren who wanted to own books, breviaries and the like, and he refused to allow it because it was against his ideal of poverty and represented worldly ambition.[102]

A vital point to appreciate about clericalism is this: that however important it is how the laity view the priest, even more important is how he views himself in relation to the laity. The parish church of Elkstone (Gloucestershire), a small but atmospheric twelfth-century church in the high Cotswolds, where sheep farming was big business in the Middle Ages, has a very fine if low chancel arch [see Plate 7]. The priest must have known how impressive he would look from the nave, celebrating Mass framed, as it were, by this arch. Iffley Church (Oxfordshire) makes my point even better. Iffley church was intended, in part, to articulate the power of Robert of St Remy, its baronial builder. But it must also have done a power of good to the morale of its resident priest. The laity would have seen him from the nave, they themselves presumably not encroaching into the chancel, which church legislation forbade.[103] From there the east end does not look at all lofty. The view looking down from the east end to the nave makes it feel much loftier [see Plates 3 and 4]. This was no accident. Robert of St Remy got a fine master mason, who had probably worked at Reading Abbey.[104] He knew what he was doing. The difference is made by the fact that from the east end, even without considering the early thirteenth-century extension, one is looking at the *downward* succession of ribbed vaults and chevroned arches, to the ornamented round window in the west wall. The church is built on sloping ground and yet an architectural illusion is created of greater loftiness looking down from the priest's end than looking up from the laity's.

We seem to get, at first sight, a very interesting glimpse of how the laity were supposed to view the priests in their most important function, the celebration of Mass, in a work entitled by its nineteenth-century editor, *The Lay-Folks Mass Book*. This was a tract composed by Jeremy, Archdeacon of Cleveland in North Yorkshire from 1171 to 1189; so yet another sign of Yorkshire being in the twelfth-century pastoral vanguard. Jeremy had come from Rouen and previously been a canon there. He wrote his treatise in French, but in the late thirteenth century it was translated into English. It is a step-by-step commentary on the Mass, and how lay people should behave and what should be in their minds during it. Jerome, or Jeremy as he is called in some English versions, was against talking during Mass, or making 'jangling'. And then, for example, 'while the priest is washing his hands, be saying the Our Father; and when he turns to ask thy prayers, knock on thy breast'. While the priest is saying the Preface to the Canon of the Mass, 'you say these words privately' in a prayer of thanksgiving:

> *In world of worlds without ending*
> *Thanked be Jesus my king*
> *All my heart I give it Thee*
> *Great right it is that it so be,*

the prayer ending:

> *Sweet Jesus grant me now this*
> *That I may come unto Thy bliss*
> *There with angels for to sing*
> *This sweet song of Thy loving.*

And when the *sanctus* is said, 'kneel thou down'. These are small samples from quite a long and detailed work.[105]

I said that at first sight this looks like an archdeacon instructing the laity on how to view and respond to the priest at Mass. But since Archdeacon Jeremy was writing in French, his treatise must have been directed to a largely aristocratic audience rather than to the ordinary peasants. There is, however, another possibility. Archdeacon Jeremy must be 40 years later than the English monoglot priest, Brihtric, at Haselbury Plucknett. By then it is likely that many parish priests could understand French. Even if they could not, there would be little point in an archdeacon, the pastor and disciplinarian of the lower clergy par excellence, writing such a book if priests themselves were not intended to know what it said; indeed, if they, the first-line instructors of the parish laity, were not intended to convey what it said to the laity. Once again therefore we are back to how the clergy viewed themselves, knowing or thinking that they were buoyed up in their celebrations by the prayers of the lay faithful.

The same point – clericalism as how the clergy viewed their own calling – may be made about a very different piece of writing, probably from about the same time as Archdeacon Jeremy's, namely the 1170s or c. 1180. It is Gervase of Chichester's commentary on the Book of Malachi. Gervase had been one of Becket's clerks or *eruditi*; he did not follow the archbishop into exile, though he preached at least two sermons about him very soon after his martyrdom, in the chapter house of Chichester Cathedral, where he became a resident canon, and died, probably as the cathedral's lecturer in theology.[106] A commentary on the Book of Malachi, the last of the

Minor Prophets, is rather a rarity. Malachi is about the need to reform the worship of the Temple and the priests who conducted it, and it gave Gervase just the starting-point that he wanted for his long-winded and repetitive outpourings on the evils of the English priests of his own day. Not that one should measure those evils by the strength of Gervase's rhetoric about them; he was a moralist, not a sociologist. He goes on and on about their avarice, drunkenness, and incontinence. No wonder he and Gerald of Wales got on so well, despite the fact that he was not in the same league as Gerald as a writer. Gervase's book is addressed to the priesthood of England, rather ambitiously considering that there is no evidence of more than three manuscripts of it – ever. With large chunks of it the priests of the cathedral and the diocese were no doubt regaled in the chapter house.

Although Gervase's is a boring book, it is an interesting phenomenon. It is all in high-blown Latin style, as are the sermons of St Bernard whom he might have had in mind as a stylist, if lacking Bernard's wit, clarity, control, and white-heat spirituality. From time to time it comes out with some good lines, e.g., 'those who carry the keys (*claves*) of the church should be sure that they do not drive nails (*clavos*) into the hands of Christ with those keys', or 'what the judge in heaven intones, the herald (i.e. priest) proclaims with his voice on earth'.[107] But just as children, and even students, are sometimes most impressed with what they do not entirely understand, however high-faluting or bombastic Gervase's language, it may well have been intended by that very fact to give the priests who heard him a heightened sense of their own vocation.

Cathedrals and parish religion

It may seem strange to include a discussion of cathedrals, bastions of the higher culture, in a chapter on parish religion rather than elsewhere, but there are fingers from them which point to both the royal court in one direction and parishes in the other. A few of the dignitaries and canons in several cathedrals were royal servants, especially of course the non-resident ones. The bishops collated most of these dignities and canonries, and there were always curialist bishops willing to oblige the king by collating some of these offices, and their incomes, to curialists. That applies particularly to bishoprics with rich canonries, or prebends, like York and Lincoln; not much to poor ones like Chichester and Exeter. But if curialist dignitaries and canons were not unimportant links with the king in some cathedral chapters, far more important were the links between the cathedrals and many parish churches of their dioceses. This was particularly so as the distinction between resident and non-resident dignitaries and canons became ever sharper during the twelfth century, with residents emerging as *the* force in the running of the cathedral and its affairs.

The income of many of the dignitaries' and canons' prebends derived from parish churches. For example, a fine study has been made by Frances Ramsey of the building up of the Wells Cathedral Chapter and its prebends in the mid-twelfth century by Robert of Lewes, Bishop of Bath (1133–66). Bath was a Benedictine monastery and the bishop, himself a Benedictine/Cluniac monk, needed a chapter to which men important to him in the running of the diocese could belong and from whose prebends they could receive their income. Bath Abbey could not supply that need; Wells Cathedral could. Some Wells prebends were endowed from the bishop's estates, others from those of the local aristocracy. And in all the endowments which represented churches and their incomes, vicarages for resident parish priests were apparently soon ordained, with the prebendary concerned being the patron of the vicarage; and these were vicarages of very good value, to judge by thirteenth-century records.[108] Bishops were not always in a position to force the specific ordinations of vicarages, but they were in a strong position to do so where the prebendal churches of their own cathedral were concerned. The laity might not have liked to have given up the patronage, effectively the power of appointing the priest, in churches which they had founded, but there were compensations apart from those of prayers. For example, when Robert de Bonville gave the church of West Lydford as a prebend to Wells (c. 1151–66) after the then priest had died (no doubt appointed by the Bonville family), the bishop gave the vicarage already ordained in the church, at Robert's request, to the latter's chaplain, Vivian.[109] Some of the Wells prebends were of churches so close to Wells, like Dulcote only one-and-a-half miles away, that they might initially have been served by the canon himself. Likewise at Chichester between 1147 and 1157, the canon who was prebendary of Eartham committed himself to have one Mass celebrated each week, obviously on a weekday, for the soul of Bishop Hilary's brother, Robert, and for all the souls of the departed – shades of the chaplain encountered by Bartholomew of Exeter! – and have prayers bid for him each Sunday.[110] The canon did not have to do these things in person, but he had to supervise them, and at six miles or so from Chichester, and riding between Chichester and Eartham, he could probably having managed them himself as a resident canon. John Henry Newman had no problem in walking to Littlemore from the centre of Oxford (over three miles) every Sunday.

My conclusions from all this are that a good deal of parish direction came from the cathedral centre, that its own prebendal churches were intended to be pastoral models, and that cathedrals acted as hinges between parish religion and the 'higher' culture. The sceptic may ask whether any of this actually worked. It is impossible to answer, but it would be excessively sceptical to assume that it did not, by and large, have its effect. One reason I would give for saying so is that canons of English cathedrals were not nearly so subject to local pressures as they were in Germany, because far fewer of them were scions of local aristocratic families.[111] Hence they were freer, if they had any ideals, to put them into practice. It is also clear, to come back to a point made earlier in this chapter, that aristocrats were not generally enemies of the pastoral effort, but rather favoured it, provided their interests were reasonably acknowledged.

In the archdiocese of York, we see similar aims if different means. There is not so much evidence in episcopal documents as there is at the diocese of Bath for the ordination of vicarages for priests actually serving the prebendal churches. But that might be the different nature of the evidence. What we do have at York is evidence of another kind that the archbishops through their cathedral wanted to direct parish religion. It is the creation by Archbishop Thurstan of a prebend in his cathedral for the Augustinian Canons of Nostell, a prebend consisting of three parish churches.[112] We have already in an earlier chapter noted the pastoral drive of Thurstan, and the centrality of Nostell to Henry I's religious side; and we shall in the next chapter give closer consideration to the Augustinian Canons as a force in English religion and in local communities. Innumerable parish churches came in the twelfth century to be run either directly by them or under their supervision. Knowing them as a pastoral force, therefore, Thurstan was involving them in the deliberations and actions of his cathedral chapter by the creation of this prebend. Archbishop Roger of Pont l'Eveque, an enemy of Becket whom he called a Pharaoh, but an alert pastor in his own diocese, confirmed Thurstan's arrangement, and at the same time confirmed to Nostell ten other parish churches, including Batley and Huddersfield, which Nostell held (and for which they were responsible) in Yorkshire.[113]

We can already see an interest in this kind of parish direction at York much earlier. In 1083 Bishop William of St Calais monasticised the cathedral of Durham and ejected the married priests. Ailred of Rievaulx's grandfather, Eilaf, suffered from this and took himself off to Archbishop Thomas I of York who at that time held the temporalities of Hexham and its area, the church of which Eilaf was priest.[114] They struck a deal. The archbishop would grant Eilaf the dilapidated church if he would restore it.

The Archbishop made the church part of the prebend of Holme in the cathedral of York, and gave the prebend to a canon of Beverley, Richard de Maton, under whom Eilaf continued to be the priest at Hexham. At present I am not concerned with the interesting question of what this says about the fluid diocesan jurisdictional relations between York and Durham, but with Hexham as an early example of York's will towards parish direction.[115]

The same will can be seen, I would argue, from early in our period at Salisbury Cathedral. It may well be that Salisbury was no exception, and that it is simply the evidence and the way that evidence has been studied that makes me single it out. Before we come to Salisbury, let it be said that there were other secular cathedrals (I am not here considering those whose chapters were monasteries like Canterbury, Winchester, or Durham) which had at least for a time learned circles of canons. Exeter was one, with the literary circle of Bishop Bartholomew (1161–84) which included Baldwin of Ford before he became a Cistercian monk and (soon) Abbot of Ford.[116] As Abbot, Baldwin wrote a treatise on the Sacrament of the Altar, a learned interest which represented the theology behind parish religion with the Eucharist at its centre. Baldwin would become Bishop of Worcester (1180–84) and Archbishop of Canterbury (1184–90). Earlier, around 1125–30, it was another canon of Exeter, Robert Pullen, later to become a cardinal at Rome, who would validate the mission of Wulfric as a recluse at Haselbury Plucknett. Wulfric had had a dream about Jesus and St Peter which ended with a vessel of oil being broken and the oil spilling down his clothes and onto the ground. Pullen came and, with the help of the Song of Songs ('Thy name is poured out as oil') and his knowledge of Bede and Gregory the Great, interpreted the dream as a presage of Wulfric's healings and other miracles – a perfect example of the continuum between the 'higher' culture and parish religion. Given that Haselbury was in the diocese of Bath, one may wonder why validation came from Exeter rather than its own diocesan centre. Surely not because Exeter was marginally the nearer cathedral. Nor because there was any conflict between Exeter and Bath over this, for the Bishop of Bath demonstrably supported Wulfric and accepted his standing. It will probably have been that at the time neither Bath nor Wells had anyone with half the learned reputation of Pullen.[117]

Other English cathedrals were notable centres of learning, such as Hereford,[118] or for a time[119] London, though none were anything like the high-powered teaching centres of Northern France, such as Paris or Laon, or in Italy Bologna; and most of them it has been said, were 'no more than glorified grammar schools'[120] (though in terms of potentially educating parish clergy such institutions had their own value). I single out Salisbury, however, because of the remarkable study of its books in the late eleventh and early twelfth centuries by Teresa Webber. Webber has shown how the canons of Salisbury built up a fine library of classical and theological works, including theological works by fathers like Hilary of Poitiers which were generally not so well represented in libraries. Many of these works were copied from exemplars by teams of canons themselves. If the canons themselves were not authors, this period of intensive library building shows that they were abreast of continental theological and biblical scholarship.[121] More to our purposes here, these theological interests flowed on into work of pastoral significance.[122] The canons produced, for example, a *florilegium*, that is a compilation of biblical and patristic extracts, which Webber calls the *Ladder of Virtues (Scala Virtutum)*. These extracts carefully avoid exclusive reference to the monastic life and are about practical virtues in the world, such as hospitality, visiting the sick, frequenting the shrines of saints, reconciliation with others. Their lessons are for 'every Christian' or even 'every man', not only for contemplative monks. The ladder of virtues cannot be ascended except with the sacraments, especially the Eucharist. The two sides of the ladder are interpreted, uniquely in this Salisbury compilation, as the receiving of baptism and the Eucharist.[123] That leads on, in this and at least one other Salisbury *florilegium*, to the validity of the orders of priests who administer the sacraments,[124] and the need for them to be, and be adjudged to be, men of pure and disciplined life.

As Webber herself says, we do not know whether, or how, any of this was translated into the practical instruction of the local clergy and laity.[125] But it seems to me inconceivable that it was not so translated in some way. Many of the Salisbury prebends consisted of churches. We admittedly lack the early evidence for vicarages in these. But the Salisbury canons would have been exceptionally incoherent people if they had had these deeply serious theological and moral interests on the one hand, and on the other hand had lacked any strong sense of their responsibilities towards the clergy and laity of their own diocese.

There were many different kinds of mutual involvement between parishes and cathedral, e.g. in the building of the cathedral itself.[126] But I should like to turn back, lastly, to Gervase of Chichester and to something which only indirectly involves parish religion. But it seems to be a nice example of the influence of one learned cathedral canon, apparently the theology lecturer in his cathedral, on what went on in his diocese. A passage in Gervase's Commentary of Malachi, a critical passage as almost always, rebukes aristocrats who out of vanity build and endow new monasteries, when they ought to be enriching and expanding and protecting the old houses built by their ancestors rather than allowing them to go to rack and ruin.[127]

In Sussex and the diocese of Chichester such an aristocrat was not, emphatically not, William of St John, patron of the Benedictine Priory of Boxgrove, three miles from Chichester. In the late 1170s William of St John asked Bishop John Greenford of Chichester to ordain vicarages in the five churches of which Boxgrove held the rectory; only Boxgrove itself was exempted – so the priory church doubled up as a parish church. The five churches were only to be given to priests who would personally minister in them and each church was to have its own priest.[128] Then in the 1180s Bishop Seffrid II confirmed their possessions and rights to Boxgrove twice over, including new grants made to them by William of St John and others (doubtless mobilised by William) to enable the number of Boxgrove monks to be raised from 13 to 15. A little later, William made further grants to enable the number to be raised from 15 to 16.[129] The three charters, that of John Greenford on the vicarages, a confirmation of possessions with additional grants by Seffrid II, and the one concerned with raising the number from 13 to 15, are all witnessed amongst others by Gervase, and with one exception, they are the only surviving bishops' charters witnessed by him. The witness list of the last (the 15 to 16 one), has not been recorded. If a copy with witnesses ever turned up, I would put heavy odds on Gervase's name being there. By his particular association with William of St John's grants to Boxgrove Priory, Gervase the canon seems to be collaborating with the baron in the whole idea of expanding a long-established monastery and making it more viable, rather than founding a new one to perpetuate William's own name.

It just happens that we catch a glimpse of how the cathedral could affect religion in the diocese here. It may well be that there was much more of this sort of influence in the twelfth century than we can now see; that what is rare is not so much *what* we glimpse as the *evidence* which in this case we have with which to glimpse it.

CHAPTER 6

The Monastic Century 1066–1216

Introduction

This chapter, about the 'long twelfth century', is entitled as it is because it would be hard to find any century thereafter in which monasteries had played anything like so large a part in the life of English, or British, society. It may surprise some that in a book entitled 'Religion, Politics and Society', there should be a lengthy chapter on monasteries. What had those whose vocation was apparently to turn their backs on the world to do with society let alone politics? In the twelfth century, as in many other ages, they had a lot to do with society and politics. The first two sections of this chapter deal with the black monks, the traditional Benedictines so called because their habits were dyed black, and the white monks, the Cistercians so called because their habits were of undyed natural wool. The great black-monk monasteries were large-scale land holding corporations whose abbots were mostly tenants-in-chief of the king. They were unavoidably involved in politics – attending court, finding knights or the means to pay knights for the king's armies, exercising great power and jurisdiction in their regions, and some of their monks being historians who were the equivalent of the most influential journalists of our own day. In 1182 when the monks of Bury St Edmunds wanted their monk, Samson to be their abbot, they needed the king's assent to their elect. This was something that mattered to the king; obviously an important man like the Abbot of Bury had to be both loyal and competent. Henry II spoke to the delegation of Bury monks, whom he received at his manor of Waltham, in the short sharp sentences which also characterised the royal writs themselves at that time. He said (and the report of this probably came from Samson himself):

*You have presented Samson to me, I do not know him. Had you
presented your Prior to me, whom I have seen and know, I would have
accepted him. As it is I shall do as you wish. But have a care. By the very
eyes of God, if you have done badly, I shall be at you!*[1]

The black-monk monasteries were mainly in significant towns. In the
most physical sense they could not withdraw themselves from the world.
They were involved in the lordships of towns, the administration of
manors, and the holding of courts. The Cistercians, new to Britain in the
1120s did turn their backs on the world in the sense that they set themselves up in the country, removed from human habitation, and they liked
to think of their monastic sites as 'places of horror and vast solitude'. They
reminded themselves of ancient hermits who had gone off into the desert
like St Anthony and the Egyptians described by Cassian in the fifth century.
But despite all this, they too were very far from having nothing to do with
society and politics. First of all, from the beginning of Christian history
those who fled the world always excited the greatest admiration and
interest of those left behind in it, who wanted to bring back into their
world something of the ascetics' spiritual power and moral authority.
Then, whatever the Cistercians said about their sites, none were far from
centres of secular power or significant roads. Many Cistercian abbeys were
sheep-farmers and their year's clip of wool soon became important to the
economy.[2] But they also held some of the best agricultural lands of central
England.[3] Above all, they never lost their sense of mission to be a salvation
to the society from which they had ostensibly removed themselves. They
took, in this, a leaf out of the book of St Bernard, the greatest Cistercian
of the twelfth century, and as Abbot of Clairvaux in Burgundy head of
the mother house of most English Cistercian monasteries. St Bernard was
a reclusive abbot for little more than a decade before his reputation for
sanctity, and his brilliant rhetoric (at first directed against laxer monks)
made their impact. After that, he was involved in, and influenced, almost
every major political upheaval of the second quarter of the twelfth century
in Western Europe. During a council concerned with the papal schism of
the 1130s he wrote to his monks at Clairvaux, protesting his misery at
being absent from them and delivered himself of the following Ciceronian
gem: 'I should like to tell you, for your consolation, how necessary my
presence here is, were it not that it would smack of boasting'!'[4]

In each section of this chapter the impact made by religious houses on
what I have called sometimes the shire communities, sometimes the knights
and upper peasants of the shires, sometimes the gentry, figures large.

Therefore I ought to put what I say into the context of the interesting discussions that historians have been having about this social group. Everyone agrees that a collective identity of this group evolved over a long period of time – say from the eleventh to the fourteenth century – the identity of a lesser nobility. Everyone agrees that the Angevin period (1154–1216), particularly through the 'legal reforms' of Henry II, was a vital period in this evolution;[5] and that even if the power of baronial lordship was still important, horizontal ties among this group were more in evidence in Angevin England than earlier.

Whether one should speak about the gentry as a homogeneous social group before the late thirteenth or fourteenth centuries is certainly questionable. As historians use the term, it applies to a more highly defined and smaller élite, one more closely tied to central government and parliamentary representation as that developed, than were our Angevin knights. Whether one should see an unbroken development from the knights of around 1200 to the gentry of around 1300 or after is also questionable, given the pressures, especially financial, on many thirteenth-century knights.[6] Whether one should speak of shire communities at all, or of the shire as a focus of loyalty in itself, may be questioned. It has been well shown that neighbourhood ties easily cut across shire boundaries. Oseney Abbey, for example, just outside Oxford, had knightly patrons and benefactors in both Oxfordshire and Buckinghamshire, whilst East Bucks families had similar links with monasteries in Bedfordshire.[7] This was not the nineteenth century when the *County* Cricket Championship began,[8] and when the high Tory Warden of Merton College, Oxford, could reproach an undergraduate by saying, 'Sir, you have let down your county!'

Nonetheless, at least for the Angevin period, we must be careful that the baby does not go out with the bath water. Because the Angevin knights and upper peasants were not yet a gentry, rather than what Peter Coss has called a 'seed bed' out of which the more sharply defined gentry would grow,[9] that does not mean that they were other than a powerful force, as some sort of community, within the shire. Whatever the pressures on such people in the thirteenth century, they still had the capacity as a group, shown in Magna Carta, to articulate their grievances and their idea of standards to which the royal government ought to adhere. That did not go away and very much re-surfaced in the Provisions of Westminster (1259).[10] And because the shire as such was not generally a focus of identity (though even this is sometimes doubtful) that does not forbid us to speak of a growing sense of community amongst knightly men and upper peasants within a shire.

The black monks

Liturgy and ritual

The great traditional English Benedictine monasteries led lives of high ritual. Their offices, such as matins and lauds, were celebrated with elaborate and meticulously performed chants. As we saw earlier (p. 38), strong feelings were aroused by these chants, which engrossed much time and could be symbols of affiliation to different Norman abbeys. When one considers the large numbers of splendid abbey churches which were built or enlarged in the Norman period, it is important not to overlook the kinds of sound which were intended to fill them. Black monks built up good libraries in this period, and albeit monasteries employed professional scribes, some of their books must have been copied by their own monks.[11] But for all that, if one asks why the scholarship emanating from these monasteries was generally of unexpectedly small account, part of the answer must be that the day was so studded with liturgical celebrations as to leave little time for cutting-edge scholarship.

The few surviving artefacts, other than books, brilliantly illuminate the ritualistic character of black-monk monasticism. An example is the superb gilt-bronze candlestick made for Gloucester Abbey in the early twelfth century, with its dragon-head feet; its figures clambering up it; its winged dragons which hold up the grease pan; its fine foliage ornament running up, and the evangelist symbols on the knop of its stem. This candlestick was commissioned by Abbot Peter of Gloucester (1104–13), as a Latin inscription on a scroll winding round its stem tell us, and it was probably one of a pair intended to stand on the altar during solemn celebrations of Mass [see Plate 2].[12] The ornament on this candlestick was likely to have matched that in the initial letters of Mass-books also placed on the altar and also the ornament stitched onto chasubles and other liturgical vestments (we have seen how fond the monks of St Albans were of their copes p. 19). No such vestments as early as the twelfth century now survive, but we have some late twelfth-century French mitres embroidered with foliage scrolls and a part of a Canterbury amice embroidered with the evangelist symbols set in roundels. These may give us some idea of how twelfth-century vestments looked.[13] When one thinks also of stone capitals with their foliage and figural ornament, one can see that the liturgy was sumptuously set in what Richard Gameson has called 'a co-ordinated artistic environment'.[14] By analogy, we may think of the co-ordinated artistic environment of a late eighteenth-century Adam dining room, whereby the swags and garlands of the plastered ceilings would be repeated on the dining table with the same motifs engraved on the silver salt cellars and pepper pots.

A group of black monks was responsible in the 1120s for putting the idea of Mary's Immaculate Conception, that Mary was conceived without stain of original sin, on the map. In this group were Geoffrey, Abbot of St Alban's, Hugh, Abbot of Reading, Osbert of Clare, Prior of Westminster, Anselm of St Saba, Abbot of Bury St Edmunds and nephew of St Anselm, and Eadmer of Canterbury. At first sight the motive behind this looks theological, but in reality it was much more liturgical. That was much more what one might expect from a group of important black monks. There was of course theology in it. Eadmer wrote a book *On the Excellence of the Virgin* arguing theologically for it. Sir Richard Southern said that his words deserved respect. But to the present writer they seem jejune, and they did not persuade St Bernard, Peter Lombard or Thomas Aquinas.[15] It is hard to see the impetus behind the Immaculate Conception as theological, particularly considering how relatively untheological the cultural background of black-monk monasteries was in that period. The impetus was liturgical, developing another great feast of the Virgin for a splendid liturgical celebration. This is shown by a letter of Osbert of Clare of Westminster written to Anselm of St Saba in December 1129. He wrote:

While we were keeping this feast, some followers of Satan decried its observance as hitherto unheard of and absurd. With malicious intentions they went to two bishops, Roger (of Salisbury) and Bernard (of St David's), who happened then to be in the neighbourhood, and representing its novelty, excited them to displeasure. The bishops declared that the festival was forbidden by a council and that the observance must be stopped. But we proceeded with the office of the day, which had already begun, and carried it through with joyous solemnity.[16]

It is not hard to guess who the so-called 'followers of Satan' were: members of the Belmeis family faction in the rival establishment to Westminster in London, St Paul's Cathedral, who were against their bishop, Gilbert the Universal who was another supporter of the Immaculate Conception.[17] But it is interesting that Roger of Salisbury, Henry I's chief minister, was displeased by it, because the canons of his cathedral really did know something about theology and he took an interest in their work (see p. 46). The principal conclusion, however, is that the emphasised words strongly suggest that what was of interest at Westminster Abbey was the celebration of the feast, a feast known in eleventh-century England but which had lapsed in recent decades.[18]

Ritual was not only worship. Ritual and symbolism engrossed the whole of life. When William, Earl of Warenne, in 1147 granted the tithes of all his demesnes to Lewis Priory, a Cluniac foundation of the late eleventh century in Sussex, his remarkable charter stated: 'and I have put them in possession (of the tithes) through hairs of my head and that of my brother Ralph of Warenne, which Henry, Bishop of Winchester cut from our heads with a knife, before the altar'.[19] The charter was simply the subsequent written record of a transaction whose essence had been represented in a ceremony. Again, a book of liturgical gospel readings made at Sherborne Abbey in Dorset contains a dossier of documents concerning a quarrel about the bishop's jurisdiction over them between the Abbey and Bishop Jocelin of Salisbury which occurred in the 1140s. The documents were not written merely onto spare leaves in the book, but were an integral and considerable part of it, as if the evidences of their rights against the bishop were under the magical protection of the sacred and publicly recited texts.[20]

The sealing of a document issued by an abbey in connection with its material affairs must always have been an act of some solemnity, all the more so because so much thought and art had generally gone into making the matrix of the seal in the first place. T.A. Heslop, for example, has shown this for the seals of black-monk monasteries, including the monastic priory of Worcester Cathedral, dedicated to the Virgin Mary. Their seals, representing Mary and her Child, show her holding a rod which signified not only a royal sceptre but also the rod of Jesse, Jesse being the ancestor from whom Mary and Jesus were sprung, and thus the Incarnation.[21] There is more to the iconography than that, but already from that we begin to see how these monasteries were by the late twelfth century presenting their public image in a biblical and theological light. As symbols and projectors of an image, these seals (which secular cathedrals, towns, and other corporations were also developing in the twelfth century) were like our present-day logos. The logos – of industrial companies, banks, insurance companies, etc. – are one of the most important features of public symbolism in our society, often devised with professional skill after widespread consultation within a company about the kind of image its directors and employees want to present.[22] Seals were also important for the legal security of a monastery. If a monastery were challenged in court with a document purportedly issued by itself and it lacked a seal, by the second half of the twelfth century the document could automatically be considered invalid. So the matrix had to be kept under lock and key. Abbot Ralph of St Albans (1146–51) one day walked into his monastery's goldsmith's workshop, saw there on the table an as yet unscupted seal, suspected (probably wrongly) his prior, Alcuin, of wanting to undermine his authority by issuing documents in the abbey's name, and promptly sacked him.[23]

Incidentally, the very fact that the abbey had a goldsmith's workshop is in itself evidence of its need of fine ceremonial objects for its ritual. The St Albans workshop was rather special, because it had as its head goldsmith a monk called Anketill, who for seven years before he joined St Albans had been moneyer to the King of Denmark.[24] Minting coins, making chalices or thuribles, and sculpting seals, were all skills practised by top metal-workers.

Material interests

One can easily get the impression that the black monks were very material-istic in their whole outlook. The chronicles of their monasteries tend to be full of accounts of law-suits and struggles to champion their rights and possessions, written sometimes in a vindictive spirit against their oppo-nents, not altogether surprising from some of the psalms which they recited regularly! *The Chronicle of Jocelin of Brakelond* is full of material concerns and Abbot Samson's cunning in pursuing them – his clever tricks to deny the Bishop of Ely certain oak trees that the abbot wanted for the building of the abbey's great tower; his attempt to charge a toll on Yarmouth herring merchants passing through the town; his raising the level of his fishpond with the consequence that the cellarer's meadow was flooded; his taking into his own administration profitably manors that had previously been leased out. Jocelin says that Samson drew up an inventory of all the dues that he was owed from courts or manors, down to every last penny and every last hen. 'Now this book', adds Jocelin, 'in which were also recorded the debts which he had paid off, he called his Kalendar, and consulted it almost every day, as if he saw there in a mirror, the image of his own efficiency!'[25]

It could be argued that the black monks were not as materialistic as such sources make them look. The monastery of Bury St Edmunds was a relatively large monastery in Samson's time, having some 90 monks. The vast majority of these were choir monks, whose principal duty was to keep the elaborate worship of the monastery going, with all the skills that that entailed – knowledge of Latin, of music, of liturgical orders, of some reli-gious literature, even of astronomy for the timing of services. Moreover we can see that their formal liturgy was intended also to include an element of more personal prayer. We can see from illustrated psalters, for example, that the recitation of the psalms was intended to bring to mind events and sayings in the life of Jesus.[26] In many passages they could be seen as relevant to Jesus. Choir monks, therefore, were engaged in a full-time occupation which in theory at least required some learning and spirituality. Only a handful of the monks were not choir monks but obedientiaries, i.e. the administrative officials of the monastery. Such, for instance, were the sacrist, the infirmarian, and above all the cellarer, who was the equivalent of a domestic bursar in a modern college or school. Such obedientiaries were important people with demanding jobs, who had their own manorial revenues from which to run their offices (only under Abbot Samson was any central control or audit established over them). Rather like some college officials, as against the general run of teaching and researching academics in our own day, the obedientiaries could easily get the impression that they were the only people in a monastery who did any real work. And the voice we hear in the black monks' own stories is the voice of the obedientiaries. We know that Jocelin of Brakelond was Cellarer at Bury St Edmunds,[27] and that the mid-twelfth-century portion of the St Albans *Deeds of the Abbots* is based on a cellarer's narrative;[28] and several other black-monk chronicle/cartularies have a cellarer-like air about them. In such sources we do not hear the voices of the choir monks, the worshipping majority. Jocelin of Brakelond is very aware of the distinction between obedientiaries and choir monks, but when occasionally he allows a voice to the choir monks, it is usually done satirically. His own urbanity and wit is that of a man of the world. During the vacancy in the abbey in 1182, he recounts how three times a week all the monks prostrated themselves in the choir and prayed that the Lord would grant them a suitable pastor, adding that there were some, who had they known who was to be abbot, would not have prayed so hard![29]

It may, therefore, be true that we are getting a one-sided picture of the black monks in their own narratives, which emphasises their materialistic side and leaves out of account the attitudes of the more religious majority. All the same, as the late Karl Leyser once pointed out to me, it would not be without significance for the nature of modern colleges if they consistently left their histories to be written by their bursars. We cannot judge the impact that their prayers and meditations had on society, but we can see what a huge impact the black-monk pursuit of their material interests had on the legal and economic development of the twelfth century.

Black-monk shrines

It was an impact also on the mental and physical health of society. This impact, in so far as we can observe it, was made above all through the black-monk cult of saints' relics and shrines. In England the rise in such cults had much to do with the conditions of the Norman Conquest, when English saints whose relics a monastery had were often seen, not least by Norman abbots, as protectors of its landed possessions and judicial rights. We have already met a striking example of this with the cult of St Etheldreda's relics at Ely (pp. 40–4). Another example is Abbot Walter of Evesham, formerly a monk of Caen in Normandy. He was not at first impressed by the cult of, to him, such obscure saints as Egwin and Wistan. But he was won over, seeing on which side his bread was buttered, and built a new shrine for them. Miracles were associated with it, and grateful patients contributed to the building of his new abbey church.[30] What some English saints needed to impress the new Norman church rulers with their claims to veneration were finer written hagiographies. Some monasteries employed a hagiographical expert in this kind of thing from Flanders, Goscelin of St Bertin. Goscelin specialised in writing up, in grandiloquent Latin, the lives of saints about whom hardly any facts were known.[31]

It should be said at once, however, that black-monk hagiography had not only to do with championing rights and possessions. It had also to do with articulating a sense of religious continuity in Britain. It was like the sense in Pope Gregory the Great's *Dialogues*, a book much read in twelfth-century English monasteries, that the sanctity and miracle-working powers of the sixth-century Italian Holy Men were still a force in the Italy of the 590s. For instance, the fifth book of William of Malmesbury's *Gesta Pontificum* (c. 1125) is devoted to a Life of St Aldhelm, the learned seventh-century Abbot of Malmesbury. A strong element of this is championing Malmesbury property rights by stressing *places* associated with Aldhelm. Yet a major theme running through the first four books is the apostolic succession in English bishoprics up to his own time. In this he thought of himself as a successor to the Venerable Bede, who in his *Ecclesiastical History of the English People* (731) attempted the same thing up to *his* own time.[32] Thus, in the hands of a great historian, could broad and local concerns arise from each other.

The biggest spate of miracle literature connected to mainly black-monk shrines occurred in the 1170s and 1180s, probably stimulated by the miracle-working shrine of Thomas Becket at Canterbury and the huge collections of miracle narratives associated with it, which were soon compiled. As we shall see more fully in a moment, so much can be learned of twelfth-century social history from such narratives that that fact in itself shows up the social impact of such shrines. For instance, the number of priests involved in hearing the confessions of the cured (repentance for sins was in itself an important basis for many a healing), or in directing them to a shrine in the first place, is eloquent testimony to the rise in influence of parish priests.[33] The kinds of illnesses cured can be seen, sometimes, as exactly what one might expect under the stress of mounting economic competition, such as insomnia or constipation.[34] Occasionally miracles of punishment light up the economic competition itself; one Geoffrey of Linby, a cutler, lost the use of two fingers by working on the feast of St Peter's Chair. He received a miraculous cure when he repented and a few months later made a pilgrimage to Canterbury.[35] Incidentally, it should be noted that one of the driving forces of sabbatarianism, going a long way back in history, was to prevent some people taking an economic advantage while others were celebrating a festival or holiday. Although women are not in the majority as the subjects of Becket's miracles, they figure notably, e.g. in problems of childbirth; but there is at least one very interesting economic miracle concerning a woman. Women in general seem not to have had a bad reputation for administration. But this particular woman went one better.[36] Thomas Becket, from his shrine, was said to have helped the wife of Ralph of Hadfield to get her beer to ferment.[37]

One element in many miracle stories which is particularly suggestive of the social impact of the saints' shrines is the ease with which crowds form when there is a cure, especially of someone described as suffering from madness. There seem to be crowds as ever ready to form as they were around the living Holy Men of the fifth and sixth century East Mediterranean, as described by Peter Brown.[38] In the miracles of St Godric's shrine, a crowd is mentioned at the cure of a mad woman, who explained to all present how her (spirit) 'possession' had occurred in the first place. At the shrine of St William of Norwich also a crowd had assembled when the cure of a madman was effected.[39] Examples could be multiplied (as also for other kinds of cure). It was almost as if a crowd were sometimes needed to validate a cure, as if their acceptance of a cure was what made it a cure in the eyes of that society. One is reminded of those rituals of healing in Nigeria which express 'the willingness on the part of the community to accept back one of its members who has had an episode of mental illness'.[40] One could imagine here that that willingness was itself part of the cure, and that some social spadework had already been done behind the scenes before that willingness was expressed ritually. This kind of miracle, one might almost call it a consensus miracle, helps one to understand what Peter Brown means by saying that a society shows its own values in what it accepts as a cure.

It could be represented that the whole business of shrines and miracles had a downside. At the very worst it could all be seen as a kind of financial exploitation of the credulous by the custodian communities of the shrines though there is little evidence for contemporaries thinking that way. Or it could be thought to take people's focus away from the sacramental heartland of the Christian religion, especially the Eucharist, and onto the peripheral – away from Christ and onto the saints. I cannot see this, either, as a strong objection in practice. But there was a clear upside also. It helped people in large numbers to cope with illness, misfortune, and guilt. On the subject of guilt, it is interesting how often a cure is recorded as happening in connection with a previous confession of sins to a priest; like a woman who had been in agony for two days in a Durham hospital, confessed her secret sins to a priest, and was then cured at St Godric's shrine;[41] or like Ida, the wife of Eustace, moneyer of Norwich, who made her confession to a priest, was laid down near the shrine of St William, screamed out in pain, and was then cured;[42] or like the father at Canterbury who was careful to confess his own sins in order to achieve the cure of his seven-year-old daughter.[43] Would that we could recover the whole human stories behind such bald narrations! But they suggest that for these people, and probably many others unseen, the assuaging of guilt, whether justified guilt or not, was an element of the cure itself. Some of the guilt was very justified. Richard, son of Eilnold, was cured of his lameness at Canterbury. His ailment was said to have been a punishment for his cruelty to a poor woman who cursed him 34 years earlier during the civil wars of Stephen's reign, for ruining the harvest in her field.[44] In seventeenth-century England, this was just the kind of woman who would have been accused of witchcraft. Keith Thomas has shown how at that time accusations of witchcraft were characteristically levelled by men and women, when illness or misfortune hit them, against poorer women whom they had refused to help and who had cursed them and made them feel guilty.[45]

Many cures at black-monk shrines have the look of people who would have recovered anyhow and whose cure had been effected by nothing more than the medieval equivalent of a modern placebo, whether by drinking water connected to the shrine or lying near it. We moderns need not rise too superior to this kind of thing. How many of us go to the doctor, receive some authoritative-sounding pronouncement about what we have got, are prescribed some pink-coloured medicine or soothing cream, and start to feel better fairly quickly? One important difference between us and our medieval forebears, however, is in the nature of the placebo. It is a commonplace to say that in the twelfth century people strongly felt that the supernatural power of the heavenly saints was principally located where their physical remains lay upon earth. Thus people who approached

a saint's shrine had the sense that they were in contact with the awesome-
ness of the holy. People felt in the vicinity of saints' shrines, and even
about objects that had touched them, something of that holiness which
characterised the holiest spaces in the Temple as expressed in the Old
Testament book of Leviticus. Very few people today have an idea that
contact with the holy is going to be an element of their cure when they
enter a doctor's surgery!

We must descend, however, from the sublime to the practical in this
matter of cures. If we take the Miracles of the Hand of St James, the great
relic and shrine of an apostle at Reading Abbey, as an example, we can see
that many of the sick arrived at Reading in the crisis of their illness. A
woman of Earley, 'swollen with dropsy', started writhing on the pres-
bytery floor as the monks began Matins, and vomited all night. A daughter
of a Sussex fisherman coughed up blood before the altar of St Mary
Magdalen. A knight called Robert of Stanford came suffering from fever,
and vomited again and again. Of another knight, Ralph Gibuin, there is a
similar tale.[46] One can see from this that the monks of Reading or their
servants might have had to spend some time mopping up after miracles,
and that a good deal of practical care of sufferers was involved. Some of
that care was after-care. Most black-monk monasteries with shrines had
hospitals for the care of the sick connected to them, or indeed founded by
themselves, where sufferers could be received beforehand or convalesce
after their 'cure'. There was less immediate magic in all this than one might
sometimes suppose. A certain female shepherd from Essex, for example,
came to Reading in a hysterical state, and it is explicitly stated that her
recovery took some time at Reading.[47] At Canterbury, a woman called
Ulviva had been 'the warden of a certain hospice' ministering to the poor
and pilgrims (hospitals were not exclusively for the sick at that time), as
well as to 'lepers', before she transferred to the life of an anchorite.[48] One
Canterbury miracle concerned a concubine of a priest who had done much
to help the poor (including surely the sick), a touching reminder of the
goodness and pastoral care of some women illegally attached to priests.
The priest had a vision at Mass after her death that she had received mercy
and at the prompting of the martyr reformed his own way of life.[49]

In the care of sufferers – and we should not assume that this care was
accorded only to the miraculously healed, any more than the medical care
at present-day Lourdes is – there was clearly an element of positivist
medicine. Not only did Canterbury have a good medical library,[50] but one
reason why Becket was said to be able to cure different types of leprosy
was perhaps because there were good diagnosticians at the Leper Hospital

of Harbledown just outside Canterbury.[51] Leprosy was a particularly grievous affliction in this period, and it would be going too far to say that twelfth-century doctors blithely called any skin disease leprosy without discrimination.[52] The Becket miracles even distinguish one kind of leprosy from another; Becket cured not only *tryriam leoninam*, but also elephantitis, and *vulpinam*.[53] One has to remember that miracle-healing shrines were up to a point in competition with each other. Every miracle collection has stories of those who sought healing at other shrines but none did the trick until they arrived at the writers' own shrine. Thus there was every inducement to the custodians of a shrine to back up a miraculous cure with their own practical medical care.

Shrines and their communities

The shrines of black-monk monasteries helped to develop urban and shire communities and their identity. Our understanding of how this happened has been considerably advanced in an important book by Simon Yarrow. It studies the miracle narratives, mainly narratives of cures, which were connected to these shrines. First of all these narratives were not 'popular culture', for their meanings and significances were constructed by élites, in particular by the monasteries who were the custodians of the shrines in their churches. Yarrow sees these narratives, telling the rituals of often very public and dramatic healings, and themselves told in a ritualistic way, as representing a kind of negotiation between a monastery and the community (of all social classes) which frequented the shrine. It was a 'negotiation' which achieved 'a shared sense of Christian identity', while the very process of 'negotiation' helped to foster social cohesion in town and shire. The word 'negotiation' here is of course a metaphor, but it seems a very fruitful metaphor to represent the idea that it took a consensus between a monastery and a wider public to develop a successful shrine and to create narratives which expressed the consensus of values.[54] For many of these tales were moral tales. And as Peter Brown has said, it is not why people sought cures but what kind of cure satisfied them which is important. 'The history of what constitutes a cure in a given society', he writes, 'is a history of that society's values.'[55] There is an implication here that who is thought worthy of a cure and who is not, and when a person is not thought worthy of a cure and when he or she is, is also a sign of the values of a society.

In his book, Yarrow has made several fine case studies. One is the shrine of Little St William at the black-monk cathedral priory of Norwich. The boy saint, William, was murdered in Norwich in 1144, and the whole case was framed up as a Jewish ritual killing. The origin of the cult and many of the narratives in Thomas of Monmouth's *Life and Miracles of St William of Norwich* (Thomas was himself a monk of Norwich) was strongly anti-Jewish in character. Thomas tells with relish the story, mercifully not represented as a miracle, of a Norfolk knight, Simon de Novers, whose squires, when he got into difficulty to repay a loan from a Jew, murdered his Jewish creditor. We take this Norwich example, in part at least because the anti-semitic bigotry about it shows that achieving social cohesion was not all sweetness and light and could be at the cost of social exclusion.

As money-lenders and money-changers for foreign merchants, the Jews of Norwich, some 200 of them living in Norwich by the 1140s, offered great opportunities to the burgeoning Christian commercial establishment of the city. But they also presented a threat to it. Being under the direct protection of the king and having to meet his heavy financial demands, doubtless made the Jews sharp towards their debtors. Indeed there is a suggestion that the initial *opposition* to the cult of St William, within both the cathedral priory and the city, was due to nervousness about the priory's and city's relationship to the king if they went ahead with something so blatantly anti-Jewish.[56] The opposition was overcome, however, by the superior 'narrative' powers of the cult's promoters! Furthermore, the Jews' superior literacy and numeracy, 'undermined the very grounds upon which the Christian clerical élites were building their own claims to an exclusive status within Christian society'.[57] Both parish priests and women played important roles in advancing the cult in their local communities, as Yarrow has shown.[58] There is also a geographical point about the cult and its development. It was much more a Norfolk and particularly Norwich cult than an overall East Anglian one encompassing the whole diocese of Norwich. Over ten times the number of pilgrims are recorded as coming to the shrine from Norfolk as from Suffolk locations. In Suffolk the shrine of St Edmund at Bury St Edmunds provided a rival attraction.[59]

Altogether, the shrine of Little St William provided a support system of the Norwich Christian economic establishment and its region. Cures were effected there for the likes of a daughter of the baronial Reginald de Warenne, a son of Robert Gresley, members of the Norfolk gentry, a son of a Yarmouth fisherman, the daughter of Eustace the Norwich moneyer as well as his wife after she had made her confession to a priest, the son of the monks' tailor, and the wife of their cook. Thus did it play its part in the social cohesion of Norfolk.[60] St William sustained the health of the Christian urban and shire community.

It should not be imagined that monks and community faced each other across the table, so to speak, as if they were two different sets of personnel, like management and workforce. The Priory itself must have been full of the friends and relatives of the wider community served by the shrine. The snatches of evidence we can by chance glean from Thomas of Monmouth's *Life and Miracles* are enough to hint at this. Peter Peverell, a Norwich monk who had been a chamberlain of Henry I, belonged to an important knightly family in Norfolk. Richard de Ferrers, who became Prior of Norwich, was of a Norfolk baronial family. William himself had been apprenticed to the skinners; his brother, Robert, subsequently became a monk of Norwich and led the accusations against the Jews. Ironically the Jews had particularly entrusted to William the repair of their best clothes. This could have been an occasion for social envy by William's family, as well as suggesting how the storm of the 1140s could have arisen suddenly out of relative peace. The cure of Hildebrand, a well-known man of Norwich, describes him as kinsman of Paul, monk of Norwich.[61]

We wrote in an earlier chapter about Ely Abbey orchestrating public opinion in Cambridgeshire around their shrine of St Etheldreda and against baronial tormentors of the abbey and their officials. The monks of Norwich were in a similar position to focus attention on their shrine and to orchestrate public opinion in the city and the shire against the Jews. It was not only their shrine, but also, as Yarrow has shown, their central importance to the economy of the region, that put them in this position. If Norwich was a negotiating community, it was also an orchestrated one.

A study of Susan Ridyard of the life and miracles of Godric of Finchale, a hermit near Durham who died in 1170, shows another way in which a Benedictine cathedral monastery might act as an agent of social cohesion in a region. Godric led his ascetic life on the bank of the River Wear under what one might call the sponsorship of the Durham church. It was a Durham monk, Reginald, who composed the *Life and Miracles*. It was very common for black-monk monasteries to have close relationships with such satellite hermits, more so than for Cistercians, who perhaps thought themselves sufficiently ascetic already. With his growing reputation for sanctity, Godric attracted many visitors seeking counsel and guidance, and these were 'screened' beforehand by the priors of Durham. Only those who carried a wooden cross as a token of the prior's permission could visit him.[62] So in a sense Godric was acting with the monastery's authority. We must remember that whereas the miracles recorded at William of Norwich's shrine were those of a dead saint, and were primarily miracles of healing, those of Godric recorded by Reginald of Durham were, while Godric was alive, the miracles of a living saint, and were many of them miracles of insight into his visitors' lives, often at a crisis in them.

One intriguing aspect of Godric's relations with those he counselled was that he seemed through them to have become the centre of a whole social network. This is well brought out by Ridyard who writes that, 'many of these relationships were long-lasting, born of or sustained in long periods of normality, though finding their most dramatic expression in circumstances of crisis': like the knight already well known to Godric, who sought his prayers when facing an important lawsuit; or like the citizen of Durham with whom Godric had close and affectionate ties.[63] Godric was welcoming and hospitable to his visitors and clearly had a gift of friendship,[64] something, as we have seen, so much the secret of Henry I's success and Thomas Becket's failure. Women valued Godric's friendship as much as men did, and far from there being any whisper of impropriety in this, he can be seen as one who upheld the values of marriage and good familial relationships.[65] When after his death his hermitage at Finchale became a priory dependent on Durham and his shrine became a resort of pilgrims there, women pilgrims, mostly in search of healing outnumbered men by two to one, a proportion only matched by the Miracles of St Frideswide, the Augustinian house in Oxford.

The monks of Durham appear to have regarded themselves as propagators and upholders of Christian moral standards in the diocese of which they were the cathedral establishment. And they regarded Godric as one of their most important agents in this mission, to judge by their encouragement and control of his visitors. Ridyard, again, calls the Durham monks 'impresarios, who helped to create and maintain Godric's reputation as a living saint'.[66] It is a paradox that a self-professed hermit should occupy, however informally, such a position. But unless we take this sort of paradox on board, we shall not be able fully to understand the relationship of religion to society in the twelfth century. It will help us to appreciate why at the time of his death in 1169, so hard-bitten an administrator as Nigel, Bishop of Ely, was supporting by his alms six hermits in his diocese.[67] Over in Germany at the same time, the Rhineland mystic, Hildegard of Bingen, exercised an extraordinary, informal moral authority over churchmen. We can see it from her correspondence.[68] We have no surviving correspondence of Godric, and see his authority only from intimations of his conversation. Hildegard's fame was based on the wonderful account of her visions; Godric's more local fame was based on his general reputation for sanctity and asceticism.

Kings and black-monk shrines

So far in this chapter, the reader may be thinking, we have had a lot about religion and society but not much about religion and politics; although any factor which helped to develop a sense of shire or urban community, as shrines did, can hardly be called unpolitical. But shrines and saints' cults could indeed be important for kings in their rule. Reading Abbey, for instance, whose great shrine/relic was the Hand of St James, almost certainly originally received this prize relic from Henry I around the time he founded the Abbey in 1125. It appears to have been a relic of the imperial treasury and to have come to England *via* Henry I's daughter, Matilda, after her husband the Emperor Henry V died – in 1125. As an imperial relic, the Emperor Frederick Barbarossa wanted it back and sent envoys to the Northampton court of Henry I's grandson, Henry II, in 1157 to ask for it back. Henry II refused the request and gave the Emperor instead, as a present, a splendid marquee (Northampton was a notable centre of tent-making at that time.)[69] Why was Henry so anxious to keep the relic? Because, being far from established in his kingship after only two-and-a-half years, and having lost the revenues of many of his royal manors, which were in the hands of those who had supported him against King Stephen, he was in a weak position. That being so, he needed every ounce of the sacrality which could enhance the mystique of his rule, and veneration by kings of important relics at great abbeys, associating themselves with the rituals of such cults, was one way of enhancing their sacrality. I do not say that a king necessarily cut a more impressive figure in the eyes of his aristocracy by such means. But if he cut a more impressive figure in his own eyes, that was already a significant gain in a vital area for rule – his own self-confidence.

Having retained the relic, Henry II did not relax in his veneration of it. In the *Miracles of the Hand of St James*, a collection of narratives written up around the end of his reign, we see Abbot Roger of Reading (1158–65), *having just taken the Hand to the king for his veneration* (possibly around the time of the outbreak of the Becket Conflict when the king needed sacrality even more), taking it out to the village of Bucklebury (Berkshire) where a plague had broken out amongst the livestock, and blessing the fields with it. We have to envisage here a portable reliquary perhaps in the shape of a hand cast in gold – such reliquaries were already known on the Continent – which could be taken from and replaced on a fixed shrine-base in the abbey church. At another point, we see two monks of Reading bringing the relic to the king when he was about to cross the Channel and wanted the Apostle's blessing before he put to sea. Perhaps most remarkable of all was not something directly connected to veneration of the relic, but which shows up the king's general devotion to Saint James, and which served him well at a critical moment in the Great Rebellion of 1173. Matthew, Count of Boulogne, and brother of Count Philip of Flanders, says *The Miracles*, tried to entice Henry to attack the castle of Driencourt on the Feast of St James (July 25), but the king refused to take up arms on that day. Matthew went ahead, got a stray arrow in his knee, and died of the wound soon after. It was a turning-point in the fighting in Normandy.[70]

The king benefited in his sacrality not only from his veneration of Reading's relic, but also from the whole reinforcement of his links to an important royal abbey. The abbey gained prestige from that too. No wonder that the author of the *Miracles* was keen to record the curing of the livestock plague at Bucklebury with the relic immediately after the Abbot had taken it to the king. It was a story that killed two birds with one stone. It pointed up the intimate connection between abbey and king on the one hand, and the help that the abbey could be to the community in its region on the other. And it was surely one of those little things, probably many but mostly unseen by us now, that all helped to carry the idea of royal sacrality deep into the twelfth-century countryside (see p. 107 above) whatever disadvantages it might also have suffered from kingly rule.

There was one shrine and one cult even more important to Henry II than the Hand of St James, and that was the cult of Edward the Confessor at Westminster Abbey. Edward had been a king and, more than that, was the son of the marriage between Ethelred II and Emma which had first joined the English kingship and the Norman duchy together dynastically. He was canonised in 1161, also in the earlier years of Henry II's reign. That was due to the joint efforts of Henry II and Abbot Lawrence of Westminster – again the collaboration in a cult between king and an abbey which had the shrine, this time an abbey at a palace already becoming the heart of royal government. In connection with the canonisation, Ailred of Rievaulx, a relative of Abbot Lawrence, wrote a life of Edward the Confessor. Ailred's prologue, attributed the canonisation to Henry II's support and authority. The actual translation of the saint's relics to a new and grander shrine took place only on 13 October 1163, after Henry returned from a four-year absence abroad.[71] That date became the saint's festival. We have already seen how offensive it was to the king that one year later in 1164 Becket would not celebrate the Mass of Edward the Confessor on that day but opted instead for a votive Mass of the Holy Spirit (pp. 86–7).

King John did not 'do' sacrality with the zest of Henry II, but even to him saints' cults were not irrelevant. Immediately after his coronation in 1199, neglecting all his other business, he went at once to the shrine of St Edmund at Bury St Edmunds according to a vow he had made. Edmund also was an English king, a king of East Anglia killed by the Danes in the ninth century, and venerated as a martyr. As a saintly king he had been of interest to Henry I, John's great grandfather. Because of John's meanness, however, the Bury monks were not pleased with his visit. Jocelin of Brakelond wrote:

We believed that he would make a big offering. He offered just one silk cloth, which his servants had borrowed from our Sacrist and have not yet paid for. He received our festive and expensive hospitality, and when he left he gave nothing at all for the honour and benefit of the Saint besides 13 pence which he offered at Mass on the day of his departure.[72]

After that it is difficult to imagine Saint Edmund bestirring himself much on behalf of King John, albeit that East Anglia would not subsequently be the main source of his troubles. But although his visit proved counter-productive, the interesting point for our present purposes is that he thought it worthwhile to make the visit in the first place.

The Cistercians

Cistercian economy and religion

The Cistercians took their name from Citeaux in Burgundy, where their first monastery was founded in 1098 as a reforming break-away from the black-monk monastery of Molesmes. The movement, if it could yet be called that after 14 years, received a great boost when the minor Burgundian aristocrat, Bernard, joined Citeaux with 30 companions (so it was said) in 1112. Bernard was a man of great charm and white-heat spirituality as well as superb rhetoric, all of which one can see from his writings. He was made Abbot of Clairvaux, one of Citeaux's earliest daughter-houses, in 1115, only three years after joining Citeaux. He became the most influential Cistercian in Europe in the second quarter of the twelfth century. During the latter part of Henry I's reign and Stephen's, the Cistercian movement spread like wildfire in England and Wales, mainly from Clairvaux.[73]

The Cistercians were in many ways a reaction to the black monks. They wanted a less elaborate liturgy, in order to be able to cultivate a more interior religion. They wanted to find God in their own souls, through a life of personal prayer and meditation. For the same reason they were against being in towns and in the trammels of worldly administration. They wanted to restore to Benedictine life – for they adamantly sought to live by the *Rule of St Benedict* – the importance that the *Rule* gave to manual labour as well as to liturgy. And out in their fields or woods, they found they could more easily pray and meditate. They felt close to nature there, and they cared about nature much more than the black monks did.[74] They had a much stronger sense of their vocation than black monks had. That does not mean that they were always better monks. Many black monks surely had a strong sense of the religious aims of their monastic life, as Orderic Vitalis had in the Norman monastery of St Evroult. But vocation was central to the whole Cistercian way of life, in a way that was not the case with the black monks. They specially stressed the provision of the *Rule* which laid down a one-year probationary period, or novitiate, before men could be professed as monks. The Cistercians were the greatest buzzers of one of the greatest buzzwords of twelfth-century religious life – vocation.

The origin of this gigantic search for one's vocation in the twelfth century is found in a religious phenomenon at its height between about 1075 and 1150, a phenomenon which has been identified most clearly by Henrietta Leyser. Communities of men or women would go off into the wilderness, the *eremita* (i.e. to the countryside, especially of France), as groups of companions dedicated to living an ascetic and prayerful life together. They were the 'new hermits', living in the *eremita* but together. These were not people seeking to avoid living by a rule; exactly the opposite. They were seeking enlightenment about which rule they were called to live by. They were in search of their vocation in religious life. They retreated from the world, the better to return into the monastic world. Their motto might easily have been, *reculer pour mieux sauter* (draw back the better to jump forward). There were large numbers of such groups, described and discussed by Leyser. Many became Cistercians, and thus the Cistercian order was constantly fed by people in search of their vocation. Many became Augustinian Canons. Some became Cluniacs; the black monks could not be written off by those considering where their vocation lay.[75]

Before long the English and Welsh Cistercians had recruited large numbers of monks and lay-brothers (conversi) and accumulated many lands of all kinds. Some historians have represented this as an early decline from their original ideals of ascetic living, not to say poverty. But Cistercian asceticism, while it might have entailed plainer architecture, vestments and ecclesiastical paraphernalia, never in the first place renounced wealth or espoused poverty. Indeed the Cistercians believed in their vocation in this world as well as in the next. And they believed that they were called to material as well as spiritual self-improvement. They were expert engineers of mill-races, drains and sewers. Anybody who sees the brilliantly constructed mill-race at Fountains Abbey or the vaulted drains/sewers of Rievaulx Abbey, both twelfth century and both in Yorkshire, will appreciate this. If an emphasis on good drains may be considered one mark of the true humanist, then the Cistercians were amongst the Christian humanists of the twelfth century. Also their belief in people's capacity to rise through their own inner spiritual resources to union with God made them so.[76]

Even from where we have got so far, it will be seen that the Cistercians were the Protestants of the twelfth century. Everything we have said about them – the interiority of their religion, the stress on vocation to salvation and vocation in this world too, the saving of time in the over-elaborate liturgy in order to accumulate wealth by working in their fields, and much else besides, all fit perfectly to the Protestant Ethic as described most famously by Max Weber. The moral conditionality which they attached to the exercise of papal and episcopal authority, which made the Yorkshire Cistercians so keen to have a Cistercian Archbishop of York, Henry Murdac, in the 1140s, was part of this 'Protestantism'.

The Cistercians quickly gathered a large workforce for their lands – the lay-brothers or *conversi*. At Rievaulx, for instance, under Ailred of Rievaulx as abbot, there were said to be 140 monks and 500 lay brothers.[77] It has been rightly observed that the numbers of men of this order, working without wages or the possibility of marriage (though not having to worry about where their next meal was coming from, and living in dry stone-built accommodation) must be an indication of a considerable demographic rise in society.[78] The sizeable lay-brothers' ranges have left their mark on the archaeology or physical remains of many medieval Cistercian monasteries. But it is vital to note the difference between the labour force of the Cistercians, and that of the black monks, essentially the peasants on their manors. The Cistercian *conversi* had their own religious vocation, their own prayers to say throughout the day, and their own monastic garb. In other words, the Cistercians did not wish in principle to live off the labour of those who did not share their religious vocation.[79] The principle was often honoured in the breach rather than the holding; the Cistercians soon came to live partly by the labour of peasants who were their tenants rather than their brethren; or worse, they would wipe out villages and 'reduce them to granges', i.e. places worked by the labour of monks. But deplorable as breaches are, and widely criticised as the avarice of the late twelfth-century Cistercians was, these things do not negate the principle.

How was the distinction made between those who would become monks and those who would become lay brothers? So far as I know, the evidence hardly allows us to answer this question. Monks had to perform manual labour, though not so much as lay brothers, for they had their choir duties and also duties of reading and writing. But the answer must lie to a considerable extent in who had the education or capacity for learning necessary to be a choir monk. It seems not to have been a purely social distinction. For we learn in passing from the Life of Wulfric of Haselbury by John of Ford, that the priest Segar, who was not the parish priest of Haselbury Plucknett and who looks rather like one of the upper peasantry in the village, had four sons in the nearby Cistercian monastery of Ford (Devon), three of them monks but one a lay brother.[80]

The Cistercian monasteries soon made a massive impact on economic life throughout Britain. We have already mentioned that they were sheep farmers on a large scale, and much of their year's clip of wool was exported. Sheep-rearing was of particular importance to the Welsh Cistercians, with their large tracts of hilly land. But there was usually much more to it than sheep. This is what David Williams has to say about Strata Florida, one of the greatest of Welsh Cistercian monasteries to which we must return shortly:

Strata Florida had a particularly diversified economy: while oats was the chief crop on its lands, wheat was grown on its lowland properties in the Aeron and Severn valleys; it had inland pools which gave it trout and eels, and sea fisheries which rendered herrings; its mountain pastures were extremely extensive [re its huge production of wool], and it owned much of Tregaron Marsh, a noted source of peat; it also had a major lead mine at Cwmystwyth; as well as several corn mills, it owned two or three fulling mills, in a part of Wales where there was a significant production of cloth.[81]

Williams also points to a significant production of coal from the Scottish Cistercian monastery of Culross, founded some time before 1217.

There would be tensions between the black monks and white monks later, but one should not imagine that from the start all was controversy and confrontation. When Henry I founded Reading Abbey as a Cluniac monastery in 1125, it was laid down in its foundation that it should owe no knight service to the king and that its revenues should not be divided between abbot and monks.[82] Both these reduced considerably Reading's involvement with secular government. Knight service involved the raising of fighting men for the king's armies and the enfeoffing of knights on the abbey's lands; the division of revenues meant that every time there was a vacancy in the abbacy, royal administrators descended on the abbey to manage the abbot's revenues on the king's behalf, with frequent arguments, naturally. To remove the abbey from the world to that degree, therefore, was a step in the Cistercian direction, albeit the Cistercians did not arrive in England until four years later.

Again, when Prior Richard of the black monk monastery of St Mary's York, together with twelve other monks, seceded to establish the Cistercian abbey of Fountains in 1133, he at first assumed that the Cistercian-inspired reforms which he wanted – more silence, less dependence on tithes, monks not living outside the monastery on its estates – could all be achieved *within* St Mary's.[83] Only when he met opposition backed up by force from Abbot Geoffrey did the secession seem necessary. The secession was backed up by Archbishop Thurstan of York, who was anything but a scourge of black monks generally. Moreover, although there is a dramatic account of the secession from the late twelfth century, written down by Hugh of Kirkstall from the first-hand memory of a ninety-year-old monk, Serlo, (incorporating Thurstan's account of it in a letter to the Archbishop of Canterbury) we should not get over-excited about it. For its context was one of secession almost as a matter of course. St Mary's York itself was the result of a break-away from Whitby, Whitby from Jarrow, and Jarrow from Evesham. These earlier break-aways were inspired not by the existence of the Cistercians (they were too early for that) but by the reading of Bede's *Ecclesiastical History*.[84] They reflected constant aspirations to a more perfect monastic life, but with minimum criticism of the monasteries from which the breaks were made.

One has only to think of Ailred of Rievaulx writing his life of King Edward the Confessor at the request of his friend and relation, Abbot Lawrence of Westminster, to support the shrine of the saint-king there, to realise that this greatest of all twelfth-century English Cistercians showed less partisan spirit towards black monks than did St Bernard.

All the same, there was a profoundly different religious ethos between the two orders. It may be illustrated by comparing their ideas of the forgiveness of sin. This may seem a rather technical issue, but it is not at all so; for it is about how people's sense of guilt in that society was assuaged, and as we know from studies of other periods such as Keith Thomas's *Religion and the Decline of Magic*, on seventeenth-century England, that is no small matter for any society. The black-monk answer was that sins could best be forgiven through the intermediation of saints' shrines and pilgrimages to them. Here it is essential to appreciate that physical healing and relief of guilt were closely associated with each other in people's minds. But shrines and relics figure rather little in Cistercianism. The Cistercians were much less interested in outer works (as Luther might have called them), and much more interested in what went on inside the mind and the soul. Ailred of Rievaulx's Pastoral Prayer, for instance, addressed to Jesus, has this: 'I ask you that in virtue of the mystery of your sacred humanity, you forgive me my sins.' Not the physical presence of the saints, not external props, but Jesus recalled to the *mind*, was how sins were forgiven.[85]

The whole nature of Cistercian prayer was to be Christ-centred and based on the powers of the mind. Much of Ailred of Rievaulx's treatise, written for his sister, about how to be a recluse, is about the kind of prayer that she should practise, and his advice was that she should try to put herself in the shoes of those around Christ, particularly the women, and meditate on their experience. This, for instance, is the passage about the woman taken in adultery:

Let the woman taken in adultery occur to your memory, *and how Jesus had asked her what she had done.* Remember *how he wrote in the ground and said, 'let him among you who is without sin cast the first stone'. When he had frightened everyone with this saying, and expelled them from the Temple,* imagine *how he raised his eyes to her and offered her forgiveness in a gentle and sweet voice.* Think *how he sighed, and with tears in his eyes, said, 'Has no one condemned you? Neither will I.'*[86]

This is all about what should go on in the mind, not about external words or forms. As we mentioned earlier this kind of prayer was not alien to black monks, but it is not nearly so articulated as with the Cistercians, nor did their whole milieu encourage its practice so much. In the early 1140s, when Ailred was novice-master of Rievaulx, he wrote a treatise on the spiritual life called *The Mirror of Love (Speculum Caritatis)* – and characteristically black-monk literature emanated from material administrators, Cistercian literature from novice masters with responsibility for moulding souls. In this book Ailred wrote of art as food for wandering eyes. The Cistercians made a great principle of the *custodia oculorum*, the control of the eyes, for the reason that all attention ought to be on the inner resources of the soul. 'What use is there for all the external pomps and shows that others love, to the man who has found Jesus's company within his own soul?' What Ailred meant by external pomps was fine hangings, marble pavements, murals that depict ancient history or even scenes from Holy Scripture, blazes of candles, glittering vessels of gold, in short the whole range of art that would please the eye and serve the liturgy and its setting in

a black-monk church. No, we must learn to find the hidden sweetness that
is signified in the words – and here comes a favourite citation of the
Cistercians – 'all the glory of the king's daughter is within' (Psalm 45,14).
But then he adds, in a moment of toleration which it would be hard to
find in St Bernard and which clearly has the black monks in mind, 'we
should examine our lives and know what we are, without having to judge
ourselves by comparison with others' (based on Galatians 6,4).[87] When we
read Walter Daniel's *Life of Ailred*, we can see that even Ailred's rule of
his monks was based on his power of mind over them, and was expressed
in his visions and prophecies about them, rather than on any enforcement
of regulations.[88]

The Cistercians were altogether keen on visions and vision literature.
Most of that will come up again shortly, but this is perhaps the place for a
particular observation about it. The idea of the bodily assumption of Mary
into heaven (as distinct from a purely spiritual assumption) took off in the
West as a result of a series of visions of Elizabeth of Schönau, a Rhineland
mystic, in the 1150s, which were written down by her brother in the 1160s.
It was above all the Cistercians who were responsible for spreading the
texts of these visions in England in the 1170s, and they spread rapidly.[89]
This in itself is interesting. The Cistercians were the great proponents of
an interiority of religion, and the less one stresses external or priestly mediation in reaching God (though the Cistercians did not of course go to the
extent of denying the necessity for priestly mediation through the sacraments, not being heretics), and the more one stresses the reaching of God
through the human powers of mind and soul, the less relevant does gender
become to the validity of spiritual experience. Thus we have in the bodily
assumption of Mary the spectacle of English Cistercian monks developing
a Christian doctrine by relying on the spiritual experiences of a woman.
The Cistercians were to a man opposed in twelfth-century England to the
idea of the Immaculate Conception of Mary, which as we pointed out was
propagated by a group of black monks; but, unlike some black monks, they
were enthusiasts for the idea of her bodily assumption. Why was that? Surely
the basic reason was that the propagation of the Immaculate Conception
primarily at that time was motivated by black-monk liturgical aims, while
the bodily Assumption arose from the spiritual experience of visions.

The Cistercians had a bad press in the late twelfth century, especially
for their avarice. But they themselves joined in the criticism of their order.
John Abbot of Ford, the biographer of Wulfric of Haselbury, in his *magnum
opus* on the *Song of Songs* (c. 1200), wrote of Cistercian abbots exhausting
their energies in material affairs, riding splendid horses and wearing fine

cloaks on their travels, engaging in too much litigation and speculation in land.[90] These criticisms were not of course exactly the criticisms that were becoming widespread against the Angevin kings in the decades before Magna Carta, but they were cognate to them: the oppressiveness and unpredictability of the royal itinerary, the corruptions and venality of royal justice, the unreasonable distraint on people's lands. If the black monks made their best contribution to society in assuaging of guilt and healing, the Cistercians, more interested in what went on in people's minds, gave to society ideas, a high moral tone, criticism of the exercise of power (they were supporters of Becket, and opponents of John), self-criticism, insistence on the rational contra the ritualistic (or indeed mumbo jumbo) in religion. Their contribution to Magna Carta was not for the most part direct, but they contributed to the intellectual and political climate which made it possible.

The Cistercians and political life

It will be noticed that we have suddenly plunged into politics. Therefore I here make three points about the lead-up to Magna Carta in 1215, the longest of the three concerning the Cistercians and politics. The first concerns money; the second the growing importance of the knightly classes and (what we have already touched upon) the upper peasants; and the third Cistercian connections to knights and their talk.

Money

In the past historians were often tempted to blame John's political problems on his personality – his temper tantrums, his sexual licence, and his effeminacy (he liked jewellery and took baths). But money had quite as much to do with it as personality. If Magna Carta marks a step on the way to English constitutional monarchy as against anything like French absolutism, then shortage of money played a large part in Magna Carta, because it forced the Angevin kings into oppressive taxation and deceitful ruses to raise it. Richard I had to finance the Third Crusade, which he led and which was hugely expensive, quite apart from the ransom for him which had to be paid to the Emperor Henry VI after he was captured on his way back. But at least his government in England was not run by foreign favourites which so exacerbated in people's eyes the evils of Angevin administration under John. John lost Normandy in 1204 to King Philip Augustus of France, and fighting to recover it when every expedition to do so had to go by sea to the South of France, was a lot more costly than holding on to it in the first place. It has been argued that the whole period 1180 to 1220 was one of inflation which put added strain on royal finance.[91] But whatever the case, John's own expeditions to Poitou in the early thirteenth century had the effect of pushing up agrarian prices mightily.

The loss of Normandy also had the effect of reducing the king's income and limiting his theatre of travel and activity. So John had nowhere to go except to travel round England, screwing more and more money out of justice and out of all classes of society by other nefarious means. It is sometimes thought that medieval people because they accepted the rightness of kingship, liked to see their king. Usually they did not. The principle that G.K. Chesterton expressed in relation to the commercial traveller was in operation here: the commercial traveller goes to see other people because they don't want to come and see him! Had it not been for the papal interdict of 1209 to 1213, which gave John the excuse to draw the revenues of large numbers of bishoprics and abbacies for several years, his parlous finances could have had the effect of bringing Magna Carta forward by many years.

Growing importance of the knightly and upper peasant classes

Sally Harvey has long since made clear how the economic and social status of such people, as a group, rose during the twelfth century.[92] These were the very people who formed the principal market, so to speak, of the shrines which we were speaking of earlier, and the very people at whom the new legal procedures under Henry II were mostly directed. They were the people making a concerted effort as they rose to secure their health and property. Henry II's legal reforms were vital in enabling these classes of people to articulate their growing political power in the localities, and in the whole development of shires and even hundreds, as political communities. They did this particularly because they all involved the use of juries. Twelve men at a time, taken from a limited but influential pool of non-baronial men in a locality, who had numerous opportunities to talk with and get to know each other, and that in circumstances when they were at the same time receiving quite a training for themselves in law and administration, in what was reasonable and what was not.[93] How large these pools of men were, and who constituted them, is a subject on which (so far as I know) not much work has yet been done, but the surviving evidence should make it possible from around 1200 onwards.[94] What is certain is that around 1200, and indeed earlier, the English shires must have been abuzz with talk.

We can sometimes capture the effects of such talk. Between 1207 and 1209 Peter de Brus, a powerful northern baron, issued a charter to the knights and free tenants of Cleveland in the Wapentake (a subdivision of a shire equivalent to a hundred) of Langbargh (North Yorkshire). In it, he promised that they would not be amerced (i.e. fined) beyond their means, what John granted by Clause 20 of Magna Carta, and that they would not be prosecuted on the unsupported charge of a bailiff but only by the legitimate public prosecutor, in effect the same as Clause 38 of Magna Carta.[95] Peter de Brus was one of the barons of Magna Carta at Runnymede in 1215. So we might almost say that a group of North Yorkshire gentlemen formulated Clauses 20 and 38. For it is obvious that it was not Peter de Brus who drafted the provisions of the Cleveland Charter in a sudden fit of philanthropy, but the knights and free tenants who wrung the concessions out of him, after discussing how to put a stop to the bad legal practices of his courts. It is a well-known fact that although Magna Carta is in the form of a privilege granted by John to his barons, there was much pressure on the barons from below, particularly from the knights. It should always be remembered that the penultimate clause of Magna Carta orders that all the liberties granted by the king to his barons, must be observed by barons towards *their* men.[96] When one looks at Magna Carta closely, while some of its clauses lay down big principles of taxation and justice, many others represent a tissue of particular local grievances. The people of Lincolnshire may not have cared much about fish-weirs on the River Thames, but they mattered to the citizens of Oxford whose trade was based on navigation of that river.[97] The citizens of Oxford may not have experienced many problems over the farms of the shires (i.e. supposedly fixed money renders to the king), but the people of Lincolnshire had,[98] and that is why trithings are mentioned in Clause 25. Only two shires had this kind of tripartite subdivision, Yorkshire and Lincolnshire.

Incidentally, Peter de Brus also granted in his Cleveland Charter that the Chief Sergeant of the Wapentake should have no more than three horses and three mounted sergeants under him.[99] This is not reflected in any clause of Magna Carta, but it is shades of John of Ford's criticism of Cistercian abbots who rode around with showy and oppressive troupes of mounted horsemen.

Cistercian connections to knights and their talk

The essence of the question about the Cistercian impact on politics is where they fit into the talk of the shires and hundreds. A historian can

never feel entirely comfortable trying to reconstruct talk, because the subject is of its nature elusive, and he or she might be tempted to compensate
for the lack of evidence by imagining what ought to have been said. On
the other hand to avoid the subject altogether, particularly in the twelfth
century, might be to miss much of historical importance. In what follows
I hope not to go in my conclusions beyond what the evidence allows. There
is no doubt that the Cistercians had manifold connections with the knightly
and upper peasant classes. Bennett Hill showed that in Yorkshire – and
the picture does not look radically different elsewhere – whereas before
1154 the Cistercians had depended mainly on baronial benefactors, in the
Angevin period after 1154, their benefactors tended much more to be
knights.[100] His interest in this is in the dangerous economic obligations
incurred by the Cistercians because of this; mine in their many connections
with this developing and often critical political class in Angevin England.

There is a very important passage in Walter Daniel's *Life of Ailred* about
Ailred's connections with the outside world and the shire community while he
was still Abbot of Revesby, a Cistercian house in Lincolnshire (1143–47).[101]
First Walter says that the bishop (i.e. Alexander of Lincoln) ordered him to
preach to the clergy in their local synods, which he did, and to correct the
lives of the priests, which he did not omit to do. Already, therefore, we see
Ailred in the swim of Lincolnshire clerical life and talk. Walter Daniel goes
on to say that the bishop also ordered him to accept grants of land from
knights, and he obeyed, Walter adding that in those chaotic times if knights
did not give their lands to monks they might lose them altogether, and also
implying that some knights actually became monks themselves. How much
the Cistercians benefited in Stephen's reign from receiving lands with dis-
puted claims or which were actually fought over is itself a matter of argument
among historians. But what is plain from this passage is how far, even in
the 1140s, knightly society and Cistercian monasteries were becoming
intertwined with each other. And Walter Daniel, as a monk of Rievaulx,
must have had all this from the very conversational Ailred himself.

It is indeed likely that Cistercian monks were almost from the start
recruited from knightly and upper peasant families. So it was with the
women of the socially similar order of Sempringham (Lincolnshire),[102]
because patrons expected the order to find a place for members of their
families, knightly families not being excluded from the general demographic
rise of the twelfth century.

The Cistercian Abbot, John of Ford, was another inveterate conversationalist, and his *Life of Wulfric of Haselbury*, written in the 1180s, was in
large part a piece of oral history. This brings us to the Cistercians and the

upper peasantry. It may be that John was actually stimulated to write it by the four sons of Segar, formerly a priest who had lived in Haselbury Plucknett, sons whom we mentioned earlier as being monks at his own abbey of Ford. In any case his work took him deep into the village society of Haselbury and other West Country villages.

If the Cistercians wanted more silence than the black monks had, they must have used their remaining periods for talking effectively. The Cistercian chronicler Ralph of Coggeshall (Essex) relied heavily on the oral testimony of eye-witnesses: Hugh de Neville for Richard I's engagement with Saracens on the Third Crusade in 1191; Anselm the king's chaplain for Richard's capture by the Duke of Austria; Milo, abbot of a French Cistercian monastery and king's almoner for Richard's death; and a variety of informants for English affairs. In fact his oral evidence was better than his documentary.[103]

The Cistercians of the late twelfth and early thirteenth centuries were interested in history, written with an eye on contemporary affairs, and with a strong moralistic streak and a fascination for visions and apparitions. Many of their vision narratives were elicited by oral testimony. For example, included in Peter of Cornwall's celebrated *Liber Revelationum*, which black monk monasteries were interested in too, were eleven visions which he got from his friend Abbot Benedict of Stratford Langthorne (Essex). King John appointed Peter and Benedict in 1210 to visit Stephen Langton, Archbishop-Elect of Canterbury, to whom John had as yet to concede his temporalities. One of the visions concerned a lay brother who was a shepherd of the monastery, 'apostasised' and returned to the world, and then, having repented, served in the infirmary for the poor of the neighbourhood until he died.[104] We do not often get such evidence of good works of Cistercian monasteries towards the outside world. It was also one way of getting to know the talk of the neighbourhood.

The story of the knightly Owen's visit to 'St Patrick's Purgatory' was written up (1180–84) by the Cistercian, Henry of Saltrey. It is mainly about the middle realms between heaven and hell (Jacques Le Goff has shown that the Cistercians were among the greatest advocates of the idea of Purgatory). The way that Henry of Saltrey presented the vision was a learned way, based on Hugh of St Victor's book on the Sacraments, which itself owed much to Pope Gregory the Great's *Dialogues*. But as Carl Watkins has shown, the details of the narrative had passed through the hands of English clerics before they came to Henry, and they reveal something about the relation of lay beliefs or experiences to theology in the twelfth century.[105]

One of the most remarkable of vision texts, because of its direct political relevance, was written down by the Cistercian Ralph of Coggeshall, the same as the chronicler. He had the narrative from an Essex peasant called Thurkill. Amongst other things, Thurkill saw in torment a famous man, known throughout England for his eloquence and knowledge of the law, but who had 'subverted many judgments by accepting bribes', just the kind of thing that Magna Carta, Clause 40, ruled out of order when it promised that to no one would the king sell justice. We can identify this famous man. He was Osbert FitzHervey, brother of Chief Justiciar and Archbishop of Canterbury Hubert Walter, who was a royal justice from 1191 to his death in 1206.[106]

Another political vision was experienced this time by a knight, Roger of Asterby (Lincolnshire). St Peter and the Archangel Gabriel appeared to him while he was walking in his fields and told him to take seven commands to King Henry II, commands which corresponded closely to later clauses in Magna Carta, and one of them again about not selling justice. This story was picked up by Gerald of Wales on one of his journeys in Lincolnshire in the 1190s so it does not come from a Cistercian source.[107] But it had often occurred to me that had the records of Lincolnshire Cistercian monasteries from the twelfth century survived better, one might have found that Roger of Asterby had his connections to one of them. And now indeed Tim Crafter has turned up a connection between the Cistercian Abbey of Louth (Lincs) and Roger. It is admittedly a connection shown up by litigation about land between them around 1200, but the strongest links are often shown up by later litigation.[108] Sir James Holt has said about Roger, that although retailed by a cleric, 'Roger's commands catered for knightly rather than clerical interests; the proper audience for this story was the knights of the shire who bore the brunt of Angevin government.'[109] Stories like that of Roger's vision must certainly have helped to knit together the knightly community of a shire when faced with the corruptions and extortions of Angevin rule. This story might simply have been borne on the talk of the knightly men of Lincolnshire. But given Roger's connection to Louth, and the Cistercians' manifold links to knightly society at that time, and Cistercian criticism of Angevin rule, it is a strong possibility that one centre of radiation for the story was from a Cistercian monastery.

Ailred of Rievaulx himself was another inveterate conversationalist, and he seems to have known everyone to judge from what Walter Daniel says about his letters, the collection of which has alas! not survived in a single copy.[110] He must have known half the knighthood of Yorkshire, if one can assume where his monks were principally recruited from, and given increasingly the origins of Rievaulx's benefactions.[111] In short, he was not only the author of a remarkable treatise on friendship but also one of the great friends in the second half of the twelfth century himself.

In the course of his treatise on friendship, Ailred has a very striking passage on the necessity of friendship in marriage. He is speaking about Adam and Eve, and Eve being created from one of Adam's ribs:

It was beautiful that the second human being was taken from the side of the first, so that nature might teach that all are equal as collaterals [lit. as of each others' sides]. For in human affairs there is neither superior nor inferior, which is the characteristic of friendship. Thus from the beginning, nature impressed upon human minds the tendency to friendship and love [or charity].[112]

At first sight this might look very unexpected and exceptionally enlightened for the twelfth century. But it was not exceptional. What Ailred said here chimed in with all those canon lawyers who were stressing free choice of one's partner and the wrong of marriage by coercion. It chimed in also with those preachers who were exhorting husbands and wives to tender affection and to agreement in everything good, 'like a pair of eyes'. There was also more of a pre-twelfth-century background in Christian writing to the idea of friendship in marriage than one might think.[113] The trouble was that the Angevin government's treatment of marriage was at odds with this whole approach. The Angevins treated the marriage of women, or the licence for them to marry, as a financial asset. The more valuable the woman (in terms of wealth, age, fewness of children, etc.) the more the king's government could charge for the licence. Or it could offer the widows and daughters of the king's tenants-in-chief to low-born foreign favourites of the king in marriage, thus disparaging them socially but providing wealth to the king's creatures at no cost to himself. The same kind of thing was repeated lower in the social scale; weight was increasingly being given to the role of parents and guardians in the contracting of marriage. And so there was a growing tension between the rising expectation of emotional satisfaction in marriage on the one hand, and the cynical coercion of women into marriages on the other hand. That is one reason why there is evidence of so much fear of marriage amongst teenage girls in the second half of the twelfth century.[114]

There was deep resentment about this treatment of marriages by the Angevin kings. It boiled up in Magna Carta, Clause 6 of which was against coercion and social disparagement in marriage, and Clause 8 against forcing widows to re-marry. These were not amongst the purely local issues in

Magna Carta. But resentment had boiled up earlier. For example, in 1189–91 the citizens of Bristol felt it necessary to seek, and they obtained a liberty from Count John (later King John) that they, their sons, their daughters and their widows should be free to marry without the licences of their lords.[115] It is hard not to suppose that such resentment was fuelled by the kinds of things that Ailred and his like were saying, or that once again Cistercians were party to criticism of the Angevins. Whether Ailred's treatise on friendship was widely read is difficult to say. But it is all likely to be the other way round: that Ailred, a well-connected and much befriended monk, wrote such things in the first place, because he knew from his own participation in talk, clerical and lay, that how marriage was and how it ought to be, was constantly being discussed. Hence we seem to be getting yet another glimpse of the Cistercians and twelfth-century talk in Ailred.

The founding of Beaulieu Abbey (Hampshire)

This section of the chapter is a continuation of what has gone before on the Cistercians. Beaulieu Abbey was founded under the patronage of King John, at Faringdon (Berkshire) in 1203 and then again at Beaulieu in 1204. It was the first time that the Angevins had shown any favour to the Cistercians. The king paid large sums for its construction, and a large-scale construction it was, as can be seen from its ruins today.[116] It came about to mark a reconciliation between the Cistercians and the king. After John was crowned in 1199 their relations had begun on the worst possible footing. When John tried to recoup the 30,000 marks which he had paid to Philip Augustus of France, partly by levying a tax on the Cistercians such as they had never had to pay before, they refused to pay it. Then in 1200 he tried to tax their year's clip of wool and they refused to pay that. The king's riposte was to order all the Cistercians' horses and pigs to be removed from royal forests and handed over to the king. The Cistercians turned, under this barrage of royal hostility, to Archbishop Hubert Walter of Canterbury to mediate between themselves and the king. The Cistercian abbots finally came face to face with the king at Lincoln in late November 1200. What followed was high drama. There are various accounts of the meeting, one of them in Adam of Eynsham's *Life of St Hugh of Lincoln*, because what had been planned as a great royal court and meeting with King William of Scotland, became the occasion of the funeral of that famous bishop in his own cathedral. But the principal account is in Ralph of Coggeshall.

After Mass on the Sunday before Hugh's funeral, 50 Cistercian abbots came into the king's bedchamber, which was by no means so private a place then as we might imagine now. They were addressed by Archbishop Hubert Walter, who told them that the king's anger was now forgotten. They sank to the ground to thank the king. The king in his turn was moved to tears and prostrated himself on the ground to ask their pardon. The king then declared that he would build a splendid new abbey for their order, where he might be remembered as long as he lived and be buried at his death (though he would in fact be buried in Worcester Cathedral). The king ended by giving the abbots the kiss of peace, and the abbots ended by asking for royal letters of protection addressed to the sheriffs of the country.[117] The whole performance was clearly intended for widespread 'publication'.

This kind of political theatre, not perhaps so common by 1200 as it had once been, was the ordinary currency of politics two centuries earlier, particularly in the German Empire. Gerd Althoff has written illuminatingly about it at that time, in a paper entitled 'Rebellion, Tears and Contrition', with observations not without relevance to John and the Cistercians. He says that such scenes rarely represent spontaneous outbreaks of emotion, without having some function. It is emotion controlled for political ends. It might underscore, he says, a determination to achieve peace without surrendering one's position.[118] Given that John did more or less surrender his position, however, another consideration has to be brought into play. The Cistercians were a highly influential group and John could ill afford to lose a propaganda battle with them as he was doing. Thus it suited him to find a way of giving in while saving his face. The problem with giving in or doing a U-turn, as we all know, is loss of face. Theatrical ritual is often a useful way to do a U-turn while saving face. John could be seen to be responding to the monks' devotion to St Hugh, by showing his own devotion to the saint. The *Life of St Hugh of Lincoln* is explicit about this. John was moved, it says, to his unexpected act of clemency towards the Cistercian abbots, and to remit permanently the tax he had exacted from them, entirely out of honour of the saint. The funeral of St Hugh was a fortuitous and fortunate circumstance in providing the occasion for the drama and the reconciliation. The *Life of St Hugh* also sets the promise to found a monastery in this context.[119]

John had excellent political antennae, and I interpret his foundation of Beaulieu as a gesture to Cistercian opinion and through that to public opinion, especially knightly public opinion. He himself well understood the political importance of the knights in their localities,[120] and he must have understood the influence of the Cistercians and their talk with this class. He had to find some way to bring the Cistercians on side.

The importance of Beaulieu to John did not stop with its foundation. Its first abbot, a monk of Citeaux called Hugh, was used by the king as his intermediary with Pope Innocent III, first in putting John's case with respect to the Interdict which Innocent imposed on England because John would not accept his nomination of Stephen Langton as Archbishop of Canterbury, and later and successfully when in 1212–13 he persuaded the pope that John was making a genuine submission. Indeed he was, for John saw that the game was up, in face of the threatened invasion of his kingdom by Philip Augustus because he (John) was excommunicated. The papal legate, Pandulf Masca, who had met John in 1211, came over to England again to receive John's submission, who then formally exhorted John's subjects to stand by him against the French invader.[121]

Thus if the foundation of Beaulieu Abbey can be seen as something of a public relations exercise on John's part, trying to mend his reputation with the Cistercians so that they might help to mend it with an aristocratic public, so Hugh Abbot of Beaulieu might be seen in his putting the case for John to the pope as something of a public relations officer. The use of Hugh in this way rather backfired on the king because it made him unpopular within the Cistercian order. At the General Chapter of 1215 Hugh was accused of extravagant living, among other things keeping a dog on a silver chain at his bedside.[122] One may suspect that these charges were overdrawn, for he was appointed Bishop of Carlisle in 1219. But whatever the case, it seems significant of John's looking to his public image that he wanted a Cistercian abbey and a Cistercian abbot to speak for him. Nor does it seem that his use of the Cistercians was a merely cynical stratagem, for he had a Cistercian confessor in Abbot Henry of Bindon (Dorset), whom he retained even after failing to get him elected Bishop of Coventry–Lichfield! It was the second rejection of a royal nominee by the monks of Coventry and prompted John's sulky remark 'you don't want to appoint anyone I like'. Abbot Henry also acted as a royal envoy at the papal curia.[123]

What I have been describing, therefore, is the social and political influence of the English Cistercians, which I have done in terms of their concern for what went on in their own and other people's minds, and in terms of their contribution of ideas, ideas which were often critical of society and government, and which led to criticism of Angevin rule, criticism often implicit and sometimes explicit. Because of their manifold connections with knightly men, an increasingly influential group in the politics of the shire communities, they may be said to have contributed to the mental climate in which Magna Carta was drafted.

The Welsh Cistercians, also, were by no means removed from politics; but in the second half of the twelfth century the relationship would have to be described in a very different way from that of the English Cistercians to politics. In the period of Stephen's reign, barons like Walter d'Espec, Robert de Beaumont, Earl of Leicester, or William de Roumara, Earl of Lincoln, undoubtedly had partly the motive in founding Cistercian abbeys to consolidate their lordships.[124] But by the second half of the twelfth century this was hardly a factor in their politics, compared to their (the Cistercians') involvement with knights, as the passage from Walter Daniel's *Life of Ailred* which we earlier cited strongly suggests. It was at the same period, however, the factor *par excellence* in the involvement of Welsh Cistercian houses in politics.

The best example is Strata Florida, as we see it from the work of David Austin of Lampeter University.[125] Strata Florida was founded by an Anglo-Norman baron in 1164, but was re-founded by Rhys ap Gruffudd, the Lord Rhys, in 1166. The latter must be considered its true patron. Rhys, ruler of Deheubarth, revived his family's power in Ceredigion, Central and South Wales, and made his court at Cardigan a pre-eminent centre of Welsh culture. He established his authority over many native rulers; he was a close ally of Henry II of England, knowing, as Rees Davies has said, how to bend without grovelling;[126] and he married two daughters to Anglo-Norman lords and his son to the daughter of the great Marcher lord, William de Braose. It would have been totally impossible by this time to expel the Anglo-Normans from South Wales, but he could prevent a renewal of Norman advance and seek to roll back Norman control at the peripheries of his kingdom.[127] The lands of Strata Florida and Whitland, the other Cistercian monastery which he patronised in a big way, can be seen as forming a bastion of his own power (he left his domain land intact), challenging and standing against the power of St David's in the South West. The well in its church, once a holy well no doubt, was probably the reason why the church of Strata Florida was located there. The Welsh Cistercians did not just seek out waste places, as Cistercian descriptions of their own sites liked to imply. The ancient holy sites of Wales were part of a political landscape which was self-consciously deployed by twelfth-century Welsh churches to emphasise their Welshness. Besides the well, gravestones have been discovered at Strata Florida carved in an older tradition than that of the twelfth century. The Lord Rhys's grandest title, *proprietarius princeps Sudwalie*, rightful prince of South Wales, survives in a charter which he gave to Strata Florida.[128]

The Augustinian Canons

As Bishop of Hippo, Augustine established a monastic community for himself and his clergy, where they led the common life of worship, refectory and dormitory. This was inspired by the ideal of the early Christian community as described by the *Acts of the Apostles*, where all property was held in common. So, Augustine thought, should all pastors do. All pastors must also combine being Mary and being Martha; they must combine a life of prayer and contemplation with the active life of the pastorate. Whichever sort of life one opts for, says Augustine in his *City of God*, 'nobody ought to be a contemplative without thinking of the needs of his neighbour, and nobody can lead the active life without needing the contemplation of God'.[129] Augustine also thought that one might opt for a combination of both lives from the start, as a third way of life of *ex utroque* (both the contemplative and active) *composito*.[130] The life composed of both contemplation and pastoral activity, the third way, may be the best description of how most Augustinian canons in twelfth- and thirteenth-century Britain lived. Thus they were inherently a social as well as a religious force.

The Augustinian Canons were regular canons, that is canons living a community life under a rule. There had been regular canons in Europe and England long before there were Augustinian Canons. Whether Augustine composed the 'rule' for his communely living clergy which passed under his name in the early Middle Ages, or whether it was put together soon after his death under his inspiration is uncertain.[131] When in the eighth century Chrodegang of Metz composed his famous and widely influential rule for the canons of his cathedral, it was far more Benedictine than Augustinian,[132] while the *Institutio Canonicorum* of the early ninth century also owed little to Augustine,[133] despite the fact that both these were inspired by the same ideal as was the Bishop of Hippo. *The Rule of Augustine*, as a text and as a direct influence, really came into its own with the Gregorian Reform. The earliest reference to it occurs at Rheims in 1067, but before that date, Gregory VII, still as Hildebrand Archdeacon of Rome, had been fostering the life of regular (i.e. communely-living) canons in his own city. The greatest propagator of the Augustinian canons was Gregory VII's loyal friend, Bishop Altmann of Passau. John Cowdrey has made the strong point that regular canons, holding their property in common, and living and worshipping in common, not only served the Gregorian ideal of a celibate clergy, but also served that related ideal of giving people pastors whose way of life and lack of avarice they could respect.[134] The latter aspect is particularly important when one considers that much anti-clericalism of late eleventh- early twelfth-century townsmen was occasioned by the perceived corruption of their clergy.

A few Augustinian houses were in existence in England before 1100, but they spread dramatically under Henry I, actively encouraged by the king and queen themselves, several of the top royal officials, and several bishops. The view was propagated by Sir Richard Southern that this is what one might expect of patrons rather mean about money, for it was much cheaper to establish a house of canons than a full-blown Benedictine monastery, while still giving a founder the kudos of a religious patron.[135] But one must also allow for an element of Gregorian religious idealism in such foundations, which often gave a new combination of the contemplative, the austere and the pastoral to their religious houses, especially in burgeoning towns like London, Bristol (1142) and Oxford (St Frideswide's transformed into an Augustinian house in 1122).

Throughout the twelfth century the Augustinian Canons were propelled by a strong pastoral drive, exemplified in various of their writings. We shall see it in the *Bridlington Dialogue* and in Prior Philip of St Frideswide's *Miracles of St Frideswide*. A remarkable example of it is Orm's *Ormulum*, a large-scale work in English by a Lincolnshire Augustinian Canon, with versifications of the gospel readings for the liturgical year, followed by what Robert Bartlett has called 'twenty-minute sermons' on each. Bartlett, noting how little heresy there was in twelfth-century England, says that Orm wrote to christianise the peasantry more thoroughly, and helped 'to naturalise the gospel stories'.[136] Again in the late twelfth century, Guy of Southwick, a Hampshire Augustinian, wrote a treatise on Confession. To this work we shall have to come back (p. 242). Here we only say that far from being a rule of thumb guide to penances which priests ought to dole out, it really helped people to come to terms with themselves.

Not all Augustinian houses of the early twelfth century, however, combined the pastoral with the contemplative. Some look more purely contemplative and quite removed from the world, like the Cistercians. Around 1130 a regular canon of Liège wrote a book entitled *Concerning the Diverse Orders and Callings in the Church*. He distinguished between those canons who established themselves as far away from people as possible in order to live a life of contemplation, like the Cistercians, and who, also like the Cistercians, earned their livelihood by their own labours;[137] and those canons who live near to people, but as strangers living in their own houses, of whom some might work in parishes.[138]

Llanthony and Nostell

A good example of the contemplative, remote house is Llanthony in the Black Mountains, before it moved to just outside Gloucester in 1136. We know of it from *The Life of Robert of Bethune* by William of Wycombe. Robert was a man of knightly family, highly educated at Laon and Paris, Master Robert indeed, although he never allowed himself to be called master after he became a canon, who was made Bishop of Hereford by Henry I in 1130. His *Life* describes romantically the 'horrors' of Llanthony's site, just as the Cistercians liked to describe their sites, often with exaggerations as places 'of horror and vast solitude', as well as his ascetic practices and manual labour. Gerald of Wales described Llanthony's site with a different kind of romanticism, with its distant prospects, as far as the eye can see, of 'mountain peaks which rise to meet the sky', and often with herds of wild deer grazing on them.[139] When Robert became prior, his rule was characterised by insight into the souls of his charges, very like that of the Cistercians Bernard or Ailred. William of Wycombe refers on more than one occasion to the 'humanity' of his conduct as bishop,[140] again very much in the spirit that would animate Ailred of Rievaulx. And he makes his long account of Robert's death at the Council of Rheims (1148) into a meditation on Christ's Passion, thus pointing up in Robert's life the Cistercian-like devotion to Jesus.[141]

Robert of Bethune took advice and devoted much thought to his vocation before he finally opted to become an Augustinian Canon. He was a perfect example of the massive search for one's vocation going on across Europe, which Henrietta Leyser, as mentioned earlier, has observed. He gave up any idea of the fame and material rewards which he could gain as a 'great master', exploring with a few mature friends where he would find quiet and contemplation, 'so that he would not make a hasty and incautious decision'. Finally he went to consult Richard, Abbot of St Albans (1097–1119) a faithful counsellor of his, who (with a magnanimity not always associated with abbots towards other monasteries and orders), put to him the question of which house of God he preferred. Robert replied: 'I do not presume to set up one order before another. Yet the Order of Canons attracts me the most, and the house of Llanthony.'[142] Given how like a Cistercian house Llanthony was in many ways, one may wonder why Robert did not choose to become a Cistercian. I can think of three possible answers to this question. One was personal contact, with Augustinians. Another was his willingness to be open to his contemplative life leading on to a pastoral one of some sort, although he put up the maximum resistance to becoming a bishop. A third, connected with the second, was that he made his choice under the inspiration of Augustine himself and Augustine's Rule, as by the twelfth century it was generally if not unquestioningly taken to be.[143]

Another example of an Augustinian house which was established on a remote site to be predominantly contemplative was Nostell Priory in the West Riding of Yorkshire, although today one hardly associates remoteness with proximity to Pontefract and Wakefield! Yet each of Llanthony and Nostell gave an excellent bishop to the English church late in Henry I's reign, namely Robert of Bethune at Hereford (1130), and Athelwold at Carlisle (1133), alongside St Osyth's in Essex, which produced William of Corbeil, Archbishop of Canterbury (1123). And, as we observed, Archbishop Thurstan of York gave Nostell a prebend in his cathedral church (1135–40), consisting of their churches of Bramham, Wharram le Street, and Lythe. Nostell must have supervised these parishes in some way, and Thurstan doubtless thereby intended to draw the Prior into the pastoral counsels of himself and his cathedral (see above, p. 126).

The *Bridlington Dialogue* and Bridlington Priory

The contemplative, prayerful side of the Augustinian vocation is powerfully represented in a commentary on the Rule of Augustine (c. 1150), the *Bridlington Dialogue*, certainly composed at Bridlington and attributed to a canon called Robert.

Bridlington, a not inconsiderable port in the East Riding of Yorkshire, had a house of Augustinian Canons founded in the reign of Henry I. That king, so often keen to effect foundations with other people's money, gave towards Bridlington's endowment a considerable amount of the royal demesne and the church belonging to his manor there. The *Bridlington Dialogue* has been called a parochial work in the extreme, 'giving no indication that a world outside Yorkshire was known to exist'.[144] But the author was also aware of a heavenly world; for the work contains two chapters on prayer, before going on to more practical matters. The first is a meditation on the Lord's Prayer; discussing the phrase 'Our Father who art in heaven', where the *Dialogue* seems to imply that the prayer of the office, and its psalms, merges with private prayer. Prayer does not need words; 'in prayer there is a turning of the heart towards God, who is always ready to give, if we are ready to take what He will have given'.[145] And then the Master in the *Dialogue* encouraged the Disciple and others to pass on from thinking of God bodily even as a body in heaven, to seeking Him in their souls.[146] When the *Dialogue* moves to the chapter on the prayer of the divine office, the whole of it is made into a biblical meditation.[147] To put the point in a nutshell, the *Dialogue* shows that contemplative prayer and communal worship represent the way of loving God from which all love of neighbour and pastoral activity ought to spring.

From its foundation, Bridlington (to continue with this useful example of the Augustinian Canons) was endowed with many parish churches. Some, like Ilkeston in Derbyshire, were far afield, but many were much closer to their own house. Historians have debated whether canons would have served as parish priests in their own churches, or whether they would rather have taken the view that a life of prayer in their own houses was their main business and that their churches should be served by secular priests or chaplains, albeit under their own appointment or presentation.[148] If the latter, the clergy who served the churches should have what they needed to live, and the Augustinian Canons would have the rest of the revenues to sustain the life of their houses. The cathedral priory of Carlisle, established by Henry I in 1124, came into this latter case with its churches. But in general we have little evidence about this matter for the twelfth century. As to general considerations, on the one hand there was the danger to a canon's chastity of allowing him to be foot-loose outside the monastery; on the other hand their order was wedded to the pastoral as well as the contemplative idea. So can we have any idea of whether Bridlington served at least some of its own churches, or whether it appointed resident priests in them? We may usefully start here with some geography. Bridlington's own priory church doubled up as a parish church. Archbishop Thurstan granted them Bessingby church, sited within Bridlington's parish. Just one mile further away was Carnaby. These were to the South West. Immediately to the west, 2$\frac{1}{2}$ miles away was Boynton, while in the other direction 3 miles to the north east, was Flamborough. If John Henry Newman in the nineteenth century could serve the church of Littlemore at least 3 miles out of Oxford, while also being Vicar of St Mary's, there seems no reason why the Bridlington Canons could not easily have served all four of these churches besides their own, from Bridlington, even if they had to go out in pairs to safeguard each other's chastity, as the *Bridlington Dialogue* proposed. Then there was a group of dependent chapels in a triangle to the north and north east, with Buckton 4 miles from Bridlington, Grindale at 5 miles and Speeton at 6. Perhaps these would be less likely served directly from Bridlington. But the Priory had substantial land in Buckton and in Speeton, certainly from the third quarter of the twelfth century and probably from before.[149] That means that Bridlington

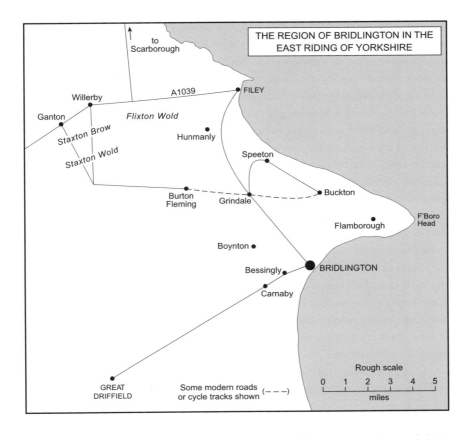

THE REGION OF BRIDLINGTON IN THE
EAST RIDING OF YORKSHIRE

could have had a house in Buckton or Speeton where two or three of their
canons could have resided and done turns of duty there. Buckton was
only 2½ miles from Speeton and 3½ from Grindale. Only 5 miles further
north from Speeton was the Canons' church of Filey, which it looks as
if they served themselves.[150] On this matter of houses where the Canons
had churches, James Bond and Kate Tiller have pointed up an apparently
analogous situation in the case of Dorchester-on-Thames (Oxfordshire),
an Augustinian house albeit of the autonomous Arrouaisian group, established as such by Bishop Alexander of Lincoln (1123–48). Their map of
Dorchester's churches and other sources of income shows that Dorchester
had land and a house as well as a church some 4 miles up the Thames at
Clifton Hampden and some 6 miles up the River Thames at Chislehampton,
to give just two examples, as well as several other churches within easy
'commuting distance' of Dorchester.[151]

Bridlington was a well-endowed house, and at the Dissolution of the
Monasteries (1535), with a valuation of £547 per annum, ranked about

twelfth out of about 170 Augustinian houses in England.[152] One may sometimes think that the dependence of Augustinian houses on churches for their income is exaggerated. Bridlington had a considerable landed endowment around its own house, as well as elsewhere. It had, for instance, a grange in Willerby, where it had a church some 12 miles north west of Bridlington.[153] This was hardly within commuting distance of Bridlington, but the land there could have provided the means, together with the revenues of the church, to enable a small group of canons to reside there and serve the church. Just 2 miles to the west of Willerby was the Canons' church of Ganton. In the other direction, south of Bridlington in the Holderness peninsula, lay, 10 miles apart from each other the Bridlington churches of Sproatley and Ottringham. Sproatley is some 25 miles from Bridlington, but once again in the twelfth century, Bridlington held considerable lands both there and in Ottringham.[154]

The reader may be thinking that although this is all very interesting, there is no direct evidence that any of it actually happened, that the Bridlington canons did serve any of their churches themselves other than their priory church which was also a parish church. Is it not all speculation about what could have happened rather than what did happen? Well, not quite all speculation.

First of all, the *Bridlington Dialogue* itself is explicit that pastoral work outside the monastery is the kind of thing that Augustinian Canons ought to be doing. True, the 'Disciple' in the 'Dialogue' between Master and Disciple, is represented as taking a hard line against those who resided at some outside post. He knew of cases where they did so for a full year. They were violators of their profession, i.e. their profession of stability. This shows that there were Bridlington Canons c. 1150 who were in the situation such as I have envisaged it at Willerby, Sproatley and Buckton. But the 'Master' will have none of this. Stability does not mean never being outside the monastery, rather than never entirely breaking his links to the house without reasonable cause:

For my part [the Master says] I have vowed to serve God for my whole life in the church which has been established at Bridlington. But whenever my superior [i.e. the Prior] arranges for me to spend a long or short time in any of the places united to the aforesaid church as limbs subject to their head (which surely must include its parish churches), I certainly believe and say that I can obey without loss to my profession, and that I ought to obey in order to avoid detriment to it.[155]

Further on, the Master adds:

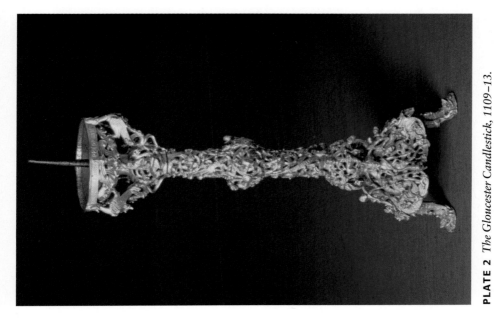

PLATE 2 *The Gloucester Candlestick, 1109–13.*

Source: © The Print Collector/Alamy

PLATE 1 *Durham Cathedral: the ribbed vaulting, c. 1100.*

Source: © Holmes Garden Photos/Alamy

PLATE 3 *Iffley Church, Oxford, 1170–80; the interior looking from west to east.*
Source: Photo by Roger Ainsworth

PLATE 4 *Iffley Church: the interior looking from east to west.*
Source: Photo by Roger Ainsworth

PLATE 6 *Melbourne Church, Derbyshire, c. 1130–40: the interior seen from the western gallery.*

Source: Courtesy of Sarah Railton

PLATE 5 *St Albans Psalter, Cathedral Library of Hildesheim, c. 1130: historiated initial letter C, p. 285, probably showing Christina of Markyate praying for Abbot Geoffrey of St Alban's and other St Alban's monks.*

Source: Courtesy of Dombibliothek Hildesheim

PLATE 7 *Elkstone Church, Gloucs, c. 1150: the chancel as seen from the nave.*

Source: © Cotswolds Photo Library/Alamy

PLATE 8 *The Chichester Roundel, c. 1250: wall painting of the Madonna and Child in the Chapel of the Bishop's Palace, Chichester.*

Source: Photo by Richard Chevis, courtesy of the Bishop of Chichester

Let me make myself clear. If a superior orders anyone subject to himself to move from the place to which he has given himself, to another place, in order to build up [edificandum] religion and divine worship there, and that brother shall live there for some time, whether to rule others or live under someone else's rule, who does not see that he ought to be obeyed?[156]

As J.C. Dickinson wrote of the view which the 'Disciple' is here made to champion, 'had it prevailed, [it] would have left the Augustinians a pale and unnecessary imitation of the Benedictines';[157] that is, it would have shorn them of their distinctive pastoral contribution which went together with their life of prayer.

One can illustrate from the churches of Willerby and Ganton, which were mentioned above, a concrete situation such as the Bridlington Dialogue had in mind. Some time in the 1120s or 1130s Archbishop Thurstan of York issued a document, the text of which is preserved in the Bridlington Cartulary, which established that Ganton, formerly a chapel, would in future be subject to the church of Willerby, both of them Bridlington churches, and that the priest of Willerby would appoint the priest resident in Ganton.[158] Now given that Ganton was a Bridlington church, it is hardly likely that Bridlington would allow anyone to be appointed there other than by a Canon of Bridlington. And given the phrase from the Dialogue that we have just quoted above, about whether a brother is sent out to rule others or live under someone else's rule, it is quite likely that the priest of Ganton would also be (after the then incumbent, Theobald, had died or moved) a Bridlington Canon. When Pope Celestine III issued a bull in favour of Bridlington in 1194, the bull said among other things that when vacancies occurred in their churches, the Canons might institute two or more of their number (again the dislike of canons outside the monastery living on their own), and present one to the diocesan bishop to be in effect parish priest.[159] There is an obvious analogy here to the institution of the Augustinian Oseney Abbey (Oxfordshire) as rector of the church of Shenstone, Staffs (1205-08) with its Canon, Master W. de Meisam, inducted into the corporeal possession of the church in the name of their whole community.[160] It looks as if in the Willerby/Ganton set-up, the parish priest was the one designated as 'the priest of Willerby', while the priest of Ganton, barely 2 miles from Willerby, may well have served the church from a canons' house in Willerby.

During the course of the twelfth and thirteenth centuries a number of Bridlington churches came to have vicarages ordained in them, that is, a portion of the revenues of the church ring-fenced for the support of the priest, presumably a secular priest rather than a canon, actually residing and ministering there. By 1291, we have the evidence of the taxation of Pope Nicholas IV for vicarages – Carnaby and Boynton, Willerby and Ganton, for instance, all had them, while Bridlington itself, Bessingby, Filey, Flamborough, Ottringham and Sproatley did not,[161] suggesting that all these latter were served directly by the Canons or by their chaplains. But much water had flowed under the bridge between Bridlington's foundation and 1291, not least the much greater supply of educated secular priests who could fill parochial cures. Even if by then vicars actually resided in the parishes, from which the canons continued to draw revenues, or if vicars did not reside and chaplains were resident priests, that did not prevent the Canons from taking a constructive interest, knowing who were the best priests to appoint (in the case of vicars to present to the Archbishop), and serving the altar (as the phrase is), i.e. celebrating Mass sometimes, preaching, and even hearing confessions.

It goes almost without saying that Bridlington, with those spiritual and pastoral ideals as stated in the *Dialogue*, and with such a swathe of churches and chapels across the East Riding of Yorkshire, must have had considerable influence in that region during the twelfth century. This was so particularly amongst the knightly people or, if one prefers the term, the gentry. When Bridlington was founded, the original patrons apart from Henry I himself were Yorkshire barons and, associated with them, knights in their Yorkshire honours; but honorial ties of knights to barons as seen in knightly benefactions quickly declined. This was part of what Hugh Thomas, in an important and incisive book, has described as the loosening of baronial honorial relationships in twelfth-century Yorkshire, whereby vassals could more easily seek out their own patrons and lords their own retinues. The links of land tenure, and the personal links which went with them were not destroyed but weakened. And knights came to form (not least by their collaborations in the administration of royal justice) more of a community in themselves (without altogether ceasing to be part of honorial communities). If I have understood Thomas correctly, honorial communities and communities of knights/upper peasantry within a shire, became overlapping communities. The baronial honour by itself, he says, could no longer function so well as 'a network of patronage and a focus of co-operation among the upper classes'.[162]

The huge Bridlington Cartulary, the book into which the Canons, in the early fourteenth century, copied all the charters which granted churches, lands and privileges to them over two centuries, recording them mainly by place, is full of grants made by knightly people and upper peasants. It leaves no doubt that for this social group as a whole, one aspect of their co-operation and shared culture in Yorkshire was their interest in and patronage of Bridlington Priory.[163] To make a useful study of these benefactors would be a gigantic task, mainly because the early twentieth-century editor of the Cartulary made no effort to date the mostly undated documents. But if dated, these documents would give an interesting conspectus of gentry society in Yorkshire, and especially its East Riding, as focused in varying degrees on Bridlington. Moreover, if one worked these documents together with the legal records of royal justice, particularly the *Curia Regis Rolls* from when they start in the mid-1190s, one would get an idea of how many of Bridlington's benefactors were also leading lights in the shire community generally. One could probably make similar studies for Guisborough in North Yorkshire and for many other Augustinian houses in the land.

Of course, as Thomas says, not all these benefactors were necessarily good Christians. Many gentry could be violent and vicious people, even sometimes using their administration of royal justice to further their own lawless ends. They could be thugs. But such things were not necessarily exclusive of pious motives.[164] Indeed, the worse people were, the more they might have felt in need of the intercessions of others for their salvation. For that society contained the paradox of much violence on the one hand together with many conscience-pricking mechanisms on the other, e.g. sermons, stories of divine punishment, and the sight of holy persons. And behind many a benefaction there may have been hidden or only half-hidden material benefits for the giver. In the main, however, one cannot doubt the strong religious motivations of benefactors.

From where were the Canons of Bridlington recruited? So far as I know there are only two direct pieces of evidence for this in the twelfth century. One is that Baldwin de Gant, a nephew of the grandson of the founder, Walter de Gant, was a Canon in the 1170s;[165] but one would think that baronial canons were always going to be unusual. Peasants must also have been relatively unusual, for what landholder was normally going to allow his labour force to be depleted? And the Augustinians had nothing like the lay brothers of the Cistercians. The most one can say here is that they may sometimes have received their most trusted chaplains as Canons. The other piece of evidence is a rare glimpse, and a fascinating glimpse, of what looks much more typical; and here we are very much in knightly social territory. In a charter of 1175–85, James de Watsand granted to Bridlington three bovates of land in Burton Fleming (some eight miles from Bridlington), which Peter de Fribois had given him for a duel which James had waged on his behalf at York, and also two bovates in Burton by Hornsea (near

Bridlington's church of Atwick, East Riding), which James's father had sold to Peter for 14 marks (two years of good income for a parish priest). James's charter continued, 'and the canons shall make my elder son a canon when he is twenty years old, and meanwhile shall find what is necessary for him'. Peter de Fribois is the first witness, and two other members of his family also witnessed.[166] The Fribois's were knightly tenants of the Gants in Yorkshire and Lincolnshire. Peter looks as if he were sponsoring James's son for a canonry, in return for James's championship of him in the duel. But it looks as if the Watsands must also have been of knightly or gentry standing. It is also interesting that it was James's elder son who was to be a canon. Was that because he was regarded as the less suitable, although the older, to be a secular heir, or the more suitable to be a canon?

If the Frisbois's and the Watsands were at all characteristic of Bridlington's recruitment, that would have been a factor giving many knightly families in the East Riding a community of interest in the Priory.[167]

St Frideswide's Priory, Oxford

We turn to another house of Augustinian Canons in a very urban setting, St Frideswide's Priory in Oxford. Once a richly endowed Benedictine monastery, it had become first a house of secular canons and was in 1122 transformed, again at the behest of Henry I, into an Augustinian house. Many Augustinian houses, like St Frideswide's had formerly been minster churches, staffed by secular canons or clergy whose pastoral activities ranged over a wide area or over many dependent churches and chapels. And many of the urban parochial churches, grandly re-built in the twelfth and thirteenth centuries, 'collegiate parish churches' as John Blair has called them, were probably descended similarly. Their architecture implies *staffs* of clergy with elaborate liturgy and pastoral responsibilities in other churches and chapels. For all we know, such churches might have been as pastorally effective as the Augustinians. The difference is simply the *stated* commitment of the Augustinians to a life of monastic prayer and community alongside their pastorate.[168]

In the early twelfth century Oxford, as already mentioned, was a centre of growing trade, production and general prosperity. This prosperity is reflected in the number of stone churches which were within a few hundred yards of its centre and existed before the scholars are known to have become a significant element in the town around 1170. They include St Mary's, All Saints, St Michael at the North Gate, St Aldates, St Peter in the Bailey, St Peter in the East, St John the Baptist, St Ebbe's and St Mary Magdalene.

The first five of these were St Frideswide's churches in the twelfth century; the last was the church of another house of Augustinian Canons just outside the town, Oseney Abbey.[169] Like Oseney itself, its church of St Mary Magdalene was just outside the town walls. We have little idea who served all these and other churches in the twelfth century, but one of the motives for the transformation of St Frideswide's in 1122 must have been that it could meet a glaring pastoral need by providing priests who could at least celebrate Mass and preach in these churches.

St Frideswide's own church, now Christ Church Cathedral, was rebuilt as a powerful and handsome late Romanesque church between c. 1160 and c. 1180. Within this church was a parish altar, whether in the nave or in the north transept is debated, whilst the chancel (without of course the nineteenth-century collegiate stalls) provided a grand space, bounded by side aisles to enhance the sense of space in it, for the performance of a splendid liturgy. Thus under one roof this church symbolised the Canons' own religious life and their pastorate. When the church was substantially complete in 1180, Prior Philip translated the putative bones of St Frideswide, an eighth-century princess, to a new shrine probably just off the north transept. Within a year, some 100 miracles had been worked at this shrine, mostly of healing, all of them recorded by Prior Philip, who acted as the shrine's 'registrar'. Some cults when deliberately established are failures; others, like St Frideswide's are a success. The factors that make the difference would be a fascinating study. In St Frideswide's case, one of the key factors in its success was that the shrine was an extension of the Canons' normal pastorate.

Prior Philip's account of the miracles of St Frideswide has a pastoral mentality written all over it. There are telling little indications of this which come incidentally into his narratives. A teenage girl called Emelina, for instance, had tried to drown herself in the River Kennet at Eddington (Berkshire), was saved, and was traumatised by the experience so that she could not talk. She was cured at the shrine and the Canons then took her on as a servant at the Priory. Again, a mad youth from Coleshill (Berkshire) raved blasphemously in the church during Mass on the feast of the Invention of the Cross (14 September), so that he was ordered to be expelled. But a Canon threw a douche of holy water in his face, which quietened him down, and eventually he was cured.[170] Whatever being cured meant in such a case, the Canons were not in the business of throwing out people who suffered from mental ill health. We get a rare insight into what kind of people the Canons might be from a reference to 'a citizen of Oxford, brother of a Canon', named Benedict Kepherin (surely Jewish), whose little son Lawrence was cured of bladder trouble after an Oxford doctor had made a mess of him.[171]

In Prior Philip's miracles, the case histories of women heavily outnumber those of men, unlike in most twelfth-century collections of miracles. Philip obviously understood the strains arising in these women from sexual fear or rebuff. One woman had had sexual intercourse with her husband and had then gone mad for three years until she came to the shrine. Another had had sexual intercourse with her husband and promptly got a headache which lasted for two years. Another had been the concubine of a priest, but having ceased to be attractive to him, was repudiated by him, and then suffered from acute internal pains and insomnia. All these things are told by Prior Philip without any censoriousness, without any tut-tuting about the only to be expected moral consequences of sleeping with a priest or with one's husband during seasons forbidden by canon law, etc., all of which might have been readily found in clerical narrators writing before the new age of – to use again the word used about the Augustinian Bishop Robert of Bethune – humanity in religion. In an age when women had far fewer outlets of fulfilling activity than men had, when they were often socially disparaged by men's purchase of marriage rights, and when stories were legion of girls who fled into vows of virginity in order to avoid arranged marriages, like the story of St Frideswide herself, it was no wonder that the teenage years were a time of unbearable anxiety to many girls, and this too shows up in several of the case histories.[172] A shrine like St Frideswide's helped to give women and girls a degree of power over their own lives.

One reason why Prior Philip had such a fund of pastoral sympathy for those who sought cures at the shrine comes out in what he wrote about a cure of his own and how he had reflected on his experience, in what Simon Yarrow describes as 'a rare first-person reflection on miracles and how they worked'.[173] The nature of his malady is not clear, but he recounts how, having seen so many of the rich and poor, lesser and great, of both sexes receive healing, he seemed to lack the faith that he felt shone in others, and he wept for it. He prostrated himself before the shrine and spent a sleepless night wracked by doubts. But, he continues, when the time of another attack of pain had passed and he had had a quiet night:

Faith conquered despair, and certainty born of the attainment of healing dissolved doubt, so that I really experienced in myself the strength of God. At the beginning of the night in which I dreaded a fifth attack of pain, I threw myself before the feretory (i.e. the shrine), so that my healing might be confirmed by repeated vigils. And truly I learned by experience what previously I had only heard: that healing given by the command of God is given totally at once. Therefore my faith was strengthened by the gift of God, so that I could more easily believe in the grace of God in others which I had experienced in myself.[174]

A modern person might ask of this how deep faith can be which depends on one's receiving a cure. But then again, what is healing is not, and was not then, an absolute; it is and was what was perceived or interpreted as healing – by an individual as well as by a society. Above all in this impressive passage, one can see a capacity to reflect on his own experience which helped Prior Philip to sympathise with and articulate the experiences of others.

Henry I and the Augustinian Canons

We might end by asking again the question why Henry I and his courtiers were so keen to establish houses of Augustinian Canons. We have already argued that it was not only their cheapness to establish, along with the prestige of founding a religious house. As to the remote or 'country' houses, we know that Roger of Salisbury, Henry's chief minister, admired Llanthony;[175] and the appointment of Robert of Bethune as a bishop makes clear that the king also did so. But in the case of the urban houses there may be more to the answer than only religious zeal and admiration for the way of life. It is clear that Henry I knew that there was money to be made out of the rising towns for the king. At the same time, however, he could see from the unrest in the Flemish and other towns across the Channel that they were dangerous places for authority.[176] In 1107 his own nominee as Bishop of Laon had been murdered. But it was not always easy, at this stage, to distinguish a sufficient authority within most towns to be entrusted with keeping order and raising royal revenue. Under Henry I, only London and Lincoln were obvious exceptions. It perhaps did not escape the king, therefore, that a pastorate conducted by religious communities whose way of life townsmen could respect, might have advantages for order as well as for royal religious patronage.

Women's religious houses

It may seem rather androcentric that after devoting so much space to male religious foundations, I now devote so little to those of women, particularly when much fine work has been done on them in the past 20 or 25 years. But the principal point I wish to make has to be seen in a context that I have already laid down (hopefully) in the earlier sections of this chapter, namely the development of shire and other local communities. A function of women's houses in these will be my point. One cannot entirely discount the effect of a few top nunneries like Wilton, Shaftesbury and Romsey (all in the South and in old Wessex) on high politics. Wilton, for instance, in the 1090s housed Matilda, daughter of King Malcolm of Scotland, who would ultimately marry Henry I. Malcolm had designed that she should marry Count Alan of Brittany, Lord of Richmond (Yorkshire); but that could have created too mighty a power block in the North for Henry I's taste and that of other barons. Malcolm rode down to Wilton and tore the veil off Matilda's head, but to no effect.[177] The whole episode shows that a top nunnery could not stand aside from royal politics, given the class of its members; as well as that even so royal and aristocratic a house as Wilton was vulnerable to male violence. There were other high aristocratic nunneries. However, for the most part, the story of women religious in our period is one that fits more modestly into society at urban or shire level, or even more locally.

Large numbers of nunneries, mostly small ones, were founded in twelfth-century England. That might seem an important way forward for women as giving them an independent role in religion and life; but it was not all to their advantage. Women's houses were dependent on men for sacramental purposes, especially the celebration of Mass, and for physical protection. Women's houses often succumbed to being dominated and ruled by male houses, as Brian Golding showed happened with the Gilbertine Canonesses.[178] In Rome itself Pope Innocent III rigorously reorganised informal groups of 'holy women' living in the city into cloistered communities.[179] The hermitage of Christina of Markyate became after her death a dependent priory of St Alban's Abbey.[180] One could multiply examples.[181] Sharon Elkins has elucidated the nature of such dependence.[182]

As Elkins herself has stressed, however, not all male helpers were equally dominant. Some nunneries of high standing in the South had male guardians or custodians with extensive powers, in fact priors alongside prioresses. But at Clerkenwell Priory in London, founded by a layman, Jordan de Breiset – to give one example – while the chaplains and the brothers were in their different capacities crucial to the continued existence of the nunnery, it was the prioress who ruled financially.[183] Nor should we think that what can look like dominance to us, necessarily represented something irksome rather than creative and helpful to medieval nuns.

Often it was a security for, and enhancement of, their religious life. A small example of this is the odd difficulty which we sometimes have in labelling women's houses as Benedictine or Augustinian. Elkins suggests that this was because women were adopting some of the customs of the orders of their male supporters; they were Benedictines perhaps who also adopted Augustinian customs, because Augustinian canons played a prominent role in their foundation or operation.[184]

Some exceptionally interesting archaeological work has enabled us to get a material impression of the way of life offered to many twelfth- and thirteenth-century women in nunneries, in some respects a distinctively female impression. For instance, at Haliwell (Shoreditch, London) or at Marrick (North Yorkshire) and elsewhere, the parish part of their churches was at the east end, whereas the nuns choir occupied the west, which would be unusual for male houses, suggesting that patronal and other families might attend Mass there. Again the nuns' dormitories were often located in 'the deepest space', i.e. the farthest away inside the nunnery from possible marauders or intruders, whereas in male communities the deepest space was often reserved for the chapter house. In women's houses the iconography of the sculpture, particularly on doorways, might mark out the spaces, with their 'degrees of permeability', as one proceeded deeper and deeper into them. Yet again, women surprisingly seem to have had less good latrine facilities than men had, perhaps, so Roberta Gilchrist has suggested, to get away from the 'locker room culture' of men![185]

As Gilchrist has pointed out, women lacked the freedom and capacity to re-structure their landscapes when they were in the country. Men were 'constantly renegotiating their economic, political and religious identities'. Women could only renegotiate theirs conceptually. And glossing this, she adds, 'the marginality of women's communities was given meaning through an eremitic vocation'.[186] This is as if to say that there was often a veering towards the eremitical in nunneries, which was already present in so many individual female religious vocations of the twelfth century. Yet, as Gilchrist herself stresses, when writing of 'small gentry foundations', that did not at all entail their being remote from their own society. She writes of such foundations that they often remained 'closely linked to gentry of their locality, people concerned with local parish and village affairs and local family ties'.[187]

We may follow up this point about local ties with two urban nunneries, gentry/ townspeople's nunneries, as we may call them: Clerkenwell (London) and Clementhorpe (York). Of Clerkenwell we have already spoken. Jordan de Breiset's family kept increasing the endowment, surely in part to secure unmarried positions commensurate with their social standing for their own womenfolk, as well as out of religious devotion. Many families at this level could hardly afford dowries for all their girls to be married. It would appear that a dowry (as we would call it) cost two or three times what a suitable donation cost to place a girl in a nunnery.[188] Clerkenwell attracted women from London but also from Essex, Cambridgeshire and even Dorset, all making entrance donations of various kinds, such as lands, woods or annual payments.[189]

Clementhorpe was founded in a suburb of York by Archbishop Thurstan, between 1125 and 1133. Its main revenues were from York rents and from its nearby land, flanking the River Ouse. It was never supervised by a male warden or custodian, thus leaving the prioress herself, as at Clerkenwell, to be the principal administrator. When the evidence becomes more plentiful in the fourteenth century, we see multiple bonds of friendship and kinship between the prioresses and the wealthier members of urban and rural society in the vicinity, while rural girls and also daughters of York merchants became nuns.[190] Many of them could well have been formidable personalities. It was all likely to have been thus from the start. Moreover, we have to remember that in various capacities well-born women in the twelfth century were no strangers to the administration of estates, and I know of no evidence that they had a poor reputation as administrators. The *Rotuli de Dominabus* of 1185 surveyed the women who could not marry without the king's licence, and their estates. But the evidence there of mismanagement seems virtually confined to estates which were farmed in wardship by rapacious crown agents or favourites.[191]

Henrietta Leyser has characterised Clementhorpe as not perhaps a place of high spirituality, 'but as an important centre for the wider community of York'. Its prioresses might not have been famed for their visions, 'but they were respected and trusted, and, in their role as executors for the citizens of York, they were left tokens of affection (such as) a silver salt cellar (or) a pair of sheets'.[192] We are getting here a picture corresponding to the kind of involvement and co-operation by a local or regional community which we have just posited for the Augustinian Priory of Bridlington (East Yorkshire). It was a focus on a religious house which itself helped to knit a society together.

Archbishop Hubert Walter and St Hugh of Lincoln: Church and King in the Late Twelfth Century

The previous two chapters have been very much about religion and society, although I hope that they have shown how difficult it is to differentiate social from political history in the twelfth century. This chapter will be much more about religion and politics. It will be good to note from the start that I am not *equating* the institution of 'the church' with 'religion'. The two principal *dramatis personae* present in many ways a contrast, but for both religious devotion played its part in how they faced the dilemmas of serving two masters, church and king.

The reader will notice that I have not used the phrase 'church and state', which was more in vogue with historians 50 or 60 years ago than it is now. It is arguable that one can hardly speak of a state, where there is no one political capital where most of the political events occurred; nor anywhere the centre of a bureaucracy was located which linked the capital with the localities, as for instance in China down the ages, or as in the Byzantine state with Constantinople as its capital. In England at least until Henry III's reign the kings exercised an itinerant rule. They were constantly on the move from one royal manor or castle to another, including in Normandy and, under the Angevins, their other continental possessions. Indeed John's loss of Normandy in 1204 was one necessary pre-condition for the development of an English state. But its immediate consequences were John's intensification of his English itinerary, and of his endeavour to make himself master of the British Isles. The development of London as a capital was a slow one![1] True, from Henry II's reign there was a permanent court of royal justices located at Westminster, though itinerant royal justice continued also; and from this reign the Exchequer was also permanently located at Westminster when in session, though the Treasury remained at Winchester until the thirteenth century. That necessitated Henry's having also another treasury at the house of the military order of Templars in London. But a decisive phase in London's evolution as a capital came only with Henry III (1216–72), who, as David Carpenter says, spent more time at Westminster than any previous king.[2] Parliament was in that reign still in an embryonic state of evolution, but, even then, when so-called parliaments were summoned, it was not necessarily (though it was usually) to London rather than, say, to the more central Oxford.

As to bureaucracy, one can hardly speak of Church and State as separate entities when there was no state bureaucracy separate from the church administrators, which there was not before the sixteenth century. In our period there was no bureaucracy having an independent existence and ethos of its own and not subject to the day to day will of the ruler, albeit some of the king's administrators were laymen. When Henry II took over a number of previously baronial castles in 1177, the people he sent out to run them were nothing like Chinese bureaucrats, or British administrators in India, who had passed their examinations. They were knights of his *privata familia*; they were his familiars, members of his household.[3] And they would have remained familiars, in the sense that when the king came into their region on his itinerary, they would have been drawn into the 'familiar' circle of his court.[4] There have always been limits to the concept of bureaucracy in England, at least up to the nineteenth century, by reason of the highly participatory character of the aristocracy, gentry and some peasants in the rule of their localities; but even allowing for that, the royal administrators of the twelfth and early thirteenth centuries cannot really be called a state bureaucracy. It was the thirteenth century before a full legal profession developed, or before a lay, professional judicature started to come into being.[5]

As to the church, the notion that the Church was a recognisable entity is a dubious one in the whole of our period. When people spoke of the *Ecclesia Anglicana*, the English Church, in the late twelfth century, they were more often than not thinking of the interests of their own local church. So it was with the monks of Christ Church, Canterbury, who were prime users of the phrase.[6] They wanted to say that the whole English church would suffer, meaning that their own Canterbury church would suffer, if the archbishops of Canterbury were allowed to set up a college of clergy, using Christ Church property, to supplant them as an electoral college. They were trying to gain the support of the papacy in the interests of their own church. We have already seen that action in the interests of one's own local church was at this time in practice far more important to most people than were the ideas of the universal or English church, though these ideas were by no means unimportant in the canon law or the thought of the time. Above all, without the great numbers of churchmen and clerics who participated in secular rule, the latter would have been unworkable. Thus the phrase 'church and state' is not a useful analytical tool for the history of c. 1200.

Nonetheless the bishops and many abbots necessarily straddled the religious and secular worlds. As we have seen earlier, bishops owed homage to the king for their lands, or baronies, as well as having the obligations of a religious pastor. Most bishops took both their secular/political and their pastoral obligations seriously, even the most hardened royal administrators like Richard FitzNeal, Royal Treasurer, author of the celebrated *Dialogue of the Exchequer*, and Bishop of London (1189–98).[7] *How* they straddled these worlds, and with what priorities, varied from one man to the next. The Third Lateran Council (1179) under Pope Alexander III forbade clergy to be involved in secular affairs.[8] That was not practicable, but how far churchmen chose to abide by or distance themselves from the spirit of Lateran III varied. Bishop Seffrid II of Chichester (1180–1204) when he first appears in English records c. 1172, having probably been studying law in Bologna, appears as Archdeacon of Chichester and a royal judge.[9] But unlike Hubert Walter or Richard FitzNeal, other than attending Great Councils Seffrid entirely ceased to be a royal servant after he became a bishop. There was a quantum leap within the clergy about becoming a bishop which Seffrid presumably felt, as Becket had very much felt it, and which Hubert Walter and Richard FitzNeal obviously did not feel to the same extent.

There is yet another factor making for the peculiar degree of intermingling between royal and ecclesiastical government in England. Whereas in twelfth-century Normandy the power of the regional aristocratic families over bishoprics and cathedral chapters was considerable and affected the choice of bishops, as Jörg Peltzer has shown – and Julia Barrow has made the same contrast in the case of Germany – in England there were for different reasons no such inhibitions on the Angevin kings in appointing their servants to bishoprics.[10] For instance, Henry II's list of nominees to bishoprics after the Becket conflict and the putting down of the Great Rebellion of 1173–74, a list ratified by the pope, was almost solid with royal servants, most of whom did not then cease to act in the royal administration.[11] A rare exception here was John, Dean of Chichester, who became bishop there; which perhaps shows, à propos of Bishop Seffrid II above, that the bishop of a relatively poor and unimportant bishopric like Chichester, with almost no significant royal servants among its canons, could afford more than most to eschew royal service and concentrate on being a bishop.

The point was made earlier, in the discussion of the resolution of the Investiture Contest in 1107 under Henry I, that how bishops managed their double lives would constitute their greatest political problem for a long time thereafter and that the contrast between Archbishop Hubert Walter and Bishop Hugh of Lincoln (though it was not in all respects a contrast) would show this up. It is time to fulfil that promise to pay.

Hubert Walter

Hubert Walter was born of a baronial family in Norfolk, probably in the early 1140s. It was only a minor baronial family, but still he was not open to the contempt which Henry II had been able to pour on Becket for his low social origins. His rise was due to his having been brought up by his uncle, Ranulf Glanvill, the Chief Justiar of Henry II in the 1180s, and Ranulph's wife. Glanvill's patronage brought Hubert into prominence in royal justice, and into the Deanship of York in 1185. He became Bishop of Salisbury in 1189, and perhaps simultaneously vowed to go on the Third Crusade, Saladin having re-taken Jerusalem for the Muslims in 1187. The Third Crusade was the making of Hubert. Its leader was King Richard I, and its spiritual leader was Archbishop Baldwin of Canterbury. When Baldwin died at Acre in November 1190, Hubert became *de facto* spiritual leader of the Crusade and much more besides. He gained a reputation as an administrator for supplying the army, for helping those crusaders in material difficulties, and, as a diplomat, for his dealings with Saladin.[12] In fact he became an international figure. He even directed military operations competently, following in the footsteps of Adhemar of Le Puy, the fighting bishop and papal legate on the First Crusade, and of the fictional Turpin in the *Song of Roland*. He also gained a reputation for genuinely caring about the religious objectives of the Crusade. The chronicler Richard of Devizes commented on how he and Archbishop Baldwin had actually fulfilled their vow to go on the Crusade, unlike those bishops who had only 'saluted Jerusalem from afar'.[13] It is not surprising, therefore, that in 1193 Richard I should have insisted that Hubert be elected Archbishop of Canterbury, and that he had also made him his chief minister, i.e. Chief

Justiciar, with responsibility for government finance and for justice, law and order.

Modern historians have tended to think of Henry II as a greater king than Richard I because of the solid weight of legal achievement in his reign, the creation of the common law indeed, with its writs, forms of legal action and expansion of the system of royal itinerant justices. Contemporaries, however, had different priorities, which made them prefer a heroic and chivalric warrior king like Richard. One sees this attitude clearly in the most important English chronicler of the late twelfth century, the royal chancery clerk Roger of Howden. But John Gillingham has been at pains to show how there was a good deal less than has sometimes been thought of impetuous romanticism and dashing bravado about Richard as a war leader, and a good deal more stress on planning, techniques of siege warfare, finance and supply lines. 'Richard', writes Gillingham, 'won his wars not simply by deeds of prowess on the battlefield, but also by being able to transform the economic resources of the Angevin Empire into military supplies and ensure that these supplies were in the right place at the right time.'[14] This was exactly the kind of capacity which recommended Hubert Walter to Richard on the Third Crusade. As the king's Chief Justiciar in England, Hubert showed himself to be a financial wizard.

Richard had been captured by the Duke of Austria while returning from the Crusade and had been handed over, a great prize, to the Emperor Henry VI. Thus a large ransom had to be paid. Hubert raised the then gigantic sum of £100,000, mostly during the year 1193, by methods some of which would probably not bear close moral inspection, and there was some unrest about it. Yet when it came to Magna Carta in 1215, Clause 15 of which promised no more taking of arbitrary taxation, one of the explicit exceptions to this was for 'ransoming the king's body'. Hubert had been in tune with Magna Carta. Hubert created a system for ensuring that the king's government would get all the money arising from 'pleas of the crown' in the localities. If a dead body were found anywhere, for instance, the king was almost always due some money – the chattels of the dead man, perhaps, or if he had been murdered the chattels of the criminal, or if he had fallen off a moving cart, the cart itself which was forfeit to the king. In short Hubert invented the office of the coroner, the keeper of the pleas of the crown in the shire.[15] He also developed a novel system for assessing the value of land before specific land taxes, or carucages, were introduced.[16] Royal government, as run by Hubert Walter for the five years 1193–98, while Richard I was mostly in France fighting to hold his continental lands together in face of the French king, Philip Augustus, is a subject of endless fascination. One can best study it in the Pipe Rolls, the account rolls of the royal Exchequer for those years, with the help of Doris Stenton's masterly introductions to the printed text. Of all English churchmen, not even Wolsey was so pivotal to English medieval government as was Archbishop Hubert Walter in the mid-1190s. He was to Richard I doubtless as Henry II had hoped that Becket would be to himself.

The Justiciar/Archbishop had his own ecclesiastical henchmen as administrators. One of them was William of Wrotham. William would subsequently become Archdeacon of Taunton (if he was not already so by 1197) and an important naval administrator under John.[17] If he was the William to whom Geoffrey of Vinsauf (a Northampton master) dedicated his *Poetria Nova*, as is quite possible, in the early thirteenth century, he must also have been a person of considerable culture.[18] In 1197, if not before, Hubert sent him to the South West as financial administrator of the Devon and Cornwall tin mines and the tax on tin owing to the king. Hubert's Assize of Weights and Measures of 1196 had its use here in enabling William to standardise the 'wheels' of tin for taxation purposes. In 1197–98, the new tax on tin, over and above the old one, brought in more than £579, the annual income of a sizeable barony, for the royal government, and in 1198–99 just short of £601.[19]

Hubert gave up the Justiciarship in 1198. That did not mean that he was excluded from a role in secular affairs, particularly as King John made him Chancellor after his coronation in 1199. But it did mean a greatly reduced role in such affairs. There is little doubt that, although Hubert himself may have wanted at some level to be relieved of administrative burdens that he had borne for nearly a decade, the decisive influence in his resignation was the election of Pope Innocent III in January 1198. Innocent had studied in the school of Peter the Chanter at Paris in the 1180s (he was only 39 in 1198) and had the distaste of that school, and of the Third Lateran Council (1179), for the involvement of clerics in secular affairs. He would choose a professor of moral theology in Peter the Chanter's school, Stephen Langton, to be Archbishop of Canterbury after Hubert died in 1205. This is what Roger of Howden says about the pressure which Innocent put on Richard I about Hubert:

The lord pope carefully admonished the lord Richard king of England, with fatherly exhortation [Richard was eleven years older than Innocent!], that for his soul's sake he should no longer permit the archbishop to engage in secular administration nor in future admit him or any other bishop or priest to secular office. He also ordered all prelates in virtue of obedience not to rashly undertake secular office.[20]

At the same time Innocent did not renew the papal legateship which Hubert had held since 1195.[21]

Howden also said that already in 1196 the Archbishop had offered to resign his Justiciarship, and that Richard had accepted this, 'although reluctantly because he had found nobody like him for preserving the laws and rights of his kingdom'. But Hubert had immediately regretted his offer, considering how much money he had raised for the king in the previous two years. Howden goes on censoriously:

*O unhappy bishop! Although he had often read, 'nobody can serve two lords', he had chosen to put the sacerdotal office second (*postponere*) rather than not adhere to the earthly king.*[22]

We may give the go-by to the question how good a position Howden himself was in to point the finger here. What this passage suggests is that Howden could appeal to a goodly sector of educated public opinion who thought Hubert Walter a scandal for the way he combined the highest ecclesiastical and secular offices.

How scandalous was Hubert? As Chief Justiciar he undoubtedly administered justice in a corrupt way and partly by these means amassed a huge fortune. At no time would that have been regarded as ethical; and it shows exactly the kind of reason why the School of Peter the Chanter disliked seeing churchmen mixed up in secular affairs. But at least he did not attempt, as did his potential rival, William Longchamp, Chief Justiciar (1190–91) and Bishop of Ely (1189–97), to use his secular position to build up a political power of his own independent of the king.[23] Nor, unlike Bishop William, was he a low-born foreign favourite when such considerations were starting to matter in English politics.

When the Third Lateran Council (1179) under Pope Alexander III forbade clergy to be involved in secular affairs, it was forwarding however impracticably a distinctive Gregorian idea – that the clergy should be like a race of purified Levites set apart from the laity. The most acute moment of crisis for Hubert in his dual role of Justiciar and Archbishop came in early April 1196 when a London demagogue called William FitzOsbert championed the so-called poor in resisting the unfair taxes to which the ruling elite of the city were subjecting them, doubtless in response to the demands of Hubert Walter and the royal government. The idea that FitzOsbert was championing the poor must have been largely rhetoric on his part, for as Tocqueville argued in his *Ancien Régime*, rebellions are not usually the work of the abject poor, and where taxation is concerned, are much more likely to be driven by those of rising prosperity who are baulked of their rising expectations. In any event when William got into hot water he took

sanctuary in the church of St Mary le Bow. Whereupon the Justiciar/
Archbishop set fire to the church, smoked him out, and had him hanged.[24]
The rebellion was soon ended and, as Christopher Cheney wrote, 'thanks
to the archbishop-justiciar the city elders could again sleep quietly in
their beds'.[25]

At exactly the same time, Richard I, having himself heard of rumblings
against the methods of collecting his ransom, sent the Abbot of Caen to
enquire into the collection. Hubert invited him to lunch at the newly built
Lambeth Palace, where the abbot became unaccountably ill at the table
and died five days later. Eight days after that, the king wrote a letter to
Hubert, meekly if not subserviently saying that he had ordered his enquiry
not out of cupidity but only to know who his friends had been.[26]

No further comment appears to surface about the Abbot of Caen's
death; but in the case of William FitzOsbert, the monks of Canterbury
were livid, because they held the patronage of the church of St Mary le
Bow (or Arches) whose sanctuary had been violated. This is what Roger of
Howden wrote about it:

The monks of Canterbury, knowing that their London church of St Mary
had been thus violated by order of their archbishop, who although he
served the king ought nonetheless to have preserved ecclesiastical rights
in tact, were indignant and heavy of heart over him, and were not on
speaking terms with him.[27]

The Canterbury monk's outrage clearly had a synthetic element to it, for
they immediately used it to good effect in appealing to the pope against
Hubert's continuing with the Lambeth chapel project as a church of
canons to the detriment of their property and archiepiscopal electoral
rights (April to May 1196).[28]

However, it may be doubted whether Hubert would have considered
himself a scandal, whatever the Parisian professors or Roger of Howden
thought, or whether he would have thought that in serving the king he was
unable devotedly to serve God, or to wield both spiritual and secular swords.
It is probable that contemporary opinions were much more divided about
him than now meets the eye. Let us consider what he or one of his learned
clerks might have been able to say about his behaviour over William
FitzOsbert. Hubert Walter was born during the Anarchy of Stephen's reign
and could have seen what a legacy of fear and disorder it had left in
Norfolk itself with its problem of criminal fugitives in the 1150s.[29] To
judge by the role he gave in his *Edictum Regium* of the previous year
(1195) to local knights in bringing criminals to book in the shires, one

may safely assume that there was a large body of opinion in the shires that no more wanted to return to those days than he did himself.[30] Then, if his critics wanted to draw on *their* learning, *he* could point to Augustine of Hippo's *City of God*, who, it was well known, maintained that it was the duty of the citizens of the heavenly city to take action in order to secure the peace of the earthly city, through which they had to pass on their pilgrimage towards their heavenly homeland.

If Hubert were then asked whether he needed to violate sanctuary and to have been so brutal in dealing with FitzOsbert, he could point out that in the absence of the king abroad, he was responsible for the king's peace which the king promised by his coronation oath to keep. How else could he have nipped so dangerous an uprising in the bud? He had no organised police force whose members' leave could be cancelled in such a situation.[31] Nor did he have magistrates' courts where such trouble-makers could be dealt with the following Monday morning (FitzOsbert was hanged on a Saturday). Who knew how the disturbance might have spread, with more loss of life, had he not been able to hang FitzOsbert before Sunday (when it *would* have been a real scandal)? We have to be careful not to judge Hubert by the standards of our own time. We only abolished capital punishment in the 1960s, and the immediacy of FitzOsbert's hanging represents, in not dissimilar circumstances, what every ship's captain did with trouble-makers as late as the eighteenth century.

As to the violation of sanctuary, Hubert would surely have agreed that it was regrettable. Sanctuary had its function where private feud, private killings and private vengeance persisted, and Paul Hyams has shown that they very much did persist up to and beyond Hubert's time. For those seeking a refuge from enraged kinsmen or neighbours, sanctuary could provide the means for a very useful cooling off period. FitzOsbert himself had just killed a man when he took refuge in the church of St Mary le Bow; thus he could look like a justified sanctuary-seeker. On the other hand he had done a lot more than kill a man; he had led a public disturbance in London. And attitudes to sanctuary were changing when it came to fugitives from public justice.[32] Besides, it could be argued that it was FitzOsbert, who was far from poor himself and seemed to be only stirring up trouble, who was guilty of sacrilege in cynically taking sanctuary, rather than Hubert Walter.

The fact is that there was a strong streak of religious devotion in Hubert's make-up, to the external eye as strong as in Becket and less tied up with his political image. His first recorded act as archbishop was to put on the black habit of the Augustinian Canons at Merton Priory, Surrey,[33] the house from which Becket's confessor, Robert of Merton, came. He was on good terms also with the Cistercians and the Carthusians. He visited on one occasion the Carthusian Priory of Witham, of which his contemporary St Hugh had been prior before becoming Bishop of Lincoln (see next section of this chapter). There he encountered the saintly monk, Master Adam of Dryburgh. After Mass he took Adam to his cell, burst into tears, confessed his sins, took off his clothes 'like a little child of Christ' to receive from him 'the discipline of the rod', and then asked Adam to compose for him a treatise on the Lord's Prayer. Later, when the archbishop was crossing the sea on affairs of state and the Prior of Witham was going to the General Chapter of his Order, Hubert took him into his own ship and sat with him alone in the stern having a conversation about spiritual matters.[34]

In 1200, after he had ceased to be Justiciar and could devote himself more to his ecclesiastical job, Hubert held a Provincial Council at Westminster. Its provisions laid a strong emphasis on the sacramental and the pastoral, e.g. instructions for parish priests about the orderly celebration of the sacraments, no heavy new pensions to the impoverishment of parish churches, no fees to be charged for sacraments, enforcement of tithe payments, provision for schoolmasters to teach without charge, rules for marriage. Cheney has said of this Council, 'the theologians of Paris rather than the lawyers of Bologna are in the background of (its) sacramental provisions'.[35] They also hark back to the Third Lateran Council (1179); in themselves they show Hubert Walter as an important reformer between the Third and Fourth Lateran Councils.[36] Moreover in Hubert's very magnificence one may detect a pastoral quality. He probably began the new Gothic Great Hall at Canterbury, now largely demolished. Its huge dimensions can be taken as a symbol of his largesse and hospitality. As with Becket, Hubert's view of magnificence was inseparable from 'the sacral quality of episcopal leadership'.[37] Hubert Walter's splendid throne at Canterbury (1200-01), with design features echoing those of the iron-work in the stained-glass windows at Canterbury, suggest that it was a symbol of reconciliation with the Canterbury monks after the archbishop had dropped the projects of the Hackington and Lambeth colleges of canons.[38]

When one surveys the evidence for Hubert's whole episcopal activity, as Bishop of Salisbury and Archbishop of Canterbury, it is hard to avoid the conclusion that he was neither more secular than religious, nor more religious than secular, but that he was always trying to hold these two aspects in a kind of tension, like the tensions in the ribbed vaults and pointed arches of gothic architecture in whose earliest age he lived. Of the three successors of Thomas Becket as Archbishop of Canterbury (Richard of Dover, 1174–84, Baldwin of Ford, 1184–90, and Hubert Walter, 1193–1205), it is not Hubert, but strangely enough Richard of Dover, Canterbury monk and previously Prior of Dover, who looks the most secularist in holding this tension. Richard consistently defended the king's role in episcopal elections (it had been great in his own election) to the irritation of Alexander III, and he gave full rein to royal participation in ecclesiastical matters.[39] But perhaps a pragmatic secularist was what was most needed at Canterbury immediately after Becket!

St Hugh, Bishop of Lincoln (1186–1200)

Hugh was born probably at Avalon in Burgundy and probably in 1140. Both he and Hubert Walter were from similar aristocratic backgrounds and were about the same age as each other. Religious concerns were of primary importance to both men, and both had close connections with the Carthusian monks, albeit Hubert was an outside admirer while Hugh was a member of the order. But whereas nobody would have thought of Hubert as a saint, or a Holy Man bishop, Hugh had that reputation with everyone when he became a bishop and while he held the office.[40] There was at that time little distinction between the public and the private lives of a bishop, any more than there was of a king. The point about Hugh as a bishop was that his holiness was an effective instrument of his public and political office, arguably more effective than Anselm's was in his case. Thus with Hubert Walter and St Hugh, two men so similar by birth and in age, there is from the start an arresting contrast in how their religion and their politics related to each other.

Hugh joined the Grande Chartreuse when he was 23, and remained a Carthusian monk there, in the mountains of the Massif Centrale, for 16 years. For the last six he was procurator, in effect bursar, so he must have had some capacity as an administrator. The Carthusians lived, worked, prayed and ate for the most part in separate cells with small herb gardens attached to each cell, but they came together on Sundays and feast days, for Mass and to eat and converse together. Thus they knew solitude but did not live in isolation. They were not solitaries. Their food was simple and excluded meat, but was not as austere as that of the ancient desert fathers. Their austerities were moderated by prudence. Their diet included fish, eggs, cheese, wholemeal bread, vegetables and wine.[41] The daily meal of each monk was passed into his cell through a hutch from the cloister. They had lay brothers to do the manual work; these baked their bread, tended their sheep, and made their shoes. What have such details to do with Hugh as the later bishop? They amounted to a way of life which was widely respected for its purity and spirituality, and which was thus perceived as a foundation for holiness.

Unlike the Cistercians, the Carthusians did not even affect to despise learning. They had good libraries and read the books in them. As a young man Hugh himself was known as a fast reader, with a facility to find quickly whatever citation he wanted from the Bible or the saints' lives or the fathers in Chartreuse's vast library (literally, 'from so great an ocean of books').[42] This is relevant to the learning, and the kind of learning, that Hugh would foster at Lincoln as its bishop. There is another point relevant to Hugh's eventually becoming Bishop of Lincoln. The Cistercian, Saint Bernard, would have liked everyone in his ideal of the world to become a Cistercian monk. The Carthusians knew that their vocation could only be for the few, but it does seem to have been thought that their way of life was a good spiritual springboard from which to share their love of God with others by becoming bishops. For although Hugh was the first (and last) Carthusian to become a bishop in England, in France there had been 32 Carthusian bishops by 1200.[43] Their prior, Guy I (1106–36), in his influential *Twelve Meditations* had written about the equality of all men, who all belong to the body of Christ, saying, 'if for whatever reason you lose the will to save one man, no matter whom, you cut off a limb from Christ's body'.[44] In this secluded life there was the propulsion towards the pastorate and not to live only for oneself. It was like the idea of the monk/pope, Gregory the Great (590–604), well known throughout the Middle Ages, that the contemplative monastic life was what best qualified monks to go out into the active life and win souls for God.

After 16 years at the Grande Chartreuse, Hugh was appointed by his prior and King Henry II to be Prior of Witham in Somerset in 1179, aged 39. It was a new house that had got off to a bad start. The king was advised in this by the Count of Maurienne, an aristocrat of Chartreuse's region with whom Henry had earlier been in negotiations about the marriage of his son John. The year 1179 was that in which Louis VII of France, accompanied by Henry, made a pilgrimage to Thomas Becket's shrine at Canterbury, so it may be that Henry's desire to make a good appointment to a house of an order which he admired was partly seen by him as further expiation for Becket's martyrdom.[45] The seven years during which Hugh was Prior of Witham laid the foundation of his reputation for holiness throughout Britain, according to his biographer, Adam of Eynsham. Part of the reason for the spread of his reputation was his continuing closeness

to Henry II. Hugh perhaps came as close as anyone to being a genuine
friend of Henry. They even looked alike, so that there were those who
thought that Hugh was a natural son of Henry, an impossibility, but an idea
revealing of their affection for each other. A mutual trust developed between
them in these years. According to Adam of Eynsham, they saw each other
frequently and Hugh freely criticised the king for keeping bishoprics and
abbacies vacant so that he could draw the revenues, or making unsuitable
appointments.[46] One is reminded here of how Roger, Bishop of Worcester,
got away with criticising Henry to his face over Becket (see p. 85). Adam
also says that Hugh helped to sustain Henry during his troubles of the
early 1180s by his consolation and his prayers – shades of Christina of
Markyate and Abbot Geoffrey of St Albans (see pp. 19–21).[47]

The reader may wonder whether I am not relying too much on the
unsupported testimony of Adam of Eynsham in all this. Adam was a monk
of the Benedictine abbey of Eynsham (Oxon), a house in the diocese of
Lincoln and under the patronage of its bishop. He was Hugh's chaplain,
but only for the last years of his life. He probably exaggerated the importance of Hugh's connection to Eynsham and it may be that there are hagiographical overstatements in his *Magna Vita*. Given, however, that Adam
was recommended as biographer by the brethren of Witham,[48] and that
Hugh had left his Priorship only eleven years before Adam became his
chaplain, returning to Witham from Lincoln for a period of prayer and
meditation every year, it is likely that he was essentially a knowledgeable
and trustworthy witness to Hugh at Witham in the 1180s.

According to Adam, Witham was not only a spiritual community under
Hugh; like the Grande Chartreuse itself, it was also a learned one, attract-
ing distinguished scholars, both secular clergy and monks.[49] So it would be
with the Lincoln Cathedral chapter when he was Bishop of Lincoln.

Henry II determined on Hugh's election to Lincoln at a royal council at
Eynsham, the actual monastery of Hugh's biographer, Adam. It was the
largest diocese and one of the richest sees in England, and it had been more
vacant than filled during the previous two decades. A number of the dignitaries and canons of Lincoln Cathedral were present. 'Some of them',
wrote Adam, 'would certainly not have refused a bishopric if pressed to
accept it!'[50] But, he continued, 'God had the heart of the king in his hand'
(for once), and the king was anxious to make up for the neglect of the see,
while drawing its revenues during its vacancy. The canons at first derided
the choice of someone so unknown (perhaps Adam exaggerated Hugh's
previous fame), and with such a foreign accent. When Hugh, however,
declared his election null and void unless he was elected in the chapter of

Lincoln according to canon law, and without the chapter's taking any account of the king's wishes or those of the Archbishop of Canterbury, the canons were so dumbstruck and impressed by this highly unusual insistence that they elected him unanimously.[51] It was the beginning of a harmonious relationship with the chapter, basic to his success as bishop. He used to call the canons 'my lords'.[52]

Although Hugh absolutely refused to take any secular office, saying once that he would obey Hubert Walter as archbishop but not as Chief Justiciar,[53] it was impossible for a bishop of an important diocese like Lincoln, by Henry II's time, not to be heavily involved in politics. As a major landholder, a bishop owed allegiance to the king as one of his tenants-in-chief. Hugh attended royal councils; he acted as an ambassador of the king to the King of France; he had to stand up to royal officials in defending the rights of his see; and when it came to laying down or lifting excommunications (for instance) it is not easy to distinguish secular and ecclesiastical politics. Thus Hugh was one of the ecclesiastics who excommunicated Count (later King) John in 1194 when he was in rebellion against his brother, King Richard I.[54]

So what difference did it make to Hugh as a bishop in politics that he was a Holy Man and known to be one? First of all he had the vital quality of strangerhood. His life of prayer and austerity as a Carthusian acted as a kind of long drawn-out ritual of dissociation from normal society, with all its suspicions, conflicts and clashes of personality. It seemed to put him above the party fray. Peter Brown has shown how this kind of strangerhood could give Holy Men of the fifth and sixth centuries in the East Mediterranean lands their authority to act as moral arbiters in their societies.[55] Hugh's strangerhood of holiness gave him freedom to speak out, a *franchise* as it has been called to say what he thought with impunity. Added to his strangerhood of holiness was his actually being a foreigner, a Burgundian, in England. Adam of Eynsham shows that Hugh himself very much stressed that he was a foreigner, an *advena*.[56] His very accent in speaking French was a constant reminder to the Anglo-Normans of this fact. We all know how a foreign accent can often be turned to the advantage of the speaker, making what he or she says the more arresting. So it probably was with Hugh. One may bet that he had his mimics in plenty.

But Hugh was also an aristocratic Holy Man, and that was important for Henry II, as we have seen from his despising Becket for his low social origins. Of course, as was pointed out at the time, aristocracy of birth was useless without aristocracy of manners to back it up. But Hugh was praised for having all the bearing, the courtesy, the considerateness of a true aristocrat.[57] Into the bargain, he was also a witty Holy Man. Thomas Becket was never known even to have essayed a joke. No doubt some people are more innately witty than others. But Becket, for all the nobility of his exile and death, was a knotted-up careerist who was probably incapable of the relaxation of personality needed to make an effective joke about anything. It was the relaxation born partly of his detached way of life that enabled Hugh to speak with boldness and wit.

A single story encapsulates most of what we have said about Hugh's personality so far.[58] Not long after he became bishop he aroused the vehement anger of Henry II by excommunicating Geoffrey, the Chief Forester, because of the harassments of his men by the king's foresters. These were the keepers of the vast tracts of royal forest, preserved for the king's hunting, a pastime with which Henry II was obsessed. It was an established rule of this king that none of his barons or officials might be excommunicated, i.e. be cut off from the life and sacraments of the church and from its members, without his permission. The Becket conflict had started with the issue of Becket's excommunications. Some of Henry's courtiers represented to him the ingratitude of Hugh (as if he had ever aspired to be a bishop in the first place!). Henry summoned the bishop, probably to Woodstock, and when he learned of the bishop's impending arrival took a number of his nobles with him to a pleasant spot – where else – in the nearby forest. When Hugh arrived, nobody returned his greeting. The king sat silently and sullenly stitching a leather bandage onto an injured finger. Hugh put his hand lightly on the shoulder of an earl who was sitting next to the king and made him give up his place. There he sat observing everything 'as though from some lofty watch-tower of inward reason'. At last he broke the silence by saying lightly, 'how you resemble your cousins of Falaise!' Henry burst into laughter, and those with him who understood the brazen joke were amazed but could not help smiling too. Most could not understand it at all. So Henry explained humorously:

You cannot understand the way this barbarian has insulted us, so I will explain. The mother of our great grandfather William, the Conqueror of this land, is reputed to have been of humble birth, and to have come from the important Norman town of Falaise, which is celebrated for its leatherwork. This giber saw me sewing up my finger and so complimented me on looking like my cousins of Falaise.

When questioned, the bishop said that he knew Henry had worked hard to make him a bishop and in return he had to look after the king's soul, and save it from the perils which would befall it if Hugh did not look after the interests of his church properly. As to not consulting the king before excommunicating his Chief Forester, he had deemed it unnecessary since the king was quite wise enough to recognise what was right! This answer was almost as brazen as the joke, but Henry accepted it and with a beaming face embraced the bishop. That was in effect the end of the matter.

One could multiply stories about Hugh's wit and boldness. One point to notice is his determination to defend the rights of his church. His aims in this were like those of Becket and all other bishops and abbots of his age; it was his means of achieving these aims that were spectacularly successful. The same thing can be seen again in 1197 when Richard I, fighting the King of France in order to hold onto Normandy, demanded of his bishops and lay magnates to provide him with 300 knights to fight for him all the year round and the money to pay for them. Hubert Walter called an assembly to agree this, but Hugh led the opposition, maintaining that as a tenant-in-chief of the king he did not owe him military service (for his estates) abroad but only in England. (Note that by now, notwithstanding that Richard was ruler of an Anglo-Norman kingdom, Normandy was beginning to be regarded as 'abroad'.) Such a thing was against the customs of his church and would be to its permanent disadvantage, so that his successor would say (quoting Ezekiel), 'the fathers have eaten sour grapes and the children's teeth are set on edge'.[59] The archbishop's lips were trembling with anger when he turned next to Herbert le Poore, Bishop of Salisbury. But Herbert followed Hugh's lead and the council was dissolved with no result. Richard I ordered the temporal possessions of both bishops to be seized in punishment, but the Exchequer officials were frightened of the Holy Man's curse, and the poor Bishop of Salisbury bore the brunt of the royal government's vengeance.[60]

Hugh's reputation for holiness must have been enhanced by his whole conduct of his episcopal office. His model was clearly Pope Gregory the Great's *Pastoral Care*, perhaps the greatest book ever written on how to be a Christian bishop, and a book universally influential in the Middle Ages. Much of this book is about how different sorts of people have to be treated in different ways to get the best out of them. That may help to explain why Hugh suspended one priest for naively, or carelessly celebrating an illegal, under-age marriage,[61] while showing a humorous toleration towards the priests who recited several gospels at once (see p. 101). It may also explain why he was notably kind to the poor, to widows and to lepers,[62] and notably protective of the Lincoln Jews when the pogroms got under way at the time of the Third Crusade in 1190,[63] while reproaching the powerful, including kings. Above all, Gregory was insistent that amidst his active pastorate a bishop should not neglect the life of prayer and contemplation. If he did not keep rekindling within himself the fire of the Holy Spirit he would freeze amidst his external works. Thus Hugh would withdraw to Witham once or twice a year for the sake of contemplation (for how long at a time is not stated). For this purpose he particularly favoured autumn, while his flock were busy gathering in the harvest.[64]

Hugh built up the cathedral chapter at Lincoln as an important centre of learning, perhaps on the model of Paris and its cathedral. For the greatest centre of learning in England by the 1190s, Oxford, was as far away from its own diocesan centre as anywhere could be (probably not entirely by accident). That diocesan centre was Lincoln itself, Lincoln was at the north-east tip of its own vast diocese, Oxford at its south-west tip. Hugh considered the office of canon to be a pastoral one, however, and would not appoint canons who would draw the revenues of their prebends as absentees. He insisted that canons should reside at Lincoln, and there is evidence that he built up the revenues of the common fund to support the resident canons.[65] Those who benefited from the endowments of the altar, he maintained, ought to serve at the altar (e.g. by celebrating Mass and by preaching).[66] He put a stop to the demands for prebends by royal clerks, or so Adam of Eynsham said; and to a distinguished theologian of Paris who said how greatly he desired to be a canon of Lincoln, Hugh replied that he would gladly have him at Lincoln if he were ready to reside – and, he added, were his virtue equal to his learning![67]

Hugh began his project by approaching Archbishop Baldwin, Hubert Walter's predecessor at Canterbury, saying that he was a foreigner who did not himself know the field. Baldwin assigned to him two of his own clerks, Master Robert of Bedford and Master Roger of Rolleston.[68] The latter was a particular success and rose to be Dean of Lincoln in 1195. Neither is known to have studied in Paris, but in general Lincoln learning under Hugh was markedly Paris-orientated. The application of a Paris theologian to be a canon implies it; so does the fact that Hugh's nephew, Reimund, when he ceased to be Archdeacon of Leicester and a canon of Lincoln in 1198, attended theology lectures in the Paris schools.[69] Paris was in the later twelfth century the greatest centre of moral theology in the West, its most famous theologian Peter the Chanter who died in 1197. The only known Paris master to reside at Lincoln under Hugh, in the 1190s, was the Englishman, Master William de Montibus. He and Peter were contemporary teachers at Paris, and though William was never apparently of Peter's school, they were similar to each other as theologians. As Joseph Goering has said, they together 'provide a valuable picture of the moral and pastoral interests of Paris theologians in the later twelfth century'.[70]

What most seems to show the Paris orientation of Lincoln under Hugh is the match between Hugh's practice as bishop and the moral teachings of Peter the Chanter's school. Hugh constantly emphasised the importance of confessing, and confessed his own sins to a priest every Saturday.[71] Peter the Chanter had the same emphasis and wrote in depth on the subject.[72] Hugh did not favour spectacular miracle stories about the Eucharist, preferring to understand the inner mystery of the sacrament.[73] Peter the Chanter was also markedly anti-superstitious and wrote against ordeals, looking for miracles, and other forms of tempting God.[74] Hugh was draconian in not allowing his chancery clerks or his officials to take bribes, to fine offenders unduly, or to oppress the laity financially in any other way. When they declared that 'the most holy archbishop and martyr Thomas [Becket] had taken fines', he replied that it was not *that* which had made him a saint![75] In other words, avarice was out. Peter the Chanter was equally adamant against financial exactions of the clergy, especially their taking personal fees for issuing documents.[76] A mark of how seriously Hugh took sacramental theology, as did Peter the Chanter's school, was the weight he attached to administering reverently the sacrament of confirmation; some bishops, Adam of Eynsham declared, administered it as they rode by, without even dismounting from their horses.[77]

Given the general idea up to Hugh's time, that the celibate life was superior to the married state, strengthened by the drive of the Gregorian Reform to set the priesthood apart, it is striking what emphasis Hugh is said to have given to the married laity. His biographer implies this at various points but is most explicit about it in reporting Hugh as saying:

When at the last the Lord shall judge every individual, he will not hold it against him that he was not a hermit or a monk, but will reject each of the damned because he had not been a real Christian. That blessed name must really represent the virtues it implies, and all sincere Christians must have loving hearts, truthful tongues and chaste bodies. The man of God often developed this further by describing and defining the properties and differences of these virtues. He taught that even married people, who never rose above the natural obligations of their state, should not be considered to be devoid of the virtue of chastity, but equally with virgins and celibates would be admitted to the glory of the heavenly kingdom. Thus the holy man impressed on the minds of ordinary people, that they

must consider themselves to be characterised by the single term Christian,
and that they must be able to explain this short and simple word to their
own people.[78]

All this represents ideas about the nobility and indissolubility of marriage
which were in the 1190s of surprisingly recent development. To put it in
context, we need a brief digression. David d'Avray, in an important book,
has referred to the twelfth century as being that of 'the Christianisation
of marriage'.[79] What does he mean by that? Something similar to what
Christopher Brooke means by pointing out that it was in the twelfth
century that the lay aristocracy of Europe allowed the Church to take over
almost completely the jurisdiction of the law of marriage.[80] Brooke's
explanation for this is that the aristocracies of Europe were coming to see
the advantage to themselves of monogamy. (Of course monogamy was
always an accepted principle of the Christian religion, but there had been
various ways in practice for aristocracies to treat it rather lightly.) His
explanation for the latter is twofold: one, to give clarity to inheritance
law and rights; the other, to give vent, as we saw earlier (pp. 161–2), to a
growing feeling that marriage was not only about procreation of children
but was also a *locus* of true love and friendship.

These developments in thought and feeling raised the question for both
canon lawyers and theologians – and their two disciplines were more intertwined in the twelfth century than they would later be: what constituted a
valid and legal marriage? The canon lawyers in particular were divided
about how much relative weight to give to the marriage promises (*verba de*
praesenti) and to the sexual consummation of the marriage, to consent or
to sexual union. Pope Alexander III (1159–81), himself previously a lawyer
at Bologna University, generally favoured consent as paramount, though
with the modification that impotence might be a ground for annulment.[81]
His thinking can be broadly traced through his decretal letters, answering
particular queries from all over Western Christendom and not least from
England. The question of what was a valid or an enduring marriage could
be a complex one. For instance, what about death-bed marriages? Or, in
an age of crusading and pilgrimage, how long after a husband had not
returned from a journey could a marriage be considered dissolved? Or,
when might a first marriage be after all valid when a second one had later
been contracted? This last was the issue on which Richard of Anstey
(Essex) fought and won his legal case to have his cousin, Mabel de Francheville, declared illegitimate so that he might take over her inheritance.[82]

Fortunately for us Richard kept a diary of his (huge) legal expenses in the early 1160s, so we know a lot about his case.[83] But, the big issue was generally consent versus consummation, and what showed consent.

All the above lay primarily in the domain of canon lawyers' arguments; but there was another aspect of validity and indissolubility of marriages,[84] where it was the Paris theologians who made the running. Until the Fourth Lateran Council, presided over by Pope Innocent III (1198–1216), church law forbade marriages within the seventh degree of kinship. Even in a society much more aware of the extended family than ours is, that extends to a huge prohibition. It means that two people who shared a great x 6 grandparent could not get married. Very few people nowadays know who their relations are beyond the third degree. The late Archbishop of Birmingham, Maurice Couve de Murville, knew who his fourth cousin was, but then he was a French prime minister of the same name! Hence people who got married, perhaps within rather closed social circles, later found that they were within the forbidden degrees and sought an annulment, claiming that the original marriage had been invalid. That was a de-stabilising factor in the institution of marriage. Indeed some men knowingly contracted marriages within the forbidden degrees, so that if they did not like their wives, they could subsequently get an annulment! All this, as well as the easy use of spiritual affinity to annul marriages, Peter the Chanter argued strenuously against as having a de-stabilising effect on marriage.[85] Being a sacrament, marriage came very much into his sacramental theology. Under Innocent III, the Fourth Lateran Council of 1215 reduced the forbidden degrees from the seventh to the fourth and refused to allow witnesses to testify about this on mere hearsay evidence, 'because from numerous instances and definite proofs we have learnt that many dangers for lawful unions have arisen from this'.[86] Innocent III had himself studied theology under Peter the Chanter at Paris.[87]

We do not have direct evidence of what Hugh had to say specifically about the forbidden degrees of kinship; but we do know that he had had to deal in high aristocratic society with at least one case of this sort.[88] We also know that he issued a constitution against under-age marriages, i.e. of children incapable of meaningful consent.[89] Hence we can see that he went in exactly the same direction as Peter the Chanter, seeking to counter everything that would undermine the validity and the stability of marriages, and to exalt the lay, married state. The Fourth Lateran Council sought by every means to bring the laity back into the full sacramental life of the church, after the effect of the Gregorian Reform had tended to be their part-exclusion.[90] Both the school of Peter the Chanter and Hugh played their part in preparing the ground for this Council. And Hugh played an important role as Bishop of Lincoln in mediating Parisian ideas and applying Parisian theology to the English church.

Conclusion

The differences between these two giants of the late twelfth-century English church are obvious. Hubert was a royal servant par excellence and brilliant at raising huge sums of money for Richard I's wars and government; whereas when Richard asked his magnates to raise a once-off aid for him, Hugh refused outright to lend himself to such exactions, saying that 'it was not for him to become the carrier of royal instructions'.[91] Like Hubert, Hugh was not averse to shows of wealth with his love of fine rings and reliquaries and his jeweller resident at Banbury;[92] but unlike Hubert he showed no disposition to build up a personal fortune.

The similarities, however, need more bringing into the open. Hugh was a saintly Carthusian; Hubert, though not a member of that order, had great feeling and admiration for it. Hugh may have channelled Parisian moral theology through Lincoln into the English church, but nothing could be more striking than the Parisian influence in the canons of Hubert Walter's provincial council at Westminster in 1200, when he had become less of a royal official and more of an archbishop. How could one more seek to bring the laity into the mainstream of the church's sacramental life than, for instance, by instructing priests to recite the words of the canon of the Mass distinctly? And anyone who remembers the days of the Latin Mass in our own times, will know that it would be a mistake to call this irrelevant where the non-latinate laity were concerned. How could Hubert be more Parisian, as well as more true to the Third Lateran Council of 1179, than by imposing strict limits on the pecuniary takings of archdeacons, rural deans and the clergy generally? How could one better try to protect marriages from the strain imposed on them by crusading and other long pilgrimages than by laying down that the latter were only to be undertaken by the mutual consent of married partners?[93] Hugh was not at this provincial council of 1200 because he was either still not back from a visit to Rome, or because he was already lying at the Temple Church, London, in his last illness. It may be, nonetheless, that he had more direct input into Hubert's canons than we can now see or define.

Above all it is emphatically not the case that whereas Hubert was a great sustainer of kingly rule, Hugh on the contrary was a 'hammer of kings'. As Karl Leyser has said, Hugh was nothing of the kind. True, he resisted the secular power, as many a twelfth-century churchman wished or tried to do when the rights and privileges of his own church were under threat. But (Leyser again), 'far from being committed to constant conflict, his opponency was occasional, and he had some understanding of his kings' predicaments'.[94] Hugh's joke about Henry II's 'cousins of Falaise', when considered closely, actually underpinned the rightfulness of the Angevin succession to the Normans.[95] And when, on another occasion he shook Richard I's shoulders because that king was denying him the kiss of peace, it showed how much he valued (if not at any cost) being at peace with his king.[96] Thus, while Hubert Walter supplied Richard I with law and order and with money, and so sustained him, St Hugh supplied Henry II and Richard I with sacrality. Henry II, as we saw in the previous chapter, for all his coarse humour and vindictiveness, knew early in his reign that he needed to give his kingship a sacral dimension. He probably felt it not less, with the rising tide of financial administration and legalism in royal government during his reign, when in 1186 he appointed a Holy Man to one of his principal bishoprics.

Intellectual Life and Culture and How They Related to Politics in the Twelfth and Early Thirteenth Century

This chapter was born of an attempt to show students how their answers to examination questions about politics could get a lift from considering the intellectual life behind politics. For politics rarely or never happens in an intellectual and cultural vacuum. Think of William Gladstone and his education as a classicist and his religious thinking as moving influences in his politics. Think of Anselm and his philosophical theology as a moving influence in his conduct of the archbishopric of Canterbury. The fact that it is not always easy to state in precise or concrete terms what that influence is does not absolve us from recognising that even the most unlikely people involved in politics, like Roger of Salisbury, are often thinking and reading people. I divide this chapter into four sections: Science and the Exchequer under Henry I; the Writing of History and Stephen's Reign; the Beginning of Legal Study at Oxford in the Reign of Henry II; and the Theologisation of Society.

Science and the Exchequer under Henry I

What lay behind the development of the Exchequer? In purely political terms, the huge dowry that Henry I had to pay for his daughter Mathilda's marriage to the Emperor Henry V must have had something to do with it. Also probably the great military and diplomatic expenses of holding on to

Normandy as a part of his kingdom once he had formally re-conquered it at the Battle of Tinchebrai in 1106. But behind that it has also to do with a learned current of interest in the sciences of calculation, which was by no means only that of the clergy, but which represented preoccupations of many members of the religious establishment. The study of arithmetic as the foundation subject in the quadrivium of the seven liberal arts, i.e. arithmetic, geometry, astronomy and music, occupied an important place in the curriculum of the cathedral school of Laon, to which Roger of Salisbury, head of the Exchequer sent his nephews, Alexander and Nigel (later Bishops of Lincoln and Ely). The same was true of the great schools of Lotharingia, such as Liège. In these schools the principles of calculating with an abacus was taught. Before Arabic numerals came into general use in the West (c. 1300), when Roman numerals were used, the abacus, with its columns of counters representing thousands, hundreds, tens and units (or on a base of eight rather than ten) was the principal way of doing calculatory arithmetic, for it is virtually impossible to do arithmetic using Roman numerals. The chequered cloth spread over the table in the early court of the Exchequer, this being a financial court to ensure that the king got all revenues due to him, was in effect a type of abacus, up and down which counters were moved to demonstrate financial calculations. It is an irony that an Arabic device was needed by the West to make calculations when for some reason it had not taken on Arabic numerals. Perhaps the reason was that while Platonist arithmetic, as represented in Boethius's *De Arithmetica*, was not calculatory, but a form of philosophical literature and of cosmology, calculatory arithmetic was mainly required in contexts where visual demonstration was all important, as in the accounting of sheriffs and other royal officials to the Exchequer.

In Henry I's reign an Exchequer clerk called Thurkill wrote a treatise on the abacus. When he came to how to do long division, he gave the example of 200 marks to be divided into a stated number of hides, 'which are the [number of] hides of the whole of Essex as Hugh of Buckland says'.[1] This is very interesting. Hugh of Buckland was notoriously one of the close circle of knightly men on whom the mechanics of Henry I's government depended, and one of those officials who was seeking to create a lordship for himself. At one time or another he was sheriff of at least six counties, including Essex.[2] While Thurkill was composing his treatise he had clearly had a conversation with Hugh, Thurkill it seems getting the facts about the hidage of Essex, while Hugh was boning up on the abacus.

When Richard FitzNeal, Royal Treasurer, composed his celebrated treatise, *Dialogue of the Exchequer*, in the 1170s, he wrote, 'the high science of the Exchequer lies not in calculations but in judgments of all kinds'. Richard was son of the Treasurer, Nigel, Bishop of Ely, and great nephew of Roger of Salisbury; he would later become Bishop of London. So he should have known what he was talking about; and indeed he represented the duel between the Treasurer and each sheriff as he took him through his accounts, making judgements about what was owing to the king, as a kind of tense chess match over the chequered cloth with its counters.[3] But it will be clear from what has just been said how much of a family business the twelfth-century Exchequer was, and Richard may here have succumbed to the temptation to make it sound as lofty a business as he could. For surely the intellectual/cultural world in which the Exchequer developed was precisely one of calculation, empiricism and scientific observation. It was a world that continued in English intellectual culture for the rest of the Middle Ages.

Three persons exemplify this world: Walcher, Prior of Malvern (Worcestershire), Adelard of Bath (not to be confused with Peter Abelard), and Petrus Alphonsi, a Spanish Jew who had converted to Christianity. They were all on the scene in Henry I's England.

Walcher was one of a number of highly educated Lotharingians who came to England before or after the Norman Conquest, reminding us that the story of eleventh-century incomers is by no means all about Normans. He had a passion for that art of calculation represented by astronomy, and for working with his astrolabe, another Arabic instrument imported into the West in the early Middle Ages and used for measuring the movements of the sun, moon, planets and other stars. In an astronomical treatise, Walcher recounts that in 1091, on a visit to Italy, he had seen an eclipse of the moon, but he was frustrated because he lacked an instrument that would give him the time of the full moon. When he got back to England and heard about the same eclipse here – one of the monks told him how that evening a servant had rushed in saying that something horrible was happening to the moon – he realised that several hours had separated the eclipse in England and in Italy. But as he still had no certainty about the time of the eclipse, he had no starting point for the lunar tables that he wanted to draw up. Walcher goes on:

Then unexpectedly in the following year on 18 October, during the same lunar cycle, the moon – as if to favour my studies and by its darkness bring me light – underwent another eclipse. I at once seized my astrolabe and made a careful note of the time of the full eclipse, which was a little more than three-quarters of an hour after the eleventh hour of the night.

*If this time is converted into equinoctial time, it will be found to be
shortly before 12.45. Hence the lunar cycle began on 3 October
at 19.30 hours.*[4]

R.W. Southern wrote of this:

*Walcher's anxiety for precision is an important indication of the existence
of a new scientific impulse. He wanted to establish by calculation and
observation the exact correlation between the phases of the moon and the
solar calendar. As soon as he got a fixed point on 18 October 1092 he
calculated backwards to 1036, when the moon's cycle began on 1 January
and constructed his table from that date to 1111 when according to his
calculation the cycle began again.*[5]

Adelard was born in Bath about 1080. He travelled widely but he had
returned to England by 1130, and the way in which he is mentioned in
the Pipe Roll of that year strongly suggests that he was then moving in
Exchequer circles.[6] He was probably a laymen rather than a cleric,[7] but
because of his learning he also moved much in clerical circles. He studied
at the then fashionable Laon, but thinking Laon standards low (like Peter
Abelard), he moved on to Sicily. He dedicated his first significant work
(before 1116), a treatise on the seven liberal arts, *De Eodem et Diverso*,
which might be translated by the Platonist, *Unity and Diversity*, to Bishop
William of Syracuse.[8] That was followed up by his *Quaestiones Naturales*,
to which we return in a moment. He certainly imbibed something of Greek
learning in Sicily, but despite his claims to have learned from the Arabs,
and though one certainly *could* learn Arabic in Sicily, he shows no clear
sign of knowing Arabic so early as in these two works.[9]

But Adelard learned Arabic, however imperfectly, later on. That is
important, because the first half of the twelfth century saw the beginning
of a movement, centred on Spain, to translate the great works of Greek
empirical science and mathematics from the Arabic in which they had been
preserved and studied (this a long story) into Latin.[10] Spain had long been
a region in which Islamic, Jewish, and in a measure Christian scholars col-
laborated, and the movement of translation from Arabic to Latin was one
in which twelfth-century Englishmen were particularly active and in which
Adelard was a pioneer.[11] How much work he did in particular on Euclid's
Elements, so important in bringing calculatory mathematics to the West, is
a matter of dispute, but he certainly translated some parts of it on geometry
from Arabic into Latin.[12] It is likely that he came to learn Arabic in Spain,
for his translation of al-Khwarizmi's astronomical tables (1126) used a

Spanish Arabic original.[13] This latter is a significant work, for we know it only from Adelard's translation, the original having been lost.

Important as all this was for the advance of empirical science, it would be a mistake to suppose that there was no other motive in it than the advance of an ideological empiricism. Late in life Adelard composed a treatise on the astrolabe for the young Henry, later Henry II, when as a boy of 9 to 13 the latter was living in Bristol (12 miles from Bath) under the care of his uncle, Henry of Blois, Bishop of Winchester and the tutelage of one Master Matthew. Very probably one interest of this for Adelard, himself not uninterested in magic and astrology, was the casting of horoscopes.[14]

To return, finally, to Adelard's earlier *Quaestiones Naturales*, while he may not yet show a knowledge of the Arabic language in the various questions discussed in this work, he does seem to share what were perhaps Arabic physiological and psychological interests in some of his questions (as Peter Abelard showed psychological interests in some of the questions discussed in his *Sic et Non* of about the same date). For instance he discussed the relation of memory to mental ability, which reminds one of the importance that the Cistercians slightly later would attach to memory in prayer, and the different temperaments of the sexes. Here the stress was on empiricism, as he insisted that human reason, not authority, was judge. 'Human science should first be listened to', he wrote, 'and only when it fails utterly should there be recourse to God.'[15] We shall meet a similar approach again in the next chapter when we look at the Franciscan scholar, Richard Rufus.

Petrus Alphonsi, our third example, was a Spanish Jew, converted to Christianity in 1106, who visited England under Henry I and became a doctor to that apparent hypochondriac, though it was said that Queen Matilda particularly trusted him. We have already noted that Roger of Salisbury disapproved of Faritius of Abingdon, another of the queen's doctors, for the kind of positivistic medicine that that Italian, and presumably also Petrus Alphonsi, practised (see pp. 10–11), although it was a similar approach which made Roger himself such a master in the world of finance. Petrus Alphonsi is best known for his *Disciplina Clericalis*, a book of moral tales derived from the Arabs. But he also wrote a *Letter on Study* which is another fine expression of early twelfth-century empiricism, in which he declared:

I do not hold with the position of intelligent men who deliver judgments on matters of which they have no knowledge, or who reject something before it is proved. Knowledge must first be grasped through 'experience' [again cf the Cistercian stress on experience in mystical prayer]. In the same way no man can consider someone to be a teacher of science (or knowledge) without first having tested him.[16]

Petrus Alphonsi also took an interest in the astrolabe and astronomical tables.[17] Considering that Adelard's translation of al-Khwarizmi's astronomical tables, and Walcher of Malvern's treatise incorporating also something on the Lunar Node and a tract on lunar cycles by Petrus Alphonsi, all appear in the same twelfth-century manuscript,[18] it is clear that all three were aware of, and quite likely knew each other.

The writing of history and Stephen's reign

We historians are often tempted to use historical and biographical or hagiographical writings as quarries of useful information, and often reasonably so. But the perceptions of medieval historical writers, not least when writing about their own contemporary scene, are usually intended to have an influence on their own world, and this goes especially for King Stephen's reign (1135–54). What sort of person should a king be and not be? To discuss this sort of question – and we may be quite sure that there was some kind of continuum between talk and writing here – was in itself to help formulate a society's ideas, and (as anthropologists say of the positive value of gossip) sustain its moral norms. It may seem that, in terms of mistrust between king and barons, for instance, John was quite as bad a king as Stephen, but the reaction to John was by then much more clearly thought out by large sectors of society than could yet be the case with Stephen.[19]

We have already touched on historical writing at black-monk monasteries (p. 138). There is a discernible kind of historical writing, not only, but quintessentially, by black monks, which reached its peak in Stephen's reign. It was distinctly personalised and focussed not least on the personality of the king. The *Gesta Stephani* (*Deeds of Stephen*), for example, which was probably composed by Robert, Bishop of Bath (1333–66), who had been Prior of Lewes, a Cluniac monastery, before he became bishop,[20] does not contain a single date,[21] but it is soon into character studies. In Book I there is a notable sketch of Stephen's own personality. He was, it says, good-natured and agreeable to all; he was reverent to those bound by religious vows; he was affable and amenable to people of whatever age:

'He was even of such a kindly and gentle disposition', continues the author, 'that he commonly forgot a king's exalted rank and in many affairs saw himself not superior to his men, but in every way their equal, sometimes actually their inferior.'[22]

The author of the *Gesta Stephani* was favourably disposed to Stephen, certainly early on; but far from commending him here, he was surely writing ironically, and he was certainly putting his finger on what was often regarded as a key weakness of Stephen. He did not behave like a king; he did not keep the necessary distance between himself and his companions; he behaved too like what he had been, a Count of Boulogne; in colloquial parlance, he wanted to be 'one of the boys'; or to put it in the literary modes of the time, he seemed to have Arthurian, round-table attitudes.

One senses here the Cluniac writer's penchant for the Old Testament. Three times the *Gesta Stephani* compares Stephen to Saul, a brave warrior, but in the end a compromised king. A comparison with Saul's successor, David, would have been more flattering.[23] Even more, perhaps, one senses the influence of the ancient classical historians, particularly the ubiquitous Sallust. No medieval Benedictine (or Augustinian) library worth its salt was without at least one copy of Sallust's Jugurthan and Catiline Wars.[24] Sallust had been pro-consul in North Africa, and the Jugurthan War was a kind of monograph with a specifically North African setting. Likewise Robert of Bath, if it was indeed he, produced what was for the most part, in its grand classical tone, a very localised story on the pocket handkerchief of East Somerset and West Wiltshire. The author imitated Sallust in what Beryl Smalley called Sallust's 'analysis of motive, informed by cynical pessism'.[25] Sallust often tried to bring out the effect of personality on history, and how human weaknesses in particular had influenced the course of events.

William of Malmesbury's brief *Historia Novella* contains a more brilliant depiction of Stephen's personality. Rodney Thomson has proved that William knew his Sallust.[26] Early on William already presents to us the brave and affable but untrustworthy person:

He was a man of energy but little judgment, active in war, of extraordinary spirit in undertaking any difficult task, lenient to his enemies and easily appeased, courteous to all. Though you admired his kindness in promising, still you felt his words lacked truth and his promises fulfilment.

Or again:

While he was a count, he had by his good nature and the way he jested, sat, and ate in the company even of the humblest, earned an affection that can hardly be imagined (William says sarcastically).

Or on his beginning military campaigns against rebels vigorously and then not following them through:

Yet he was not broken in spirit by any man's rebellion but appeared suddenly now here, now there, and always settled the business with more loss to himself than his opponents, for after expending many great efforts in vain he would win a pretence of peace from them for a time by the gift of honours or castles.[27]

Even were it possible for this to be dismissed as propaganda for Earl Robert of Gloucester, William's patron and as the Empress Matilda's half-brother the greatest of Stephen's opponents, it would still be a very effective sketch of a character. But it cannot be so dismissed, because it accords too well with other evidence and with the impressions of other writers. Not least was Stephen's habit of receiving his enemies peacefully or with a smiling face, and then, when they were supposed to be enjoying the protection of his court, engineering a scene in which hands were clapped on them and they were thrown into prison. He did it with Bishops Roger of Salisbury, Alexander of Lincoln and Nigel of Ely in 1139; and again with Geoffrey de Mandeville in 1143, and with Earl Ranulph of Chester in 1146.[28]

However much historians have liked to dwell, quite reasonably, on the social/structural problems between king and aristocracy at that time, this personal untrustworthiness of Stephen was an important factor in the politics of his reign. Had it not been for this character defect, William of Malmesbury considered that he might have surmounted the problem of what he, William, thought of as his unlawful acquisition of the kingdom.[29] But he lost the author of the *Gesta Stephani*, and other clerics like Henry of Huntingdon, with his arrest of the bishops.[30] It was too like Saul not showing due respect to his priests.

The greatest importance of Stephen's untrustworthiness lies deeper. Had it not been for the rebellions against Stephen in the first four years of his reign, the Empress Matilda would not have had the troubled waters in which to fish when she landed in England to fight for her inheritance, as she thought it, in 1139, and there would not have been – to change the metaphor – the breeding ground for so much of the conflict which followed. Virtually all those early rebels were familiars, or 'new men', of Henry I. Henry had hugely built up the lands and offices of Robert of Gloucester, David of Scotland also Earl of Huntingdon, and Roger of Salisbury, if not to the same extent as he had built up Stephen himself. They were all rebels against Stephen in those early years. So were others whom Henry had built up, like Baldwin de Redvers at Exeter or Miles de Beauchamp at Bedford. Why was it the charmed circle of Henry I who caused so much early trouble to Stephen? Various reasons have been given, but underlying them all was that here was the greatest member of the charmed circle suddenly standing among them as their king, and they already knew that he was not to be trusted! In the Treaty of Winchester of November 1153, laying down the conditions on which Duke Henry of Normandy, son of Matilda, would succeed to Stephen's kingdom after his death, Stephen is made to anticipate in the text what would happen if he went back on his promises.[31] By the end of his reign everyone knew what the others of Henry I's charmed circle already knew at the beginning!

In the historical writers of Stephen's reign we are in the heartlands of the twelfth-century Renaissance and its humanism. There was an interesting divergence about what twelfth-century humanism meant between R.W. Southern and David Knowles. In a famous essay, Southern took the term to mean the whole build-up of confidence in human intellectual power and human capacity to understand and master the world and the cosmos, a build-up in the twelfth and thirteenth centuries which comprehended God, law, medicine, human psychology, mathematics and astronomy, ethnography, etc., and which culminated in the great scholastic achievements of the thirteenth century, above all Thomas Aquinas's *Summa Theologiae*.[32] The great sweep of Southern's concept has appealed to many. Not incompatible with it, but much more restricted, was David Knowles's concept, wherein one recognises the scholar who originally trained as a classicist. The very fact that Knowles's concept was more closely defined makes it in a way more useful to historians.

Knowles described twelfth-century humanism as a phenomenon particularly of the period c. 1120–60, a period characterised by an especial love for, and intensive study of, the ancient Latin classics – for instance the Cistercian Ailred of Rievaulx taking Cicero's treatise on friendship as the starting point of his own work on *Spiritual Friendship*; or Héloise, in tears, expressing her suffering at separating herself from Abelard, for his sake, in the words of Cornelia's lament as given by Lucan. In particular, twelfth-century people like these followed the classics in the importance which they attached to a rather introspective examination of their emotions.[33] Mid-twelfth-century historians followed classical historians in trying, as it were, to light up from inside, the personalities of actors on the historical stage. Exactly the same phenomenon can be observed in the art of the period, for example, the attempt to light up the inner soul by the outward expression of sculptured figures on the early Gothic west portal of Chartres

(c. 1150);[34] or, I might add, the attempt to capture on the face of one of the sisters in the Chichester sculpted reliefs of the Raising of Lazarus (also c. 1140) the moment when grief is turning into astonishment.

The contrast between the representation of Stephen and earlier depictions of a king's character could not be better made than by citing the Monk of Caen's description of William the Conqueror, written probably within a few years of his death (1087).[35] William was undaunted by danger; he was temperate in eating and drinking; he was never downcast in adversity nor had his head turned by good fortune; his voice was harsh, but he spoke persuasively. Historians used to say: an excellent thumb-nail character sketch by a man who must have known the king. Until somebody noticed that it was lifted almost word for word from Einhard's much earlier description of Charlemagne, which itself came mostly from Suetonius's *Lives of the Caesars*. A further point is that the Monk of Caen's picture more or less exemplifies the four cardinal virtues of fortitude, temperance, prudence and justice, the virtues traditionally associated with rule. The whole picture is much more stylised than it at first looks.

There is nothing stylised about the way the historians of Stephen's reign present him. We can be sure of that not least because of the explanatory stress which they put on his personal weaknesses. Stephen's reign falls plumb in the Knowles period of twelfth-century humanism. For once with a medieval ruler, the culture in which his history was written gives us some assurance that a character is coming over that is actually useful for political understanding.

The reader might well ask what all this has to do with *religion* and politics. Well, it is not only that Stephen's character is mediated to us by clerics through a culture of Christian humanism. It is also that the disapproval of Stephen is a particular, clericalist disapproval, which not everyone shared. We must briefly look at the less clericalist view.

It is an inescapable fact that even at the nadir of Stephen's fortunes in 1141 he had many supporters amongst the aristocracy. Going into the siege of Lincoln, he had six earls on his side,[36] not to mention 'a number of barons of notable loyalty and courage'.[37] His 'approval ratings' in this class were not negligible. One can only assume that many people liked his style – that of a dashing, brave and not particularly calculating war leader, generous to his followers, and with round-table manners. One may describe it as a chivalric or Arthurian style. Geoffrey of Monmouth represented this style to perfection, writing about King Arthur in his best-seller, *History of the Kings of Britain*. The Arthurian legend was really floated on the Western world under Henry II with his all-British ambitions; but

Geoffrey completed his book about 1138, so that it reflects at least some people's expectations of a king and attitudes to kingship in Stephen's time. Ironically, two of its dedicatees, Robert of Gloucester and Waleran of Meulan, would be on opposite sides at the Battle of Lincoln where Stephen was taken captive by Earl Robert in 1141. In the legend Arthur was similar to Stephen, liking to feast with his men on as equal terms as possible;[38] notable for his personal bravery in battle and particularly when things were going against him;[39] and generous with his rewards to his followers, not least with earldoms.[40] Some historical commentators on Stephen have been distressed by his profligacy, as they see it, in this last point.[41]

Above all, with Arthur there was serious war-making on the one hand, and there was playing at battles (the *ludus belli*) on the other, the latter centred mostly on the rising aristocratic functions of jousts and tournaments (different from each other but connected). Arthur's knights, as seen in Geoffrey of Monmouth, were amongst the earliest lovers of tournaments. After a certain feast:

They all went out into the meadows and split up into groups ready to play various games. The knights planned an imitation battle and competed together on horseback, while their womenfolk watched from the top of the city walls and aroused them to passionate excitement by their flirtatious behaviour.[42]

Likewise with Stephen, there was serious war, and there were war games; and as Maurice Keen has remarked, 'the line could indeed be thin between mock war and the real thing'.[43] At the Battle of Lincoln in 1141, Stephen had broken off the siege of the castle in order to offer battle with Earl Roger, the leader of Matilda's forces. That was already a chivalric way of behaving. Then the royalists at first treated Roger's attack as an opening game (*proludium*), a form of jousting, until they saw how in deadly and professional earnest the Earl's forces were.[44] That is just the kind of thing that *attracted* so many aristocrats to Stephen; he was quintessentially chivalric.

William Clito, another of Henry I's nephews, a constant rebel against Henry in Normandy in the latter's later years, was not at all a shrewd politician, but he likewise attracted many young nobles to his side by his dashing, almost quixotic, generalship. One of these was Waleran of Meulan, a dedicatee as we have mentioned of Geoffrey's book, who started on Stephen's side at Lincoln in 1141 (albeit he let down his chivalric ideals by fleeing),[45] and who had joined Clito's rebellion against Henry I in 1122–23. Henry had brought together a troop of hard-nosed professional knights, the very opposite of Clito's style. According to Orderic's idea, as put by David Crouch: 'Waleran was seduced by romantic visions of the knightly life; the young count's head was filled with chansons and ambitions of military glory.'[46]

What we are getting, therefore, with the *Gesta Stephani* and William of Malmesbury, is only one side of the argument about kingship, a rather solemn, churchy side. The other side was a more secular, chivalric side. Churchmen condemned tournaments and jousts from the start.[47] St Bernard saw the causes of the failure of the Second Crusade (1147–48) in the crusaders' wretched state of mind as evidenced by their having tournaments everywhere on their return.[48] Of course Geoffrey of Monmouth was himself a churchman,[49] as were (on the church side) the Bishop of Bath, William of Malmesbury, and also Henry of Huntingdon and Orderic Vitalis. A third of his dedicatees was his neighbour in Oxford, Walter of Coutances, Archdeacon of Oxford. Many twelfth-century churchmen were interested in secular literature to varying degrees and in various ways. The church and its clergy were not a monolith.

The beginnings of legal study at Oxford in the reign of Henry II

The question here is in reality what was the context, or a part of the context, of the legal reforms of Henry II. In England during the twelfth century there were no cathedral schools of anything like the importance of several in Northern France. London during the episcopate of the learned Gilbert the Universal (1128–34), so called because he was thought to know everything, looked as if it might become important; but after Bishop Gilbert's death the promising shoots came to almost nothing. Exeter and Hereford built a modest significance, the latter being where the notable scientist Robert Grosseteste studied.[50] This whole situation was perpetuated by most people going abroad to study, whence they returned, often to be absorbed by the rising administrations of king, bishops, monasteries, and lay aristocracy.

At least two important schools developed, however, which had nothing to do with cathedrals, namely Oxford and Northampton. Both were far away from their diocesan centre of Lincoln, Oxford especially being at the opposite end of the largest diocese in England. Both, much more importantly, were placed at or near key centres on the *royal* itinerary. Oxford was near Henry II's favourite hunting lodge of Woodstock; Northampton had a royal castle and was so called in distinction from Southampton, the major channel crossing-point between England and Normandy, where Henry II's yacht was kept.[51] Northampton and Southampton were linked by a major arterial route, nowadays the A34. It has long been appreciated by historians that Northampton, already by the mid-1170s when Oxford was still only a fledgling place of teaching and learning, had an important school for mathematical sciences and for law.[52] If we were to get into my time machine and land on the streets of either town around 1175 or a little earlier, and ask people which of the two, Northampton, a great modern centre of shoe production, or Oxford, with its early guild of shoe-makers, would become famous for its university and which for its shoes, it would have been quite reasonable of them to answer Northampton for its university and Oxford for its shoes!

When did Oxford become a major centre of higher study, particularly of legal study? In his masterly contribution to the History of the University of Oxford, the late Sir Richard Southern argued that Oxford was a promising centre of intellectual activity in the early 1130s, when Robert Pullen (later a cardinal of the Roman church) taught there; that after his departure in 1133 circumstances were not favourable to academic growth; that the period from 1135 to 1185 is an 'exasperating blank'; and that it was only around 1190 or just before that masters really began to congregate in Oxford, at first very much as teachers of law; and that only from then could one speak of a continuous history of teaching and higher learning at Oxford.[53] My own submission is that all this began at least a decade earlier, in the 1170s, and I shall come shortly to why that decade makes a big difference.

We are here dealing with a time nearly a century before colleges, as we know them, were thought of, and well before there was even any known faculty organisation. Masters were entrepreneurs, setting up as teachers where they could attract students, and students found accommodation where they could, perhaps in houses or halls owned by their masters. One sees this kind of entrepreneurship very clearly from the story of Peter Abelard in France in the earlier decades of the twelfth century.[54]

As might be expected of a period with gaping gaps in the evidence, and of an institution (Oxford University) with no formal constitutional beginning and thus no formal record-keeping, my evidence for the 1170s comes from a most unexpected place. It is in the Cartulary of the Augustinian Canons of Guisborough (North Yorkshire), that is the book in which the medieval canons of Guisborough copied out their title deeds and other documents relevant to their rights and properties, a book owned by Sir Robert Cotton in the seventeenth century and now in the British Library. There is the text of a document, dateable to some time between 1174 and 1180, issued by three papal judges-delegate (John Bishop of Chichester, Adam Abbot of Evesham, and Baldwin Abbot of Ford) to settle a lawsuit which had been raging between Archbishop Roger of York and the Canons of Guisborough about rights over Kirklevington church and its dependent chapel of Eston (North Yorkshire). The settlement was made, as the text of the document itself informs us, at Oxford, by the advice of many men learned in the law (*plurimorum jurisperitorum*).[55] The names of some of these are given as witnesses. They are:

1. Master John of Cornwall
2. Thomas, Archdeacon of Wells
3. Jocelin, Archdeacon of Chichester
4. Geoffrey, Precentor of Salisbury
5. Master Gilbert of Northampton
6. Master Godfrey of Lanthony
7. Geoffrey *de Lardaria*
8. Richard, Prior of Newburgh
9. Master Osbert of Arundel
10. and others, the cartulary copy of the original document adds, not naming these others who were probably named in the original twelfth-century document.

In this list, nos 2, 3, 4 and 8 must have been present in some way to support the judges or parties, e.g. Richard, Prior of Newburgh to support his fellow Yorkshire Augustinian Canons. But nos 1, 5, 6, 7 and 9 cannot be explained in this way, and they must represent the earliest known list of Oxford scholars. Master Osbert of Arundel had in the 1150s and 1160s, it is true, been a Canon of Beverley and a confidante and frequent witness to the documents of Archbishop Roger of York.[56] But by the second half of the 1170s he had apparently ceased to witness them, and by then he was probably in Oxford as a scholar in his own right, though doubtless a supporter of his old friend the archbishop. Geoffrey de *Lardaria*, only a little later than this, was apparently doing legal work for the Cistercian Abbey of Bruern in Oxfordshire, and witnessed several of their documents, styled as *Master* Geoffrey de *Lardaria*.[57]

When a man was styled 'Master' – and more and more men were coming to use that title in the twelfth century – it means that he had completed a long and gruelling arts course somewhere, and had earned the *jus ubique docendi*, the right to teach anywhere, and to go on to the 'higher' studies of law or theology or medicine if he wished. The title was rather like our 'doctor' virtually never used when it had not been earned, but sometimes dropped when it had been earned.

Southern made generous acknowledgement of the Guisborough document; in fact he used it to point to Oxford's central geographical position and its development as a convenient place for bringing judges and parties together to resolve judicial disputes, which was one factor in its becoming a centre of legal study.[58] But he stuck to his overall argument that not before about 1190 did Oxford become such a centre. He probably thought, à propos the list of masters from Guisborough, that one swallow did not make a summer. Yet that is a strange saying, for if one sees a swallow, one can take a shrewd guess at what season it is. Similarly, if an authentic document says, without any axe to grind about things in Oxford (as distinct from in North Yorkshire), that a case was settled with the advice of many men learned in the law, that suggests a context of legal study in just the same way as seeing a swallow suggests a context of summer. Likewise is the mention, in a collection of Oxford 'miracles' (1180) of a student from the York region residing in the Oxford schools.[59] York had flourishing schools (for the liberal arts) at this time.[60] Why should a York man want to go to Oxford if there were no context of higher study already there?

We return to the question of why it matters whether Oxford became a centre of legal learning only in the late 1180s or already in the 1170s. It matters because politically and ecclesiastically the 1170s was one of the great decades in the history of English law. After Thomas Becket was martyred in 1170, the system of jurisdictional appeal to Rome and the appointment of papal judges-delegate to hear and determine cases in England took a new leap forward. At the same time, the 1170s was the decade of vital development in the procedures (*novel disseisin* was discussed in Chapter 5) which formed the basis of English Common Law, backed up by regular and comprehensive judicial eyres, and with even something like a royal court of appeal being introduced in 1178. An Oxford of legal learning in the 1170s, therefore, looks much more like a stimulus to, and even a shaper of, the current preoccupations of the ruling élite, and much less like a mere reflector of them, than an Oxford for which the earliest evidence would come from the late 1180s.

One might take it from the character of twelfth-century legal treatises, with their scholastic methods, that anyone who attended the legal schools of the 1170s, whether at Bologna or Northampton or Oxford, would be studying a subject of deep intellectual interest, and in fact a training of the mind. They would also be studying a subject of practical usefulness as twelfth-century society grew by leaps and bounds in litigiousness. A neat illustration of the latter comes from the Chronicle of Battle Abbey (Sussex). In 1176, when Odo, Abbot of Battle was locked in a dispute with Godrey de Lucy over rights in the Church of Wye (Kent), he wished he could draw on legal expertise within his monastery. All the expensive lawyers he approached refused his brief for fear of offending the king or Godfrey's father, who was the Chief Justiciar, Richard de Lucy. Whereupon one of Odo's kinsmen, a monk it seems, said to the wretched abbot: 'My lord, if you had only spent enough on me and your other relatives so that we could have attended the schools, we should long since have been knowledgeable in the law and the decretals (canon law), and could have been your defence in this and in other necessities.' To which the abbot was said to have replied, 'it is judgment on me for not having studied the law myself!'[61] This conversation of 1176 would have been almost nonsensical if there had been no good law schools nearer to home than Bologna by the 1170s.

Incidentally, for practical purposes litigants were always likely at this time to need both secular and canon law, particularly for cases involving the legitimacy of marriages and thus of inheritances (e.g. Richard of Anstey, c. 1160, having to appear in both secular and ecclesiastical courts), or the status of churches, etc.

The most interesting person in the list of witnesses to the Guisborough charter is the first, Master John of Cornwall. He had studied the liberal arts and theology at Paris, and though his connection with Oxford as early as the 1170s would otherwise be unknown, he is considered to be the first master known to have taught theology/law at Oxford. He knew the Welsh language, not perhaps surprisingly considering the links between Wales and Cornwall; he was a friend of Walter of Coutances, another Cornishman, who was Archdeacon of Oxford from about 1175 until he became Bishop of Lincoln in 1183 (and Archbishop of Rouen in 1184); and he was distinguished enough to be proposed for the bishopric of St David's in 1176.[62]

Several decades ago, two distinguished scholars turned up a manuscript of Gratian's *Decretum* (c. 1140), the standard work on canon law in the twelfth century, where two glosses in the margins, amazingly, had reports of John's Oxford teaching, c. 1190, one on the celebration of Mass, the other on marriage. These were two highly charged and socially important subjects at the time, in both of which canon law and sacramental theology touched each other closely. This is the gloss on marriage:

A certain fornicator on his death bed, not wishing to renounce his fornication, took his concubine to wife notwithstanding his knowledge that he could never thereafter have sexual intercourse with her [most medieval canon lawyers considered consummation a vital part of a validly contracted marriage]. Was this a marriage? John of Cornwall (Jo Cornub) says that it is a marriage (and brings in past intercourse, not to legitimate it but as indicating consent). John of Tynemouth (Jo de Ti) says that won't do, but raises the question whether any children whom they may have had previously should be considered for the future legitimate. It seems so, and (thus) in so far as it was so to the parties, it was a marriage.[63]

This poignant echo is the first known sound from the halls of disputation in Oxford. It was obviously part of a scholastic exercise. But it raises principles of great practical importance for judging the validity of a marriage and the legitimacy of children. It also envisages a particularly humane sort of death-bed repentance, unlikely in the normal way to have found a place in any of the text books. No wonder that John was taken out of the Oxford schools for the last two years of his life (c. 1196–98) to be Archdeacon of Worcester! He must have made a sensitive archdeacon.

The theologisation of society

The first thing to make clear about the title of this section is that it is not about the actual moral standards of the age. Anyone who knows theologians in any numbers will know that they are like hairdressers or bus drivers, or like other kinds of academics. There is the same mixture of good people and not so good people amongst them. Of course there are always many theologians who hope that what they say or write will raise the moral levels of their own society. But around 1200, we have no means of gauging their effects. Hence we are not speaking about moral improvement, though the Almighty might know whether such a thing occurred. We are speaking about a 'big idea' projected on to society by theologians. Let me give an analogy from the Reformation period. Diarmaid MacCulloch has acknowledged the importance of Eamon Duffy's contribution to Reformation history and his showing that the late medieval church, anyhow in England, was not as corrupt and ineffective as Protestants had tended to portray it; but MacCulloch argues, rightly, that

that only highlights the importance of the *ideas* which the Reformers put forward.[64] Similarly it was argued in Chapter 2 above that moral reform was not even the primary objective of the so-called Gregorian Reform in the late eleventh century rather than that it was about revolutionising how people thought about 'the right order of the world'. Perhaps the theologising of society c. 1200 was more about moral reform than the Gregorian Reform was, but we should be very sceptical about characterising one historical period as morally worse than or superior to another. 'Moral standards' are not really a useful analytical tool in the study of history.

The advances in preaching and confession are a major part of this theologisation, but they will be left mainly to the next chapter on the Friars. Here we may start with the king. Once again we have to rid our minds of royal sacrality as it might be talked about for the tenth century, with a panoply of art and ritual to sustain a quasi-sacramental mystique of God-given kingship. Ernst Kantorowicz called this sacral idea Christ-centred kingship, because it projected onto the king that he was a ritualised Christ-figure in his rule. We can see how much that was gone, by the way monastic writers wrote about King Stephen. Kantorowicz saw an idea of law-centred kingship succeed in the twelfth century to that of Christ-centred.[65] Magna Carta (1215) and the arguments leading up to it show how barons and churchmen were by then seeking to bring the king under the law and 'good' customs, as knights and others were trying to do with barons and churchmen.[66] But bringing ideas of law into it is not quite the same thing as bringing in theology.

We must proceed now with many small brush strokes rather than with one or two great sweeps of the pen. Stephen Langton, Archbishop of Canterbury, was one of a number of Englishmen who had played a prominent role as a professor of moral theology in the Paris school of Peter the Chanter, a school which very much applied theology to contemporary issues.[67] The old notion that Langton played a significant constitutional part in the production of Magna Carta has been effectively put to rest.[68] But he had already made a contribution to the intellectual climate behind Magna Carta before he was nominated to the archbishopric in 1206 by Pope Innocent III (who had himself studied in the Chanter's school).[69] One small but telling example of this comes in his commentary on Deuteronomy (17,17: the king shall not have immense weights of silver and gold). Langton says:

This is plainly against modern kings, who collect treasure not in order to sustain necessity, but to satiate their cupidity . . . Note that the author

says 'immense', that is beyond the measure of necessity, therefore
whatever goes beyond necessity is evil, that is, a sin.

David d'Avray says of this that for Langton the doctrine of necessity was a theological one.[70] Of course the Angevin kings were notorious for always claiming that they were in urgent need of more money, but it is doubtful whether their claims would have carried much weight in Paris, where their enemies, the Capetian kings, ruled. We may also note that Langton calls going beyond necessity a sin (i.e. cupidity), for as pope, Innocent III consistently claimed his duty to intervene in worldly politics where there was a case of sin.[71]

Another small brush stroke about the application of theology to kingship comes in the form of a fine psalter, made probably at St Augustine's Abbey, Canterbury, c. 1210–20. Every psalm text in this book begins with a small, historiated initial. Many of these small initial letters are adorned with images of kings, and almost all of these are the initial letters of psalms which emphasise God's forgiveness and support for just rulers. Noting this, Stella Panayotova argues persuasively that the images reflect the tone of reconciliation between John and the Pope (May, 1213), after the pope's Interdict caused by John's not accepting Langton as archbishop. It is now not possible to tell for which patron this Psalter was made; but Panayotova suggests that the likeliest answer is for King John himself. (This is reminiscent of the Psalter prepared by Herbert of Bosham for Thomas Becket to study.) Master Alexander, who became Abbot of St Augustine's Canterbury in that same year, 1213, was close to the king.[72] And John, one of the most learned rulers of medieval England, was interested enough in theology to borrow several theological works from Reading Abbey in 1208 during the Interdict.[73] It goes to prove our earlier assertion that theology and great sins are not incompatible with each other!

Parisian moral and religious influence, especially the influence of Peter the Chanter's school, is everywhere apparent in Britain at the turn of the twelfth and thirteenth centuries. We have already seen it at St Hugh's Lincoln of the 1190s and in Hubert Walter's Provincial Council of 1200. The Lincoln mediation can be seen in the *Life of St Gilbert of Sempringham*, completed by the end of 1200. The Gilbertines were an order centred on Lincolnshire, and the author of this *Life*, composed for the canonisation of Gilbert by Innocent III in 1202, was a canon at Sempringham.[74] The work was submitted for correction to the Paris master, William de Montibus, when he was Chancellor of Lincoln Cathedral.[75] A small but telling example of Parisian influence in the *Life* is what the author says about Gilbert's sticking up for Becket against Henry II, because 'the archbishop took his stand on divine law and the liberty of the universal church'. The Gilbertines were indeed staunch supporters of Becket, and they provided him with guides and servants and even found him hiding places before he went into exile from England.[76] But whether Gilbert in the 1160s would have expressed himself in these terms is doubtful. Much more likely they express what was said to his hagiographer while writing, perhaps by a Parisian master, around 1200. For they almost exactly correspond to what Peter the Chanter was reported as saying while arguing in Paris that Becket should truly be considered a martyr.[77]

The whole matter of canonisation of saints by the pope was in itself taking to its logical conclusion the views of Peter the Chanter against using saints' relics and the veneration of saints to raise money. And it is worth noting that saint's cults were a matter of intense debate in the Middle Ages, and not one of general acquiescence in what the Reformation would call Romish practices. The Fourth Lateran Council (1215), in so many ways Paris theology writ large by Innocent III, says (c. 62) that ancient relics ought not to be shown outside their reliquaries (note all the fine enamelled reliquaries for Becket's relics made in the decades after his martyrdom), or put up for sale. As for newly discovered relics, they were not to be venerated publicly without the authority of the Roman pontiff. Nor should people be deceived into venerating them, and giving alms, by 'vain fictions or false documents'.[78] In other words, before papal authority was given, accredited dossiers were required like that of the *Life and Miracles* of, and letters about, Gilbert of Sempringham. Thus as papal canonisation became enlarged under Innocent III, so the pope became more and more the arbiter of what was holiness in society. And in Innocent III's case, his function as arbiter was based on principles that went back to Pope Gregory the Great (590–604), a powerful influence in the Chanter's school. There were two requirements for canonisation in Innocent's view – proof of a good and pious life and confirmation of this by miracles after death. The second was of no value without the first. The *Life* of Gilbert of Sempringham stresses the same Gregorian point.[79]

When Gerald of Wales, who had himself studied at Paris, wrote his *Gemma Ecclesiastica* in the late 1190s, he followed to a considerable extent Peter the Chanter's *Verbum Abbreviatum* (1191–92, shortened version by 1197–99). Peter's book was a popular manual of ethics;[80] it was a pioneer in bringing in examples (*exempla*) to illustrate moral points, which would become so much the basis of the friars' preaching methods; and it was very popular, surviving in over 90 manuscripts.[81] Gerald wrote his none too abbreviated book to try and raise the moral standards of his clergy in the archdeaconry of Brecon; this was not a popular success. Despite its being a fascinating read and written in a racy style, it survives in only one copy! Hence we can hardly study its effects, but it reflects interestingly on the Parisian *mind* of an educated and active churchman.

But Gerald did not slavishly follow the points made by Peter. His mind was always on what most applied to Brecon. Peter, thinking of the sins of urban Paris, had much on the sin of usury. Gerald, thinking of rural Breconshire, was more concerned with the illiteracy of the clergy,[82] for example the hapless priest who owed to some grasping English prelate (Gerald was down on that sort also) 200 eggs (*ova*), and instead promised him 200 sheep (*oves*)![83] Peter knew all about the dangers of prostitutes to Parisian scholars. Gerald was more concerned about priests' concubines, who, in A.L. Poole's translation, 'kindled their fires but extinguished their virtue'.[84] Peter, with his sacramental approach, stressed the need for priests who celebrated Mass to lead continent lives. Gerald, however, had many more examples than Peter had of the evil influence of women. In addition, Gerald reworked some of Peter's stories for Welsh audiences, for example changing an anecdote about the Carthusian order to one about the Cistercians, who were more popular in Wales.[85]

Peter the Chanter exercised his influence also on architecture in England. His *Verbum Abbreviatum* includes a chapter against superfluity (or extravagance) of buildings, in which, quoting Seneca extensively, he passes animadversions against the luxury of the moderns as against the simplicity of the ancients.[86] Paul Binski has taken Salisbury Cathedral as an example of this attitude. Bishop Richard Poore (1217–28, when he was translated to Durham) moved his see from Old Sarum on Salisbury Plain, where it was cheek by jowl with the castle and the city, and in 1220 began the building of the cathedral by the River Avon, on a site so well known from Constable's paintings. Bishop Richard and his successor built it in an architecture of clean and pure lines, which were emphasised by the use of dark marble, and plain moulded capitals.[87] According to a contemporary poem about the new construction, Richard saw it as a liberation from the secular world of Old Sarum, a 'Langtonian emancipation from the old order', Binski calls it.[88] Salisbury was far away from the architecture of Wells Cathedral, for instance, dating from a few decades earlier, with its rich use of stone carving. Binski refers in this to the architecture of the Langtonians. As he rightly points out, the 'Langtonians' were not the only examples of high moral purpose in architecture. Others had earlier said similar things about architecture. All the same, Langton had been a pupil

of Peter, and Richard Poore of Langton, in Paris.[89] Peter had stood for
simplicity in the affairs of the church generally, for instance against
legalism and logic-chopping. Such also was the architecture of Salisbury.

The early thirteenth century saw a theological deepening in the preaching of crusade. In the twelfth century the principal concentration was on
indulgences, remission of punishment for sin, and the justice of the cause.
In the early thirteenth century the stress shifted to a theology of salvation –
the fact of sin itself, the consequent need for redemption, and the saving
nature of the Cross. An anonymous tract of about 1216, *On Preaching the
Holy Cross in England*, illustrates this tendency. It was probably written to
help preachers of the Fifth Crusade compose their sermons.[90] (Previously,
only the Third Crusade had been intensively preached in Britain.) The Fifth
Crusade was a top priority for Pope Innocent III. There is a case for saying
that, to him, the Fourth Lateran Council of 1215 was intended to set the
Church's house in order as a preparation for this greatest of enterprises.[91]
Galvanised by the pope, the preaching of this crusade was done with
extraordinary drive and efficiency, not least in England. Our anonymous
tract said that, in sermons, the purpose of *exempla* (i.e. illustrative anecdotes)
was to attract the listener's attention, prevent boredom, inspire contrition,
and encourage rejection of earthly riches and vanities. It contained meditations on the allegorical interpretation of Christ on the Cross.[92]

With this tract we seem to be back to the influence of (now) theological
study at Oxford on society. For it is very likely that it was written by
Master Philip of Oxford, whom Innocent had appointed in 1213 to be one
of three executors in England for recruiting crusaders.[93] We noted that
John of Cornwall, as an Oxford master, had been part canon lawyer part
theologian. Since his time Oxford had grown apace as a centre of theological study. There was, for example, Alexander Nequam, former Paris
scholar and himself a distinguished exponent of the art of preaching (as
well as being a scientist);[94] and there was Edmund of Abingdon, who
'incepted' as a theologian in Oxford around 1214, and who would in 1234
become Archbishop of Canterbury. In the 1200s Edmund himself was
a notable preacher of crusading, with a penchant for addressing large
open-air meetings.[95]

Even the reader who may be persuaded to think that there is something
in the idea of theologisation, horrible as the word is, may yet jib at the idea
that there was any 'such thing as society'. What notion of 'society' could
people have had who made only the crudest of class distinctions which
implied little sense of a whole structure, whose only idea of the meaning of
societas for the most part was a religious body or confraternity, and who

had no means of making social measurements but only of conveying impressions? In those circumstances what can it mean to say that theologians sought to imprint a theological idea of itself *on society*?

There seems to be no easy answer to this question. Wherever one thinks one might find an answer to what is meant by society in anything like our sense, it is not quite there. John of Salisbury in his *Policraticus* has a concept of the political body, the *res publica*, and the duty of princes to be just and promote the good of their subjects,[96] deriving from the Fathers and the classics; but that is not quite the same thing as a concept of society. The posthumous miracles recorded of Gilbert of Sempringham for his canonisation bring in a wide social spectrum – noblemen, knightly men and women (including a niece of Gilbert himself), villagers male and female, a doctor, a weaver, a boy servant at the mill of Sempringham, etc;[97] an impressive sweep until one remembers that this may be an old hagiographical cliché. Pope Gregory the Great in his *Dialogues* (590s), a work very much used by the Gilbertine author of this *Life and Miracles*, created a similar picture in describing the following of St Benedict. So a concept of society is not necessarily implied here either.

Perhaps in the end we have to be satisfied with there being no society that could perceive itself by sociological analysis, rather than one which could perceive itself as a people with differing conditions and needs though with some common purposes. And yet there is at least one piece of writing, a brilliant piece, in which we may discern a certain developing concept of society, namely Gerald of Wales's *Description of Wales* (*Descriptio Cambriae*, 1194 or a little before). Of this work, and a similar one on Ireland, Rees Davies wrote that Gerald's 'massively pioneering achievement should not be concealed beneath the cultivation of his even more massive ego'![98] One would not say this about the positive achievement if one considered only the clichéd image of the barbarian in the work, or the anecdotal method by which it is expounded (*exempla*, as in sermons). But there is much more to be said. First of all, it is perhaps the first medieval effort to describe a people in its totality – its geographical environment, its language, its manners and customs, its moral qualities, its music and religion. Moreover, in describing such things Gerald often tells us what all classes shared, being bold of speech, having regard for family descent, and having warrior instincts ('sound the trumpet for battle and the peasant will rush from his plough').[99] And he envisages a society which had been in all its parts influenced for good by its religion.[100] This is something much more sociological than it is another cliché of the age, i.e. the cliché of the unity of the Church in its ordered hierarchy.

There is something even more innovative in Gerald's *Description*, and that is his use of the scholastic method to bring out the whole truth about the Welsh. This is where his intellectual training at Paris must come in. The two fundamentals of the scholastic method were: (i) to break a subject down into its component parts of subdivisions in order finally to build up the whole, the *Summa* as one might say; and (ii) to apply to each question in each sub-division the *Sic et Non* method of ranging up the arguments which could be put for and against any proposition (yes and no), the idea being to bring conflicting considerations into the open before determining the truth. The scholastic method reached its culmination in Thomas Aquinas's *Summa Theologiae* (Paris, 1260s), but it is already to be seen in Ivo of Chartres's work on canon law in the early twelfth century, and in Peter Abelard's *Sic et non* (1120s).

In respect of the first point of scholasticism sub-dividing to build up as total a picture as possible – Gerald must have been stimulated in part by a classical ethnographic tradition; but it could only have been in part.[101] He can truly be called the father of medieval ethnography. Fifty years later the Franciscan John of Plano Carpini, also Paris trained, wrote a similar book about the Mongols after making an epic journey to their kingdom.[102] As an old man, he was probably amazed to come back to Europe still alive! On the second point, however – putting arguments and counter-arguments in such a work – Gerald was pretty much unique. Having in Book I, he wrote, described the good points about the Welsh, in Book II, *more historico* (in the way of history), he would say what was less praiseworthy or virtuous about them.[103] *More historico*? Classical and medieval historians often tried to give a balanced account of personalities or a fair appraisal of enemies. But I cannot think of another earlier medieval historical writer who does anything like it with this degree of formalism. This formalism, however, perfectly answers to how a theological or moral or legal *quaestio* would be debated in the schools. It would seem that this was Gerald's way of trying to reach the truth about the Welsh by scholastic procedure. Some scholars have been tempted to attribute the so-called ambiguities of Gerald's attitude towards the Welsh to his being himself half-English, half-Welsh. But most of these ambiguities fade away (Gerald loved the Welsh) when one appreciates what he is doing – applying a method developed in connection with theology to the description of a people. I am not saying that his *Descriptio* in itself represents an attempt to theologise society, in the way that Gerald's *Gemma Ecclesiastica* does; only that it helps us to understand what an intelligent person might in the 1190s make of what we call a society.

CHAPTER 9

The Early English Franciscans

Poverty

Two great orders of Friars sprang up in the early thirteenth century, the Franciscans and the Dominicans. The reason why the Friars are distinguished from the Monks and even from the Augustinian Canons is that, though like these they had vows of (personal) poverty and chastity, they did not live in such stable communities. They were much more mobile in their work of evangelisation; their establishments needed little in the way of endowments; and they were wedded to communal as well as to personal poverty. The very term 'friar' was one of humility compared with the oft-used title of 'dominus' for a monk. The Dominicans were the Order of Preachers; the Franciscans, even more self-abasing, were known as the Friars Minor. It may seem surprising to the reader that this chapter is largely about the Franciscans, for in the history of the thirteenth-century Western church as a whole, the Dominicans did not make a lesser impact. But although Dominicans had arrived in England earlier than Franciscans – and were of help to their co-friars – the Franciscans were more important than the Dominicans in English learning and politics, and even possibly in the hearing of confessions, in Henry III's reign.

St Francis was born in Assisi in the early 1180s, the son of a merchant who often travelled to France, hence his name. As a young man he was affable, well-dressed and flighty. Then, around the age of 24 he had a serious illness and underwent a deep religious conversion. He sold his clothes, gave the money, which he now hated to touch, to an Assisi priest, repaired churches, went around wearing a kind of hermit's dress, and served and even embraced lepers. He was deliberately identifying himself with the marginalised (not necessarily the poor) of Assisi. When, attending Mass, he once heard the gospel about Christ sending out his disciples with nothing, he gave up shoes and replaced his leather girdle with a plain cord around his one tunic. He begged for his bread, hence his order was known as the Mendicants, the beggars. He quickly attracted followers.[1] Francis would later specialise in creating disorder and embarrassment of every kind. If invited to a meal at the house of great persons, for instance, he would beg for scraps of bread beforehand and then, disdaining the fine food he was offered, would make a picnic of his scraps at the table.[2] It was all a reaction to the development of orderly government and the intellectually rational modes of scholasticism. Both government and a training in scholasticism could make people a lot of money.

Francis had a special rapport with nature and a great affection for animals; he took creation seriously.[3] It was perhaps partly a release from the throttling effects of human institutions. He spoke of Brother Wolf and Brother Fish, etc; and he once caressed a hare which had been caught in a trap 'with maternal affection'. He began to preach to the birds, and when they listened to him with great attention, he charged himself with negligence for not having preached to them earlier, 'being now by grace become simple, though he was not so by nature'.[4] In other words he had had plenty of social *savoir-faire*, and knew how to behave normally rather than like a mad-hatter. His was divine simplicity, not simple-mindedness.

When Francis had some followers, he applied to Pope Innocent III to recognise them as an order with a Rule (1210). The Rule was nothing that could be used for the institutional organisation of an order. It was little more than a chain of citations from the Gospels where the evangelic life of Christ and apostolic poverty were highlighted.[5] But its recognition by the pope gave Francis and his followers the freedom to preach their message. It is tempting for historians sometimes to think that if Francis had had to choose between following a life of apostolic poverty which was all in all to him, and obedience to the Church, which later wanted to compromise that ideal in order to stabilise and institutionalise him, Francis would have chosen apostolic poverty, i.e. the perfect following of the Gospel. But the point is that under Innocent, at least, he did not have to choose. The church authorities had learnt to be less paranoiac than Alexander III had been with religious movements of 'poor men and women', like the Poor Men of Lyon or the Waldensians, and had learnt not to run them into an extreme position. That may in itself have been partly Paris influence and Paris distaste for shows of ecclesiastical wealth. To Alexander III or churchmen of his time, the poor man Francis might have looked dangerously like an anti-clerical heretic. However, the learning was not all on one side. Those seeking poverty had also learnt something. Unlike the anti-clericals of the early twelfth century, Francis had the utmost veneration for church buildings; for priests and bishops and pope; for apostolic authority; and for the sacraments, not least confession, the last in line with what would be an emphasis of the Fourth Lateran Council.

The Franciscans arrived in England in 1224. They were wedded to voluntary poverty and one naturally asks how they related to *in*voluntary poverty. The strange thing, at first sight, is the difficulty to find the real poor, the sufferers from involuntary poverty, at that time, or in the decades immediately before their arrival. In Robert Bartlett's still recent book, *England under the Norman and Angevin Kings, 1075–1225*, despite its political-sounding title a superb and massive sweep of social history, the index contains neither the words poor nor poverty. Bishops making grants often use the formal phrase, 'for the use of the poor', but with never an indication of who these poor were.[6] Their grants to hospitals for lepers and the like are no evidence for a problem of poverty as such. There is little evidence of poverty in the miracle collections (the subjects of miracles are far more likely to be the upwardly mobile receiving health cures), or chronicles or hagiographies. William FitzOsbert is said to have set himself up in 1196 as the champion of the so-called poor of London.[7] But when the poor are equated, as in this case, with people over-burdened with taxation, one wonders whether Tocqueville's thesis might not apply: that it is not the abject poor, but those baulked by taxation of their rising material expectations, who particularly engage in rebellion and revolution.

One could think, with the long rise in population of the twelfth and thirteenth centuries, that Malthusian checks would already have begun to bite by the 1220s. But the possibilities of further economic expansion or management seemed able to cope with this problem until later than that time.[8] Paul Hyams has shown in royal court records of the early thirteenth century that men were often excused from paying amercements (i.e. fines) on the grounds that they were poor. But as he says, poor did not necessarily mean destitute.[9] What this looks like is the operation of a principle laid down in Magna Carta (Clause 20) that no free man or unfree peasant should be so amerced as to lose his livelihood. Actually kings needed there to be poor people, whether there were any or not; for one of the functions of a model king according to the Old Testament was to protect the *pauperes*, or poor, from the *potentes*, or powerful. Bishops, too, needed there to be poor people, whether there were any or not, in order to fulfil one of their traditional roles, part of a bishop's image, of assigning a proportion of their revenues to 'the poor'.

Of course there were poor people; there always are. In the countryside this came about especially because partible inheritance of peasant holdings made some, perhaps many, holdings too small to support a family. There were no doubt also genuine urban poor who had come into towns to escape rural poverty.[10] But in the countryside it could be that opportunities for paid labour, provided by landlords who were ceasing to lease out their lands and were taking them into direct administration, helped to keep many families from destitution. Again in the towns, apart from the opportunities which towns offered poor people to make good, the more that towns flourished, the more the demand for paid labour. Unfortunately, the demand for paid labour and its usefulness to the poorest families is almost impossible to quantify around the 1220s.

In any event, it is hard to see a *structural* problem of poverty, rather than impoverishment of some families, at this time. The Franciscans, and their sermons and confessions, were probably more needed by the upwardly mobile, guilt-ridden tradesmen and merchants, than by 'the poor', whom in any case they could not at all help materially, because of their own espousal of voluntary poverty.

A stimulating book by Kenneth B. Wolf, *The Poverty of Riches: St Francis of Assisi Re-considered* (2003), shows up the ironies inherent in Francis's ideal of voluntary poverty. As coming from a wealthy background he could *choose* to be poor; the involuntary poor could not. By espousing poverty himself he could do nothing to alleviate other people's poverty; he could not be like the 'civic saint', Raymund of Piacenza, who founded a hospice for the sick, the poor, and pilgrims. Indeed, as has been said, he competed with the poor for alms; rich people could salve their consciences by giving to him and at the same time investing in a saint who would intercede for them.

Wolf's book, however, lacks any attempt to assess how great or of what nature the problem of poverty was in Assisi itself, and how far perhaps helped by church or commune or individuals. The marginalised who Francis principally encountered were lepers, and he aligned himself with them by staying in their houses.[11] So there were leper houses – provided by whom? Francis is also occasionally said to have encountered (real) beggars. But one such meeting is instructive. Francis rebuked a brother who insulted a poor man begging for alms. The brother had doubted the real poverty of the beggar. Francis upbraided the brother for his bad manners, not for being wrong![12] Wolf criticises Francis for the inadequacy of his preaching to the involuntary poor; but there seems little or no evidence for there being many such people. The problem of involuntary poverty is not equally acute in every society. If the poor were relatively thin on the ground, in early thirteenth-century Assisi or England, then my own hypothesis might kick in: that voluntary poverty is best suited to conditions where there is not too much involuntary poverty.

Poverty and learning

When the Franciscans arrived in England in 1224 and made for the towns, they at once attracted men of learning. The attraction was no doubt to their religious zeal, and partly perhaps to their giving scholars in a highly competitive and careerist world an opportunity honourably to opt out of the rat race. But the principal attraction to scholars might well have been the strong evangelising drive of the Franciscans, as of the Dominicans, from the start, where Francis himself had recognised the value of learning and education if properly harnessed to humility and poverty. The question then arose in an acute form: could learning and poverty go together?

This was never a serious problem for the early Dominicans. Dominic and his followers had begun by preaching against the Cathar heretics in Southern France. Their austerity of life was intended to recommend their preaching to those who were disillusioned with the showy materialism of the church and its representatives amongst them, a 'channel of communication' as this austerity has been called. But Dominic became convinced that the only satisfactory way to convert heretics was to engage in the deepest possible study of orthodox theology. Thus on 15 August 1217, he announced the dispersal of his order to the towns in Europe with the best universities. This was the first and last dramatic gesture of his life; 15 August was the feast of Mary's Assumption into Heaven, and it was as if his order were being apotheosised along with Mary.[13] From the start, therefore, the Dominicans put learning first, with poverty an adjunct to its communication. From 1217, also, Dominic's personality became completely submerged in his order, while Francis's personality never was in his. For the Franciscans it was poverty that was of the essence; and for long after Francis's death the discussion about poverty in his order remained fixed, if not fixated, on the personality and apostolic ideal of Francis himself as the very exemplar of holiness.

Francis himself was characteristically ambiguous about whether learning was compatible with the poverty of the Gospel. He allowed Anthony of Padua to teach theology to the friars. But when 'a certain minister' asked for some 'ambitious' and valuable books to be kept, he replied, 'I am not going to lose the book of the Gospel, which I have promised to obey, for the sake of your books. Do however what you will, for my permission shall not be made a snare.'[14] Confusing in every sense of the word! There were other times also when he reacted strongly against friars owning books. In Anthony of Padua's case, Francis clearly made an *ad hominem* judgment. Anthony had already proved himself to be a man great in the spirit of poverty and in a virtue closely allied to voluntary poverty, namely humility. Nobody at his hermitage near Forli had thought of him as other than a simple brother willing to perform any menial task, until on a visit to Forli he was unexpectedly required to preach, when his high intellect and articulateness became known.[15] And Francis greatly honoured true theologians, though not friars who out of ambition wanted to improve themselves.

What were Francis's problems with learning? First, it needed books, and books at that time were expensive; they were no sign or symbol of poverty. Second, books and study needed solid buildings, of the sort that Francis would not countenance; and study needed warmth and proper food. Third, learning was associated with making a lucrative living. Making money was what the monastic orders did, against whose wealth the Franciscans were reacting.

After Francis's death in 1226, however, the balance in the order began to shift from the lay brothers for whom poverty presented no problem of principle, towards the learned element, the provincial ministers of northern Europe, and the like. This happened particularly during the five years when John Parenti was Minister-General of the order (some of the earliest years of the Franciscans in England), and while the pope was Gregory IX. As Cardinal Hugolino, Gregory had been Francis's protector in Rome, but he always tried to pressurise Francis to institutionalise the order more than he wanted, to make it look safer to the papal curia. Perhaps the key moment in the shift came with Gregory's bull of 1231, *Quo Elongati*, which allowed Franciscans to have the *use* of houses, albeit these were not to be formally *owned* by themselves but by so-called 'spiritual friends'.[16] Francis, for whom shacks sufficed, would surely have disapproved of this legal technicality. But such a measure was arguably necessary to secure the very continuation of the order, at least as a force for learning.[17] After John Parenti, Elias, the favoured disciple of Francis himself, became Minister-General for a second time. The *putsch* against him in 1239 virtually sealed the victory of the learned element, not that Elias himself was against learning, but he represented the large element of Italian lay brothers in the order, and was regarded as high-handed in dealing with the learned element.

In the 1240s and 1250s, the learned element who had won, themselves felt obliged to grapple with the question: how could learning and Francis's ideal of poverty go together? Almost a scholastic *Sic et Non* developed. Hugh de Digne argued on the one hand that Francis reverenced theologians and that he, Hugh, was not about to strip himself of his learning in order, to use a favourite saying of Francis, as a naked man to follow the naked Christ. On the other hand he wrote two works on poverty, arguing against superfluities, etc.[18] Another example seems to be the biographer of Francis, Thomas of Celano. Celano was not unlearned. He wrote one Life of St Francis before his canonisation of 1229, and then he wrote a second many years later in 1244–45. The greatest difference between the two Lives is that in the second the ideal of poverty in relation to Francis is driven much harder than it is in the first. In the second Life Francis is seen actually pulling down buildings. And on a journey, someone asked him, so this Life says, whether he would visit 'the house of the brethren' at Bologna. On hearing the phrase 'house of the brethren', he was so affronted that he by-passed Bologna altogether.[19] One could think of Celano's Second Life as a kind of rearguard action against the learned element in the order after they had won. Celano was at that time in close touch with the 'Companions' of St Francis, who self-consciously kept the banner of the saint's ideal of poverty flying. But I prefer to think of it as Celano's trying to stress the poverty side of the *Sic et Non* going on within the order in the 1240s, because it still needed stressing, while being well aware of the learning side of the argument also.

St Bonaventure was the greatest of all Franciscan theologians and he took part in this Yes and No debate too. In his *Apologia Pauperum* of probably the late 1250s, Bonaventure argued that poverty was less important than charity, but that as cupidity was the enemy of charity, poverty was still vital. Christ was poor, he said, in order to render his poverty lovable (*amabilem*) to the world.[20] This was written at a time when Bonaventure was Minister-General, and his front-line preoccupation then must have been to be conciliatory in the embittered debates at Paris between secular masters and friars, which began in earnest in 1252–53. But given that he went to Paris to study the arts subjects in 1235 when he was a young man of 18, that he sat there at the feet of one of the friars' great masters, Alexander of Hales, that Paris was centre stage in the events of the *putsch* against Elias (1239) and its aftermath, and that he himself became a Franciscan probably in 1243 when he began his theological studies,[21] he must also have had an eye on the events of 1239–40.

Poverty and learning in England

The principal source for the earliest Franciscans, or Friars Minor, in England, is Thomas of Eccleston's vivid *On the Coming of the Friars Minor to England*. Eccleston wrote probably in 1258, but says that he had been collecting material orally for 26 years, which takes us back to 1232, within a decade of the Franciscans' arrival in England. He was not a front-line theologian, but he had studied in Oxford, had learning, and clearly associated himself with the learned element in the order and with the northern Provincial Ministers. By the time he wrote he could have had his eye on the acrimonious debates between Friars/Mendicants and Secular Clergy at the University of Paris in the 1250s. The Seculars maintained that begging or mendicancy was not true apostolic poverty, which was giving up one's possessions (and one's professorships!) and earning one's bread by manual labour or by going into a monastery. Haymo of Faversham at least, as English Provincial Minister, would partly accept this argument when he encouraged the friars to extend their sites (as at Gloucester) so that they could cultivate their own vegetables.[22] The Seculars regarded as hypocrisy the Franciscans having property legally owned by others. But in his one reference to the Paris quarrels, Eccleston seems to keep his distance from them.[23] Paris was on the periphery of his interests. He was very Anglo-centric. He approved of John of Parma's efforts to achieve reconciliation in Paris, but what he most approved of in this Minister-General was his admiration for the English province. He quoted John as saying frequently, 'would that such a province were situated in the middle of the world so that it could be an example to all!'[24]

Nonetheless Eccleston thought that things were changing for the worse. When he wrote he felt that the ideal of poverty was being disregarded, as was becoming increasingly apparent in the friars' buildings. The friars, so Eccleston thought, were starting to be too lenient to the rich in their confessions, and to make honourable provision for persons of distinction who joined the order.[25] 'Wake up to your great and poverty-honouring past!', Eccleston seems to say to his province. Furthermore, if one put the crucial question of whether poverty and learning could go together, Eccleston's answer seems to be that they very much could do so in principle and practice, if one considered the golden age of the Province in the 1220s and 1230s.

Eccleston has been taken to be weaving together a series of good examples or 'pleasant' vignettes, examples for the Franciscans of his own times;[26] and it is true that illustrative examples were a vital element of the friars'

whole approach to preaching.[27] In his brief Prologue he makes this *the*
point. But he was more artful than all this implies. His chapters are called
collationes, or conferences, his own word. This suggests that he modelled his book in some sense on the famous and widely read fifth-century
compilation of stories about the Egyptian fathers, Cassian's *Collationes*.
Cassian wrote to inspire and edify Western monks of his day, Eccleston
the English friars of the 1250s. Then again, Eccleston liked to give an
impression of spontaneity about the earliest English Franciscan foundations, as if they were upwellings of pure trusting spirituality, of taking no
thought for the morrow in the true spirit of evangelical poverty (Matthew,
6, 34). The stories spring up *in medias res*, like some pieces of romantic
music such as the opening of Mendelssohn's Italian Symphony. But this
was artifice. David Lamb has effectively shown how much careful advance
planning was needed even for simple foundations like theirs – designation
of sites, acquisition of timber, operation of patrons. All this could not
simply happen.[28]

When the Franciscans, on their arrival, moved into the towns, they at
once attracted the learned to themselves. Eccleston is glowing about the
poverty in which the early friars lived, at Cambridge and especially at
Oxford, as well as elsewhere. At Cambridge there was a chapel so humble
that a carpenter knocked it up in one day from 15 split tree trunks.[29] At
Oxford the friars were so keen on hearing the theology lectures that they
visited the schools daily in winter, barefoot, in bitter cold and deep mud,
and at night they huddled together like piglets for warmth. The infirmary
was so low that a man could hardly stand upright in it.[30] The first Oxford
novice, with whom Eccleston had spoken directly, was the youthful
Brother Solomon. Of him Eccleston says:

While he was still a novice, he was made procurator and came to the
house of his sister begging for alms. As she brought him the bread she
averted her gaze, saying, 'cursed be the hour that I ever saw you'.
But he took the bread and went away rejoicing.[31]

An anecdote from Oxford which particularly appealed to Eccleston
concerns Brother Walter of Madeley. It comes within a chapter, or *collatio*,
which was supposed to be about a rather dry-sounding subject, the organisation of the English province into 'custodies', and it occupies a good third
of that chapter by itself. This is Eccleston's narrative:

It chanced that Brother Walter of Madeley had found a pair of
sandals [Eccleston has just said that the Oxford brethren neither

*normally used pillows to sleep nor sandals to walk at that time], and
had put them on when he went to Matins. It seemed to him, therefore,
that he stood more comfortably at Matins than usual. But later,
when he had gone to bed and was sleeping, he dreamed that he had to
go through a certain dangerous pass between Oxford and Gloucester
called Baisaliz [as yet unidentified but possibly Besselsleigh], where
there were wont to be robbers. When he came down into the deep valley,
these ran up to him from either side of the way, shouting 'Kill, Kill!'
Whereat, greatly terrified he said he was a Friar Minor. But they replied,
'You lie, for you walk not unshod.' But he, believing himself to be as
usual unshod, said, 'Nay, but I do walk unshod,' and when he calmly
stretched forth his foot, he found, in the robber's presence, that he
was wearing these said sandals. Then forthwith, roused from sleep
by extreme confusion, he threw the sandals far away into
the fields.*[32]

The English province, with Robert Grosseteste, from early on the friars'
teacher at Oxford, had a high reputation for learning all over the Franciscan
world, including with Minister-General Elias. In the 1230s Elias caused
Brothers Philip of Wales and Adam of York to be appointed Readers at
Lyon.[33] This reputation was by no means due solely to Oxford. But the
province had an equally high reputation for poverty. Eccleston tells how
Francis himself once 'seemed to come' to an English friary and sat in
silence looking around him for a long time. The custodian eventually said
to him, 'Father, what are your thoughts?' Francis replied, 'look around
you at this house', which the Custodian did, and the whole house was of
wattles, daubed with mud. 'Such ought the houses of the Friars Minor to
be', Eccleston has the saint say.[34] This story illustrates not only Eccleston's
idea of the English reputation for poverty, but also how the ideal of
poverty went on and on being discussed with reference to the person of
Francis himself.

Thomas of Eccleston, writing of England in the 1230s and 1240s, with
all the events and clashes of 1239 to 1244 in the order behind him,
obviously had in mind one of the central questions that convulsed the
early Franciscans: could voluntary poverty and learning go together? A
major motive of his writing was to give the answer 'yes' to this question. If
one held up to view the early history of the English province, this seemed
to be a perfect example of a true marriage between poverty and learning.
A fleeting example, perhaps, but one to which Eccleston wanted to recall
the friars. Nonetheless, the English province had shown the whole order
how it could be done.

This does not appear as merely a surfeit of English patriotism on Eccleston's part. The real hero of his book is the highly influential Englishman Haymo of Faversham. Haymo had been the friars' Reader at Tours, Bologna and Padua; and none other than Pope Gregory IX, St Francis's one-time special protector in the papal curia, had sent him on a mission to the Byzantine Empire. He was an authoritative theologian, a renowned preacher, and an international figure within the order. He was also ardent for poverty. As English Provincial Minister, he would sit on the ground at meals during provincial chapters, wearing a mean and torn habit, with those at the farthest end of the refectory.[35]

Haymo was the principal architect, amongst North European Provincial Ministers, of Brother Elias's downfall in 1239. Eccleston is quite explicit about this. Elias had received a special blessing from Francis and had been the saint's nominee to be first Minister-General of the order. But his personality seemed to have needed the sustaining power of Francis's spirituality and idealism. After Francis's death he failed to uphold the ideal of poverty in his personal life. He hob-nobbed with the Emperor Frederick II; he had a chef; he received his friars reclining before a crackling fire in winter; he rode around on a charger. Part and parcel of all this was the resentment of the northern Provincial Ministers at the high-handedness with which Elias dealt with the enlightened elements in the order.[36] Thomas of Celano had mentioned his being blessed by Francis in his first *Life*, but he completely dropped him from the second.

Haymo initiated an appeal against Elias in the Provincial Chapter of 1236 at Paris, after one from Oxford. When the whole issue came to a hearing before Pope Gregory IX, it was a witty speech by Haymo, and the unseemly interruptions of Elias himself, which turned the Pope against the latter. 'Albeit the brethren had said to Elias that they wished him to eat gold', said Haymo 'they had not said that they wished him to have a treasury. Albeit they had said that they wished him to have a horse, they had not said that they wished him to have a palfrey or a charger.'[37] The almost immediate result of the events of 1236–39 was that Haymo became Minister-General of the order in 1240, and remained so until his death in 1244.

Thus Thomas of Eccleston's belief, expressed from his knowledge of the English province, that learning and apostolic poverty could go together, was a belief vital to the success of the learned element in the order as a whole in 1239 – through Haymo of Faversham. We get very used in our historical thinking to the idea, almost the assumption, that England, or Britain, always takes its tune from Europe. But in early Franciscan history it was the other way round. England played a decisive role in the development of the whole order.

Confession

By confession, I mean the private confession by an individual to a priest of his or her sins or sinfulness, and their receiving (normally) absolution. It should be added that nobody in the Middle Ages could justifiably think that it lay in the power of the priest to forgive sins. That lay with Christ alone. The priest could be no more than a mediator between Christ and the penitent or, perhaps better, a church-appointed spokesman of Christ. The penitent's absolution marked his or her reconciliation not so much directly with Christ as with the Church. And the penance imposed, whether it was the reciting of one Our Father or the undertaking of a lengthy pilgrimage, was therefore an ecclesiastical penalty not a God-given one. Of the actual sins confessed, however, the priest was bound by the strictest possible seal of secrecy, as though they were a matter solely between the penitent and Christ himself. If a priest thought that it was strongly in the interest of a public that a sin should be revealed, his only option was to make his absolution conditional on penitents themselves revealing it.

The practice of private confession was becoming much more widespread than previously in the twelfth century and apparently almost universal in the thirteenth-century church. It was a powerful instrument in the advance of Christian morality, and even of social control by the Church. In that respect it was like preaching, and preaching to the laity also became organised to an unprecedented degree in the thirteenth century. Historians have naturally concentrated more on the history of preaching than on that of confession, because besides there being manuals for both preachers and confessors and canon law prescriptions for both, many sermons and collections of sermons survive as historical sources, whereas because of the seal of confession, we hardly ever know what went on in the 'confessional box'. The paradox of this whole subject is that although the tangible evidences of preaching are plentiful, the intangible influence of confession was almost certainly as important. And that for one simple reason. People can readily go to sleep or switch off during a sermon; they can hardly do so when their own sins are under discussion in the one-to-one situation of confession. The fourteenth-century carver at Norwich Cathedral, in his roof boss of John the Baptist preaching, represented most of the Baptist's congregation asleep, or at least with their eyes half closed.[38] As a college tutor giving one-on-one tutorials to undergraduates who read out their essays, I noticed that their attention often wandered when the tutor talked about the subject of their essays, but never when it was their own essays that were under discussion!

During the course of the twelfth century and into the early thirteenth, a sea change in the whole approach to confession came about. First of all it grew in importance. In the first half of the twelfth century, some bishops at least already had diocesan penitentiaries, individuals responsible for organising the hearing of confessions on a diocesan basis. Gilbert of Sempringham was one of these under Bishop Alexander of Lincoln, 1123–48, and incidentally also one of the great Exchequer bishops. Alexander Murray has noted astutely that England was exceptionally early in its degree of emphasis on confession, not least as a necessary concomitant to miraculous remedies of ills deemed to have been caused by sin. (But confession itself must often have been *the* remedy.) Equally, Murray has observed the major role that was obviously played by the early English Augustinian Canons in this emphasis.[39] Once again our story has taken us back to the Augustinian Canons and their pastorate.

The second point to make about the changing approach to confession is that whereas previous to the twelfth century the idea of guidance to confessors had been mainly to present tariffs of penance for a multitude of sins, now more attention came to be given to understanding the psychology, intention, and situation of penitents and to giving them deep-seated oral guidance. There is a parallel between this and what Prior Philip of the Augustinian Canons of St Frideswide, Oxford, had to say about the psychology of those receiving miraculous cures at the shrine there (see pp. 177–9). It is always important how people in a society try to cope with their sense of guilt,[40] and confession here played a vital role for the twelfth century. The preaching of the Second Crusade in the 1140s was probably instrumental to this changing approach. The First Crusade (1090s) had concentrated on the remission of penance due to sins for those who took on the warrior pilgrimage to Jerusalem. Pope Eugenius III, under the influence of his fellow Cistercian St Bernard, when he preached the Second Crusade, dwelt much more on the need for an inner state of contrition in those who hoped to reap the religious benefits of crusading.[41]

A landmark in this changing approach to confession was the *Penitential* of Bartholomew of Exeter, composed probably either in the late 1150s when he was Archdeacon of Exeter or in the early 1160s after he had become bishop (1161).[42] In his work, Bartholomew favoured moderation rather than rigidity in the application of penances, and insisted that the confessor should take account of different circumstances. In cases of parricide, for instance, which he defines, the penances should 'have regard for persons, places and times, but especially for the causes and whether perpetrated accidentally or deliberately'.[43] Bartholomew, who had studied at Paris in the early 1140s, relied much on those two great canonists of the earlier twelfth century, Ivo of Chartres and Gratian; but not apparently in the passages which I have just cited.

After Bartholomew we come to William de Montibus, another Parisian who wrote his *Speculum Penitentis* (Mirror of the Penitent) probably while Chancellor of Lincoln Cathedral in the 1190s. Here William discussed how priests should positively enquire about penitents' sins and their nature, emphasising the eliciting of unrecognised faults, and he wrote of hearing confessions as an art.[44] After William we can come to another English member of the school of Peter the Chanter in Paris, Thomas of Chobham, whose *Summa Confessorum* dates from about 1215.[45] It is intriguing that just at the time of Magna Carta, this English professor at Paris should be writing about the *nature* of morality and immorality in human conduct, and also about different kinds of people and their situations, just the kind of thing that Magna Carta was trying to do, for instance in its Clause 20 on how different kinds of people should be amerced (fined) or not amerced. We can go on into Wales where about 1230 Bishop Cadwgan of Bangor (1215–36) wrote his *De Modo Confitendi*.[46] Cadwgan had had a colourful career, if we trust the disparagements of Gerald of Wales, before he became bishop; but he is known, by chance, to have sent a ship to Ireland to collect grain for distribution to the poor of his diocese,[47] and he was no mean scholar, who used his scholarship to try to raise the level of education amongst his flock. His treatise on confession was an aspect of this. He too has much on the penitent's right state of mind and how he (or she) should be questioned, guided and advised by a confessor. But by 1230 he could rely not only on William de Montibus, but also on a raft of other, early thirteenth-century texts.

Augustinian Canons are part of this trail through treatises on confession around 1200. Guy of Southwick (Hampshire) wrote one such for William de Vere, Bishop of Hereford (1186–98) and a discerning patron of learning, with whom Guy had discussed the subject in London, doubtless at a council.[48] He dealt with the right state of mind for confession, saying that confession was not efficacious unless one conveyed one's intimate thoughts; and he gave advice on what to confess and why. Around 1215 Robert of Flamborough wrote the first *Summa* for confessors.[49] Similar things may be said about it to what we have said about the others. Robert was a canon of the church of St Victor in Paris, and the Victorines were similar to the Augustinians in their combination of learning, contemplation and pastoral work. However he presumably came from Flamborough in East Yorkshire, whose church we noted to be almost certainly under the direct management of the Augustinian Canons of Bridlington, so it is likely that he received some of his youthful education under them. Several English Augustinian abbeys had early copies of Bartholomew of Exeter's *Penitential*, and one, Leicester, had Bartholomew and William de Montibus bound together.[50]

We should say, incidentally, that several black-monk houses had copies of Bartholomew, e.g. Bury St Edmunds, Ramsey, St Augustine's Canterbury, and Peterborough.[51] This may have had partly to do with the association between miraculous healings at shrines and the need to confess one's sins, which we mentioned above. But there was probably more to it than that. It may be that monk-priests often heard confessions. Bishop William of Norwich (1146–74) had a monk of Norwich called Wichermann to be his deputy for hearing confessions in the diocese, in other words a penitentiary.[52] Moreover, when monasteries took seriously the supervision of the parish churches of which they were rector or to which they had the right (and duty) of appointment – and presumably some if not most monasteries did take this seriously – a Penitential might have been a useful book from which to advise their priests.

The great watershed in the history of confession was the Fourth Lateran Council of 1215. Indeed this Council was altogether a watershed. Its provisions stimulated much development in Western religion and the church, and its provision about confession could not have been effectively implemented had not the orders of friars just come into existence. But it also articulated much that was already happening. Metropolitans, i.e. archbishops, it said, were to hold provincial councils annually.[53] Archbishop Hubert Walter held an important council in 1200 which was like a mini Fourth Lateran Council in its anticipations, and in the influence on it of the School of Peter the Chanter (albeit there is no evidence for Hubert that this was an annual event). The Fourth Lateran Council provided for the education of the clergy. Every cathedral was to have a master to teach Latin grammar and other subjects to the clergy and other poor scholars without charge; and every metropolitan cathedral was to have a prebend assigned to a theologian to teach the Scriptures to the clergy.[54] Even a cathedral so low in prestige and endowments as Chichester actually had amongst its canons a theology teacher in Gervase of Chichester before the end of the twelfth century. Perhaps through his agency, Bishop Hilary had given its chapter a copy of Peter Lombard's *Sentences*, *the* theology textbook of its time, within 10 or 15 years of its being composed at Paris.[55] Where confession was concerned, we see the drive to educate priests to conduct this sacrament intelligently for many decades before the Council.

This is what the Council had to say about confession:

Every Christian of either sex after reaching the years of discretion shall confess all his sins at least once a year privately to his own priest [the friars were not yet effectively on the scene for this purpose] and try as hard as he (or she) can to perform the penance imposed; and receive with reverence the sacrament of the Eucharist at least at Easter. [As we have observed, the Council sought to bring the laity back into the sacramental heart of the Church.] . . . As for the priest, he should be discerning and prudent so that like a practised doctor he can pour wine and oil on the wounds of the injured, diligently enquiring into the circumstances both of the sinner and of the sin, from which to choose intelligently what sort of advice he ought to give and what sort of remedy to apply, various means availing to heal the sick. Let him take the utmost care not to betray the sinner in any measure by word or sign or any other way whatever . . . He who presumes to reveal a sin disclosed in the confessional we decree is to be not only deposed from his priestly office but also shut up to do penance for life in a monastery of strict observance.[56]

Such a canon was all very fine, but where were the priests to be found skilful and educated enough to carry out so ambitious a scheme? Indeed with the penitentials which we have just been considering, we have no idea what proportion of the parish clergy were capable of benefiting from their advice. Bishop Richard Poore, conscientious implementer of Lateran IV's decrees, laid down in his Salisbury synodal statutes (1217–19) that people were to go to confession not once but three times a year, and to their own priest (the friars were not yet on the English scene).[57] This was positively quixotic! The friars, with all their zealous, learned and intelligent recruits, were obviously a godsend in this situation. Without them, the Fourth Lateran decree on confession might have been virtually unfulfillable.

Although the title of this chapter has the word Franciscans, the rest of what we say about confession must equally apply to the Franciscans and the Dominicans. But the whole institution of confession fitted quite as well to the Franciscan as to the Dominican ethos. Francis rejected urban commerce on his conversion, and yet the spirituality which the Franciscans developed 'belonged unmistakably to the very society that they rejected'.[58] An early Franciscan work on poverty had the allegorical title *Holy Commerce*. In this thought-world, confession could be seen, and was so in some thirteenth-century manuals of confession, as a kind of commercial negotiation between confessor and penitent (having of course nothing to do with actual money).[59]

The evidence of friars coming into urban and rural parishes to preach and hear confessions is not unequivocally favourable; where it exists it sometimes suggests that initially there were parish clergy who resented such incursions into their own domain. But whatever initial resistance there may have been, bishops quickly realised their potential to help raise standards amongst the parish clergy themselves, and they also took steps to protect the material interests of the parish clergy and the standing of the clergy in their parishes. Thus at Winchester in the 1260s, a synodal decree forbade parishioners to confess to a friar in Lent or outside it without the permission of their parish priest and provided they paid their customary offerings.[60] This, or something like it, was decreed in many other dioceses. The need for such regulations in themselves point to the popularity of the friars as confessors. The reference in the Winchester case to customary offerings shows that there was a pecuniary interest here, not of course in the simoniacal sense of paying for a confession, but in the sense that the annual confession (likely to happen in Lent just before Easter) was in some way associated with the altar offerings that laity owed to their priests at Easter time. On the other hand, were the priests assured of their offerings, this means that they were likely to give their permissions for friars to hear confessions. For the better qualified the confessor, the higher the standard of religious observance was likely to be, and that could only be of advantage to the parish clergy.

In any case, the evidence suggests that by far the greater clash of interests, when one occurred, between friars and parish priests, was over profitable rights of burials, whether they were to be in the friars' cemeteries or in the parish cemeteries.[61] This was surely something that Thomas of Eccleston would have had in mind when regretting the lapses from apostolic poverty by the English Franciscans.

In general, the evidence leaves no doubt that the friars were almost everywhere as confessors. Bishops were unanimous in wanting to receive the friars in their dioceses with honour and reverence because of the fruitfulness of their preaching and confessions.[62] When Bishop Grosseteste, the special protector of the Franciscans and their teacher at Oxford, came into a rural deanery in his diocesan visitations of 1238–39, the clergy and people gathered together, and a Dominican or Franciscan preached, after which four friars heard confessions and enjoined penances.[63] It is interesting, incidentally, and suggestive of the rising religious education of the laity, that Grosseteste could envisage both clergy and laity together listening to such sermons. In the end the friars had designated licensed confessors. One reason for that can be seen in a Chichester statute of 1289 complaining of fake friars, dressed for the part, coming into villages and preaching and hearing confessions.[64] This is late evidence, but it shows that such visits of real friars must have been commonplace long before 1289.

There was a particular advantage that to many people the friars must have had over the parish clergy in hearing confessions. They were strangers to the communities into which they came, outsiders with their own communities. Moorman saw this as a disadvantage. Surely, he thought, it was better for the parishioners to have a wise priest who knew them and was always there to look after them rather than a stranger, here now and gone tomorrow.[65] But Alexander Murray put the opposite, and undoubtedly better, point. Friars 'were not part of the parish: so a penitent could bare his heart with less embarrassment'. However, as he also shows, there were many complaints in the thirteenth century, made for instance by the Franciscans Bonaventure and Anthony of Padua, that the seal of confession had been broken, especially in the matter of adultery.[66] It is difficult to tell what lay behind such complaints. No sin has never happened. But I think that even in the thirteenth century priests who knowingly broke the seal of confession were an extreme rarity. Anthony Kenny in his marvellous autobiography, *A Path from Rome*, writes that in his experience as a former Catholic priest, amidst all the faults of many Catholic clergy (gambling, drunkenness, fornication, etc.), he had never once known of a case where the seal of confession had been broken.[67] Of course it was always possible that an inadvertent remark of a priest might give a clue.

It is possible, however, to suggest why people confessing to a parish priest might think that the seal had been broken, when in fact it had not been. Gossip, in towns as well as villages, was rife, and a resident parish priest could not avoid being part of it. Other people are always more aware of someone else's sins than the sinner thinks. Thus what one confesses may often be known or suspected in any case. That was the advantage of having as one's confessor a stranger like a friar, particularly in the early days after Lateran IV which had sought to institutionalise confession on a parish basis. It was an advantage to the priest as well as the penitent. In a closed community it relieved him of suspicion of having broken the seal, whether deliberately or inadvertently. The strength of the friars was their combination of involvement and strangerhood.

Near the beginning of this discussion of confession we said that in social terms confession was as important as preaching. The truth is more, perhaps, that they were intimately tied up with each other. The kind of advice and questioning that priests gave and conducted in the confessional had to go hand in hand with the lines that they took in their sermons. I refer here to both friars and parish priests. Bishops in the thirteenth century started (to our knowledge at least) to lay down schemes of preaching for parish priests, as they are not known to have done in the twelfth century. Thus Grosseteste, around 1239, gave a Lincoln diocescan instruction that parish priests must preach to the laity 'in a common idiom' (i.e. in the vernacular and understandably) on the Ten Commandments, the Seven Deadly Sins, the Sacraments and the Apostles' Creed.[68] The Bishops of Worcester (1240), Norwich (1240–43), and Wells (1258), for instance, followed suit.[69] Bishops must have expected friars in their preaching also to conform to some extent with such a scheme. It looks, depressingly to our modern eyes, as if sexual morality figured large in such a scheme; although David d'Avray has shown that in so many marriage sermons a more positive aspect of this subject was presented, involving human relationships more broadly.[70] He also says that sexual sins were more likely to be considered in the confessional than in the pulpit.[71]

Shining like a jewel amidst these schemes is that of the saintly Bishop Richard Wych of Chichester (1245–53). His scheme indeed ends with the item that all sexual intercourse outside marriage is a mortal sin, but before that he instructs priests to preach frequently on the Trinity, the Incarnation and Nativity of Christ, on his Passion, Resurrection and Ascension, and in general on the rising of the dead.[72] Given Richard's known and close connections with both Dominicans and Franciscans,[73] and given the early Franciscans' striking devotion to Christ Crucified,[74] one cannot help reading Franciscan influence particularly behind this for its time exceptional scheme. The Dominican biographer of Richard, Ralph Bocking, says of his preaching and teaching that 'he often strove to fulfil this duty in person but he sometimes did so through the Friars Preacher or Friars Minor'.[75]

Learning and politics

With all their learning, the friars were also very political animals, the Franciscans quite as much so as the Dominicans. Their scholarship was first and foremost biblical, and especially New Testament scholarship, and that in itself was almost bound to make them politically radical. In Paris, Peter the Chanter was their St John the Baptist, as Beryl Smalley said, the voice crying out before them. They were welcomed there by 'Chanterites'. And the Chanter had faced the question of how Gospel teaching could be reconciled with current political and ecclesiastical practice, not least, as we have already seen, as regards the church's wealth. In his *Summa* on the sacraments he often advised people to follow Gospel teaching against secular and canon law; he was against the easy absolving from oaths; against hunting rights and forest laws, he advocated an idea of human rights; and, as the Franciscans would be, he was much exercised by the problem of evangelical poverty. As Bery Smalley, again, said, the Chanter helps to explain why reforming scholars welcomed the Mendicant Orders to Paris (1217 and 1219), before jealousy would later (especially in the 1250s) endanger their status there.[76]

The whole preaching of the thirteenth-century friars was inescapably political. Friars were often found in royal and aristocratic courts, in that way as in the trust between them and the papacy like the sixteenth-century Jesuits. They thought of cities, in which they were principally located, as associated with royal power – there was a royal city in the kingdom of the conscience, said one of them.[77] They used political imagery to make their points; and they had a strong sense of the cohesiveness of political society, perhaps from the middle of the century reinforced by their study of Aristotle. The thirteenth-century Parisian, Thomas Lebreton compared the Lord to a good prince.[78]

The actual political impact of the friars on the thirteenth-century West can hardly be exaggerated. But if one takes England and France, say from about 1230 to 1270, the difference in this impact is striking. In France the friars practically *were* the rule of King/Saint Louis IX; in England, particularly the Franciscans represented much more the opposition to Henry III.

In 1247, before Louis went on crusade he sent *Enquêteurs* (inquisitors) round his kingdom, before whom people could make direct complaints about the oppressions and injustices of royal officials – a concession off his own bat which Henry III had to have wrung out of him in 1258 when the Justiciar, Hugh Bigod's eyre performed a similar function. And who were the *Enquêteurs*? Friars.[79] Louis was trying to put his house in moral order before he undertook the Crusade. Although Louis's crusade failed in its main aim to recapture Jerusalem, he himself gained great cachet from it. The brilliant Joinville represented it as the height of chivalric endeavour; but to Louis himself it was much more (under the influence of the friars, whom Joinville hated) an attempt to spread Christianity and to pay a debt to his conscience. He meant Jerusalem to be a springboard for the conversion of the Mongols.[80] After his return to France he sponsored the journey of William of Rubruk to the land of the Mongols with a brief, amongst other things, to comment on the chances of converting them to Christianity.[81] William was a Franciscan. Also after Louis' return to France, one response to his failure was to develop a deepened sense of moral responsibility in his rule. Thus in 1254 he issued the *Grande Ordonnance*, with edicts against usury, prostitution and blasphemy, an ordinance which followed age-old Carolingian precedents. It was largely based on the ordinances (1249) of his brother, Alphonse of Poitiers for his South French appanage. Two of the authors of Alphonse's and Louis's ordinances were Franciscans.[82] Louis's financial policy, to pay for crusading, etc., was to tax church lands and benefices heavily, a policy that caused the Archbishop of Tours to complain to the pope in 1262. As Favier pointed out this was a friars' policy. The friars were against ecclesiastical displays of wealth, and they had little to lose by it themselves.[83] Alongside all this, Louis consistently supported the friars against their critics amongst the secular masters in the University of Paris, on his doorstep.[84] The friars had a lot to do with projecting the image of Louis as a saintly king by their very participation in his rule.

Henry III of England may have looked less robust than the chivalric Louis IX of France. Under him a man held land in Hampshire, as a sergeanty, for the service of holding the king's head whenever he crossed the channel, and the present writer once heard the late Naomi Hurnard observe that he was surely the first English king for whom such a service can have been necessary.[85] But he cannot have looked much less devout or religious. By his bed in the king's bed-chamber at Westminster, and also in Winchester castle, he had painted the Guardians of Solomon's Bed, and he liked to present his rule like that of the wise Solomon. He was appropriating an image of King Solomon to his rule.[86] At Westminster the paintings date from the 1260s, when his rule was in fact under the greatest pressure from baronial rebellion. He made at least eleven pilgrimages to the shrine of Our Lady at Walsingham, as well as pilgrimages to other Marian shrines, gave and received costly presents of images of Mary, and attended Mass regularly on her festivals.[87] On a visit to Paris in 1259 (to finalise the Treaty of Paris, whereby Louis granted Henry to hold Gascony, despite having lost it to Louis militarily), Henry was said to have been unable to resist passing a church on the way without attending Mass there, and to have been the butt of Louis IX's humour for arriving late in consequence.[88]

Much of what Henry III did under the impetus of religious fervour, however, seemed to go off at half cock. Above all this was the case with his putative relic of Christ's Holy Blood. Henry acquired this relic to rival Louis's acquisition of the Crown of Thorns, to house which he built the glorious Sainte-Chapelle in Paris. Henry had both his goldsmith, Edward of Westminster, and Master Henry, his mason, go and study the Sainte-Chapelle in the 1240s, which strongly influenced his re-building of Westminster Abbey, in part at least to house his relic.[89] But despite the

pomp and ceremony with which he celebrated the solemn handing over of
the relic to Westminster in 1247, nobody outside that abbey seemed to
accept that a relic of Christ's blood could quite 'cut the mustard' in the way
that a relic of the Crown of Thorns could. There were doubts about it,
and cults could not succeed without a degree of consensus about them.
In any event, the Crown of Thorns flourished as a cult, while the Holy
Blood languished.[90]

So why did Franciscans gravitate to the opposition against Henry III's
rule while they and the Dominicans were such important agents of Louis
IX's? There were two principal reasons. First, English government and
administration, secular and ecclesiastical, were much more developed than
French, and the king had therefore much more patronage to offer. But
he had far greater claims on his patronage, most of all from his Poitevin
half-brothers, the Lusignans and their hangers-on. The Lusignans and the
Savoyards, the relations of Henry's queen, Eleanor, have had a worse press
than they deserved, or so various historians have argued. Some of them,
ecclesiastics like Aymer of Lusignan, bishop-elect of Winchester for ten
years,[91] and laymen like Peter of Savoy, were able and serious administrators who were not mere featherers of their own nests. But they were
in the main bitterly unpopular, as foreign favourites, in England.[92] They
were part of the reason, as were many English placemen of Henry III, why
reforms of royal officials which Louis IX was seen to offer spontaneously
had to be wrung from Henry III when he had descended into a financial
crisis in 1258. And above all, they left no space for the friars to play the
sort of role in royal government which they played in France.

Second was the friars' deep friendship with Simon de Montfort. It is
doubtful whether Simon was already a primary leader of opposition when
the Provisions of Oxford were agreed by the barons in 1258, imposing
constitutional constraints on the king. But 18 months later he had emerged
as its leader. Simon had been a friend of Robert Grosseteste when he
became Earl of Leicester in 1231 while Grosseteste was still Archdeacon of
Leicester before he became Bishop of Lincoln (1235–53). This was decisive
for Simon's links with the Franciscans in particular, because of Grosseteste's
being at that time the Franciscans' lecturer in Oxford. From the start the
two men recognised each other as kindred spirits, zealots who both disliked compromise. Matthew Paris has it that Simon regarded the bishop as
his father confessor and was on terms of intimate friendship with him.
Grosseteste drew his friend into a circle of Franciscans, the most important
of whom was Adam Marsh, lecturer of the Oxford Franciscans (1245–50)
who became a public figure.[93] From early on Adam shared his thoughts

and fears about his role in public life, for instance his anxiety that he had incurred the king's displeasure through one of his sermons.[94]

It is significant that Grosseteste was considered Simon's confessor, for the latter's spiritual advisers saw confession and the cultivation of conscience as key to the pastoral mission of the Franciscans, to instructing the laity and saving their souls. If vocation was one of the great 'buzz-words' of the twelfth century (see p. 149), conscience was so for the thirteenth. The friars wanted bishops like Grosseteste and Walter Cantilupe of Worcester, and others of their friends, to instruct the laity on how to confess and scrutinise their consciences. Simon, with his religious intelligence and finely tuned conscience, was their ideal pupil; but a pupil who still needed teaching.[95] Marsh remonstrated with him when he went to be Governor of Gascony in 1242 for taking the Chancellor of Salisbury's resident vicar at Oldham (Hampshire), who had the cure of souls there. How could he have put the priest's flock in such danger by depriving the church of their vicar, Marsh wondered.[96] One point in particular where Grosseteste and the Franciscans helped Simon to work through his conscience was on the subject of vows. Vows mattered to Simon. His conscience was constantly troubled by the fact that when he married Eleanor, Henry III's sister, she had previously taken a vow of chastity.[97] This seemed actually to make him the more determined to keep the vows he took. When so many barons were breaking their vows to support the Provisions of Oxford – perhaps feeling that one could not continue to constrain a king like that – he never deviated in fulfilling his vow.

When Grosseteste built up the Franciscans as a learned community as their first Lecturer at Oxford, he built it up pre-eminently as a community of biblical study. It was through the Bible, and especially the Gospels, that their teaching mission to the church was to be fulfilled. Adam Marsh wrote a letter to Simon de Montfort exhorting him to study the scriptures. 'The less will those darts strike us which we anticipate', he wrote referring to Gregory the Great, 'and we shall take the evils of the world more tolerably, if we are fortified against them with the shield of providence.'[98] There follow a string of scriptural quotations to make his point, as if he assumed that he was writing to a person who had already formed scriptural interests and knowledge. Grosseteste died in 1253 and about that time Adam Marsh's letters to Simon dry up. But there were other Franciscans with whom he continued to be intimate. One of these was Thomas Docking, the Franciscan Lecturer at Oxford from about 1262 to 1265, the crucial period in Simon's leadership of the opposition to Henry III. In his commentary on Paul's Epistle to the Galatians, Docking wrote with what John Maddicott has taken, surely with good reason, to be a direct commendation of Simon's government:

It seems to me . . . that if some man who is prudent and well fitted for the business of rule, seeing God's people endangered by defect of government, should aspire to the dignity of ruling, solely for the love of God and the benefit of his subjects, his aim is good and he desires to do a good work.[99]

Franciscan learning and political opposition interacted with each other most in the poem known as *The Song of Lewes*; or rather they *probably* interacted, because the *Song* was probably composed by a Franciscan.[100] It is an outright polemic in support of Simon de Montfort from between his victory at the Battle of Lewes (1264) and his being killed at the Battle of Evesham (1265), a year in which he was virtually ruler of England. It has the learning of the schools, as well as the hatred of foreign favourites, written all over it. It is actually cast in the form of a scholastic *quaestio* which first puts the case against which it is arguing and then the case for. The king's case, his *ratio*, is therefore put first. He is free to choose whom he wanted for his ministers and councillors, like an earl who was *compos sui*, entirely in charge of his own affairs, and was free to dispose of his castles, revenues, etc. as he wished. (We remember here that Simon was an earl, and that his friend Bishop Grosseteste had written a treatise on estate management.) 'But now', the poet continues, 'let my pen be turned to the opposite argument', the barons' case (*propositum*). Unlike the king's foreign counsellors, who are steering the ship of state straight for the rocks, the barons seek to magnify the royal status (*statum*). The king thinks he can choose his own helpers without constraint. (Louis IX thought this too, in his arbitration of 1264, the Mise of Amiens.) But the king may need to be forced to be free, because he has a responsibility to the community of the realm as a whole. He is God's helper (*adminiculum*) and in that capacity he has to be of advantage to his whole people. In other words, unlike an earl, he is more like an estates steward than an outright owner of property. The kingdom ought to be directed in the way of truth, rather in the sense that Aquinas at the same time was saying, adapting Aristotle, that the political community should be directed towards its highest good by the king. The *Song* then brings in the Pauline idea of the interdependence of all the members of the political body.[101]

There is probably an influence of the twelfth-century John of Salisbury and his *Policraticus* in the *Song's* strong idea of the king's being subject to law, as there is of the lawyer Bracton.[102] The idea of authority as a stewardship is already powerfully expressed by Pope Gregory the Great in his *Pastoral Care* (c. 595), and indeed in *The Rule of St Benedict*. As we have just noted, there is probably a streak of Aristotle in the thinking; Aristotle's *Politics* was the latest of his works to become known in the West – in the mid-thirteenth century.[103] The *Song of Lewes* is a panoply of the highest contemporary biblical and secular learning.

The *Song of Lewes*, which survives in only one manuscript, could not have had much general political impact, particularly considering Simon de Montfort's death within a year of its composition. But like most polemic and propaganda, its primary purpose must have been to reinforce the self-confidence of, and to justify in their own eyes, the side for which it argued, rather than to convert the other side. In that respect it was not isolated, but was the culmination of Franciscan support for Simon. Adam Marsh was dead by 1264, though the *Song* could easily have been composed at that time by a Franciscan like Thomas Docking (see above pp. 251–2). But back before 1253, when Robert Grosseteste died, Adam Marsh, whose zeal for the pastoral care of the laity against careerists and absentees among the clergy matched Grosseteste's, wrote to the latter: 'I return to your lordship that short treatise which you wrote on the rule of a kingdom and tyrannical rule as you sent it with the signature of the Earl of Leicester.'[104] No trace of this treatise survives, but Marsh's letter shows how far the shared zeal of Simon and the Franciscans for political reform went back.

Everything that we have written about Simon de Montfort and foreign favourites may have occasioned surprise. For had not Simon himself been the greatest of all foreign favourites when he married Henry III's sister and settled in England thirty years earlier? But foreigners in England have often had the habit of forgetting that they themselves were foreigners while remembering it about everyone else!

One point should be made absolutely clear. If the author of the *Song of Lewes* was indeed a Franciscan, his detestation of foreign favourites was an issue of good counsel and righteous government rather than xenophobia. There was a lot of xenophobia around at that time; some of it may help to explain, ironically, why the foreigner Simon de Montfort had difficulty to keep his supporters. But no such thing afflicted the learned elements of the friars. They were the great internationalists of the thirteenth century, amongst English friars particularly in respect of their relations with the University of Paris. Jeremy Catto has written that 'Oxford theologians (of the century) tended to be an amphibian breed, migrating from the *terra firma* of the Oxford schools to the international waters of Paris';[105] and he proceeds to unfold a remarkable story of the friars' to-ing and fro-ing between Oxford and Paris, bringing the latest learning on Peter Lombard's *Sentences*, biblical studies, and moral theology from Paris to England and not infrequently giving something of their own ideas back to Paris in their turn.[106]

One of these friars, whose studies were divided between Paris and Oxford, was the Franciscan Richard Rufus of Cornwall. He joined the Friars Minor probably in 1238; at Paris he came to know the greatest of all Franciscan scholars, St Bonaventure; and after his own Commentary on Peter Lombard's *Sentences* (c. 1250), he produced an Abbreviation of Bonaventure's Commentary on this book (c. 1256) to make it more easily digestible to an English audience, together with some further remarks of his own.[107] Richard Rufus is of interest to us because he played a part in a revolution of thinking about how creation ought to be studied, and that revolution could not but affect political attitudes.

The great challenge that thirteenth-century intellectuals had to face was the new availability in Latin translation of Aristotle's scientific writings, and they knew it. It was a challenge almost like Darwin in the nineteenth century. And here were the friars, Franciscans and Dominicans, to meet it. One might almost say of the thirteenth century: no friars, no Aristotelians. Grosseteste, the teacher of the Franciscans in Oxford who owed very little to Paris, took Aristotle on board in one way; Richard Rufus took him on board in quite another way.

Grosseteste was a traditionalist theologian. He considered theology to be primarily the understanding of Scripture, and that understanding depended on the allegorical method, i.e. seeing the visible realities of the Bible as being outward signs to the deeper, hidden meaning with which God had endowed creation. Thus Grosseteste followed Augustine's *De Doctrina Christiana*, holding that the more one knew about the properties of animals, plants and natural phenomena mentioned in the Bible, the richer the allegorical interpretations that would lead one to a deeper understanding of the spiritual truths that lay behind them.[108] An example which Augustine gave was hyssop, a modest-sized plant with deep roots which could be taken to signify the virtue of humility. And Aristotle's science had given people a wealth of new knowledge with which to enlarge their perceptions of the action of God in his universe. Of course Grosseteste thought that the study of created things and their properties not only provided stepping-stones to such perceptions but were useful and interesting in themselves. As a genuinely experimental scientist he was interested in rainbows and optics as such, but he also saw light, emanating from God, as the unifying principle of the whole universe down to the tiniest particle of matter. However, in the study of creation, he would not break the great continuum between God and Creation, expressed most clearly and fully in his *Hexaemeron*. Even a tiny speck of dust, the most perfect form known in nature, was a treasury of all the primary mathematical constituents from which the whole universe was constructed and a mirror of the Creator in its unity and trinity (of potentiality, form and the union of the two).[109] That continuum, that unity of God and creation, was the overarching reason for studying natural philosophy, or science as we call it.

Quite otherwise was it with Richard Rufus by the mid-thirteenth century. He of course believed in God and in that continuum as much as Grosseteste had. But for him Aristotle had provided the means to study nature as an entity in itself.[110] It was as if he no longer thought that justice could be done to the whole panorama of Aristotelian learning by stuffing it all into a container, so to speak, which was far too small to take it, namely the allegorical interpretation of the Bible. Visible reality, to follow the argument of Peter Raedts in his book on Richard Rufus, is no longer valued for its symbolic properties; it has acquired a consistency, and its study a validity of its own. Harmony and participation have made room for clear-cut distinctions and a science of causes.[111] Richard was not, like Grosseteste and the Pseudo-Dionysians, interested in the mystical theology of light, but only in the light we see.[112] Nor, like the neo-Platonists, was he interested in mathematics and astronomy as the basis of the divine unity of the universe. He had the ontological and empirical approach of Aristotle. In a universe whose study was governed by the laws of nature, Richard had to re-define God's place in it. He did so not through a notion of participation by the natural in the supernatural, but through a strong emphasis on God's will and grace (thus setting the scene for the fourteenth-century scholars of Merton College, Oxford).[113]

Although Richard Rufus had an original mind, he was not a solitary genius. St Francis himself took nature seriously in a humanistic sense, that being the most obvious way in which the Franciscans may be seen as successors to the Cistercians. Going further back, Gerald of Wales often gave naturalistic explanations of the phenomena of creation, particularly in his earlier writings, sometimes alongside miraculous ones; and John of Salisbury used the phrase 'law of nature' to refer to the causal chains of the physical universe.[114] Writing of the different attitude to miracles in the age of Bede and in the twelfth century, Benedicta Ward has described the latter as when heaven and earth became in a sense unbound from each other, and nature came to be considered 'an entity in itself'.[115] In less scholastic form, therefore, the approach of Richard Rufus to creation and the autonomy of its study had long been in the air.

If nature could be detached from the supernatural and be considered as an entity in itself, so surely could politics be so. One may think that Aristotle's *Politics* gave political philosophers an instrument to do this. But the *Politics* was one of the last of Aristotle's works to become known in the West, and so there could have been little 'take' on it before the end of our period. Aquinas knew it well when he wrote his *De Regimine Principum* (c. 1260), but he himself could not by any means shake the supernatural out of his political thinking. Whereas Aristotle clearly preferred rule by aristocracy to that of monarchy or polity, the other satisfactory forms of constitution to his mind, Aquinas preferred monarchy because he saw the king as the image of the one God on earth. He also argued that it was peculiarly the business of the king to lead his people to the blessedness of heaven; thereby he substituted a supernatural 'end' of human society for Aristotle's earthly 'end', namely the good life.[116]

In England, however, the thinking of the *Song of Lewes* was to politics what the thinking of Richard Rufus (only a little earlier) had been to creation. Above all that was because in practice it stripped the kingship of its sacrality in order to subject it to the scrutiny of reason; also because in the community of the realm, a phrase it uses more than once, the king should be limited by having to use his 'natural' counsellors, the barons. The phrase 'natural counsellors' is not actually used in the *Song of Lewes* (and is probably Bracton's), but it is implied over and over again in the *Song*.[117]

An earlier example of what we might call the Richard Rufus mentality of detaching nature, and thus politics, from God is none other than Magna Carta itself. Its final clause (61) lays down that 25 barons are to be appointed to enforce the provisions of the Charter and if any of the 25 were absent or if there were disagreement amongst the ones who were present, whatever a majority of those present and voting should decide was to be regarded as fixed and established.[118] In fact this soon became a dead letter, but it is the idea that is interesting. The idea almost certainly came from the practice of the city of London when it set up committees to reform its Commune in the earliest years of the thirteenth century.[119] This is so far as I know the earliest example of the straight majority principle in the Middle Ages. Previously, whenever unanimity could not be achieved and decisions had to be taken by a majority, it was always laid down that the *maior et sanior pars* should prevail, the larger and more sane part; and what could *sanior* mean in most cases except more in accord with the divine will, as though it would be obvious what that was? In 1179 Pope Alexander III laid down in the Third Lateran Council that a two-thirds majority of the cardinals constituted a valid election to the papacy. But in a divided papal election that was no doubt because there was no superior power to determine which was the *senior pars*, though one could assume that they would be included in so large a majority as two-thirds.[120] But to have a straight majority as in Magna Carta was a radically new and humanistic idea; nobody had divine approval on their side in a one man one vote system. Politics here was not in continuity with the action of God in the world. A go-ahead, vibrant, flourishing town like London was just where one might expect so novel and secularist an idea to come from!

One last point should be made about the impact of the friars' learning – more this time on English society than on politics. It is particularly about the education of the parish clergy. When Walter de Merton founded Merton College at Oxford in 1264, he founded it in the first place to educate his kinsmen. Walter, who had become the thirteenth-century equivalent of a billionaire, largely by land transactions some of which would hardly bear close moral scrutiny, was one of eight siblings who survived into adulthood, and all the other seven were girls. That gave him a passion to have his nephews educated. He was a churchman and they would have been his heirs, but rather than divide up his inheritance between them he preferred to found a college which would enable them by their education to rise to good positions in church and state, as he had done (he was King's Chancellor when Merton College was founded, and would later become Bishop of Rochester). The amazing thing about the early statutes of the college is this: that after its scholars had completed their arts course (with no doubt a fair measure of Aristotle) at least 14 of the 20 of them were required to go on to study theology. In this and in other ways he looked to the recently founded college of Robert of Sorbonne in Paris. Here is a hard-bitten speculator, administrator and politician, and he attaches enormous importance to theology! In fact he thought of establishing his college in Surrey where most of his estates lay; he almost certainly decided for Oxford because there his scholars could sit at the feet of the friars, people like Richard Rufus, to study.[121]

What Walter de Merton's primary careerist aims for his scholars were is made clear by his acquisition for his college of many advowsons, that is the right of the college to present clerics to the bishop to become vicars or rectors in parish benefices. Of course some such people would be absentees in royal service or as scholars engaging in further studies; others would quickly rise to higher things. But Walter's very intention is interesting, because it shows how much the standing of the parish clergy had risen by the end of our period. Little more than peasants around 1086, they had become (at least often) the equivalent of well-established professional people in our own day. We have already observed how the programmes of Peter the Chanter and the Fourth Lateran Council required well-educated clergy to put them into effect. Merton College both reflected that the need was being met and helped to meet it further. The friars were a fundamental ingredient in both processes.

CHAPTER 10

Changes and Continuities under Henry III

Pope, king and church

In Chapter 9, I have written much of what I wanted to say about the thirteenth century up to 1272, particularly as to what changed through the friars' involvement. This chapter, therefore, might have the appearance of an epilogue but there were other changes and also significant continuities which deserve an airing, and which are not unimportant in my scheme of things.

First we pick up again John's submission to the papacy in 1213, before Magna Carta, effected at least partly through the mediation of the Cistercian, Hugh of Beaulieu. That marked a change in the whole configuration of English ecclesiastical politics, with the papacy gaining a new degree of influence compared to previously. The period from the Norman Conquest to Magna Carta was characterised by Z.N. Brooke as one in which two rival masters, king and pope, competed with each other for control of the English church. And if at 80 years distance this now looks in some ways an over-simplification, it has proved a useful basis for discussion. John's submission to Innocent III, however, changed everything. Thereafter, king and pope were much more each other's allies or, rather, with Henry III, the king was much more in the pope's pocket.

What happened in 1213 was dramatically reinforced between 1216 and 1219 after John died. Prince Louis, later Louis VIII of France, invaded the kingdom in support of the rebels against John (and to prosecute his own claim to the kingship) and the eight-year-old Henry III was left as a minor and a papal ward. This wardship was at first in effect exercised by Cardinal Guala, who came to England as papal legate in 1216. Guala's three aims were to end the civil war, secure Henry III, and punish the rebels against the king, especially clerical rebels like Simon Langton, brother of the Archbishop, and the distinguished architect, Elias of Dereham, who were 'despoiled' of their benefices.[1] In the second of these aims, securing Henry III, Guala had considerable success. As C.H. Lawrence has said, under Guala the nominal overlordship of the papacy (created by John's submission) was converted into a political reality.[2] And after 1227, when Henry declared the end of his minority, he never forgot what he owed to the papacy (often to his political cost). Thus Guala's aims were much more political than religious in character. That has a bearing on the implementation in England of the reforms of the Fourth Lateran Council. This owed more in the early years of Henry III to Bishop Richard Poore's influential Salisbury statutes of 1219 and Stephen Langton's provincial constitutions of 1222 than to Guala's legateship. In other words it owed more to the direct influence of people who had earlier experienced the Paris School of Peter the Chanter. Indeed the two areas in which Guala did most to strengthen ties between England and Rome, collation of English benefices to Italians and dispensations to pluralists from residing in their benefices, were not notably in the pastoral spirit of Lateran IV.[3]

Around 1200 the young Emperor Frederick II had also been a ward of the pope, namely Innocent III. It is interesting to compare the effect this fact had on the two rulers. Henry III supported the papacy through thick and thin, including financially, in its wars against Frederick II. This is what landed him in the financial mess which sparked off the baronial rebellion of 1258; particularly when after Frederick's death he fell in with the pope's plan that his younger son, Edmund, should assume the kingship of Sicily and oust Frederick's Hohenstaufen successors from there.[4] It may be, however, that Frederick's wardship had more effect on him than at first meets the eye. The papacy had to fight against him because of his claims to world rule and because of where he sat, sandwiching the papal states between his kingdom in Sicily and South Italy and his claimed power to overlordship over the communes of North Italy. Yet when Frederick seemed to have Rome itself at his mercy in 1239, he would not invade it, partly at least because of a respect for the papacy born of his wardship. Both Henry and Frederick incurred the enmity of the Franciscans, the great new propaganda engine of the papacy, for very different reasons. That did not cost Henry the support of the papacy, though it helped to move England on its way to becoming a limited, constitutional monarchy, as the friars' support for Louis IX helped to move France on its way to becoming a theocratic monarchy. But the Franciscans' enmity blew the Hohenstaufen, as imperial rulers, out of the water.

To pursue English relations with Rome further it is necessary to consider briefly what was happening in Rome itself. Two related developments occurred: one was the enormous growth of papal bureaucracy during the thirteenth century, and the other was the institutional development of the college of cardinals. As we said in an earlier chapter, from Gregory VII's time the Rome curia became increasingly a jurisdictional centre of Western Christianity, and by 1200 the administration of the papal states in Italy was also making heavy demands on the papacy. The resulting bureaucracy was organised into many departments of treasury clerks, tax collectors, judges and notaries, etc. There was even a tribunal called the Audience of Contradicted Letters. Concurrently, the college of cardinals developed as a consultative body and a kind of cabinet, sharing executive power with the popes. As ever since the late eleventh century, the principal links between Rome and the regions were papal legates, and when one of the college's members was chosen to be a legate *a latere*, which only a cardinal could be, there were extraordinary rituals involving the whole college to mark his departure from Rome and return to it. Thus was expressed the corporate responsibility of the pope and cardinals.[5]

There were two principal consequences of this for English/papal relations, again related to each other. The first was that the salaries of whole cohorts of papal officials and cardinals' kinsmen had to be paid for, and this was done by providing church benefices for them across Western Christendom, from which they would be largely absentees but would draw the revenues while working for the papacy, i.e. the system of papal provisions. The second was that dealing with Rome became so complex that it required expertise; hence any cathedral church, or monastery, or other institution or person anticipating canon law litigation would be well advised to have at least one proctor in Rome. And in that highly litigious age, when benefices or elections or marriages or inheritances or buildings of churches or canonisations could all be involved, nobody could afford not to anticipate canon law litigation. If one were not minded to appeal to Rome oneself, one could be sure that one's opponent would be. Thus the king himself, and many churches, who disposed of benefices in their patronage, had a ready asset if they wanted to meet the salaries of useful Romans.

The king could be especially useful in providing well-endowed cathedral canonries, where he had influence, for papal nominees (though such men did not spurn the richer parish benefices). Master Marinus of Eboli, for instance, vice-chancellor of Pope Innocent IV, held a canonry in Salisbury (which was doubtless useful for Salisbury), as well as other benefices.[6] But there was also advantage to the king. Cardinal John of Toledo, an

Englishman who had studied in Toledo, over a thirty-year period in the curia secured benefices by papal provision for many royal clerks.[7] For example, a papal mandate of 1236 ordered the Bishop of Lincoln to allow Hugh de Pateshull, royal treasurer, to be absent from his benefices in that diocese, provided they were properly served.[8]

The whole system of papal provisions rested on the idea that the papacy disposed freely of all benefices in Christendom. This idea was the culmination, or as some might see it the *reductio ad absurdum*, of the Gregorian Reform idea that all church appointments should be independent of lay power and that the pope was the spiritual head of Christendom. There was much opposition to the system in England, particularly because it clashed with a well-developed system of patronage here,[9] and also particularly when it was seen to be allied to papal tax collectors who came in with Henry III's support to collect money for the so-called crusade against the Emperor Frederick II. Many thought the whole system a by-word for venality, and it stoked up the widespread xenophobia. In 1231, for example, a young Yorkshire landholder, Robert Tweng, having been denied his right of presentation to a church, gathered a band of sympathisers who ranged the country from Yorkshire to Hampshire, armed and masked; they issued manifestoes, ordered those who farmed the lands of churches held by alien absentees (so not men like Pateshull) to withhold their rents, and molested Italians setting fire to their barns.[10]

Before we consider the confrontation between Robert Grosseteste and Pope Innocent IV over this whole subject in 1250, however, it is only right to give the positive side to papal influence in Henry III's England. First, we may notice that in the mandate in favour of Hugh de Pateshull's leasing out his benefices, the pope (Gregory IX) insisted that the pastorate must be properly provided for. He was not undermining the pastoral effort which we described in Chapter 5. Second, if a papal legate went too far in despoiling clerks of their benefices or promoting his own kinsmen to benefices, the pope might be bombarded with complaints about him which would weaken the legate's position in the curia. Elias of Dereham, a distinguished clerk albeit a rebel against John, Louis VIII and Henry III, appealed to Pope Honorius III against being despoiled of his benefices by Guala in 1218, and he was back in them within a year.[11] The papacy had strong reason not to raise resistances unnecessarily. Third, the system of papal provisions could be used to raise the standard of educated clergy. Benefices sometimes, perhaps often, went under this system to English clerks who were continuing their university studies. And fourth, if we bring papal influence in episcopal elections into the equation, it is striking how enlightened many appointments were. During the minority of Henry III, outstanding and well-educated bishops such as Richard Poore at Salisbury and William de Blois at Worcester owed their promotion to the pope, as did the learned, saintly and pastoral Edmund of Abingdon to Canterbury in 1233, and others later.[12]

A most instructive episcopal election, in terms of the working of papal and royal influence, was that of St Richard of Wych to be Bishop of Chichester in 1244–45. When Richard's predecessor died in February 1244, the Chichester chapter soon elected Robert Passelewe, a notorious royal administrator and justice of the forest, to replace him. They wanted an effective protector of their interests who had royal favour and Henry III quickly gave the royal assent. Passelewe must have 'seemed home and dry', but he had reckoned without Boniface of Savoy, archbishop-elect of Canterbury, and Robert Grosseteste, Bishop of Lincoln. Boniface was a foreigner who spent much of his time on the Continent, but when in England showed considerable pastoral drive. He and five of his suffragans, including Grosseteste examined Passelewe in June; Grosseteste plied him with questions too hard for him; and he was found insufficiently qualified to be a bishop.[13] Passelewe, with his secular involvements, was just the kind of cleric of whom Grosseteste most disapproved, and he was not the first bishop of Lincoln to object particularly to forest officials (see pp. 197–8 above).[14] In his place the bishops chose Richard of Wych, a learned man previously Chancellor of Oxford University, a deeply pastoral man, and a friend of the friars. Henry III took the temporalities into his own hand and refused to release them to Richard, earning for this a letter of reproach from Innocent IV, to whom Richard had taken his case.

At first it might look as if this were a rare clash between Henry III and the papacy, but in reality the element of conflict was minimal, and that is what is so instructive about it in terms of king/pope relations at the time. Innocent IV naturally supported Richard's cause, and indeed consecrated him as bishop himself on 21 July 1245. But Henry III, even while he kept Richard out of Chichester now, had his proctors working hard at Rome to keep the pope favourable to Passelewe. It came off. At the end of May, some weeks before he consecrated Richard, the pope granted Passelewe as Archdeacon of Lewes, an indult to enable him to be elected a bishop in principle (although this never happened and Passelewe died as Archdeacon of Lewes).[15] Innocent had no option but to support Richard of Wych, yet he did what he could, and more than Grosseteste would have liked, for Henry III and Robert Passelewe.

One area where the pope could usefully support English royal power was the Scottish church. In Chapter 5 we remarked in passing that the suppression of King William the Lion's rebellion against Henry II in 1173–74 postponed the independence from England of the Scottish church for some time. That statement needs modification. After lengthy disputes about who should exercise metropolitan authority over the Scottish dioceses (St Andrews, Glasgow, Dunkeld, Dunblane, Brechin, Aberdeen, Moray, Ross and Caithness – not Whithorn/Galloway which remained loyal to York), in particular whether it should be York or St Andrews raised to metropolital status,[16] the celebrated bull of Pope Celestine III, *Cum Universi Christi* (1192), brought about a singular resolution. The nine dioceses of the *Scoticana ecclesia* were henceforth to be directly under the authority of the pope himself.[17] Their councils would be gathered under legates, either Scots or persons sent directly from Rome. Such was to be the constitution of the Scottish church.

But that did not rob the English king of all influence over the Scottish church, once John had made his peace with Innocent III in 1213. The Scottish bishops who had opposed John had in 1218 to seek absolution from the papacy.[18] When King Alexander in 1221 urged the Legate, James of St Victor, to perform an unprecedented coronation ceremony, the pope forbade it unless and until the young Henry III and his counsellors agreed to it.[19] Legates to Scotland would be based in England and that too would give the English king influence. Indeed Cardinal Otto, legate in England 1237–41, with a separate commission as legate to Scotland, actually made peace between the two kings at York in September 1237.[20] Later, in 1251, the young King Alexander III would be married to Henry III's daughter, Margaret.[21] And besides royal influence, Scottish reforming decrees, in pursuit of Lateran IV, were heavily indebted to the reforming decrees of Richard Poore at Salisbury.[22]

The greatest clash between England and the Papacy in Henry III's reign came in 1250, essentially about papal provisions to English benefices, not between Henry and the pope, but between Robert Grosseteste, Bishop of Lincoln, and the papal curia under Innocent IV. Grosseteste was an ardent papalist. As the sun is to moon and stars, he thought, so is the pope to other bishops, and bishops to their inferiors. But in the last phrase lay the rub. Grosseteste, ever an extremist, was, even more than in his papalism, ardent about his pastoral responsibilities as a diocesan. And through the system of papal provisions countless souls stood in danger of hell. He recognised that the pope had the power to dispose freely of all benefices, but only if he provided suitable clergy. He did not have the strong feelings against aliens as such that some had; the acid test was whether they were qualified to be pastors. He even had no objection to absentees as such, priests who were doing valuable work for the church in ecclesiastical or secular government, or who were extending their education. But they had to understand the pastorate, otherwise how could they have the necessary judgement to recognise the right qualities in their substitutes? Men like Robert Passelewe, the forest judge were unsuitable for a parish cure, let alone a bishopric.[23]

Grosseteste's criticisms of the papacy reached a climax when he made a speech to Innocent IV and the cardinals at Rome on Friday 13 May 1250, just two days before Pentecost. It is hard to think of anyone else in the thirteenth century who would have had the combination of intellectual trenchancy, daring, experience and loyalty needed to make that speech. It had something of the *franchise* of a holy man about it, of a St Martin addressing his emperor. There was nothing the slightest Lutheran or Reformational about it, precisely because it was made by a *loyal* critic, someone who fully accepted the papal primacy. The more fully he accepted it, indeed, the more the papacy's proneness to criticism pained him. That had been the position of St Bernard one hundred years earlier and of St Boniface four hundred years before that. Grosseteste prepared his speech carefully in advance, and distributed copies beforehand to the pope and some of the cardinals, one of whom read the text to the assembly. This text was initially preserved among Grosseteste's papers in the Franciscan library at Oxford.[24] It would have taken about an hour to read out.

In his speech Grosseteste attributed the whole malaise of the church in neglecting pastoral care to the papal curia. It had allocated benefices to its members on the basis of private interests rather than pastoral ones. That was what had caused a drying up of the sap (as a scientist Grosseteste was interested in deciduous trees) and the dessication of the word of God in pastoral care. He attributed limitations on his diocesan power to investigate the sins of this flock to secular authority indeed, but as exercised with papal connivance.[25] The stunned silence at the end of the speech may well be imagined!

It may be tempting to discuss the speech as nothing more than the wild overstatements of a fanatical old man (Grosseteste was 80 in 1250). Two considerations should make us take it more seriously. First, a whole intellectual world is here trained onto a pastoral point of great practical importance. Grosseteste's life-long study of the scientific works of Aristotle, which largely became known in the West only in the twelfth century, had taught him to look for one underlying root cause of phenomena, and to look for it always *within* the system of which its effects formed a part. His Platonist universe itself was one homogeneous whole.[26] We have already met this same thing in Grosseteste's belief that there was a continuum between the divine order as revealed in the Bible and the natural order, for instance between divine light and optical light (see above pp. 254–5). Second, as we have also seen, the speech represented ideas about the pastorate which had long been maturing in his mind – at least since his undertaking to teach the Franciscans in Oxford and since Simon de Montfort became his friend.

It will now be apparent why I have made so much of it. Grosseteste saw the development of papal provisions in the thirteenth century as threatening the pastoral drive of the twelfth century and of his own time. Furthermore, I have written earlier about the constant dilemma of bishops, the constant tension, in how they straddled the religious and secular worlds, how they sought to combine their service of church and king, how differently from one another they, and other churchmen, tried to hold the balance between secular and clerical office. It could be seen in the discussion of investiture in Chapter 3, and again where Hubert Walter and Hugh of Lincoln were concerned in Chapter 7. Grosseteste raised this dilemma in an acute form, throwing his weight, with little compromise, on the religious side.

Parish clergy revisited

The subject of parish priests will now be revisited. In Chapter 5, I observed that if many twelfth-century parish churches were served not by rectors or vicars who had the security of benefices, but by chaplains of monasteries or of lay patrons, that did not necessarily mean that such chaplains were poor, ill-educated or ill-regarded. I also observed that when we come into the thirteenth century and have the evidence of priestly ordinations by bishops and of those who got benefices, evidence from bishops' registers which we do not have for the twelfth century, we see that there was a huge disparity between numbers ordained and the far fewer numbers who got benefices. But I added that did not necessarily mean that there was a mass of unprovided-for, poverty-stricken clergy milling about in a state of dangerous rebellion (see pp. 114–15). Fortified by fuller evidence in the thirteenth century, I can elaborate on this.[27]

In some ways this evidence suggests that the issue of adequate and per-petual vicarages for resident pastors, which so exercised twelfth-century bishops, though still remaining, had been overtaken by another issue – the adequate provision for chaplains who actually served the churches and who were sometimes at least referred to as parish priests (*presbyteri parochiales*).[28] Rectors, and now vicars also, were frequently absentees, and not always for bad reasons. They might be given leave to undertake further study. They might be involved in what was regarded as important work in diocesan or royal administration. They might be pluralists, which was a way of giving some clergy higher salaries, and higher salaries then as now were not always thought to be undeserved. Moreover, priestly chaplains were needed to serve dependent chapels, which often functioned, for practical purposes, like parish churches. Such institutions as hospitals also needed chaplains. When St Mark's Hospital, Bristol, was established in 1259, its foundation deed provided for three chaplains.

At least from the late twelfth century onwards, nobody could be ordained without 'title', i.e. without demonstrating to the bishop ordaining him that he had adequate and guaranteed material provision. Whether this always worked in practice is a moot question. We do know, however, that one way in which such people got their titles, was from the clergy to whom they were acting as assistants; and it is clear that such clergy were often in a good position to know the priests, particularly when they were local men, whom they were taking on.[29] That was also true of monasteries providing chaplains for their churches, as mentioned in the case of Bridlington Priory (see above p. 174). All of which suggests that the granting of titles was generally done by those who took the parish pastorate seriously.

Whether this provision of and for chaplains always worked well in practice is doubtful. The Cathedral Register of Salisbury, for instance, has the documentation for Dean William Waude's visitation of the dependent churches of Sunning (Berkshire), whose perpetual vicar was called Vitalis, and their chaplains. It was an abysmal picture. Only one of the chaplains was any good. The others were largely illiterate and totally incapable of passing their Latin test, Latin being then the language of the Mass. One of them, when asked what word in the opening of the Canon of the Mass (*Te igitur clementissime Pater*) 'governed' (grammatically) the word '*Te*', produced the famous one-liner, '*Pater*, for the Father governeth all things!' Vitalis, who had been vicar for over thirty years, was admonished by the Dean, who declared that if there was no improvement he would take the benefices into his own hand.[30] However, we must note that this appears as an isolated case in the Salisbury records; that the Dean was a great admirer of his bishop, Richard Poore, who was *the* principal propagator in England of the pastoral aims of the Fourth Lateran Council; that in consequence William de Waude took apparently decisive action to remedy the situation; and that the likely reason for his visitation in the first place was that Sunning was less a normal case than a particularly notorious pocket of incompetence.

It is striking how some of the clearest evidence for providing chaplains and assistant clergy in the parishes comes from Walter Cantilupe, Bishop of Worcester (1236–66), in his diocesan statutes of 1240. Cantilupe was someone who *par excellence* brought together the political and parochial worlds in thirteenth-century England. He had been a high-level diplomat for Henry III before he became bishop. As a bishop he was a leading opponent of Henry III and that king's absolutist tendencies.[31] He was on the committee which devised the abortive but radical 'Paper Constitution' of 1244, designed to restrain those tendencies.[32] He was the chief clerical opponent from 1255 of Henry's acceptance of the Sicilian crown for his second son, Edmund, and the leading clerical opponent of the king in the baronial revolt of 1258. He had been a friend and ally of Robert Grosseteste before the latter died in 1253, and thus was a participator in the great pastoral agendum for English society which was mentioned in the previous chapter, with Grossseteste, Simon de Montfort and the Franciscans the driving force behind it. He remained a loyal supporter of Simon de Montfort to the end, celebrating Mass for his friend on the morning of 4 August 1265, when Simon was killed at the Battle of Evesham.[33] Comparing the English and Italian churches of the thirteenth century, Robert Brentano says that good English bishops tended to be scholars and high administrators; good Italian bishops were likely to be more local, more military and even more saintly.[34] Cantilupe was one of the best of the English type.

In his Worcester statutes of 1240 Cantilupe ruled that assistant priests, deacons and subdeacons were to be provided through his archdeacons and officials, unless rectors could do this more quickly. Following his predecessor as bishop he said that large parishes should have at least two resident chaplains in case one fell ill, in addition to assistants in lower orders. He envisaged clearly a local recruitment network for chaplains and assistant clergy, i.e. in particular for clergy known to and trusted by priests who provided titles for them. He ordered the compilation of lists of all clergy licensed to celebrate Mass in his diocese, separate records to be kept of those of dubious repute. And he ordered his own treatise on confession to be copied and to be observed by all chaplains hearing confessions, 'because it was too long to be published in the present synod'.[35] Had every bishop the same pastoral drive as Cantilupe? Perhaps not, but there are plenty of indications that many had the same aims. Even a bishop in England less popular in his own time and with historians, the foreigner and ruthless financier, Peter des Roches at Winchester (1205–38), was surprisingly serious about the religious and pastoral sides of his post.[36]

Cantilupe sympathised with some pluralists, and that may be one reason why, in line with Grosseteste's thinking, he stressed that absentee rectors should find their own assistant priests, where this could be done quickly. When Cardinal Otto, presiding over his legatine council of 1237, pronounced his statute against pluralists who held many benefices with cure of souls, contrary to the Lateran Council, Cantilupe got up, set aside his mitre and said that many of his kinsmen had obtained many benefices and were not yet dispensed, of whom some were advanced in age and until now had lived honourably, dispensing hospitality as they could and disbursing alms at their open doors, and that it would be excessively hard on them to be despoiled of their benefices and driven into ignominious poverty. That is perhaps why the text of Cardinal Otto's canon made this a matter for consultation rather than statute.[37]

The principal function of the parish clergy was to administer the sacraments, foremost among them the Eucharist. The feast of Corpus Christ, the Body of Christ in the Eucharist, was established in the Western church during the thirteenth century. As with the idea of the bodily Assumption of Mary in the twelfth century (see above p. 154), the idea for this feast originated in the visions of a saintly woman, in this case Juliana of Cornillon (Liège). Liège was the centre of a region where religion flourished, thanks in no small part to the numbers of communities of women Cistercians and Beguines, with their especial devotion to the Eucharist. The idea of the feast was supportively taken up by the Dominicans at Liège in the 1230s and 1240s, and the festival itself was formally instituted by the bishop there in 1246.[38]

The feast of Corpus Christi only arrived in England, formally speaking, in the early fourteenth century. But given their manifold trading and cultural connections to Lower Lotharingia, English people could not have been unaware of the devotion earlier. In thirteenth-century England, a growing place was in fact accorded to the Eucharist. Synods paid great attention to how the Eucharist, i.e. Mass, was celebrated. Chalices were to be of gilt or enamelled metal or ivory; cloths were to be held under the chins of communicants to catch any crumb of the consecrated wafer that fell. A visitation of parish churches appropriated to St Paul's Cathedral, c. 1250, revealed a sorry state of chalices and pyxes.[39] This shows that synodal decrees did not guarantee their own success; but it also suggests a continued exercise of cathedral influence on parish life. The gifts of lords and patrons of churches were crucial for worthy liturgical vessels, vestments and lighting. The fact that when a patron failed in this kind of generosity it was noted in visitations,[40] suggests that it was a normal expectation. Not surprisingly, with the growth of reverence for the Eucharist came also new opportunities for superstition. Stories circulated such as how the crumbs of a consecrated host were used by a woman to fructify her bees; and the prophylactic purposes to which hosts could be put were legion.[41] Nonetheless legislation and visitations showed the efforts being made by churchmen, following the teaching of the Parisian School of Peter the Chanter, to bring the laity closer into the central sacramental life of the church. Interestingly, Thomas of Chobham, sometime pupil and master in this school, had a long association with Salisbury Cathedral, *the* centre from which the decrees of Lateran IV radiated in England, and became Bishop's Official there 1214–17.[42]

That applied not only to the Eucharist, but also to confession. I said in Chapter 9 that the Friars were a vital instrument in spreading effectively the practice of confession, as envisaged by the Fourth Lateran Council. Moreover, bishops evidently hoped that the impact of the Friars would raise the standards of the parish clergy as confessors. Now I must add another important factor in the spread of the practice during the thirteenth century. That factor is the development of a highly influential theological idea in the High and Later Middle Ages, namely purgatory. Purgatory is one of the most humane ideas which has arisen within the concept of Christian salvation. It broke the almost intolerable starkness of the alternative between heaven and hell, between eternal blessedness and irrevocable damnation. Augustine of Hippo had drawn up four moral categories of human being: the entirely good and the entirely wicked; the not entirely good and the not entirely wicked.[43] The vast majority of people would surely think of themselves in one of the two last categories. Were such people to be consigned to hell for sins which had been confessed in all contrition but for which penance was still outstanding? (For the idea that penance, e.g. in pilgrimage, fasting and alms, was still vital for the full expiation of sins persisted despite the change in the nature of the 'Penitentials'.) Was hell the only punishment for their lesser or venial sins, surely a disproportionate punishment?

The idea of purgatory, as a state or place in the after-life and located in time between an individual's death and the Last Judgment, where penance and purgation could continue with the certainty of ultimate salvation in heaven, went back in some form at least to Augustine and Gregory the Great. It developed greatly in the twelfth century, and even more in the thirteenth. The popularity of the twelfth-century text about St Patrick's

Vision of Purgatory, as written up by the Cistercian Henry of Sawtrey, shows that the need for such an idea was strongly felt. In fact it was a twofold need, as is shown by there being *two* versions of St Patrick's Purgatory written up into Latin in late twelfth-century Britain. Gerald of Wales, struggling to improving clerical morals in his archdeaconry of Brecon, wrote of evil spirits inflicting punishments of fire and water so severe that anyone who underwent them would not have to endure the pains of hell, except for some very serious sin. In contrast, Henry of Sawtrey emphasised the more spiritual side, contrition being achieved through divine grace, and trust in Christ being what put the devils to flight.[44] It is almost as if these versions appealed to the Catholic and Protestant ethics respectively!

In both twelfth and thirteenth centuries the Cistercians, with their interest in relations between the living and the dead, and in vision literature (*re* praying for the dead and *re* ghostly apparitions as moral examples), did altogether much to further the idea. Another factor which advanced the idea of purgatory was indeed prayers for the dead. The desire of people, from the early Middle Ages, to pray for their departed families or patrons, was a fundamental instinct of medieval religion. But there was no point in praying for souls in hell; their eternal fate was already fixed. There was, however, every point in praying for souls in purgatory; their sufferings could be reduced in time and intensity by this means, and they were ultimately assured of heaven. All the stories of ghostly apparitions may be seen to have two principal functions, a spur to pray for the dead, and a spur to confess and do penance for one's own sins. Jacques Le Goff sees the great take-off in the emergence of purgatory as a cross-fertilisation between the Cistercians and the late twelfth-century Parisian masters.[45]

One of the Paris masters of the thirteenth century was William of Auvergne, who became Bishop of Paris (1228–49). In the 1230s, before Bonaventure and Thomas Aquinas, William wrote powerfully about purgatory, conceiving it as a continuation of earthly penance, as had Thomas of Chobham.[46] And this makes quite clear the connection between the idea of purgatory and the spread of confession. The more opportunities there were to repent of and confess one's sins and to do penance for them, the more insistent seemed the problem of those who did not deserve hell, but only deserved to enter heaven after some further process of penance and reconciliation in this life and the after-life. The more one confessed and did penance in this life, the less would be one's sufferings in the after-life, just as prayers and Masses for the dead offered by the living could diminish them.

There was a highly important ingredient in all this which should not
be overlooked. It was the growing significance of corporeality alongside
spirituality in medieval religion from the twelfth century onwards, as
Caroline Walker Bynum has brilliantly shown. Characteristic of twelfth-
century dualist heretics was the belief that spirit and matter were two equal
principles struggling for mastery of the world and that spirit was good
and God-created, while body or matter was evil and the work of the devil.
The church had to respond to this. One response was the ever greater
stress on Christ's bodily presence in the Eucharist. But 'all the religiosity
of the period was animated in deep ways by the need to take account of
(rather than merely to deny) matter, body and sensual response'. The idea
of purgatory was posited on human corporeality and its persistence into
the after-life. Amongst the speculations of thirteenth-century theologians
about the state of purgatory was whether the 'fires' of purgatory were
physical or only metaphorical. There was general agreement that they
were physical. And if one asks how that could be, when people's skeletons
were known to be in their graves, the only answer I can give is Bynum's:
that preachers, hagiographers and schoolmen saw nothing fundamentally
inconsistent in depicting bodily tortures of disembodied spirits, particularly
given the widespread belief that the soul itself had some sort of material
body, 'though they sometimes admitted it was odd'.[47] Time, also, was essential to any concept of purgatory – the idea that one 'did time' in purgatory
and that one might be released from purgatory before the Last Judgment,
which marked the end of time.[48] And to any concept of time, corporeality
is of the essence.

One mark of the growing self-confidence of the parish clergy in the
thirteenth century is their increasing willingness to act collaboratively to
champion their perceived rights. During the 1230s in Sussex the rectors or
vicars of Westout, Patcham, West Lavington and Barcombe all went to law
against Lewes Priory and its claims to exact tithes from them. These are
cases which surface in the historical record, but it is clear that already from
around 1220 onwards the Priory was facing much trouble from Sussex
clergy over tithes and also pensions from churches. Over pensions, the
clergy of Stoughton, Upmarden and Stedham had already been challenging
the Priory by 1220, and there was no doubt more below the surface. The
Priory had to forge documents to defeat these clergy, which they did effectively, but not before allowing us to see the parish clergy of Sussex flexing
their muscles threateningly.[49] Some of the places concerned were in close
proximity to each other, e.g. West Lavington, Stoughton, Upmarden and
Stedham, and again so were Barcombe and Patcham, though these were

separated by some distance from the other four. One may see here the effect of rural deans' synods, bringing clergy together who thereby had an opportunity to discuss such matters.[50] The same applies to the county-based archdeacons' courts, or in the case of Sussex, divided into two archdeaconries, the effect of Chichester diocesan synods. From 1215 to 1217 none other than Richard Poore was Bishop of Chichester before being translated to Salisbury, and that great protagonist of the Fourth Lateran Council would hardly in principle have wanted to see the resources of parishes depleted by the exactions of rich monasteries.[51]

Another instance of parish clergy power is even more striking, because it involved confronting face to face the papal tax collector, Pietro Rosso, to resist papal taxation. Again this resistance was ultimately not successful, probably for the basic reason that Henry III was on the pope's side. I refer to the protest of the Rectors of Berkshire in 1240. Rosso came to England to collect money for the pope's war against Frederick II. He got these rectors together after bishops and archdeacons had put up resistance to him, trying to use them as a moral lever on their superiors, and with sermonising, threats and promises (so goes the story of the anti-papalist Matthew Paris), he sought to raise a contribution. But these rectors, who obviously had powerful advice behind them, replied (again according to Paris) that they were not obliged to contribute to a war against the emperor, who though excommunicated, had not been judged a heretic nor had he occupied the Roman patrimony. Moreover, just as the church of Rome had its own patrimony, so other churches had theirs, by the generosity of kings and magnates, and did not owe tribute to the Roman church.[52] In fact they trounced the legate. One of the longest traditions of the Roman curia, however, is that no member of it can be trounced by argument alone. And here diplomacy won the day for the pope.

Who 'the Rectors of Berkshire' were is not entirely clear. But leaving aside corporate rectors like monasteries, not apparently involved, what we have just said about the clergy of Sussex shows that a county could have enough parish priests (rectors, vicars, and even chaplains who might sometimes have been responsible for finding the taxes due from their churches) to stand up for their rights, ever more often brought together by archdeacons and rural deans as they were.

Monasteries

Finally I may do a little updating of the monasteries from where we left them in the early thirteenth century. One could easily get the impression that the monasteries, especially the Benedictines entered a period of dignified senescence during the thirteenth century, or that they entered a stagnant phase. But that impression would be somewhat misleading. Their political role may have become diminished by the thirteenth century,[53] but there were other new shoots of life. According to the Fourth Lateran Council (c. 12), a general chapter of abbots was to be held every three years in every province of the church. That this was intended to apply particularly to the black monks is clear from the fact that these chapters were initially to invite in Cistercian abbots to advise them, since the Cistercians had long held such chapters and knew how to do it.[54] And forthwith, in England, these chapters happened; their minutes have been preserved and now long since edited. They were held in various places at or near which there were important Benedictine monasteries: Southwark, Oxford, Evesham and Reading are amongst those named. Their debates were concerned with many matters which were thought to need correction, and with some, such as whether or not meat should be eaten, which related closely to ideals of living which defined the monastic way of life. I cannot go into all these debates.

There is one subject, however, in the acts of these chapters which has an important bearing on the vibrancy and adaptability of the thirteenth-century black monks, and that is the place of learning. The rituals of the Benedictine monastic office became so elaborate and time-consuming that they left little time for anything else, and the chapter meetings were acutely aware of the fact. At Southwark in 1249, it was laid down that the monks ought not to be burdened with excessive psalmody, 'as is the custom in some places'. At Evesham in 1255 it was said that superiors might cut out the superfluities in the divine office, so that other things could be more easily learned by the brethren and attention might be given to reading on sacred subjects (*sacris lectionibus*), meditation, and other such matters. And then in 1277 at Reading there was a clause which began with the prolixity of the office beyond what the Rule required, and ended by the abbots saying that monasteries should have a suitable house in Oxford where the monks of their monasteries could study.[55] So began, just after our period, the monastic colleges in Oxford, founded from such houses as Canterbury, Gloucester and Durham. As institutions these colleges all disappeared at the Reformation, though medieval buildings of Gloucester College still form part of Worcester College, while the location of Canterbury College is still remembered in the quadrangle of that name at Christ Church.

It is never easy to judge the effect of such legislation (or recommendations) as we have just cited. But if one considers Reading Abbey, it was already happening. Their medieval book collections finely studied by Alan Coates, show in the thirteenth century an interest to keep up with front-line university studies (perhaps their relative proximity to Oxford helping here), as in a similar way do those of Durham Cathedral Priory.[56] At the same time they were important contributors to the study and composition of polyphonic music, thus influencing how thirteenth-century England *sounded*.[57] Put briefly, Reading wanted its monks to have the same educational opportunities as secular clerks were getting. In addition the abbey had what is the only surviving manuscript of the *Song of Lewes*, suggesting that it was not divorced from political concerns (as does their compilation of annals), and they had a copy of Adam of Eynsham's widely dispersed version (1197) of Edmund of Eynsham's *Vision of Purgatory*.[58] Similar studies would probably reveal that Reading was not exceptional amongst Benedictine houses. Both Glastonbury and Peterborough, for instance, had Latin translations of Aristotle's *De Anima* by the mid-thirteenth century, while from the late twelfth century St Alban's had part of Aristotle's Nichomachean Ethics.[59]

Not only had the black monks their new chapters in the thirteenth century, but this was also the first century of systematic visitation of monasteries by bishops. Such visitations threw up a new kind of source for historians and brought to light, of course, some scandals and some financial mismanagement; although from this new kind of evidence, and from the evidence altogether, David Knowles drew the general conclusion that for the monasteries, 'the period was one neither of fervour nor of widespread decadence'.[60] I suspect that we could say worse of them at their worst, and better of them at their best.

One remarkable sign of life in thirteenth-century English Benedictine monasticism lies in the foundation of the oldest Cambridge college, Peterhouse. Peterhouse was founded after our period, in 1284, by Hugh de Balsham, who had then been Bishop of Ely for 27 years, but before that had been monk and sub-prior of Ely Cathedral Priory, and as bishop remained on good terms with the monastery. Balsham's statutes were based, for the practical workings of his new college, on the earlier statutes of Merton College, Oxford. But what they say about the *tone* of Peterhouse is suffused with the *Rule of St Benedict*. When the scholars were engaged in formal disputations in arts or theology, for instance, they were not to do so 'clamorously' but in a civil way. They should not interrupt each other or be quarrelsome and offensive. The Merton Statutes had nothing like this, but the *Rule of St Benedict* had quite a lot, including (on humility) that when a monk speaks he should do so gently and 'without clamour'. Or again, the college porter was to show a discernment of persons (in whom he let in and whom he did not), very like the discernment that the *Rule* requires the abbot to show towards his monks. Or again, like the *Rule*, the Peterhouse statutes emphasised how there should be no 'murmuring' amongst the scholars. To be subprior in a Benedictine Cathedral monastery was the equivalent to being a prior in another monastery, since the bishop was technically the abbot, and thus the prior was in effect abbot. A prior was not responsible for the material administration but for the monastic observance of a house. And here was a Benedictine monk and subprior, who so many years after he had become a bishop, could still be sufficiently inspired by his *Rule* to impress its tone on a new collegiate community.[61]

On the thirteenth-century Cistercians I am going to be even more selective in what I say than on the black monks. By around 1200, the Cistercians had become an important element in the British economy mainly but by no means only because of their production of wool. Not surprisingly, that made them an object of envy and resentment in some quarters, and they acquired a reputation for ruthless acquisition of land and wealth, not to say avarice. That such criticisms were at least partially justified is implicit in the way that John of Ford, himself a Cistercian abbot, wrote in self-criticism of his own order around the turn of the century. Our principal evidences for the thirteenth-century Cistercians are their charters (i.e. grants and legal agreements, etc.) and their administrative records. David Knowles's chapter on them in his *Religious Orders* is all about their agrarian economy.[62] Here he did not use the misleading cliché that the Cistercians declined from their primitive ideals, misleading in its implication that they had ever espoused corporate poverty in the first place; though he rightly pointed out that once their monasteries got going as businesses they needed a cash income. (Do we see in this development something that the Franciscans particularly reacted against?) What he did say, however, was that the white monks made no stand against the forces that drew them back into the world, and that they were soon 'knots in the great web of commercial life that had its centres in Flanders and Brabant, Tuscany and Lombardy'.[63] But as we saw in Chapter 6, there are some senses – religious, political and social – in which it is doubtful that they were ever withdrawn from the world.

The remainder of this brief discussion about the thirteenth-century Cistercians will consider one of their abbots, Stephen of Sawley (Yorkshire), who incidentally was not mentioned by Knowles. Stephen had been novice and monk at Fountains Abbey, and was Abbot of Sawley from 1223–34. In 1234 he was elected Abbot of Newminster (Northumberland), the mother-house from which Sawley was founded, and early in 1248 he became Abbot of Fountains itself (he died in 1252).[64] These elections show that we are not only dealing with an isolated individual, but with qualities in a man that were valued by at least three monastic communities. Those qualities included administrative ability, since he was elected to Sawley from being cellarer (comparable to a domestic bursar in our day) of Fountains for a number of years. As a Cistercian abbot, Stephen also had considerable experience of attending the General Chapters at Cîteaux and of visitations of other Cistercian houses in England. He was not at all simply a reclusive mystic removed from the world.

In many ways Stephen followed in the finest twelfth-century traditions of Ailred of Rievaulx, Gilbert of Hoyland (both of whose writings he imbibed) and their like. Like Ailred his meditation was Christ-centred, and he shared Gilbert's delight in the Song of Songs. He wrote a 'Mirror' for Novices; this shows psychological insight and human sympathy which are anything but formulaic.[65] His most original achievement, however, was his *Meditations on the Fifteen Joys of the Virgin Mary*, which became very popular. Writing of this work, André Wilmart, who brought it to light in 1929, said that Stephen had the qualities of an excellent witness both to his time and to his order.[66] All religious orders had a pronounced devotion to Mary in the twelfth century, but this intensified in the thirteenth, e.g. the extreme devotion to her of Henry III himself.[67] One has only to consider the tenderness of the Virgin and Child depicted in the Chichester Roundel (c. 1250), a wall-painting in the chapel of the Bishop's Palace, to see this [see Plate 8].[68] Given that this comes probably from when Richard of Wych was bishop, with his connections to the Dominicans and St Dominic's proverbial devotion to Mary, that may have something to do with it. But essentially this kind of tenderness all goes back to Stephen of Sawley, as the late Val Flint pointed out to me.

Stephen starts his *Fifteen Joys* by saying that the meditations are divided into three groups of five each. He goes on:

Each of the fifteen contains: first a meditation of the joy; second an expression of that joy directed to the Virgin; third a petition of the person meditating; fourth the angelic salutation plus certain devout words (in effect the Ave Maria or Hail Mary). And after each group of five there are pauses so that the meditator can (in his or her mind) recapitulate.[69]

Stephen was not primarily a scholar though he was quite well read, but here he shows a positive predilection for the methods of scholasticism with their subdivisions and categorisations, as had St Bernard. The first three meditations have all to do with the Annunciation, the fourth is on how the

Holy Spirit overshadowed the Virgin 'with inexpressible sweetness',[70] and the fifth concerns the *Ave*, or salutation of Elizabeth to Mary on the latter's Visitation. The sixth meditation is on the Nativity of Christ, and is so much in the spirit of the later Chichester Roundel that some of it is again worth quoting [see Plate 8]:

Oh wise boy, oh squawking Word (!), Oh humble majesty, Oh noble weakness. Oh happy shepherds, who deserved to see such great mysteries. But happier virgin to whom alone it was granted not only to contain the lord of all things in her womb, but also to fondle him on her lap, to press him to herself with her embraces (hugs), to kiss him with her sacred lips, and to comfort him with her heaven-filled breasts.[71]

The 'joys' of Mary also include the sufferings of Christ, like the Crucifixion which she witnessed, a joy because it led to the deliverance of souls from purgatory and the opening of the gates of heaven to the whole world.[72]

Anyone familiar with the devotion of the rosary will see that we have not yet arrived at it. There are no beads and no Our Father. The Hail Mary, not yet in its final form, is not repeated ten times for each of the fifteen mysteries or joys, but only once at the end of each of the fifteen. The joys, or mysteries, or meditations, though similar, are not yet exactly the same in subject as those of the fifteen mysteries of the rosary. But equally Stephen's work has to be regarded as a significant step in the evolution of the rosary. For as Anne Winston has remarked (without bringing in Stephen of Sawley), it is not beads and repetitions of Hail Marys which constitute the essence of the rosary in its fully developed form, but the combination of verbal prayer and an accompanying set of mental meditations.[73] This she rightly says developed from the recitation of the Psalter. That makes it interesting that Stephen also wrote a work on how to meditate while reciting the psalms.[74] Stephen's immediate audience was one of Cistercian monks. But it is hard to think that, so far at least as the *Joys of the Virgin* was concerned, his audience stopped at monks for long, given the climate of intense Marian devotion in his time, and given what we have argued in Chapter 6 about how wide a public beyond themselves Cistercian ideas and Cistercian religion earlier reached. Anne Winston, again, in commenting on how far-reaching the effect of the rosary was on extraliturgical piety, has said that 'the devotion shaped, and was shaped by, the demands of the laity for new, more individual and private forms of religious observance'.[75] Thus did a thirteenth-century English Cistercian monk influence the whole nature of later medieval religion.

Some readers may ask what a spiritual writer like Stephen of Sawley, little known in the world, can have to do with religion, politics and society. I am unrepentant. Part of my idea in this whole book has been to write about things which *must* have been influential – like talk, or confession, or prayer – but whose full effect it is impossible to gauge. It is a risky policy, but no more risky than it is to ignore them on the grounds that their effect cannot be known in any detail or precisely measured. In a fine paper delivered to the annual Reichenau Conference of 2003, the distinguished German historian, Hagen Keller, spoke of concepts of order, new horizons of human experience, and understanding of the world, in the cultural mutation of the twelfth/thirteenth centuries. The very title of his paper indicates that Keller sees these two centuries in a continuum (as had Sir Richard Southern in his famous essay 'Medieval Humanism'). One of his themes is what he calls the growing *Weltlichkeit* of the period – perhaps better translated as worldly-wise rather than worldliness, though neither is ideal. There was a widening of worldly experience, developed not least by actual journeys whether for pilgrimage or trade or crusading. But such journeys were not only geographical. Purgatory, says Keller, was seen as the terrible journey of purification to the blessedness of paradise.[76] Horizon-broadening journeys may also be ones of inner experience. That is where Stephen of Sawley could have helped many.

Notes

Chapter 1

1 Miller, 'England in the twelfth and thirteenth centuries'; Miller and Hatcher, *Medieval England*, esp. cc. 6, 7.

2 Southern, *Western Society and the Church*, esp. 258–9.

3 Miller and Hatcher, 46–8; Titow, *English Rural Society*, 73–8, but at page 74 failing to recognise where Barbara Harvey is coming from.

4 King, *Peterborough Abbey*, c. 4.

5 Lennard, 'Demesnes of Glastonbury'; Postan, 'Glastonbury Estates', *Econ. Hist. Rev.* 5 (1952–53), 8 (1956), 9 (1956–57).

6 Hallam, *Settlement and Society*, 16.

7 Faith, *English Peasantry*, 225–34, citing also B.K. Roberts.

8 For example, MTB ii, 96; i, 44; and for insomnia also Life of Wulfric, c. 29, p. 46.

9 Miller and Hatcher, 204–13; Faith, 184–5, 205. For a marvellous study of how one great ecclesiastical landlord ran its estates, see Barbara Harvey, *Westminster Abbey*, the early part of most chapters for our period.

10 The sum paid to John, clerk of the Queen of Spain (Henry II's daughter), probably a mathematician, for residing in the schools of Northampton, starting in 1176, was 2 shillings a week, or £5:4 shillings a year, PRS 26, 23 Henry II, 89. Similarly for several more years.

11 *Jocelin of Brakelond*, 33; Greenway et al. (eds) *Tradition and Change*, 30.

12 Mayr-Harting, 'Functions of a twelfth-century recluse', 340, 343; on Glastonbury Abbey as coloniser of new land in Somerset, see Faith, 187.

13 Reynolds, *English Medieval Towns*, 59.

14 Beresford, *New Towns*.

15 P.D.A. Harvey, *Banbury*.

16 Roth, *Jews of Medieval Oxford*, 3–10.

17 PRS 10 Henry II, 1164, p. 8, *pro corveisariis*, apparently for the first time.

18 Lobel and Carus-Wilson, *Bristol*, 3–7.

19 *Jocelin of Brakelond*, 76–7; Greenway et al. (eds) *Tradition and Change*, 68.

20 PRS 18 Henry II, 1171–72, pp. 71–2.

21 Roth, *Jews of Medieval Oxford*, 7.

22 Davis, 'Ford, river, city'.

22a Nicholl, *Thurstan*, 31–2.

23 For references to most of the above, see Mayr-Harting, 'Functions of a twelfth-century recluse'.

24 *Life of Christina of Markyate*, 34–79.

25 Life of Wulfric, 13–15.

26 Ibid., 82 (*ars culcitariae*).

27 Life of Godric, c. 49, p. 46.

28 *Life of Robert of Knaresborough*, 118, 116.

29 Life of Godric, 25, 29–30.

30 Brown, *World of Late Antiquity* (1971), 101.

31 Mayr-Harting, 'Jesus scourge of money-grubbers', TLS, 26 December 1986.

32 Southern, *St Anselm and His Biographer*, 77–121.

33 Ibid., 290–6; Brooke, in *History of St Paul's Cathedral*, 24–5.

34 Vision of Thurkill.

35 Walter Map, p. xix.

36 Ibid., 206–7.

37 Bartlett, *England under the Norman and Angevin Kings*, 614.

38 Walter Daniel, *Life of Ailred*, 46–8.

39 Gransden, *Historical Writing in England*, 125.

40 *History of the Church of Abingdon*, p. xlix.

41 V. Saxer, *Le Culte de Marie Madeleine en Occident* (1959).

42 E.A. Webb, *Records of St Bartholomew's Priory* (1928), i, 385–92.

43 Bartlett, *England*, 603.

44 Moore, *Formation of a Persecuting Society*, c. 2.

45 Gervase of Canterbury, i, 258–9.

46 EEA 20, York 1154–81, nos 117–27.

47 Chichester Acta, no. 107.

48 Mansi, *Concilia* xxii, col. 230.

49 Moore, *Formation*, 75–8; Stanley Rubin, *Medieval English Medicine* (1974), 159–60, on excavations at South Acre (Norfolk); EEA 20, York 1154–81, no. 119.

50 *Rotuli Curiae Regis*, ed. F. Palgrave (1835), ii, 89.

51 Talbot and Hammond, *Medical Practitioners*.

52 R.M. Thomson, 'Liber Marii de Elementis', *Viator* 3 (1972), 179–89; B. Lawn, *Salernitan Questions* (1963), 58–66.

53 Rather as described in the Nigeria of the 1960s by Una Maclean, *Magical Medicine* (1974), esp. cc. 4, 7.

54 MV ii, 221.

55 Davis, 'An Oxford Charter of 1191', 54.

56 Britnell, *Commercialization*, 80.

57 Life of Godric, c. 42, 101–2.

58 *Book of St Gilbert*, 74–5.

59 PRS 15 Henry II, 1168–9, 151. See also 16 H II, 135, and 17 H II, 133.

60 N.R. Ker, *English Manuscripts in the Century after the Norman Conquest* (1960), 11.

61 So one may conclude from Pierre Chaplais, 'Westminster Charters', in *Early Medieval Miscellany for D.M. Stenton*, PRS, NS, 36 (1962), 95–7.

62 *Life of St William of Norwich*, 138, 143. Instances of candles given are too many to enumerate.

63 Cf. Moore, *Origins of European Dissent*, 108–9.

64 Bartholomew of Farne, 315.

65 R. Rogers, *Latin Siege Warfare* (1992) 50, 61, cc. 2, 4.

66 PRS 25, 22 Henry II, 1175–76, p. 60, 1. 15.

67 Bartlett, *England*, 254.

68 EEA 6, Norwich 1070–1214, no. 89, p. 77. 1. 3; no. 94.

69 R.F. Hunnisett, 'The origins of the Office of Coroner, TRHS 5th Ser. 8 (1958), 88–104.

70 Howden, iii, 299. I recollect John Prestwich speaking of professional knights in his Oxford lectures of 1956–57, which is how I originally came to the point.

71 Howden, iv, 46.

72 Miller and Hatcher, *Medieval England*, cc. 7, 8; Britnell, 'The Winchester Pipe Rolls', 2; Drew, 'Manorial accounts of St Swithun's, Winchester', EHR 62 (1947), an old but brilliant study.

73 *Records of the Templars*, lxx–lxxi.

74 Saltman, *Theobald*, 100–23, and for Theobald more generally as primate, Morey and Brooke, 88–95.

75 Walter Map, 22–23.

76 Ibid.

77 Greenway, 'False *Institutio*'; Ramsey, 'Robert of Lewes, Bishop of Bath'.

78 Brooke, 'The archdeacon and the Norman Conquest', esp. 7–10, 13–15.

79 John of Salisbury, *Policraticus*, I, 353–5.

80 *Letters of John of Salisbury*, ii, 24–5.

81 *Life of Christina of Markyate*, 33–103.

82 *Gesta Abbatum S. Albani*, i, 73.

83 *Life of Christina of Markyate*, 171.

84 Ibid., 149, 173.

85 Ibid., 117.

86 Bynum, *Holy Feast and Holy Fast* (1991), 253.

87 *Gesta Abbatum S. Albani*, i, 74–80.

88 *Life of Christina of Markyate*, 138–41.

89 Jane Geddes, 'The St Albans Psalter', in *Christina of Markyate*, 199–200 and plate 1.

90 Eadmer, *Historia Novorum*, 33.

91 Chichester Acta, no. 38, p. 100.

92 Leyser, *Medieval Women*, 201.

Chapter 2

1 Karl Leyser, 'On the eve of the first European revolution', in his *Communications and Power in Medieval Europe: the Gregorian Revolution and Beyond* (1994), c. 1, esp. 16–17; Moore, *Origins of European Dissent*, esp. 40–5, 65–7; Moore, *The First European Revolution*, esp. 14–16.

2 Cowdrey, *Gregory VII*, 27–8.

3 Southern, *Making of the Middle Ages*, 139–42.

4 Cowdrey, *Gregory VII*, 325, 529–34.

5 Ibid., 249–53.

6 These two cases are discussed powerfully in I.S. Robinson, *Authority and Resistance*, 165–6, 170.

7 *Register of Pope Gregory VII*, 104–6, 194–5; Robinson, as in note above, 170; cf. R. Schieffer, on background of simony cases in *Historisches Jahrbuch* 92 (1972) 19–60.

8 Gerd Tellenbach, *Church State and Christian Society* (Engl. trans. 1940), p. 1 for this phrase. See also Walter Ullmann, *The Growth of Papal Government in the Middle Ages* (1955), cc. 9–12.

9 Henry Chadwick, *The Circle and the Elipse* (1959).

10 Robinson, *Authority and Resistance*, 22–3.

11 Henry Mayr-Harting, *Church and Cosmos in Early Ottonian Germany* (2007), 139, with refs in footnotes.

12 P. Fournier and G. Le Bras, *Histoire des Collections Canoniques en Occident*, ii (1932), 28–9; Kathleen Cushing, *Papacy and Law in the Gregorian Revolution* (1998), esp. cc. 1–3.

13 Fournier and Le Bras, *Histoire des Collections Canoniques en Occident*, ii, 8–14, 31–5, 46–51; Cushing, *Papacy and Law in the Gregorian Revolution*, e.g. 71, 87–8.

14 This is entirely compatible with the paucity of texts from Gregory VII in the content of canon law, Cushing, 90.

15 Morris, *Papal Monarchy*, 93–4; Cowdrey, *Gregory VII*, 592–6. For Hildebrand as Archdeacon of Rome, Morris, 90–1; Cowdrey, *Gregory VII*, 38–9.

16 St Bernard, *De Consideratione*, I, cc. 3–6, *Sancti Bernardi Opera* 3, eds J. Le Clercq and H.M. Rochais (Rome, 1963), 397–401. Various translations, e.g. by George Lewis (1908), 17–25.

17 I.S. Robinson, 'The Friendship Network of Gregory VII', *History* 63 (1978), 15–18.

18 *Register of Gregory VII*, I, 62, pp. 65–6; but this translation by E. Emerton, in *The Correspondence of Pope Gregory VII* (1966), 27.

19 Ibid., II, 67, p. 161; trans. Emerton, 72.

20 Morris, *Papal Monarchy*, 114.

21 Cowdrey, *Gregory VII*, 680–1.

22 *Register of Gregory VII*, VIII, 21, p. 394; trans. Emerton, 173.

23 Southern, *Western Society and the Church*, 102–4; Morris, *Papal Monarchy*, 112.

24 Gibson, *Lanfranc of Bec*, 193.

25 Matthew, *Norman Conquest*, 172.

26 *Life of Herluin of Bec*, in Robinson, *Gilbert Crispin*, 98.

27 Henry Mayr-Harting, *The Coming of Christianity to Anglo-Saxon England* (3rd edn, 1991), 270–3.

28 Cowdrey, *Lanfranc*, c. 7. Also Matthew, *Norman Conquest*, 173; Golding, *Conquest and Colonization*, 150–4.

29 Matthew, *Norman Conquest*, 208–9; Brett, *The English Church under Henry I*, 109–11.

30 Hugh the Chantor, 3. See also Walker, *The Normans in Britain*, 43–4.

31 Hugh the Chantor, 3–4.

32 Cowdrey, *Lanfranc*, 93–103, esp. 99.

33 Golding, *Conquest and Colonization*, 152, 154.

34 *Letters of Lanfranc*, no. 13, pp. 80–3.

35 Ibid., no. 50, p. 160.

36 Ibid., nos 9 and 10, pp. 66–72; Gibson *Lanfranc of Bec*, 121–31.

37 Cowdrey, *Lanfranc*, 38, cf. 55.

38 *Letters of Lanfranc*, no. 59, p. 174.

39 For Ethelwold in general, Patrick Wormald, 'Aethelwold and his Continental Counterparts'.

40 Cowdrey, *Lanfranc*, 89–90, cf. 103.

41 Ibid., 101–2.

42 EHD 1042–1189, no. 99, p. 645.

43 *Letters of Lanfranc*, no. 38, pp. 128–31.

44 Z.N. Brooke, *English Church and Papacy*, c. 5, esp. 68–73.

45 Matthew, *Norman Conquest*, 186–7; EEA 10, pp. xxiv–xxv; Frances Ramsey, 'Robert of Lewes, Bishop of Bath', 253.

46 Z.N. Brooke, 68–9; *Letters of Lanfranc* no. 47, pp. 150–3.

47 Trinity College, Cambridge, Ms. B. 16.44.

48 The whole in translation, EHD 1042–1189, no. 84, pp. 609–24.

49 Symeon of Durham *Libellus de Exordio*, 221–57; R.H.C. Davis, 'Bede after Bede', in his *From Alfred the Great to Stephen* (1991), 9.

50 Mark Philpott, 'The *De Iniusta Vexatione Willelmi Episcopi Primi* and Canon law in Anglo-Norman Durham', *Anglo-Norman Durham 1093–1193*, eds David Rollason et al. (1994) esp. 130–5.

51 R.A.B. Mynors, *Durham Cathedral Manuscripts* (1939), 32–45, and plates 16–32.

52 H. Fichtenau, 'Riesenbibeln in Österreich und Mathilde von Tuszien', in his *Beiträge zur Mediävistik* i (Stuttgart, 1975), 163–86; esp. I.S. Robinson, 'The Metrical Commentary on Genesis of Donizo of Canossa', *Recherches de Théologie Ancienne et Médiévale* 41 (1974), esp. 12–15; Henry Mayr-Harting, *Ottonian Book Illumination* ii (1991), 175–8; Walter Cahn, *Romanesque Bible Illumination* (1982), esp. 102–3.

53 The clear implication of Symeon of Durham, *Libellus de Exordio*, 212–13, 236–7. Implicit also in M.W. Aird, *St Cuthbert and the Normans* (1998), 115–16, 119, 124–5.

54 Gibson, *Lanfranc of Bec*, 54–61.

55 Ibid., 81–97.

56 *The Monastic Constitutions of Lanfranc*, ed. David Knowles (1951), 1.

57 Wormald, 'Aethelwold and his continental counterparts', 38.

58 *De Abbatibus Abendoniae*, ii, ed. J. Stevenson (RS 1858), 283–4, and *History of the Church of Abingdon*, ed. John Hudson (2002), pp. xl–xlii, xxi–xxiii; for Turold, Knowles, *The Monastic Order*, 114, 118, and *The Chronicle of Hugh Candidus*, trans. C. and W.T. Mellows (1941), 40, 43–4.

59 David Hiley, 'Thurstan of Caen and Plainchant at Glastonbury', *Proc. Brit. Acad.* 72 (1986), 57–90, esp. 82; and William of Malmesbury, *Gesta Pontificum*, i, pp. 308–11.

60 William of Malmesbury, *Gesta Pontifcum*, p. 426; *Life of Wulfstan*, Camden Series 40 (1928), 46.

61 *De Abbatibus Abendoniae*, as in note 58 above, p. 283, bottom 3 lines.

62 *Liber Eliensis*, p. 196.

63 Ibid., pp. 200–2, 220–1.

64 Matthew, *Norman Conquest*, 290–5. Similarly, but less critical of William of Malmesbury, Williams, *The English and the Norman Conquest*, 172–3.

65 Williams, 3, 196–200.

66 Brian Golding, 'The religious patronage of Robert and William of Mortain', in *Belief and Culture, Studies Presented to Henry Mayr-Harting*, eds Richard Gameson and Henrietta Leyser (2001), 213–18.

67 Ibid., 211, 221–30; Golding, *Conquest and Colonization*, 175.

68 *Liber Eliensis*, pp. 225, 150.

69 Ibid., pp. 212–13.

70 John Gillingham, *Sunday Times Colour Supplement*, 23 March 1986, pp. 36–40.

71 John Crook, *The Architectural Setting of the Cults of Saints* (2000), 167.

72 Patrick Geary, 'Humiliation of saints', in *Saints and their Cults*, ed. Stephen Wilson (1983), 123–40, esp. p. 133.

73 *Liber Eliensis*, p. xlix.

74 Jean Dunbabin, *France in the Making* (1985), 94–5, 215.

Chapter 3

1 Southern, *St Anselm*, 163–4.

2 *Brett, The English Church under Henry I*, 112.

3 *Life of Robert of Bethune* c. 11.

4 Orderic Vitalis, xi, 43, vol. VI, 174–6.

5 Webber, *Scribes and Scholars at Salisbury Cathedral*, 45, 82.

6 Most graphically described in Henry of Huntingdon's disillusioned *De Contemptu Mundi*, see Karl Leyser, 'Kings and Kingship', *Medieval Germany and its Neighbours* (1982), 258.

7 Notably R.W. Southern, 'King Henry I', *Medieval Humanism*, 216–17. It should, however, be noted that of all religious orders the Cluniacs took pride of place, and Henry's most important foundation, Reading Abbey, was a Cluniac house, Green, *Henry I*, 170–2, 278.

8 Green, *Henry I*, 279.

9 Ibid., 257.

10 Julian Haseldine (ed.), *Friendship in Medieval Europe* (1999), esp. Introduction and contributions, Haseldine, McEvoy, Cassidy, White, Hirata and Robinson. Also Colin Morris, *Discovery of the Individual*, 97–108.

11 William of Malmesbury, *Gesta Regum*, I, 742.

12 Orderic Vitalis, xii, 22, vol. VI, 278 (in amicitiam os benigniter recepit); and for Ranulph Flambard, ibid., 142.

13 C. Warren Hollister, 'Henry I and the Anglo-Norman Magnates', in his *Monarchy, Magnates and Institutions* (1986), 181–2.

14 Abingdon Chronicle ii, 234, cf. R.C. Van Caenegem, Royal Writs.

15 R.R. Davies, 'Henry I and Wales' in *Studies Presented to R.H.C. Davis*, 139. Occasionally, but only as a last resort, Henry led military expeditions into Wales, ibid., 141.

16 R.R. Davies, *The Age of Conquest: Wales 1063–1415*, 179–91.

17 Ibid., 183–4. For Urban of Llandaff, David Walker, *The Normans in Britain* (1995), 67–9.

18 Southern, *St Anselm*, 165–8, 176.

19 Hagen Keller, 'Die Investitur', *Frühmittelalterliche Studien* 27 (1993), 59–65.

20 Quoted by Gerd Tallenbach, *Church, State and Christian Society* (1940), 87, from Radulph Glaber's *Histories*.

21 Keller, 64–5.

22 Ibid., 66.

23 Cowdrey, *Gregory VII*, 548–50.

24 C.N.L. Brooke, *The Investiture Disputes* (Hist. Assoc. 1958, 1969), 11.

25 R.W. and A.J. Carlyle, *History of Medieval Political Theory in the West*, iv (repr. 1970), 97.

26 Quoted ibid., 97–9.

27 Hugh the Chantor, 14.

28 Some of this *pace* Norman Cantor, *Church, Kingship and Lay Investiture in England, 1089–1135* (New York, 1969), 234, but his discussion of Hugh of Fleury, 226–34, is illuminating. The most relevant passage from Hugh of Fleury is quoted in R.W. and A.J. Carlyle, 102–3, note 2.

29 Southern, *St Anselm*, 167.

30 Ibid., 159–60.

31 Ibid., 164.

32 Ibid., 171.

33 Hugh the Chantor, 13–14.

34 Christopher Brooke, *Europe in the Central Middle Ages, 962–1154* (1964), 287.

35 On the whole subject of Henry I's episcopal appointments, Brett, *The English Church under Henry I*, 110–12, is excellent; as is Green, *Henry I*, 264–5.

36 John Gillingham, *Richard I* (1973), 168.

37 Henry of Huntingdon, 470; Hugh the Chantor, 109; Green, *Henry I*, 178–9.

38 Morey and Brooke, *Gilbert Foliot and His Letters*, 92–3.

39 Warren, *Henry II*, 311–12.

40 Saltman, *Theobald, Archbishop of Canterbury*, 106–7.

41 Henry of Huntingdon, 752–4.

42 Hugh the Chantor, 13.

43 Ibid., 7–8.

44 Or rather Richard de Lucy, Henry II's Chief Justiciar and the abbot's brother in effect said this for Walter, *Chronicle of Battle Abbey*, 180. For the monks behind Abbot Walter, ibid., 172. More than one third of this Chronicle is taken up with Walter's legal fights to retain every jot and tittle of Battle Abbey's rights, ibid., 142–266.

45 Chibnall, *The World of Orderic Vitalis*, 15–16, 28–41, 223–4.

46 For example, on Canterbury, Southern, *St Anslem*, 248–52.

47 Nicholl, *Thurstan Archbishop of York*, 37.

48 Hugh the Chantor thought Henry I a capable double-dealer, e.g. 39, 52, 74.

49 Brett, *The English Church under Henry I*, 36–50; he also explains at 45–6 why Henry and Canterbury were willing to receive John of Crema in 1125.

50 Green, *Henry I*, 274–6; Brett, *The English Church under Henry I*, 79–82. Perhaps I emphasise more than these writers do the connection with papal legates.

51 Hugh the Chantor, 29.

52 Green, *Henry I*, 262.

53 Hugh the Chantor, 56.

54 Nicholl, *Thurstan Archbishop of York*, 44.

55 Hugh the Chantor, 43–4.

56 Eadmer, *Historia Novorum*, Bk 5, p. 288.

57 Hugh the Chantor, 46.

58 Ibid., 68–72.

59 Ibid., 80.

60 Ibid., 77.

61 Ibid., 79 (Fili dulcissime).

62 Nicholl, *Thurstan*, 68–73.

63 Ibid., 73. In his discussion of the whole Thurstan story, Karl Leyser characteristically comments on Henry I's fear of loss of face, 'Kings and Kingship' (see note 6), 257.

64 Ibid., 95–7.

65 Ibid., 79–82, based on Eadmer's *Historia Novorum*.

66 Barrow, *The Kingdom of the Scots*, 154–5.

67 Nicholl, *Thurstan*, 137.

68 Richard Sharpe, *Norman Rule in Cumbria 1092–1136*, 15–20.

69 Judith Green, 'King Henry I and Northern England', TRHS 6th Ser. 17 (2007), 53.

70 Ibid. It is difficult to give specific pages, for I take this to be a message of this whole important article.

71 Green, 'King Henry I and Northern England', 48.

72 Ibid., 45; Sharpe, *Norman Rule*, 51.

73 Green, 'King Henry I and Northern England', 43.

74 On John of Glasgow, whom Barrow has described as 'one of the outstanding prelates of medieval Scotland', see Barrow, *The Kingdom of the Scots*, 207–8, and for the building, endowments and resident clergy of Glasgow Cathedral, ibid., 208–13.

75 Arnold of Bonneval, *Vita Prima* of St. Bernard, II, 1, 4, PL 185, col. 271 A–B.

76 This fourth section of the chapter is largely based on my lecture to the Friends of Melbourne Church given at Melbourne in March 2004, *Melbourne Church in its Earliest Historical Surroundings*, published by the Friends of Melbourne Parish Church. But I wrote the lecture partly with the present book in mind. Philip Heath has helped me with his local knowledge.

77 Richard Gem, 'Melbourne church', *Archaeological Journal* 146 (1989), *Supplement on the Nottingham Area*, 24–9.

78 Rita Wood, 'The Romanesque Church at Melbourne', *Derbyshire Archaeological Journal*, 126 (2006), 127–68. The case is made particularly with reference to the scheme of sculpture.

79 Osney Annals, 1130, in *Annales Monastici* iv, 19, Rolls Series 36/4.

80 Karl Leyser, 'England and the Empire', in his *Medieval Germany and its Neighbours* (1982), 193, quoting Henry of Huntingdon, 456.

81 Matthew, *Norman Conquest*, 300, and illustration facing 113; Rodney M. Thomson, *Manuscripts from St Albans Abbey 1066–1235*, (1982) i. 26.

82 Otto Lehmann-Brockhaus, *Lateinische Schriftsquellen zur Kunst in England*, etc. 901–1307 (1955–60), ii, no. 3632.

83 Leyser, 'The Anglo-Norman Succession, 1120–25', in *Communications and Power in Medieval Europe*, ed. Timothy Reuter (1994), ii, esp. 106–14.

84 Leyser, 'Kings and Kingship', *Medieval Germany and its Neighbours*, 258; Suger, *Vie de Louis VI*, ed. Henri Waquet (1964), 190.

85 Green, *The Government of England under Henry I*, 38–43.

86 Esp. J.O. Prestwich, 'The Military Household of the Norman Kings', EHR 96 (1981), 1–35.

87 E.g. William of Eynesford, see Green, *Government*, 201, 203, 208; or Sharpe, *Norman Rule in Cumbria*, on Odard the Sheriff, 15–20, 33.

88 Sharpe, *Norman Rule*, 21–2, 55–6.

89 Henry Summerson, 'Athelwold the Bishop and Walter the Priest', *Trans. Cumberland and Westmorland Antiquarian and Archaeol. Soc.* 95 (1995), 85–93.

90 Green, 'Henry I and Northern England'.

91 Barrow, *David I of Scotland*, 17.

92 Ibid.

93 Henry Summerson, *Medieval Carlisle*, I (1993), 40–1.

94 Ibid., 41.

95 Haseldine (ed.), *Friendship in Medieval Europe* (1999), xvii–xxiii; id., 'Friendship and Rivalry: the Role of Amicitia in Twelfth-Century Monastic Relations', *Journ. Eccl. Hist.* 44 (1993), 390–414; id., 'Friends, Friendship and Networks in the Letters of Bernard of Clairvaux', *Cîteaux*, 57 (2006), 243–80.

96 David Knowles, 'The Humanism of the Twelfth Century', in his *Historian and Character* (1963), 16–30.

97 Ibid., 17.

98 Ibid., 29.

Chapter 4

1 Duggan, *Thomas Becket*, 96.

2 *Letters of John of Salisbury*, i, pp. xxxvii–viii, 197–8, 221–5; Barlow, *Thomas Becket*, 61.

3 Matthew, 'The Letter-Writing of Archbishop Becket', in *Belief and Culture*, 297.

4 Life of Godric, 237.

5 Duggan, *Becket*, 26–7, 34. See also, Barlow, *Becket*, 72, 82–3.

6 MTB iii, 252–3; Barlow, *Becket*, 84.

7 Ibid., 42.

8 *Gesta Abbatum S. Albani*, i, 150–1.

9 Duggan, 'Henry II, the English Church and the Papacy', in *Henry II*, ed. Harper-Bill and Vincent, 161–9.

10 *Letters and Charters of Gilbert Foliot*, no. 148, pp. 193–4.

11 D.J.A. Matthew, 'The letter-writing of Archbishop Becket', in *Belief and Culture*, 293.

12 EHD 1042–1189, 719–20.

13 Cartulary of Castle Acre (BL Harl. 2110), fo 112v, cf. EEA 1, no. 93, pp. 63–4.

14 EHD 1042–1189, 719–20.

15 MTB iii, 44.

16 Excellent on this issue is Duggan, *Thomas Becket*, 48–58, cf. Charles Duggan in the *Bull. Inst. Hist. Research* 35 (1962), 1–28.

17 PRS 8 Henry II, 1161–2, p. 40.

18 H. Mayr-Harting, 'Henry II and the Papacy, 1170–1189', esp. 39, 41–2.

19 Ibid., 40.

20 Duggan, *Becket*, 50–4.

21 EHR 51 (1936), 215–36.

22 MTB iii, 42–3. For Henry's capacity suddenly to drop his friends, see, e.g., Vincent, 'The Court of Henry II', 316.

23 *Gesta Abbatum S. Albani*, i, 163.

24 Richard Vaughan, *Matthew Paris*, 182–3.

25 EHD 1042–1189, 750–1; on Robert de Broc, Barlow, *Becket*, 125.

26 Knowles in his *Historian and Character* (1963), 121.

27 Ibid., 127.

28 Southern, *St Anselm and His Biographer*, c. 4; Brett, *English Church under Henry I*, 35–40.

29 For example, *Correspondence of Thomas Becket*, i, no. 93, pp. 374, 378; no. 96, pp. 434–6; no. 109 (*Multiplicem*), pp. 512, 524, 532–4.

30 Morey and Brooke, *Gilbert Foliot and His Letters*, 174–7.

31 Ibid., 59–69; Smalley, *Becket Conflict*, 168–78 and generally cc. 3–7.

32 *Correspondence of Thomas Becket*, i, no. 95, pp. 394–5.

33 Matthew, as in note 11 above, 291–2.

34 Knowles, *Episcopal Colleagues*, 171–80, esp. 180; Morey and Brooke, *Gilbert Foliot and His Letters*, 166–87.

35 Morey and Brooke, *Gilbert Foliot and His Letters*, 160.

36 Barlow, *Becket*, e.g. 54, 235.

37 William FitzStephen, in MTB iii, 104–6; Barlow, *Becket*, 208.

38 Barlow, *Becket*, 25.

39 Julian Haseldine, 'Thomas Becket: Martyr, Saint – and Friend?, *Belief and Culture*, as in note 11 above, esp. 309–17.

40 Timothy Reuter, 'Symbolic acts in the Becket dispute', 178–97. In general on ruler ritual and the 'rules of play' in public communication in the medieval empire, see Gerd Althoff, *Die Macht der Rituale* (2003), c. 4, and *Spielregeln der Politik* (1997), esp. 229–57. For uses of anger by kings, Jolliffe, *Angevin Kingship*, c. 4.

41 William FitzStephen, MTB iii, 50; Reuter, as in note above.

42 Barlow, *Becket*, 98.

43 Reuter, 'Symbolic acts', esp. 182.

44 Jennifer O'Reillly, 'The double martyrdom of Thomas Becket: hagiography or history', *Studies in Medieval and Renaissance History*, 7 (1985), esp. 218–24.

45 *Correspondence of Thomas Becket*, no. 74, pp. 292–3, and ibid., note 1.

46 *Letters of John of Salisbury*, no. 168, pp. 110–13.

47 A.L. Poole, *Domesday Book to Magna Carta* (1951), 198.

48 Z.N. Brooke, *English Church and Papacy*, 193.

49 Smalley, *Becket Conflict and the Schools*, c. 5.

50 Ibid., 113.

51 Ibid., 114.

52 Ibid., 117.

53 Ibid., 115.

54 Knowles, *Historian and Character*, 100.

55 Ibid., 113–14.

56 Herbert of Bosham, MTB iii, 41; Barlow, *Becket*, 219.

57 O'Reilly, as in note 44 above, 189–97; Binski, *Becket's Crown*, 7–9.

58 Cited by O'Reilly, 197.

59 Ibid., 198.

60 Powicke, *Stephen Langton*, 58, 60–2, 144–5; Baldwin, *Masters, Princes and Merchants*, 146–7, 181, 256–7.

61 Smalley, *The Becket Conflict*, 20, 30.

62 O'Reilly, as in note 44 above, 199.

63 Morey, *Bartholomew of Exeter*, Part I, c. 2, and Part II, c. 1.

64 Knowles, *Episcopal Colleagues*, 30, 104–5.

65 R.W. Hunt, 'English learning in the late twelfth century', in *Essays in Medieval History*, ed. R.W. Southern (1968), 118.

66 Southern, *St Anselm and his Biographer*, 77–121.

67 Gervase of Canterbury, i, 171.

68 *Magistri Petri Lombardi Sententiae* 2 vols (Grottaferrata, 1971), Book I.

69 Stella Panayotova, 'Tutorial in images of Thomas Becket', 77–86.

70 Smalley, *Becket Conflict*, 135–7.

Chapter 5

1 Redfield, *Peasant Society and Culture*, esp. c. 3, pp. 42, 45–6, 52.

2 Life of Wulfric, c. 36, p. 53.

3 Redfield, *Peasant Society*, 49.

4 Gerald of Wales, *Gemma Ecclesiastica*, I, 35, pp. 109–10.

5 Ibid., 107.

6 Isidore of Seville, *Etymologies*, ed. W.M. Lindsay (1911, many reprints), VII, v, 17, and XI, iii.

7 Watkins, *History and the Supernatural*, esp. c. 1, but the whole book is important.

8 Benedicta Ward, 'Miracles and history', in *Famulus Christi*, ed. Gerald Bonner (1976), 71.

9 William of Malmesbury, *Gesta Regum*, no. 225, p. 410.

10 Thomson, *William of Malmesbury*, 23–4.

11 Blair, *The Church in Anglo-Saxon Society*, 510.

12 Ibid., 368–74.

13 Ibid., 397–401, 498–504; Reynolds, *Kingdoms and Communities*, 92–3.

14 Blair, 370.

15 Reynolds, *Kingdoms and Communities*, 87–90; Introduction, *Minsters and Parish Churches*, ed. John Blair (1988), 8–9; Blair, *Church in Anglo-Saxon Society*, 498–504.

16 Bartlett, *England under the Norman and Angevin Kings*, 214–15.

17 Doris M. Stenton, *English Justice 1066–1215* (1965), 168.

18 *Stubbs' Charters*, 9th edn, ed. H.W.C. Davis (1913), 252.

19 Glanvill, *Tractatus de Legibus*, ed. G.D.G. Hall, 30, 167.

20 Gerald of Wales, *Gemma Ecclesiastica*, I, 48, pp. 126–9.

21 Life of Wulfric, c. 36, p. 53; Mayr-Harting, 'Functions of a twelfth century recluse', 344.

22 D.M. Stenton, *English Justice* (as in note 17 above), 170–1 (the whole case, with English translation, 148–211).

23 Bartlett, *England*, 489.

24 *Jocelin of Brakelond*, 33; Greenway and Sayers, 30.

25 *Rotuli de Dominabus*, ed. J.H. Round, PRS 35 (1913); A.L. Poole, *Obligations of Society*, 100–1.

26 Warren, *Henry II*, 335–42; Donald Sutherland, *The Assize of Novel Disseisin* (1973), esp. cc. 1 and 2.

27 Glanvill, *Tractatus de Legibus*, 167–8.

28 R.C. Van Caenegem, *Royal Writs from the Conquest to Glanvill*, Selden Society 77 (1959), 261–316, esp. 284–7.

29 Sutherland, as in note 26 above, esp. 47–50; Milsom, *The Framework of English Feudalism*, esp. 11–25; Brand, 'Milsom and After', 212–16, 222–4.

30 Glanvill, *Tractatus de Legibus*, 168–9; and see Sutherland, 51.

31 For example, *Jocelin of Brakelond*, 131; Greenway et al. (eds), *Tradition and Change*, 116.

32 Van Caenegem, as in note 28 above, esp. 294–7.

33 Jolliffe, *Angevin Kingship*, cc. 11 and 12.

34 *Facscmiles of Early Charters from Northamptonshire Collections*, ed. F.M. Stenton, Northants Record Society 4 (1930), 97, 136.

35 For example, from the Pipe Roll of 1160 (PRS 2, 1884), the Count of Flanders and Richard de Lucy in Oxon, p. 8; Robert de Dunstanville in Wilts, p. 17; Robert FitzHarding in Bedminster, Somerset, p. 57. Also Emilie Amt, *the Accession of Henry II in England* (1993), esp. 157–67.

36 On Henry II and Ireland, Warren, *Henry II*, 187–206; Marie Therese Flanagan, *Irish Society, Anglo-Norman Settlers, Angevin Kingship* (1989), on Strongbow, c. 4.

37 Warren, *Henry II*, 108–36.

38 R.A. Brown, 'Royal castles, 1154–1216', EHR 74 (1959).

39 Jolliffe, *Angevin Kingship*, cc. 3–4, esp. 96–7; examples in Warren, *Henry II*, 366, 387.

40 *Gesta Henrici II*, i, 60–2; William of Canterbury, MTB i, 487; Diceto, i, 378; Warren, *Henry II*, 130–1.

41 *Gesta Henrici II*, I, 68. These two incidents are mentioned in passing by Warren, *Henry II*, 131, 134.

42 Ralph of Diceto, i, 379.

43 William of Newburgh, i, 183–9.

44 Ibid., 183–5.

45 Peter Brown, 'The rise and function of the Holy Man in late antiquity' (1971), reprinted in his *Society and the Holy* (1982), 103–52, esp. 118–21.

46 *The Letters of Arnulph of Lisieux*, ed. Frank Barlow, Camden 3rd Series 61 (1939), pp. xi–lxvi.

47 *Historia Pontificalis of John of Salisbury*, ed. and trans. Marjorie Chibnall (1956), 55–6.

48 *Letters of Arnulph*, xxxi–xlvii; Barlow, *Thomas Becket*, e.g. 96, 133, 189–90.

49 *Letters of Arnulph*, no. 42, esp. p. 74.

50 Herbert of Bosham, MTB iii, 478.

51 Bartlett, *England*, 465.

52 EEA 20, York 1154–81, nos 122–3, pp. 136–7.

53 *Book of St Gilbert*, 18–21.

54 Mayr-Harting, 'Functions of a twelfth-century recluse', 349.

55 *Life and Miracles of St William of Norwich*, 228.

56 Walter Map, *Courtiers' Trifles*, ii, 30, pp. 206–7.

57 William of Canterbury, MTB i, 486.

58 Quoted in Sussex VCH, ii, 5.

59 EEA 10, nos 115–34, pp. 87–100, and listed in no. 218, pp. 165–7.

60 Lennard, *Rural England*, 329–30.

61 John of Salisbury could have thought of himself in this way (Letters, i, pp. xii–xix). His letter, in Archbishop Theobald's name (ibid., no. 98) seems to be about a royal clerk promised some benefices in the diocese of Worcester (1158–60). John approved of uncorrupt clerics involved in secular government, thinking of Samuel as both priest and *quasi* itinerant justice (*Policraticus*, V, 16, ed. Wells, i, 357–8).

62 Mansi, Concilia 21, col. 285.

63 Also in Scotland from at least the 1190s, N.F. Shead, 'The administration of the diocese of Glasgow in the twelfth and thirteenth centuries', *Scottish Historical Review* 55 (1976), esp. 129–30.

64 EEA 24, no. 27, pp. 24–5.

65 *Llandaff Episcopal Charters*, no. 34, pp. 32–3.

66 c. 32, EHD, 1189–1327, 658.

67 Howden, iv, cc. 10 and 5, pp. 134, 131–2.

68 Chichester Acta, no. 137, pp. 188–9.

69 Howden iv, 131–2, Hubert Walter's Council of 1200, c. 6.

70 Simon Townley, 'Unbeneficed Clergy in the Thirteenth Century', 60.

71 Morey, *Bartholomew of Exeter*, 80–1.

72 Brett, *The English Church under Henry I*, 212–14; Brian Kemp, 'Acta of English Rural Deans', *Studies Presented to David Smith*, ed. Philippa Hoskin et al. (2005), e.g. 140, 151.

73 Kemp, 'Miracles of the Hand of St James', 11–12.

74 William of Canterbury, MTB i, 307.

75 Bartlett, *England*, 451–4.

76 C and S I, Part 2 (1066–1204), pp. 1070–1.

77 Morey and Brooke, *Gilbert Foliot and his Letters* 212–16.

78 For example, places like Huntingdon or Dunstable. See also Orme, *English Schools*, 64–5.

79 John of Salisbury, *Policraticus*, ed. C.C.J. Webb (1909) ii, 28, vol. 1, p. 164, 474a, ll. 14–21; Clanchy, *From Memory to Written Record*, 192–97.

80 EEA 24, Durham 1153–95, no. 26, pp. 22–3.

81 Henry Mayr-Harting, *The Venerable Bede, The Rule of St Benedict, and Social Class* (1977), 15.

82 EEA 1, and my review in *Lincolnshire History and Archaeology* 16 (1981), 51.

83 For example, Peter des Roches, see EEA 9, Winchester 1205–38, esp. pp. xxxi–iii, lvi–lix.

84 C.N.L. Brooke, 'Gregorian Reform in action: clerical marriage in England, 1050–1200', *Cambridge Historical Journal* 12 (1956), 1–21.

85 Julia Barrow, 'Hereford bishops and married clergy, c. 1130–1240', *Historical Research* 60 (1987), 1–8, esp. 7. And for the advancing formalization of marriage already in C12, Jean Scammell, 'Freedom and marriage in medieval England', *Economic History Review* 27 (1974), 523–37.

86 Life of Wulfric, pp. xxviii–xxxiii, with references to the text.

87 *Walter Daniel's Life of Ailred*, ed. F.M. Powicke, pp. xxxiv–xxxix; Aelred Squire, *Aelred of Rievaulx* (1969), 8–12.

88 *Letters and Charters of Gilbert Foliot*, no. 86, p. 121.

89 R.I. Moore, *The First European Revolution, c. 970–1215*, 5–6, for the nub of the book's argument.

90 R.W. Southern, 'Lanfranc of Bec and Berengar of Tours', *Studies in Medieval History pres. to F.M. Powicke* (1948), 27–48 (still a good short introduction).

91 Bartlett, *England*, 385.

92 *Anselmi Opera* iii, ed. F.S. Schmitt, 182–3.

93 Henrietta Leyser, *Hermits and the New Monasticism* (1984), most explicitly, e.g. 3–5, 21–2, 45–6, 49–51 (*re* women's vocations), 61, and c. 9.

94 *Policraticus*, trans. Cary J. Nederman (1990), 166–8, 201.

95 Ruth Mellinkoff, *The Horned Moses* (California, 1970), 1–2, 77–8, 26.

96 Ibid., esp. 94–6.

97 Bartlett, *England*, 485.

98 Ibid., 485–6.

99 Gerald of Wales, *Gemma Ecclesiastica*, 331–2.

100 Life of Wulfric, c. 27, p. 45.

101 *Life and Miracles of St William of Norwich*, 201–2.

102 See below, pp. 233–4.

103 Gerald, *Gemma Ecclesiastica*, I, c. 42, ii, 118–19.

104 Ruth Nineham, *Who built Iffley Church?*, Iffley Local History Soc. 5 (2001), 24.

105 *Lay Folk's Mass Book*, pp. xli–li, 4, 24, 28.

106 See below, p. 128.

107 Christine Appel, *Gervase of Chichester*, 129, 145.

108 Frances Ramsey, 'Robert of Lewes, Bishop of Bath', *Belief and Culture*, 251–63; and EEA 10, Bath and Wells 1061–1205, pp. lxii–lxiii.

109 EEA 10, no. 48, pp. 37–8.

110 Chichester Acta, no. 28, p. 93.

111 Julia Barrow, 'Cathedrals, provosts and prebends', 536–64; and her 'Education and the recruitment of cathedral canons in England and Germany 1100–1225', *Viator* 20 (1989), esp. 132–3, 135.

112 See below, p. 169.

113 EEA 20, York 1154–81, no. 132, pp. 148–9.

114 *The Priory of Hexham*, ed. James Raine, *Surtees Society* 44 (1864), 49–50, 191–2.

115 Ibid., lvi–vii.

116 Morey, *Bartholomew of Exeter*, c. 6.

117 Life of Wulfric, c. 11, pp. 24–5.

118 Clanchy, *England and its Rulers*, 177–8.

119 C.N.L. Brooke, in a *History of St Paul's Cathedral*, eds W.R. Matthews and W.M. Atkins (1957), 25–6.

120 Barrow, 'Education and Recruitment', as in note 111 above, 131.

121 Teresa Webber, *Scribes and Scholars at Salisbury Cathedral*, cc. 2 and 4.

122 Ibid., c. 5.

123 Ibid., 116–23.

124 Ibid., 122, 129.

125 Ibid., 131.

126 For example, Ramsey, 'Robert of Lewes', as in note 108 above, 254, 257, 258.

127 Appel, *Gervase of Chichester* (as in note 107 above), 129–30, from Royal Ms. 3 B.X. fos. 86v–87r.

128 Chichester Acta, no. 58, pp. 116–18.

129 Ibid., nos 76–8, pp. 134–41.

Chapter 6

1 *Jocelin of Brakelond*, 23; Greenway and Sayers, *Tradition and Change*, 21.

2 Howden iii, 210 (1193).

3 For example, Hill, *English Cistercian Monasteries*, 35–6.

4 *Opera S. Bernardi*, vii, 345–6, Ep. 144, trans. Bruno Scott James (1945), no. 146.

5 Especially Jean Scammell, 'Formation of English social structure: freedom, knights, and gentry, 1066–1300', *Speculum* 68 (1993).

6 J.R. Maddicott, 'Magna Carta and the local community, 1215–59', esp. 26–43; Peter Coss, *Origins of the English Gentry*, c. 4.

7 Anne Polden, 'The social networks of the Buckinghamshire gentry in the thirteenth century', *Journ. Medieval Hist.* 32 (2006), esp. 376–83.

8 The point is Michael Prestwich's, in *English Politics in the Thirteenth Century*, 59–60.

9 Coss, *Origins of the English Gentry*, 44.

10 *Documents of the Baronial Movement of Reform and Rebellion, 1258–1267*, eds R.F. Treharne and I.J. Sanders (1973), 20–5, 136–57.

11 For example, Rodney Thomson, Manuscripts from St Albans Abbey 1066–1235, i (1982); N.R. Ker, *English Manuscripts in the Century after the Norman Conquest* (1960), cc. 2, 3.

12 Charles Oman, *The Gloucester Candlestick* (1958).

13 *English Romanesque Art, 1066–1200* (Arts Council, 1984), nos 490–2, p. 357.

14 Richard Gameson, *The Role of Art in the Late Anglo-Saxon Church* (1995), 118–26.

15 Southern, *St Anselm and His Biographer*, 294–5.

16 *The Letters of Osbert of Clare*, no. 7, p. 65.

17 C.N.L. Brooke, in *A History of St Paul's Cathedral*, eds W.R. Matthews and W.M. Atkins (1957), 24–26.

18 Edmund Bishop, *Liturgica Historica* (1918), c. 10.

19 EYC viii (Warenne), ed. C.T. Clay, Yorks Archaeol. Soc. 6 (1949), no. 32, pp. 84–5.

20 Francis Wormald, 'The Sherborne Chartulary', *Fritz Saxl Memorial Essays*, ed. D.J. Gordon (1957), 101–20.

21 T.A. Heslop, 'The Virgin Mary's regalia and 12th century English seals', in *The Vanishing Past: Studies pres to Christopher Hohler*, eds A. Borg and A. Martindale (1981), esp. 56–9.

22 Wally Olins, *Corporate Identity* (1989).

23 *Gesta Abbatum S. Albani*, i, 107.

24 Ibid., 83–7; and *The St Alban's Psalter*, ed. Otto Pächt et al. (1960), 172–7.

25 *Jocelin of Brakelond*, 71–2, 76–7, 131, 133, 29; Greenway and Sayers, *Tradition and Change*, 63–4, 68, 116, 27.

26 Henry Mayr-Harting, 'The reception of the Bible in twelfth-century English prayer', in *Essays in Honour of Henry Wansbrough*, ed. Philip McCosker (2006), 175–9.

27 *The Kaledar of Abbot Samson*, ed. R.H.C. Davis, Camden Series 84 (1954), pp. li–vii.

28 Vaughan, *Matthew Paris*, 182–3.

29 *Jocelin of Brakelond*, 11; Greenway and Sayers, *Tradition and Change*, 11.

30 Matthew, *Norman Conquest*, 202, 204.

31 D.W. Rollason, *The Mildrith Legend* (1982), 58–68; and *Saints and Relics* (1989), 229–30.

32 For William's *Gesta Pontificum*, see Select Bibliography.

33 For example, MTB ii, 125–6; ibid., 48–9; MTB i, 289; *Life of St William of Norwich*, 154–5; ibid., 228.

34 For example, *Miracles of St Frideswide*, c. 97, p. 586; MTB ii, 96, 97, and Life of Godric c. 202, p. 454.

35 MTB ii, 240.

36 See below, pp. 161–2.

37 MTB ii, 253.

38 Peter Brown, 'Rise and function of the Holy Man', 113.

39 Life of Godric, c. 112, p. 407; *Life of St William of Norwich*, 204, also 225, 227.

40 Una Maclean, *Magical Medicine* (1974), 80; Mayr-Harting, 'Functions of a twelfth-century recluse', 342.

41 Life of Godric, c. 23, p. 378.

42 *Life of St William of Norwich*, 154–5.

43 MTB ii, 125–6.

44 MTB ii, 79.

45 Keith Thomas, *Religion and the Decline of Magic* (1971), esp. 660–9. See also Peter Brown, 'Rise and function of the Holy Man' as 'an allayer of anxiety', 145.

46 Kemp, 'Miracles of the Hand of St James', nos 2, 20, 24.

47 Ibid., no. 8.

48 MTB, ii, 49.

49 MTB i, 294–5.

50 M.R. James, *Ancient Libraries of Canterbury and Dover* (1903), 55–62.

51 Benedicta Ward, *Miracles and the Medieval Mind* (1982), 96.

52 Moore, *Formation of a Persecuting Society*, 75–8.

53 MTB i, 333.

54 Yarrow, *Saints and Their Communities*, esp. 13–23.

55 Peter Brown, 'Rise and function of the Holy Man', 142.

56 Yarrow, *Saints and Their Communities*, 140–4.

57 Ibid., 144, following Moore, *Formation*, 100–1.

58 Yarrow, *Saints and Their Communities*, 147–8, 155–6.

59 Ibid., 151–2.

60 Ibid., 160–3.

61 *Life of St William of Norwich*, 129, 142–3, 91–2, 15, 159.

62 Ridyard, 'Functions of a twelfth-century recluse revisited: the case of Godric of Finchale', 240.

63 Ibid., 240, 243, 246.

64 Ibid., 244, 250.

65 Ibid., 242, 247.

66 Ibid., 249.

67 PRS 16 Henry II, p. 96.

68 Sabina Flanagan, *Hildegard of Bingen* (1989), cc. 8 and 9, and esp. 172.

69 K.J. Leyser, 'Frederick Barbarossa, Henry II and the hand of St James', EHR 90 (1975), repr. in his *Medieval Germany and Its Neighbours* (1982), c. 9.

70 Kemp, 'Miracles of the hand of St James', nos 14, 25, 26.

71 B.W. Scholz, 'The canonization of Edward the Confessor', *Speculum* 36 (1961); Ailred's *Life of Saint Edward* is translated into English by Jerome Bertram (1990). For Abbot Lawrence of Westminster's part, see Mason, *Westminster Abbey*, 52–4.

72 *Jocelin of Brakelond*, 116–17; Greenway and Sayers, *Tradition and Change*, 102–3.

73 Knowles, *The Monastic Order*, cc. 13, 14, 20; Burton, *The Monastic Order in Yorkshire*, c. 4.

74 For example, *Walter Daniel's Life of Ailred*, 12–13.

75 Leyser, *Hermits and the New Monasticism*.

76 Etienne Gilson, *The Mystical Theology of St Bernard* (1940), esp. cc. 3, 4 (pp. 101–18), 5.

77 *Walter Daniel*, 38.

78 Southern, *Western Society and the Church*, 250–61.

79 Cf. Christopher Holdsworth, 'The blessings of work: the Cistercian view', *Studies in Church History* 10 (1973), 59–76. But by 1200, no doubt for practicality's sake, John of Ford accepted the ownership of villeins.

80 Life of Wulfric, 38.

81 Williams, *The White Monks in Wales*, 23.

82 Reading Abbey Cartularies i, ed. B.R. Kemp Camden Series 31 (1986), 18, 33–5. On Reading's remarkable colletion of relics, representing a whole

conspectus of Christian culture, see Denis Bethell, 'The making of a twelfth-century relic collection', *Studies in Church History* 8, eds G.J. Cuming and Derek Baker (1971), 61–72.

83 Knowles, *Monastic Order*, 234; *Memorials of Fountains*, ed. J.R. Walbran, Surtees Society 42 (1863), 21, lines 6–10, 16, 18–25.

84 Denis Bethell, 'The Foundation of Fountains Abbey and the State of St Mary's York in 1132', *Journal of Ecclesiastical History* 17 (1966), 11–27.

85 André Wilmart, 'L'oraison pastorale de l'abbé Aelred', *Auteurs Spirituels* (1932, 1971), p. 293, ll. 84–5.

86 Ailred, *De Institutione Inclusarum, Opera Omnia*, i, 665. Further, Mayr-Harting 'Reception of the Bible' as in note 26 above, 168–75.

87 Ailred, *De Speculo Caritatis* ii, 24, *Opera Omnia*, i, 99–100; *The Mirror of Charity*, trans Geoffrey Webb and Adrian Walker (1962), 74–6.

88 *Walter Daniel*, e.g. 24–5, 30–2, 37, 51.

89 Henry Mayr-Harting, 'The idea of the Assumption of Mary in the West, 800–1200', *The Church and Mary, Studies in Church History* 39 (2004) ed. R.N. Swanson, 105 with references to earlier work.

90 C.J. Holdsworth, 'John of Ford and English Cistercian writing, 1167–1214', TRHS 11 (1961), 132.

91 Holt, *The Northerners*, c. 9; P.D.A. Harvey, 'The English inflation of 1180–1220', *Past and Present* 61 (1973), 3–30. Tyerman, *England and the Crusades*, 75–85, would somewhat play down the financial factor in the Third Crusade.

92 Sally Harvey, 'The knight and the knight's fee', *Past and Present* no. 49 (1970), 3–43.

93 There was much discussion at this time about what was 'reasonable', e.g. Holt, *Magna Carta* 1st edn, 78, 2nd ed., 92; Poole, *Obligations of Society*, 96.

94 But see Coss, *Origins of the English Gentry*, 46–59.

95 Holt, *Magna Carta*, 1st edn, 58–60, 2nd edn, 67–70.

96 EHD 1189–1327, cl. 60, p. 323.

97 R.H.C. Davis, 'The ford, the river and the city', in his *From Alfred the Great to Stephen*, 285–8.

98 Holt, *The Northerners*, 155–6, and *Magna Carta*, 2nd edn, 62–3.

99 Holt, *Magna Carta*, 1st edn, 58, 2nd edn, 68.

100 Hill, *English Cistercian Monasteries*, 64–77.

101 *Walter Daniel*, 28.

102 Golding, *Gilbert of Sempringham and the Gilbertine Order*, 147–52.

103 Gransden, *Historical Writing*, 324–5.

104 C.J. Holdsworth, 'Eleven Visions . . . Stratford Langthorne', (Essex), *Citeaux* 13 (1962), 185–204, esp. 193, 196.

105 Carl Watkins, 'Doctrine, politics and purgation . . . the Vision of Owen at St Patrick's Purgatory', *Journ. Medieval Hist.* 22 (1996), 225–36.

106 Bartlett, *England*, 610–11.

107 Gerald of Wales, *De Principis Instructione, Opera* viii, 183–6.

108 *Earliest Lincolnshire Assize Rolls, 1202–1209*, ed. D.M. Stenton, Lincs Record Soc. 22 (1926), p. 12, no. 74. Roger also had connections with the Gilbertine house at Alvingham (Lincs), *Transcripts of Charters relating to Gilbertine Houses*, ed. F.M. Stenton, Lincs Record Soc. 18 (1920), p. 106, no. 8; p. 111, no. 17. References thanks to Tim Crafter. See also J.C. Holt in EHR 69 (1955), 10, note.

109 Holt, *Magna Carta*, 1st edn, 61; 2nd edn, 73.

110 *Walter Daniel*, 42.

111 For example, Janet Burton, *Monastic Order in Yorkshire*, 208–9, 211.

112 Ailred, *De Spirituali Amicitia*, Opera i, 298–9.

113 For example, J. Leclercq, *Monks on Marriage* (New York, 1982), 44–5.

114 Mayr-Harting, 'Functions of a twelfth-century shrine: miracles of St Frideswide', 199–201.

115 *Earldom of Gloucester Charters*, ed. R.B. Patterson (1973), no. 10, p. 37. Reference thanks to Paul Hyams.

116 Hockey, *Beaulieu, King John's Abbey*, 12–13. Also Christopher Brooke's Foreword, ibid., p. xii.

117 Ralph of Coggeshall, *Chronicon*, 107–10.

118 Gerd Althoff, 'Empörung, Tränen, Zerknirschung: Emotionen in der öffentlichen Kommunikation des Mittelalters', in his *Spielregeln der Politik in Mittelalter* (Darmstadt, 1997), 258–81, esp. 265–7.

119 MV ii, 232.

120 Holt, *The Northerners*, c. 4.

121 Hockey, *Beaulieu*, 23–4; C.R. Cheney, *Pope Innocent III and England* (1976), 329–31.

122 Hockey, *Beaulieu*, 25.

123 Cheney, *Innocent III and England*, 130, 323.

124 For example, for William de Roumara and Revesby Abbey (Lincolnshire), 1141–42, Burton, *The Monastic Order in Yorkshire*, 116.

125 I rely here mainly on a brilliant lecture given by David Austin (Lampeter University) several years ago on Strata Florida at the Department of Archaeology in Oxford.

126 Davies, *The Age of Conquest*, 223.

127 Ibid., 222.

128 Ibid., 219–21.

129 Augustine, *City of God*, xix, 19 (CCSL 48, p. 686, ll, 12–14). See also Henry Chadwick, *Augustine of Hippo: A Life* (2009), 52–3.

130 *City of God*, ibid., l. 9.

131 *The Rule of St Augustine*, eds T.J. Van Bavel and R. Canning (1984), esp. 6–7.

132 Jerome Bertram, *The Chrodegang Rules* (2005), 16–22.

133 Dickinson, *Origins of the Austin Canons*, 20.

134 Cowdrey, *Pope Gregory VII*, 249–53.

135 Southern, 'Henry I' in his *Medieval Humanism*, 216–17; Brett, *The English Church under Henry I*, 138–40, where also their pastoral importance is recognized.

136 See above, p. 116. The phrase '20-minute sermons' comes not from Bartlett's book but from his Ford Lectures delivered at Oxford in 2005.

137 *Libellus de Diversis Ordinibus*, 56–69.

138 Ibid., 72–97.

139 Gerald of Wales, *Itinerarium Kambriae* I, I, p. 38; trans. Thorpe, 97–8.

140 *Life of Robert of Bethune*, cc. 19 and 25 (*humanitas*).

141 Ibid., c. 25 and esp. c. 26.

142 Ibid., c. 5.

143 *Libellus de Diversis Ordinibus*, 72.

144 Dickinson, *Origins of the Austin Canons*, 66. For Bridlington's foundation, Burton, *Monastic Order in Yorkshire*, 69–71.

145 *Bridlington Dialogue*, 78.

146 Ibid., 81.

147 Ibid., 95–109.

148 Brian Kemp, 'Monastic Possession of Parish Churches', *Journ. of Eccl. Hist.*, 31 (1980), 145–6.

149 EYC ii, ed. W. Farrer (1915), no. 1161 p. 453; *Chartulary of Bridlington*, p. 41.

150 There being no mention of a vicarage in the Taxation of Pope Nicholas IV in 1291, *Taxatio*, p. 304a.

151 *Dorchester Abbey*, ed. Kate Tiller (2005), 29–30 (map, 30).

152 Dickinson, *Origins of the Austin Canons*, 120, 291.

153 VCH Yorks, East Riding, ii, 332–3.

154 VCH Yorks, East riding, vii, 100; EYC iii, ed. W. Farrer (1916), no. 1306, pp. 34–5; *Chartulary of Bridlington*, 327–44.

155 *Bridlington Dialogue*, 31–33.

156 Ibid., 33.

157 Dickinson, *Origins*, 219.

158 EEA V, York 1070–1154, no. 46, pp. 42–3.

159 *Chartulary of Bridlington*, 436–7.

160 Brian Kemp, 'Acta of English Rural Deans', as in chapter 5, note 72, above, no. 19, p. 156.

161 *Taxatio*, pp. 303–4.

162 Hugh Thomas, *Vassals, Heiresses, Crusaders and Thugs: Gentry of Angevin Yorkshire*, 27–40, citation p. 40.

163 *Chartulary of Bridlington*. In this whole discussion I am much influenced by John Nightingale, *Monasteries and Patrons in the Gorze Reform* (2001), and his discussion of the relation of aristocratic society to monasteries in tenth-century Lotharingia.

164 Hugh Thomas, as in note 162 above, pp. 63–85, 151.

165 EYC ii, no. 1229, p. 501; cf. ibid., no. 1136, p. 429.

166 EYC iii, no. 1356, pp. 72–3.

167 Cf. Nightingale, as in note 163 above.

168 John Blair, 'Clerical Communities and Parochial Space', in *The Church in the Medieval Town*, eds T.R. Slater and G. Rosser (1998), 272–94, esp. 280–2.

169 Taxation of Pope Nicholas IV, *Taxatio*, p. 30.

170 *Miracles of St Frideswide*, nos 31, 25.

171 Ibid., no. 110.

172 Mayr-Harting, 'Miracles of St Frideswide', esp. 199–201, 203; and cf. Peter Brown, *The Cult of Saints* (Chicago, 1981), 44.

173 Yarrow, *Saints and their Communities*, 187.

174 *Miracles of St Frideswide*, no. 106.

175 Gerald of Wales, *Itinerarium Kambriae* I, 3, pp. 39–40; trans. Thorpe, 99.

176 Reynolds, *English Medieval Towns*, 104–5; Moore, *Origins of European Dissent*, 63–6.

177 Henrietta Leyser, *Medieval Women*, c. 9, here, 189, also 81–2.

178 E.g. Golding, *Gilbert*, 101–11; Thompson, Women Religious, 213–16.

179 Ibid., 190.

180 Elkins, *Holy Women*, 52, 47.

181 For example, Thompson, *Women Religious*, 25.

182 Elkins, *Holy Women*, 46–54.

183 Ibid., 67.

184 Ibid., 66–7.

185 Gilchrist, *Gender and Material Culture*, 101–3, 113–15, 126, 153–5, 163–7.

186 Ibid., 91.

187 Ibid., 50; cited by Leyser, *Medieval Women*, 203.

188 Bartlett, *England*, 436.

189 Elkins, 68.

190 R.B. Dobson and Sara Donaghey, *History of Clementhorpe Priory* (1984), 9–20.

191 Poole, *Obligations of Society*, 101–2.

192 Leyser, *Medieval Women*, 202.

Chapter 7

1 Clanchy, *England and Its Rulers*, 117.

2 Carpenter, *Struggle for Mastery*, 44.

3 *Gesta Henrici II*, i, 160.

4 Jolliffe, *Angevin Kingship*, 146–9.

5 Paul Brand, *The Origins of the English Legal Profession* (1992), c. 4; John Maddicott, *Law and Lordship: Royal Justices as Retainers*, Past and Present Supplement, no. 4, 1978.

6 For example, *Epistolae Cantuarienses*, ed. W. Stubbs RS, (1865), 109, 110.

7 EEA 26, pp. lxxxvii–xc.

8 Cheney, *From Becket to Langton*, 22.

9 Henry Mayr-Harting, *The Bishops of Chichester 1075–1207: Biographical Notes and Problems* (1963), 14–16.

10 Peltzer, *Canon Law, Careers and Conquest*, esp. c. 5; Barrow, as in chapter 5 above, and c. 5, note 111.

11 See *Henry II: New Interpretations*: Duggan, 'Henry II, the English Church and the Papacy, 1154–76', 180–1; Vincent, 'The Court of Henry II', 294–5.

12 Cheney, *Hubert Walter*, 36–7. For an example in many ways similar to Hubert see on William of Saint-Mère Eglise, Bishop of London, in Ralph V. Turner, *Men Raised from the Dust*, (1988) c. 2.

13 Tyerman, *England and the Crusades*, 64.

14 John Gillingham, *Richard Coeur de Lion: Kingship, Chivalry and War in the Twelfth Century* (1994), esp. cc. 2, 3, 5, 6, 10 and 11; and for the quotation, Gillingham, *Richard the Lionheart* (1978), 287.

15 R.F. Hunnisett, 'The Origins of the Office of Coroner', TRHS 5th Ser. 8 (1958), 88–104.

16 *Stubbs Charters*, 9th edn, ed. H.W.C. Davis (1913), 249–50, 255.

17 Bartlett, *England under the Norman and Angevin Kings*, 260–1.

18 *Poetria Nova of Geoffrey of Vinsauf*, trans. Margaret F. Nims (Toronto, 1967), 11–12.

19 PRS 1198 (NS, 9, 1932), 181; PRS 1199 (NS, 10, 1933), 242; PRS 1197 (NS, 8, 1931), 15, shows that he must have gone there in 1196 or early 1197.

20 Cheney, *Hubert Walter*, 100.

21 Ibid., 120–3.

22 Howden, *Chronica*, iv, 12–13.

23 Christopher Tyerman, *Who's Who in Early Medieval England* (1996), 267.

24 Howden, iv, 6.

25 Cheney, *Hubert Walter*, 94.

26 Ralph of Diceto, *Imagines Historiarum*, ii, p. lxxix.

27 Howden, iv, 6; cf. Gervase of Canterbury, i, 532–3.

28 Howden, ibid.; Gervase of Canterbury, i, 534.

29 See a number of Henry II's writs in *Register of St Benet of Holme*, ed. J.R. West, I (Norfolk Record Society 2 (1932), 10–28, esp. p. 19, no. 28 about the return to the abbot's land of fugitives who had fled in Stephen's time. Other similar writs can be found elsewhere.

30 Howden, iii, 299.

31 Hyams, *Rancor and Reconciliation*, 194.

32 Ibid., 95, 195–6, 135.

33 Cheney, *Hubert Walter*, 51.

34 Ibid., 179–81.

35 Ibid., 66–7.

36 Binski, *Becket's Crown*, 36.

37 Ibid., 40–1.

38 Ibid., 37–8.

39 Tyerman, *Who's Who*, 232; and Mayr-Harting, 'Henry II and the papacy', 43–4, 50–1.

40 MV i, 94.

41 Henrietta Leyser, 'Hugh the Carthusian', in Mayr-Harting ed., *St Hugh of Lincoln*, esp. 4–5.

42 MV i, 39, 76.

43 Henrietta Leyser, 'Hugh the Carthusian', 13–14.

44 Ibid., 17.

45 ODNB on Hugh of Lincoln, 292.

46 MV i, 70–2.

47 MV i, 72.

48 Ibid., i, p. x.

49 Ibid., 77–9.

50 Ibid., 93.

51 Ibid., 92–6.

52 Ibid., 124.

53 MV ii, 29.

54 ODNB on Hugh of Lincoln, 293.

55 Peter Brown, 'The rise and function of the Holy Man', 103–52, esp. 130–7.

56 Leyser, 'The Angevin kings and the Holy Man', in Mayr-Harting (ed.), *St Hugh of Lincoln*, esp. 51; MV i, 62–3, and 94, where his accent (*loquela*) is commented on.

57 Karl Leyser, ibid., 57–8.

58 MV i, 113–19.

59 MV ii, 98–100; Howden, iv, 40.

60 Leyser, 'The Angevin kings and the Holy Man', 61–4.

61 MV ii, 24.

62 Ibid., 13, 20, 48.

63 MV ii, 17, 228.

64 MV ii, 44–5.

65 EEA IV, nos 100, 106, 107.

66 MV i, 120.

67 Ibid.

68 MV i, 110–13.

69 MV ii, 156.

70 Goering, *William de Montibus (c. 1140–1213)*, 11–12.

71 For example, MV ii, 118–19.

72 Baldwin, *Masters, Princes and Merchants*, i, 50.

73 MV ii, 95.

74 Baldwin, *Masters, Princes and Merchants*, i, 326–7, ii, 219.

75 MV ii, 38, 112, 142–3.

76 Baldwin, *Masters*, i, 181–2.

77 Leyser, 'The Angevin kings and the Holy Man', 52.

78 MV ii, 46.

79 d'Avray, *Medieval Marriage*, 14.

80 Christopher Brooke, *The Medieval Idea of Marriage*, 126.

81 Ibid., 137–8.

82 Ibid., 148–52.

83 EHD ii (1046–1189), 456–7.

84 For medieval discussion of indissolubility, see the magisterial chapter 2 of d'Avray, *Medieval Marriage*.

85 Baldwin, *Masters*, i, 332–7.

86 EHD iii (1189–1327), 665–6.

87 Kenneth Pennington, 'The Legal Education of Pope Innocent III', *Bulletin of Medieval Canon Law*, 4 (1974), 70–7. Morris, *Papal Monarchy*, 418.

88 EEA IV, no. 40A.

89 Ibid., p. 206, no. 39.

90 On this part-exclusion, see, for instance, R.W. Southern, 'The church of the Dark Ages', in *The Layman in Christian History*, eds Stephen Neill and H.-R. Weber (1963), esp. 93, 103.

91 MV ii, 105.

92 For example, MV ii, 167–8.

93 Howden iv, 128–35. Here mentioned are c. 1, pp. 128–9; cc. 5 and 8, pp. 130–1, 133; c. 11, p. 135.

94 Karl Leyser, 'The Angevin Kings and the Holy Man', 72.

95 Ibid., 59.

96 MV ii, 101.

Chapter 8

1 C.H. Haskins, *Studies in the History of Medieval Science* (1927), c. 15, and esp. p. 328.

2 Judith Green, *The Government of England under Henry I*, 41, 139, 166, 169, 171, 196, 197, 199, 201, 237. A similar figure was Geoffrey de Clinton, R.W. Southern, 'King Henry I', in his *Medieval Humanism* 211–17.

3 *Dialogue of the Exchequer*, ed. C. Johnson (1950), 15, and e.g. 85.

4 Haskins, as in note 1, 113–17, cited in translation in Southern, *Medieval Humanism*, 166–7.

5 Southern, ibid., p. 167, n. 2.

6 *Pipe Roll of 31 Henry I*, ed. Joseph Hunter (1833, repr. 1929), 22; Haskins, 34.

7 Margaret Gibson, 'Adelard of Bath', in *Adelard of Bath*, ed. Charles Burnett (1987), 7–9.

8 Alison Drew, in *Adelard*, ed. Burnett, 17–24.

9 Haskins, 38, 40.

10 R.N. Swanson, *The Twelfth-Century Renaissance* (1999), 50–4; De Lacy O'Leary, *How Greek Science Passed to the Arabs* (1980).

11 Later examples were Robert of Ketton/Chester; and Daniel of Morley, who came to study mathematics in Toledo, where he heard that his subject was better taught in Northampton! At that time in the 1170s a John, clerk of the Queen of Spain, was being paid by Henry II to teach there. Henry's daughter, Eleanor, was betrothed to Alfonso VIII of Castille in 1170, R.W. Hunt, 'English learning in the late twelfth century', TRHS 1936, 23–4. And for John, see above, chapter 1, note 10.

12 Haskins, 25; Menso Folkerts, 'Adelard's Versions of Euclid's *Elements*, *Adelard*, ed. Burnett, 55–65.

13 Haskins, 22–3; Gibson, in *Adelard*, ed. Burnett, 13–15; Raymond Mercier, 'Astronomical tables in the twelfth century' in *Adelard*, ed. Burnett, 88–9.

14 Haskins, 28–9; Gibson, 'Adelard', 15–16.

15 Haskins, 37, 40–1.

16 Quoted in *The 'Disciplina Clericalis' of Petrus Alfonsi*, trans. and ed. Eberhard Hermes, and trans. into English, P.R. Quarrie (1977), 59.

17 Mercier, as in note 13, 95–6.

18 Oxford, Bodleian Library, Ms. Auct. F. 1.9; Mercier, 102; Haskins, 114.

19 J.C. Holt, *Magna Carta*, 2nd edn, esp. cc. 3 and 4.

20 *Gesta Stephani* (1976), R.H.C. Davis on its authorship, pp. xviii–xl.

21 Bartlett, *England under the Norman and Angevin Kings*, 620.

22 *Gesta Stephani*, 22–3.

23 David Crouch, *The Reign of King Stephen* (2000), 101.

24 One need only open almost any index of authors in the volumes of the Corpus of British Medieval Library Catalogues (British Academy/British Library) to see this.

25 Beryl Smalley, 'Sallust in the Middle Ages', *Classical Influences*, ed. R.R. Bolgar (1971), 172; and eadem, *Historians in the Middle Ages* (1974), 19–20, 46.

26 Rodney Thomson, *William of Malmesbury* (1987) 29, 58.

27 William of Malmesbury, *Historia Novella* 16, 18, 22–3.

28 Henry of Huntingdon, *Historia Anglorum*, 718–21; 742–3; 748–9; *Gesta Stephani*, 76–7, 80–1; 160–3; 196–7.

29 William of Malmesbury, HN, 20.

30 As in note 28, *Historia Anglorum*, 718–21; *Gesta Stephani*, 74–79.

31 *EHD, 1042–1189*, 405–6.

32 R.W. Southern, title esay, in his *Medieval Humanism*, c. 4.

33 David Knowles, 'The humanism of the twelfth century' in his *Historian and Character*, c. 2.

34 Adolf Katzenellenbogen, *The Sculptural Programs of Chartres Cathedral* (1959), 43–4.

35 *EHD, 1042–1189*, 279–80.

36 Henry of Huntingdon, *Hist. Angl.*, 728–31; William of Malmesbury, HN, 48–9.

37 William of Malmesbury, ibid. Similar to some of this and following paragraphs, the discussion in Donald Matthew, *King Stephen* (2002) c. 3

38 Geoffrey of Monmouth, *History of the Kings of Britain*, 229, ll. 4–6.

39 Ibid., 224–5.

40 Ibid., 225–30.

41 See R.H.C. Davis's critique of such in his *King Stephen* (1967), 129–32.
    Crouch, *Stephen*, 84–90, takes the view that earls had military and
    administrative functions in their shires, but does imply that patronage
    and reward were also part of such promotions, ibid., 87.

42 Geoffrey of Monmouth, 229–30.

43 Maurice Keen, *Chivalry* (1984), 85, and c. 5 generally.

44 William of Malmesbury, HN, 49.

45 Orderic, vi, 542.

46 David Crouch, *The Beaumont Twins* (1986), 15.

47 Keen, *Chivalry*, 87.

48 St Bernard Letter 376, PL 182, col. 581; trans. Bruno Scott James, *The
    Letters of St Bernard of Clairvaux* (1953), no. 405, p. 476. For St Bernard's
    condemnation of tournaments generally, E. Vacandard, *Vie de Saint
    Bernard* i (Paris 1920), 249–52.

49 A.G. Rigg, *A History of Anglo-Norman Literature, 1066–1422*, 41–4.

50 Clanchy, *England and Its Rulers*, 177–8, excellent on Hereford; Julia
    Barrow, 'William de Vere', *Viator* 18 (1987), 186–7; R.W. Southern, *Robert
    Grosseteste* (1986), esp. c. 5. On Exeter, Adrian Morey, *Bartholomew of
    Exeter* (1937), c. 6.

51 For example, PRS 21 (20 Henry II, 1173–4), 135; PRS 27 (24 Henry II,
    1177–8), 112 (*esnecca*).

52 H.G. Richardson, 'The schools of Northampton in the twelfth century',
    EHR 56 (1941), 595–605.

53 R.W. Southern, 'From schools to university', *The History of the University of
    Oxford*, i, ed. J.I. Catto (1984), c. 1.

54 D.E. Luscombe, *The School of Peter Abelard* (1969), 5–9. Abelard tells us
    himself how successful he was in attracting students in his autobiographical
    Historia Calamitatum, trans. J.T. Muckle (1964) or in the Penguin Classics.
    There was clearly a market for teaching in the arts and theology amongst the
    sons of the demographically rising knightly classes, i.e. people like Abelard
    himself.

55 Printed in *Cartularium Prioratus de Gyseburne*, ed. W. Brown,
    Surtees Soc. 89 (1891) ii, 81–3; and Chichester Acta, no. 130 (1965),
    pp. 123–5.

56 EEA 20 (York 1154–81), p. xlviii, and numbers as given ibid., note 13.

57 For much of this section, see Henry Mayr-Harting, 'The role of Benedictine
    abbeys in the development of Oxford as a centre of legal learning', in
    Benedictines in Oxford, ed. Henry Wansbrough and Anthony Marett-Crosby

(1997), 11–19, 279–80. For Mr Geoffrey de Lardaria, ibid., 17–18, and for the references to the Bruern charters witnessed by him, ibid., p. 280, note 20.

58 Southern, 'From schools to university', 14–16, and 16, note 2.

59 Ibid., 10, and 10, note 4.

60 EEA 20 (York 1159–81), pp. xxxviii–xl.

61 *The Chronicle of Battle Abbey*, ed. and trans. Eleanor Searle (1980), 322–5.

62 Eleanor Rathbone, 'John of Cornwall: a brief biography', *Recherches de Théologie Ancienne et Médiévale* 17 (1950), 46–60.

63 Cambridge, Gonville and Cauis College, Ms. 676 of fo. 196 rb; Stephan Kuttner and Eleanor Rathbone, 'Anglo-Norman canonists of the twelfth century', *Traditio* 7 (1949–51), esp. 317–21, and for the text, Rathbone, 'John of Cornwall', 51. On consummation, David d'Avray *Medieval Marriage* (2005), c. 4. For John of Tynemouth, Kuttner and Rathbone, 317–25.

64 Diarmaid MacCulloch, 'The Reformation, 1500–1650', in *Christianity: Two Thousand Years*, eds R. Harries and H. Mayr-Harting (2001), 134–5. The phrase 'big idea', was written by me here before the General Election campaign of 2010!

65 Ernst Kantorowicz, *The King's Two Bodies*, cc. 3 and 4.

66 J.C. Holt, *Magna Carta* (2nd edn, 1992), cc. 3 and 4.

67 F.M. Powicke, *Stephen Langton* (1928, 1965), cc. 2 and 3.

68 Holt, *Magna Carta*, 268–70, 280–7.

69 Jane Sayers, *Innocent III*, 17–23; Morris, *The Papal Monarchy*, 418.

70 David d'Avray, 'Magna Carta: its background in Stephen Langton's biblical exegesis', *Studi Medievali*, 3rd Ser. 38 (1997), esp. p. 427.

71 R.W. and A.J. Carlyle, *History of Medieval Political Theory in the West*, v (1929, repr. 1971), esp. pp. 165–75; Morris, *The Papal Monarchy*, 433.

72 Stella Panayotova, 'Art and politics in a royal prayerbook', *Bodleian Library Record*, 18, no. 5 (April, 2005), 440–59, esp. 449–54.

73 Alan Coates, *English Medieval Books: the Reading Abbey Collections*, 119.

74 *The Book of St Gilbert*, pp. lxii–iii, lxxi–ii.

75 Ibid., 8–9.

76 Ibid., 70–3.

77 Powicke, *Stephen Langton*, 58.

78 EHD, 1189–1327, pp. 669–70.

79 Eric Kemp, *Canonization and Authority in the Western Church* (1948), 104–5.

80 Baldwin, *Masters, Princes and Merchants*, i, 13.

81 Ibid., i, 14; d'Avray, *The Preaching of the Friars*, esp. 66–70.

82 Eva Matthews Sanford, 'Giraldus Cambrensis' debt to Petrus Cantor', *Medievalia et Humanistica* 3 (1945), 16–32, esp. 19. I owe my knowledge of this article to the kindness of Christine Appel.

83 *Gemma Ecclesiastica* II, c. 34, pp. 331–2.

84 A.L. Poole, *Domesday Book to Magna Carta* (1951), 224–5.

85 Sanford, as in note 82, esp. 25–8.

86 Binski, *Becket's Crown*, 31, 45.

87 Ibid., 65–73.

88 Ibid., 69.

89 Ibid., 70–2.

90 Simon Lloyd, *English Society and the Crusade, 1216–1307*, 66.

91 Sayers, *Innocent III*, 177–8.

92 Tyerman, *England and the Crusades*, 163–4; Lloyd, 62–5.

93 Lloyd, 66.

94 R.W. Hunt, *The Schools and the Cloister: the Life and Writings of Alexander Nequam (1157–1217)* (1984). Paris, 5; Peter the Chanter, 100–2; teaching at Oxford in the 1190s, 7–8; scientist, 66–83.

95 C.H. Lawrence, *St Edmund of Abingdon* (1960), 118–24; Lloyd, 62–3.

96 *John of Salisbury, Policraticus*, ed. C.C.J. Webb (1909), esp. Books 4 and 5, i, pp. 234–368, sections 513a–588b. Trans. Cary J. Nederman (1990), pp. 27–102.

97 *The Book of St Gilbert*, e.g. 289, 305, 317, 273, 285 (Gilbert's niece), 297, 323, 277, 317.

98 R.R. Davies, *The First English Empire*, 116.

99 *Giraldi Cambrensis Descriptio Kambriae*, Opera vi, ed. James F. Dimock (RS, 1868) e.g. I, c. 15, p. 192; I, c. 17, p. 200; I, c. 8, p. 179 (also II, c. 10, p. 226). Trans. by Lewis Thorpe (1978, 2004), pp. 245, 251, 233 (and 274).

100 Ibid., I, c. 18, pp. 202–3, trans. 253–4.

101 Robert Bartlett, *Gerald of Wales, 1146–1223*, 179–80. Tacitus was little if at all known in C12, and Sallust was not enough in himself.

102 English translation in *The Mission to Asia*, ed. Christopher Dawson (1955, 1980), 3–72.

103 Gerald, *Descriptio Kambriae*, as in note 99 above, Book II, Preface, p. 205; translation, p. 255, though 'as a serious historian' is not a satisfactory translation of *more historico*.

Chapter 9

1 Brooke, *The Image of St Francis*, cc. 1 and 2.

2 II Celano, ii, 42. The Latin texts of Celano's *Lives* are printed in *Analecta Franciscana* X (1926–41), 1–331. There are various translations into English. My citations, apart from being to chapters, are of that of A.G. Ferrers Howell (1908), here pp. 214–15.

3 Roger D. Sorrell, *St Francis of Assisi and Nature* (1988): wolf, p. 20; fish, p. 95. Sorrell rightly relates Francis to long-standing traditions of Christian asceticism.

4 I Celano, c. 21, p. 58.

5 Morris, *The Papal Monarchy*, 444.

6 Of many possible examples, see EEA 18 (Salisbury, 1078–1217), nos 154, 179, 181, 232.

7 Howden, iv, 5.

8 Edward Miller, 'England in the twelfth and thirteenth centuries: an economic contrast?', *Econ. Hist. Review* 24 (1971), 1–14.

9 Paul Hyams, *Kings, Lords, and Peasants in Medieval England* (1980), 52, 53, 76, 149 note 109; and at p. 76 note 43, following M.T. Clanchy.

10 Miller and Hatcher, *Medieval England: Rural Society and Economic Change, 1086–1348*, c. 6, esp. p. 149; c. 3, esp. p. 71.

11 Wolf, *The Poverty of Riches*, c. 1, esp. pp. 14–15; I Celano, cc. 7, 15, pp. 18, 40.

12 Wolf, *The Poverty of Riches*, p. 28.

13 Christopher Brooke, 'St Dominic and his first biographer', TRHS 17 (1967), repr. in his *Medieval Church and Society: Collected Essays* (1971), c. 11.

14 J.R.H. Moorman, *Sources for the Life of St Francis* (1940), 22; II Celano, c. 62, p. 204.

15 Brooke, *Image of St Francis*, 322–3.

16 Rosalind Brooke, *Early Franciscan Government* (1959), I, c. 3. Malcolm Lambert on how *Quo Elongati* blocked the way back to poverty as lived by Francis and the Companions, *Franciscan Poverty* (1961), 83.

17 Brooke, *Image of St Francis*, citing Francis's *Testament*, 323.

18 Ibid., 91–4.

19 II Celano, c. 28, p. 201.

20 *S. Bonaventurae Opera Omnia*, VIII (1898), esp. p. 272, 1–3, and p. 274, 7. See also Gordon Leff, *Paris and Oxford Universities* (1968), 265–7.

21 Brooke, *Image of St Francis*, 246–7.

22 For the disputes over professorships, see Leff, *Oxford and Paris Universities*, 39–40. For extensions of sites, *De Adventu*, c. 10, pp. 44–5, trans. 62. In his *Testament*, Francis had approved of manual labour while also being committed to begging, Rosalind Brooke, *The Coming of the Friars* (1975), 118.

23 The implication of his *De Adventu Fratrum Minorum in Angliam*, c. 13, p. 74, trans. E. Gurney Salter, 88–9. See further, Brooke, *Early Franciscan Government*, 267–8.

24 *De Adventu*, c. 15, p. 98, trans. 120.

25 Ibid., p. xxiv, with references to the text.

26 Knowles, *Religious Orders in England*, i, 139–43.

27 D'Avray, *The Preaching of the Friars* (1985), esp. 66–70.

28 David Lamb, 'Service, image and leadership: the first century of the Franciscan settlement in the West Midlands', *Midland History* 27 (2002), 16–37.

29 *De Adventu*, c. 4, p. 22, trans. 31.

30 Ibid., c. 6, p. 27, trans. 38. This presumably at least includes the early Oxford friars. Also c. 3, p. 13, trans. 18; c. 10, p. 44, trans. 61.

31 Ibid., c. 3, p. 12, trans. 17.

32 Ibid., c. 7, p. 35, trans. 49–50.

33 Ibid., c. 11, p. 49, trans. 67.

34 Ibid., c. 10, p. 46, trans. 63–4.

35 Ibid., c.14, p. 86, trans. 104. For Haymo generally, see Brooke, *Early Franciscan Government*, 195–209.

36 Brooke, *Early Franciscan Government*, esp. 151–2, 170; and for resentments against Elias, ibid., 154–61.

37 *De Adventu Fratrum Minorum*, c. 13, p. 68, trans. 80–1.

38 Martial Rose and Julia Hedgecoe, *Stories in Stone* (1997), 124.

39 Alexander Murray, 'Confession before 1215', TRHS (1992), 51–81, esp. 76–9.

40 Masterly discussion of this theme *re* seventeenth-century England in Keith
   Thomas, *Religion and the Decline of Magic* (1971), c. 4, and see above, c. 6,
   note 45.

41 Giles Constable, 'The Second Crusade as seen by contemporaries', *Traditio* 9
   (1953), esp. 248–52.

42 Adrian Morey, *Bartholomew of Exeter*, 108.

43 Ibid., 195, 215; also, 172–3.

44 Joseph Goering, *William de Montibus, c. 1140–1213: The Schools and the
   Literature of Pastoral Care* (1972), 179–210.

45 J.W. Baldwin, *Masters, Princes and Merchants*, i, 34–6.

46 Joseph Goering and Huw Pryce, 'The *De Modo Confitendi* of Cadwgan,
   Bishop of Bangor', *Medieval Studies* 62 (2000), 1–27.

47 Ibid., p. 6.

48 A. Wilmart, 'Un opuscule sur la confession composé par Guy de Southwick
   vers la fin du XIIᵉ siècle', *Recherches de Théol. Ancienne et Médiévale* 7
   (1935), 337–52. For the interesting and widely connected William de Vere,
   Julia Barrow, 'A twelfth-century bishop and literary patron: William de
   Vere', *Viator* 18 (1987), 175–89; and for Guy of Southwick's connection to
   him, ibid., 185.

49 *Robert of Flamborough, Liber Poenitentialis*, ed. J.J. Francis Firth (1971),
   esp. pp. 10–20.

50 Morey, *Bartholomew*, pp. 164–5, nos 2, 6, 8, 10. For the Leicester
   manuscript, *The Libraries of the Augustinian Canons*, eds T. Webber and
   A.G. Watson (Corpus of British Medieval Library Catalogues 6, 1998), A20,
   337 d and e. The Leicester catalogue is fifteenth century, but the binding
   together of the two works is likely to have been early thirteenth century.

51 Morey, Bartholomew, 164–6.

52 *Life and Miracles of St William of Norwich*, I, 8, and II, 7, pp. 30, 84.

53 EHD, 1189–1327, c. 6, p. 648.

54 Ibid., c. 11, p. 651.

55 N.R. Ker (ed.), *Medieval Libraries of Great Britain: a List of Surviving Books*
   (2nd edn, 1964), 51, 246. From the 1220s the rich prebend of West Wittering
   in Chichester Cathedral was appropriated to the theology lectureship.

56 EHD, 1189–1327, c. 21, pp. 654–5.

57 C and S ii, 72.

58 Barbara H. Rosenwein and Lester K. Little, 'Social meaning in the monastic
   and mendicant spiritualities', *Past and Present* 63 (1974), 23.

59 Ibid., 23–4.

60 C and S ii, 706.

61 Moorman, *Church Life in England in the Thirteenth Century*, 391–2.

62 For example, C and S ii, 133, 595, 706.

63 Ibid., 265.

64 Ibid., 1088, c. 38.

65 Moorman, *Church Life*, 391; Murray, 'Confession as a historical source in the thirteenth century', 285.

66 Murray, 'Confession as a historical source in the thirteenth century', 282–4.

67 Anthony Kenny, *A Path from Rome: an Autobiography* (1985), 155–6.

68 C and S ii, 268, c. 1.

69 Ibid., 304, c. 34; 345; 610, c. 43.

70 David d'Avray, *Medieval Marriage Sermons* (2001), esp. 9–15.

71 Ibid., p. 9.

72 C and S ii, 455, c. 23.

73 David Jones, *Saint Richard of Chichester* (Sussex Record Society 79, 1995), 6, 18, 67 (many bequests to the friars in his will), 76, 163, 181.

74 For example, in England, Thomas of Eccleston's *De Adventu Fratrum Minorum*, c. 5, p. 26; trans. of EGS, 35–6.

75 Jones, *Saint Richard of Chichester*, 105, 181.

76 Beryl Smalley, 'The Gospels in the Paris Schools', *Franciscan Studies*, 39 (1979), esp. 232–49.

77 David d'Avray, *Preaching of the Friars* (1985), 217–22, esp. 218.

78 Ibid., 220.

79 W. Chester Jordan, *Louis IX and the Challenge of the Crusade* (1979), 55–64.

80 G.-A. Bezzola, 'Orient et Extrême-Orient', *Le Siècle de Saint Louis*, ed. Regine Pernoud (1970), 230–7; J. Richard, 'La Politique Orientale de Saint Louis', in *Septième Centenaire de la Mort de Saint Louis*, ed. Louis Carolus-Barré (1976), 197–207.

81 *The Mission of Friar William of Rubruck*, ed. Peter Jackson, Hakluyt Society no. 173 (1990).

82 Louis Carolus-Barré, 'La Grand Ordonnance de 1254', *Septième Centenaire de la Mort de Saint Louis*, ed. Louis Carolus-Barré (1976), 85–96.

83 Jean Favier, 'Les Finances de Saint Louis', ibid., 133–40, esp. 140.

84 M.-M. Dufeil 'Le Roi Louis dans la querelle des mendiants et des séculiers', ibid., 281–9.

85 Derived from a lecture of Miss Hurnard, heard by the author in 1956.

86 Paul Binski, *The Painted Chamber at Westminster* (1986), 42–4.

87 Nicholas Vincent, 'King Henry III and the Blessed Virgin Mary', *The Church and Mary*, ed. R.N. Swanson, *Studies in Church History* 39 (2004), esp. 133–9.

88 Vincent, *Holy Blood* (2001), 36.

89 Robert Branner, *Saint Louis and the Court Style* (London, 1965), 124–26.

90 Vincent, *Holy Blood*, cc. 2, 3, 5 and 7.

91 H.W. Ridgeway, 'Ecclesiastical Career of Aymer de Lusignan', *The Cloister and the World: Essays in Medieval History in Honour of Barbara Harvey*, eds John Blair and Brian Golding (1996), 148–77.

92 Michael Prestwich, *English Politics in the Thirteenth Century* (1990), c. 5, for an admirably balanced discussion.

93 Maddicott, *Simon de Montfort*, 79–93.

94 *Letters of Adam Marsh, Monumenta Franciscana* i, ed. J.S. Brewer (RS 4, 1858), no. 143, p. 275.

95 Maddicott, *Simon de Montfort*, 84–5.

96 *Letters of Adam Marsh*, Ep. 136, pp. 262–3.

97 Maddicott, 38–9, 86–7.

98 *Letters of Adam Marsh*, Ep. 140, pp. 266–8.

99 Maddicott, 254.

100 Ibid., 279.

101 *The Song of Lewes*, ed. C.L.Kingsford (1890), esp. ll. 485–786.

102 Ibid., pp. 105–6, 109–10, 114–15, 118–19, 132–3; and for Bracton, pp. 138–9.

103 Ibid., pp. 110–11, 119.

104 Quoted ibid., p. 138, n. 3, from the *Letters of Adam Marsh*, Ep. 25, p. 110.

105 J.I. Catto, 'Theology and theologians 1220–1320', *History of the University of Oxford*, i: *The Early Oxford Schools*, ed. J.I. Catto, 471–517, the quotation at 471.

106 For example, Peter Raedts, *Richard Rufus of Cornwall* (1987), 79–81.

107 Ibid., 61, 247, and c. 3.

108 Southern, *Robert Grosseteste*, 179.

109 Ibid., quoted from Grosseteste's *Dictum*, 216–17.

110 Raedts, *Richard Rufus*, 180; and for the whole contrast between Grosseteste and Rufus, cc. 6–7.

111 Raedts, 160.

112 Ibid., 199.

113 Ibid., 169; and W.A. Pantin, *The English Church in the Fourteenth Century* (1955), 136–40.

114 Robert Bartlett, *Gerald of Wales* (1982), 138–40, and in general, c. 5.

115 Bendicta Ward, 'Miracles and history', *Famulus Christi*, ed. Gerald Bonner (1976), 71; and see her *Miracles and the Medieval Mind* (1982), 8–9.

116 *Aquinas: Selected Political Writings*, ed. A.P.D'Entrèves (1959), 10–13 (c. 2), 50–1, 78–9 (c. 15).

117 See Walter Ullmann, *Principles of Government and Politics in the Middle Ages* (1961), 152–4; E.H. Kantorowicz, *The King's Two Bodies* (1957), 152.

118 EHD, 1189–1327, pp. 323–4.

119 J.C. Holt, *Magna Carta* (1965, 1st edn), 48; (2nd edn, 1992), 56; also Christopher Brooke, *London, 800–1216* (1975), 51.

120 Good discussion of the *maior et sanior pars* in Jörg Peltzer, *Canon Law, Careers and Conquest: Episcopal Elections in Normandy and Greater Anjou c. 1140–1230* (2008), 38–48.

121 See especially Roger Highfield's introduction to *The Early Rolls of Merton College Oxford*, ed. J.R.L. Highfield (1964), 1–78 (on advowsons, 43–6). Also J.R.L. Highfield, 'The early colleges', in *Hist. Univ. Oxford*, i, ed. J.I. Catto, c. 6; and G.H. Martin and J.R.L. Highfield, *A History of Merton College* (1997) cc. 1 and 2.

Chapter 10

1 *Letters and Charters of Cardinal Guala*, pp. xli–lxvi.

2 Lawrence, 'Thirteenth century', 131.

3 *Letters and Charters of Cardinal Guala*, pp. lxxxi–iii.

4 Carpenter, *The Struggle for Mastery*, 345–47; Maddicott, *Simon de Montfort*, 128–9.

5 Lawrence, 'Thirteenth century', 138; and for legates, Robinson, *Papacy*, 146–78.

6 Lawrence, 'Thirteenth Century', 125–6.

7 Ibid., 125.

8 EHD, 1189–1327, p. 734.

9 *Letters and Charters of Cardinal Guala*, p. lxxiii.

10 F.M. Powicke, *The Thirteenth Century* (1953), 45–6.

11 *Letters and Charters of Cardinal Guala*, pp. xlvii–l; Adrian Hastings, *Elias of Dereham* (1997), 9–10.

12 Lawrence, 'Thirteenth Century', 146.

13 E.F. Jacob, 'St Richard of Chichester', *Journ. of Eccl. Hist.* 7 (1956), 180–2; Jones, *Saint Richard of Chichester*, 13–14, 95–8, trans. 172–4.

14 Southern, *Grosseteste*, 267–9.

15 Jacob, 'St Richard', 181.

16 Watt, *Medieval Church Councils in Scotland*, 19–29.

17 Ibid., 29, 44; Barrow, *Kingdom of the Scots*, 133.

18 Watt, 37–8.

19 Ibid., 42.

20 Ibid., 48–9.

21 Ibid., 72.

22 Ibid., 59–60.

23 W.A. Pantin, 'Grosseteste's Relations with the Papacy and the Crown', in *Robert Grosseteste*, ed. D.A. Callus (1955), esp. 184–95.

24 Southern, *Grosseteste*, 277, note 7, for the MS source of the text.

25 Ibid., 276–81, and on deciduous trees, 161–3.

26 Ibid., 216–19, 275–9, 284.

27 Townley, 'Unbeneficed clergy in the thirteenth century', 48–58.

28 Ibid., 49.

29 Ibid., 53.

30 *Register of St Osmund*, ed. W.H. Rich Jones, i (RS, 1883), 304–7.

31 Excellent summary account of Henry III's style of kingship in Clanchy, *England and Its Rulers*, 222–30.

32 C.H. Lawrence in ODNB (2004), vol. 9, 959–61. For the 'Paper Constitution' of 1244, Carpenter, *Struggle for Mastery*, 358–9.

33 ODNB, 9, 960–1.

34 Brentano, *Two Churches: England and Italy in the Thirteenth Century*, esp. 204–13.

35 C and S, II, i, 309, 320.

36 Vincent, *Peter des Roches*, esp. cc. 1, 5, 10, 13.

37 C and S, II, i, 243–4; and see c. 13 of the 1237 Council, ibid., 251.

38 Miri Rubin, *Corpus Christi* (1991), 166–76.

39 Rubin, 'What did the Eucharist mean to thirteenth-century villagers?' 50–1.

40 Ibid., 52.

41 Ibid., 53–4.

42 Baldwin, *Masters, Princes and Merchants*, i, 34–6.

43 Le Goff, *Birth of Purgatory*, 220, 222.

44 Watkins, *History and the Supernatural*, 191–92.

45 Le Goff, *Birth of Purgatory*, esp. 168.

46 Ibid., 242–5.

47 Caroline Walker Bynum, *The Resurrection of the Body* (1995), esp. 281.

48 Ibid., 282–3; also Le Goff, 229, and for the fire of purgatory, Le Goff, 254.

49 Chichester Acta, pp. 62–70.

50 For example, ibid., p. 64, n. 4.

51 EHD, 1189–1327, p. 658, c. 32.

52 Matthew Paris, *Chron. Maiora*, iv, 38–43.

53 For example, Philippa Hoskin, 'Diocesan politics in the see of Worcester', esp. 430–6.

54 EHD, 1189–1327, pp. 651–2.

55 *Chapters of the English Black Monks, 1215–1540*, ed. W.A. Pantin, i (Camden Series 45, 1931), 44, 55, 64, 74.

56 Alan Coates, *English Medieval Books: The Reading Abbey Collections*, 76–8.

57 Ibid., 72–4.

58 Ibid., 72, 75–6, 157, nos. 67, 162, no. 97 (where the *Song* is in interesting company!).

59 Corpus of Brit. Medieval Library Catalogues, 4. *English Benedictine Libraries*, ed. R. Sharpe, et al. (1996), p. 202; Corpus etc., 8, *Peterborough Abbey*, ed. K. Friis-Jensen and James Willoughby (2201), pp. 117–18; Rodney Thomson, *Manuscripts from St Alban's Abbey* (1982), i, pp. 64, 111.

60 Knowles, *Religions Orders* i, 112. Also C.R. Cheney, *Episcopal Visitation of Monasteries in the Thirteenth Century* (1931), though this is about procedure and legal disputes concerning visitation, rather than about the findings.

61 Henry Mayr-Harting, 'The foundation of Peterhouse, Cambridge (1284), and the Rule of St Benedict', EHR 103 (1988), 318–38.

62 Knowles, *Religious Orders* i, c. 7.

63 Ibid., 67.

64 André Wilmart, 'Méditations d'Etienne de Salley', 317–20.

65 *Stephen of Sawley, Treatises*, 83–122.

66 Wilmart, 'Méditations', 324.

67 Nicholas Vincent, 'King Henry III and the Blessed Virgin Mary', *The Church and Mary*, ed. R.N. Swanson, *Studies in Church History* 39 (2004), 126–46.

68 See plate 8 of this book, and Walter Oakeshott, *The Sequence of English Medieval Art* (1950), Plate 6 and p. 21. For similar tenderness, see also the thirteenth-century wall-painting of the Visitation at Chester Castle, pictured on the front cover of Caroline Babington, et al., *Our Painted Past* (English Heritage, 1999).

69 Wilmart, 'Meditations', 339. I have used my own translations, but the work is well translated, as in n. 65 above.

70 Ibid., 343.

71 Ibid., 344, 345.

72 Ibid., 351, line 452, cf. 341, ll. 66–7.

73 Anne Winston, 'Tracing the origins of the Rosary: German vernacular texts', *Speculum* 68 (1993), 621.

74 *Stephen of Sawley, Treaties*, 125–84.

75 Winston, as in note 73, 619.

76 Hagen Keller, 'Ordnungsvorstellungen, Erfahrungshorizonte und Welterfassung im kulturellen Wandel des 12/13 Jahrhunderts', p. 14.

Select Bibliography

Note: a number of the books and sources and many of the articles cited in the end notes have not been repeated in this select bibliography. Three or four works, not cited in the notes, which have influenced me, are included here.

Primary sources

Ailred of Rievaulx, *Opera Omnia*, eds A. Hoste and C.H. Talbot, CCCM 1 (1971).

Aquinas: Selected Political Writings, ed. A.P. D'Entrèves (1959).

Bartholomew of Farne, *Vita Bartholomei Farnensis*, by Geoffrey of Coldingham, in *Symeonis Monachi Opera Omnia*, ed. Thomas Arnold, RS75 (1882), i, 295–325.

Benedict of Peterborough, *Miracula S. Thomae*, MTB ii, 21–281.

The Book of St Gilbert, eds Raymonde Foreville and Gillian Keir (1987).

The Bridlington Dialogue: An Exposition of the Rule of St Augustine for the Life of the Clergy, ed. and trans. A Religious of C.S.M.V. (A.R. Mowbray & Co. 1960).

Brooke, Rosalind, *The Coming of the Friars* (1975).

I and II Celano: Lives of St Francis by Thomas of Celano, printed in *Analecta Franciscana* 10 (1926–41), 1–331. Translation, e.g. by A.G. Ferrers Howell (1908).

Chartulary of Bridlington, ed. W.T. Lancaster (Leeds, 1912).

Chichester Acta: *The Acta of the Bishops of Chichester 1075–1207*, ed. H. Mayr-Harting, Canterbury and York Society no. 130 (1965).

Chronicle of Battle Abbey, ed. and trans. Eleanor Searle (1980).

Correspondence of Thomas Becket, Archbishop of Canterbury, 1162–1170, ed. Anne Duggan, 2 vols (2000).

De Adventu, see Thomas of Eccleston.

The Dialogue of the Exchequer, ed. and trans. Charles Johnson (1950).

The Disciplina Clericalis of Petrus Alfonsi, trans. P.R. Quarrie (1977).

Eadmer, *Historia Novorum*, ed. M. Rule, RS81 (1884).

EEA, see abbreviations.

EHD, see abbreviations.

Geoffrey of Monmouth, *History of the Kings of Britain*, trans. Lewis Thorpe (1966).

Gerald of Wales, *Gemma Ecclesiastica*, ed. J.S. Brewer, *Giraldi Cambrensis Opera* ii RS 21 (1862).

Gerald of Wales, *Itinerarium Kambriae* and *Descriptio Kambriae Giraldi Cambrensis Opera*, vi, ed. J.F. Dimock, RS 21 (1868).

Gervase of Canterbury, *Opera Historica*, ed. W. Stubbs, RS 73, i (1879).

Gesta Abbatum S. Albani, ed. H.T. Riley, i RS 28/4, (1867).

Gesta Henrici Secundi, ed. W. Stubbs, 2 vols RS 49 (1867).

Gesta Stephani, eds K.R. Potter and R.H.C. Davis (1976).

Gilbert of Sempringham, see *The Book of St Gilbert*.

Glanvill, *Tractatus de Legibus et Consuetudinibus Anglie*, ed. and trans. G.D.G. Hall (1965).

Goering, Joseph, and Pryce, Huw, 'The *De Modo Confitendi* of Cadwgan, Bishop of Bangor', *Medieval Studies* 62 (2000), 1–27.

Henry of Huntingdon, *Historia Anglorum*, ed. and trans. Diana Greenway (1996).

Herbert of Bosham, *Vita S. Thomae*, MTB iii, 155–534.

History of the Church of Abingdon, ed. John Hudson (2002).

Howden: *Chronica Magistri Rogeri de Hovedene*, 4 vols, ed. W. Stubbs, RS 51 (1868–71).

Hugh the Chantor, *History of the Church of York, 1066–1127*, ed. Charles Johnson (1961).

Jocelin of Brakelond, Chronicle of, ed. H.E. Butler (1949); trans. Diana Greenway and Jane Sayers, Oxford World Classics (1989).

John of Salisbury, see Letters of.

John of Salisbury, *Policraticus*, ed. C.C.J. Webb, 2 vols (1909); translation of parts, Cary J. Nederman (1990).

Kemp, Brian, 'The Miracles of the Hand of St James', trans. with introduction, *Berkshire Archaeological Journal* 65 (1970), 1–19.

Lay Folk's Mass Book, ed. Thomas F. Simmons, EETS 71 (1879, repr. 1968).

Letters of Adam Marsh, Monumenta Franciscana i, ed. J.S. Brewer RS4 (1858).

The Letters and Charters of Cardinal Guala Bicchieri, Papal Legate in England 1216–1218, ed. Nicholas Vincent, Canterbury and York Society 83 (1996).

Letters and Charters of Gilbert Foliot, eds Adrian Morey and C.N.L. Brooke (1967).

Letters of John of Salisbury, i, eds W.J. Millor and H.E. Butler, revised by C.N.L. Brooke (1955); ii, eds W.J. Millor and C.N.L. Brooke (1979).

The Letters of Lanfranc, Archbishop of Canterbury, eds and trans. Helen Clover and Margaret Gibson (1979).

The Letters of Osbert of Clare, Prior of Westminster, ed. E.W. Williamson (1929).

Libellus de Diversis Ordinibus et Professionibus qui sunt in Aecclesia, eds and trans. G. Constable and B. Smith (1972).

Liber Eliensis, ed. E.O. Blake CS 92 (1962).

Life of Christina of Markyate, A Twelfth Century Recluse, ed. and trans., C.H. Talbot (1959).

Life of Godric: *Vita et Miracula Godrici Hermitae de Finchale auct. Reginaldo Monacho Dunelmensi*, ed. J. Stevenson, Surtees Society 20 (1847).

The Life of Robert of Bethune by William of Wycombe, ed. and trans., B.J. Parkinson (Unpublished Oxford B.Litt. thesis, 1952). The text was published by Henry Wharton in his *Anglia Sacra* ii (London, 1691), 293–321, minus the miracle narratives, of which Wharton disapproved!

Life of Robert of Knaresborough, ed. Joyce Bazire, EETS 228 (1953).

The Life and Miracles of St William of Norwich, eds A. Jessop and M.R. James (1896).

Life of Wulfric, *Wulfric of Haselbury*, John of Ford, ed. Maurice Bell, *Somerset Record Society* 47 (1933).

Llandaff Episcopal Acta 1140–1287, ed. David Crouch (1989).

Matthew Paris, *Chronica Maiora*, ed. H.R. Luard, 7 vols, RS 57 (1872–84).

Miracles of St Frideswide, Acta Sanctorum, October, viii, 567–89.

MV, see abbreviations.

Orderic Vitalis: *The Ecclesiastical History of Orderic Vitalis*, ed. and trans. Marjorie Chibnall, 6 vols (1969–80).

The Ormulum, with the notes and glossary of Dr R.M. White, ed. Robert Holt, 2 vols (Oxford, 1878).

Ralph of Coggeshall, *Chronicon Anglicanum*, ed. J. Stevenson, RS 66 (1875).

Ralph of Diceto (Diss), *Imagines Historiarum*, ed. W. Stubbs, 2 vols, RS 68 (1876).

Records of the Templars in England in the Twelfth Century, ed. Beatrice A. Lees (1935).

The Register of Pope Gregory VII, 1073–1085, An English Translation, ed. H.E.J. Cowdrey (2002).

Register of St Osmund, ed. W.H. Rich Jones, 2 vols (RS, 1883, 1884).

The Song of Lewes, ed. C.L. Kingsford (1890).

Stephen of Sawley, Treatises, eds and trans. Jeremiah O'Sullivan and Bede Lackner, Cistercian Fathers Series 36 (Kalamazoo, Michigan, 1984).

Symeon of Durham, *Libellus de Exordio Dunhelmensis Ecclesiae*, ed. and trans. David Rollason (2000).

Taxatio Ecclesiastica of Pope Nicholas I, 1291, eds S. Ayscough and J. Caley (London, 1802).

Thomas of Eccleston, *De Adventu Fratrum Minorum in Angliam*, ed. A.G. Little (1951). Trans. by E. Gurney Salter, *The Coming of the Friars Minor* (1926).

Vision of Thurkill: *Visio Thurkilli, relatore, ut videtur, Radulpho de Coggeshall*, ed. Paul Gerhard Schmidt (Leipzig, 1978).

Walter Daniel's Life of Ailred of Rievaulx, ed. F.M. Powicke (1950).

Walter Map, *De Nugis Curialium (Courtiers' Trifles)*, ed. and trans. M.R. James, revised by C.N.L. Brooke and R.A.B. Mynors (1983).

William of Canterbury, *Vita S. Thomae*, MTB i, 1–136; *Miracula S. Thomae*, i, 137–546.

William FitzStephen, *Vita S. Thomae*, MTB iii, 1–154.

William of Malmesbury, *Gesta Pontificum Anglorum*, i (text and translation), ed. M. Winterbottom (2007).

William of Malmesbury, *Gesta Regum Anglorum*, i, eds and trans. R.A.B. Mynors, R.M. Thomson, M. Winterbottom (1998); ii, ed. R.M. Thomson, General Introduction and Commentary (1999).

William of Malmesbury, *Historia Novella*, ed. and trans. K.R. Potter (1955).

William of Newburgh, *Historia Rerum Anglicarum*, in *Chronicles of the Reigns of Stephen, Henry II, and Richard I*, i, ed. Richard Howlett RS 82 (1884).

Wilmart, André 'Les Méditations d'Étienne de Salley (i.e. Sawley) sur les Joies de la Vierge Marie, in his *Auteurs Spirituels et Textes Dévots du Moyen Age Latin* (Paris, 1932, 1971).

William of Norwich, see *The Life and Miracles of St William of Norwich*.

Books and articles

Adelard of Bath, ed. Charles Burnett (1987).

Appel, Christine, *Gervase of Chichester and the Applied Theology of the Priesthood in Late Twelfth-Century England* (unpublished Oxford D.Phil. thesis, 1999).

Baldwin, J.W., *Masters, Princes and Merchants: The Social Views of Peter the Chanter and his Circle*, 2 vols (Princeton, 1970).

Barlow, Frank, *Thomas Becket* (1986).

Barrell, Andrew D.M., 'Scotland and the papacy in the reign of Alexander II' in *The Reign of Alexander II, 1214–49*, ed. Richard D. Oram (Leiden, 2005), 157–77.

Barrow, G.W.S., *David I of Scotland (1124–1153): the Balance of New and Old*, Stenton Lecture 1984 (Reading, 1985).

Barrow, G.W.S., *The Kingdom of the Scots: Government, Church and Society from the Eleventh to the Fourteenth Century* (2nd edn, 2003).

Bartlett, Robert, *Gerald of Wales, 1146–1223* (1982).

Bartlett, Robert, *England under the Norman and Angevin Kings, 1075–1225* (2000).

Belief and Culture in the Middle Ages: Studies Presented to Henry Mayr-Harting, eds Richard Gameson and Henrietta Leyser (2001).

Beresford, M.W., *New Towns of the Middle Ages* (1967, 1988).

Binski, Paul, *The Painted Chamber at Westminster* (1986).

Binski, Paul, *Becket's Crown: Art and Imagination in Gothic England, 1170–1300* (2004).

Bisson, Thomas, *The Crisis of the Twelfth Century* (Princeton, 2009).

Blair, John, *The Church in Anglo-Saxon Society* (2005).

Brand, Paul, *The Origins of the English Legal Profession* (1992).

Brand, Paul, 'Milsom and after', in his *The Making of the Common Law* (1992), c. 9.

Brentano, Robert, *Two Churches: England and Italy in the Thirteenth Century* (1968).

Brett, Martin, *The English Church under Henry I* (1975).

Britnell, Richard, *The Commercialization of English Society, 1000–1500* (2nd edn, 1996).

Britnell, Richard, 'The Winchester Pipe Rolls and their historians', in *The Winchester Pipe Rolls and Medieval English Society*, ed. Richard Britnell (2003).

Brooke, C.N.L., 'The earliest times to 1485', in *A History of St Paul's Cathedral*, eds W.R. Matthews and W.M. Atkins (1957), 1–99.

Brooke, Christopher, 'The archdeacon and the Norman Conquest', *Tradition and Change: Essays in Honour of Marjorie Chibnall*, eds Diana Greenway, Christopher Holdsworth and Jane Sayers (1985), 1–19.

Brooke, Christopher, *The Medieval Idea of Marriage* (1989).

Brooke, Rosalind, *Early Franciscan Government* (1959).

Brooke, Rosalind, *The Image of St Francis* (2006).

Brooke, Rosalind and Brooke, Christopher, *Popular Religion in the Middle Ages: Western Europe 1000–1300* (1984).

Brooke, Z.N., *The English Church and the Papacy from the Conquest to the Reign of John* (1931).

Brown, Peter, *The World of Late Antiquity* (1971).

Brown, Peter, 'The rise and function of the Holy Man in Late Antiquity', *Journal of Roman Studies* (1971), reprinted in his *Society and the Holy in Late Antiquity*, (1982), 103–52.

Burton, Janet, *The Monastic Order in Yorkshire, 1069–1215* (1999).

Bynum, Caroline Walker, *The Resurrection of the Body in Western Christianity, 200–1336* (New York, 1995).

Carpenter, David, *The Struggle for Mastery: The Penguin History of Britain 1066–1284* (2003, 2004).

Catto, J.I., 'Theology and theologians, 1220–1320', *History of the University of Oxford, i, The Early Oxford Schools*, ed. J.I. Catto (1984), 471–517.

Cheney, C.R., *From Becket to Langton: English Church Government, 1170–1213* (1956).

Cheney, C.R., *Hubert Walter* (1967).

Cheney, C.R., *Pope Innocent III and England* (Stuttgart, 1976).

Chibnall, Marjorie, *The World of Orderic Vitalis* (1984).

Christina of Markyate, eds Samuel Fanous and Henrietta Leyser (2005).

Clanchy, M.T., *From Memory to Written Record: England 1066–1307* (1979).

Clanchy, M.T., *England and Its Rulers, 1066–1272: Foreign Lordship and National Identity* (1983).

Coates, Alan, *English Medieval Books: the Reading Abbey Collections* (1999).

Coss, Peter, *The Origins of the English Gentry* (2003).

Cowdrey, H.E.J., *Pope Gregory VII, 1073–1085* (1998).

Cowdrey, H.E.J., *Lanfranc, Scholar, Monk and Archbishop* (2003).

Crouch, David, *The Beaumont Twins: The Roots and Branches of Power in the Twelfth Century* (1986).

Crouch, David, *The Reign of King Stephen, 1135–1154* (2000).

Davies, R.R., *The Age of Conquest: Wales 1063–1415* (1987).

Davies R.R., *Domination and Conquest: The Experience of Ireland, Scotland and Wales 1100–1300* (1990).

Davies, R.R., *The First English Empire* (2000).

Davies, R.R., 'Henry I and Wales', *Studies in Medieval History Presented to R.H.C. Davis*, eds Henry Mayr-Harting and R.I. Moore (1985), 133–47.

Davis, R.H.C., *King Stephen* (1967).

Davis, R.H.C., 'An Oxford Charter of 1191', *Oxoniensia* 33 (1968), 53–65.

Davis, R.H.C., 'The ford, the river and the city', *Oxoniensia* 38 (1973), 258–67.

Davis, R.H.C., *From Alfred the Great to Stephen* (1991).

d'Avray, David, *The Preaching of the Friars* (1985).

d'Avray, David, *Medieval Marriage Sermons* (2001).

d'Avray, David, *Medieval Marriage: Symbolism and Society* (2005).

Dickinson, J.D., *The Origins of the Austin Canons and their Introduction into England* (1950).

Duggan, Anne, *Thomas Becket* (2004).

Duggan, Anne, 'Henry II, the English Church and the papacy, 1154–76', in *Henry II: New Interpretations*, eds Christopher Harper-Bill and Nicholas Vincent (2007), 154–83.

The Early Rolls of Merton College, ed. J.R.L. Highfield (1964).

Elkins, Sharon, *Holy Women of Twelfth-Century England* (1988).

Faith, Rosamond, *The English Peasantry and the Growth of Lordship* (1997).

Favier, Jean, 'Les Finances de Saint Louis', *Septième Centenaire de la Mort de Saint Louis*, ed. Louis Carolus-Barré (Paris, 1976), 85–96.

Finucane, Ronald C., *Miracles and Pilgrims: Popular Beliefs in Medieval England* (1977).

Gibson, Margaret, *Lanfranc of Bec* (1978).

Gilchrist, Roberta, *Gender and Material Culture: The Archaeology of Religious Women* (1994).

Gillingham, John, *Richard I, The Life and Times of* (1973).

Gillingham, John, *Richard Coeur de Lion: Kingship, Chivalry and War in the Twelfth Century* (1994).

Gillingham, John, *The English in the Twelfth Century: Imperialism, National Identity and Political Values* (2000).

Goering, Joseph, *William de Montibus (c. 1140–1213): the Schools and the Literature of Pastoral Care*, Studies and Texts 108 (Toronto, 1992).

Golding, Brian, *Conquest and Colonisation: the Normans in Britain 1066–1100* (1994).

Golding, Brian, *Gilbert of Sempringham and the Gilbertine Order, c. 1130–1300* (1995).

Gransden, Antonia, *Historical Writing in England, 550 to 1307* (1974).

Green, Judith, *The Government of England under Henry I* (1986).

Green, Judith, *Henry I: King of England and Duke of Normandy* (2006).

Greenway, Diana, 'False *Institutio*' in *Tradition and Change: Essays in Honour of Marjorie Chibnall*, eds Diana Greenway, Christopher Holdsworth and Jane Sayers (1985).

Hallam, H.E., *Settlement and Society: A Study of the Early Agrarian History of South Lincolnshire* (1965).

Harvey, Barbara, *Westminster Abbey and its Estates in the Middle Ages* (1977).

Harvey, P.D.A., *Banbury*, in *Historic Towns*, ed. M.D. Lobel (1969).

Haseldine, Julian, ed., *Friendship in Medieval Europe* (1999).

Haskins, C.H., *Studies in the History of Medieval Science* (Cambridge, MA, 1927).

Henry II: New Interpretations, eds Christopher Harper Bill and Nicholas Vincent (2007).

Hill, Bennett D., *English Cistercian Monasteries and their Patrons in the Twelfth Century* (Urbana, IL, 1968).

Hockey, Frederick, *Beaulieu, King John's Abbey* (1976).

Holt, J.C., *The Northerners: A Study in the Reign of King John* (1961).

Holt, J.C., *Magna Carta* (1st edn, 1965; 2nd edn, 1992).

Hoskin, Philippa, 'Diocesan politics in the See of Worcester, 1218–1266', *Journal of Ecclesiastical History* 54 (2003), 422–40.

Hyams, Paul R., *Rancor and Reconciliation in Medieval England* (Cornell, 2003).

Jolliffe, J.E.A., *Angevin Kingship* (1955).

Jones, David, *Saint Richard of Chichester*, Sussex Record Society 79 (1995).

Kantorowicz, E.H., *The King's Two Bodies* (Princeton, 1957).

Keen, Maurice, *Chivalry* (1984).

King, Edmund, *Peterborough Abbey, 1086–1310: A Study in the Land Market* (1973).

Knowles, David, *The Monastic Order in England, 943–1216* (1940); *The Religious Orders in England* i (1962).

Knowles, David, *The Episcopal Colleagues of Archbishop Thomas Becket* (1951).

Knowles, David, *Historian and Character and Other Essays* (1963).

Lambert, M.D., *Franciscan Poverty* (1961).

Lawrence, C.H., *St Edmund of Abingdon* (1960).

Lawrence, C.H., 'The thirteenth century', in *The English Church and the Papacy in the Middle Ages*, ed. C.H. Lawrence (1965), 117–56.

Le Goff, Jacques, *The Birth of Purgatory*, trans. Arthur Goldhammer from French (1984).

Lennard, Reginald, *Rural England, 1086–1135* (1959).

Leyser, Henrietta, *Hermits and the New Monasticism* (1984).

Leyser, Henrietta, 'Hugh the Carthusian' in *St Hugh of Lincoln*, ed. Henry Mayr-Harting (1984), 1–18.

Leyser, Henrietta, *Medieval Women: A Social History of Women in England, 450–1500* (1995).

Leyser, Karl, 'The Angevin Kings and the Holy Man', in *St Hugh of Lincoln*, ed. Henry Mayr-Harting (1984), 49–74.

Lloyd, Simon, *English Society and the Crusade, 1216–1307* (1988).

Lobel, M.D. and Carus-Wilson, E.M., 'Bristol', in *Historic Towns*, ed. M.D. Lobel (1975).

Maddicott, J.R., 'Magna Carta and the local community, 1215–59', *Past and Present* no. 102 (1984), 25–65.

Maddicott, J.R., *Simon de Montfort* (1994).

Mason, Emma, *Westminster Abbey and its People, c. 1050–1216* (1996).

Matthew, D.J.A., *The Norman Conquest* (1966).

Matthew, Donald, *King Stephen* (2002).

Matthew, D.J.A., 'The letter-writing of Archbishop Becket', *Belief and Culture*, 287–304.

Mayr-Harting, Henry, 'Henry II and the papacy, 1170–1189', *Journal of Ecclesiastical History* 16 (1965), 39–53.

Mayr-Harting, Henry, 'Functions of a twelfth-century recluse' (Wulfric of Haselbury), *History* 60 (1975), 337–52; reprinted in his *Religion and Society in the Medieval West, 600–1200: Selected Papers* (2010), c. XIV.

Mayr-Harting, Henry, ed., *St Hugh of Lincoln* (1987).

Mayr-Harting, Henry, 'Functions of a twelfth-century shrine: the miracles of St Frideswide', in *Studies in Medieval History presented to R.H.C. Davis*, eds H. Mayr-Harting and R.I. Moore; reprinted in his *Religion and Society*, c. XV.

Mellinkoff, Ruth, *The Horned Moses* (1970).

Miller, E., 'England in the twelfth and thirteenth centuries: an economic contrast?', *Economic History Review* 24 (1971), 1–14.

Miller, Edward, and Hatcher, John, *Medieval England: Rural Society and Economic Change 1066–1348* (1978).

Milsom, S.F.C., *The Framework of English Feudalism* (1976).

Moore, R.I., *The Origins of European Dissent* (1977).

Moore, R.I., *Formation of a Persecuting Society* (1987).

Moore, R.I., *The First European Revolution c. 970–1215* (2000).

Moorman, J.R.H., *Church Life in England in the Thirteenth Century* (1945).

Morey, Adrian, *Bartholomew of Exeter, Bishop and Canonist: A Study in the Twelfth Century* (1937).

Morey, Adrian and Brooke, C.N.L., *Gilbert Foliot and His Letters* (1965).

Morris, Colin, *The Discovery of the Individual, 1050–1200* (1972).

Morris, Colin, *The Papal Monarchy: The Western Church from 1050–1250* (1989).

Murray, Alexander, *Reason and Society in the Middle Ages* (1978).

Murray, Alexander, 'Confession as a historical source in the thirteenth century', *The Writing of History in the Middle Ages: Essays presented to Richard William Southern*, eds R.H.C. Davis and J.M. Wallace-Hadrill (1981), 275–322.

Murray, Alexander, 'Confession before 1215', TRHS 43 (1993), 51–81.

Nicholl, David, *Thurstan Archbishop of York, 1114–1140* (1964).

Orme, Nicholas, *English Schools in the Middle Ages* (1973).

Panayotova, Stella, 'Tutorial in images of Thomas Becket', *The Cambridge Illuminations: The Conference Papers*, ed. Stella Panayotova (2006), 77–86.

Peltzer, Jörg, *Canon Law, Careers and Conquest: Episcopal Elections in Normandy and Greater Anjou, c. 1140–1230* (2008).

Prestwich, Michael, *English Politics in the Thirteenth Century* (1990).

Poole, A.L., *Obligations of Society in the Twelfth and Thirteenth Centuries* (1946).

Powicke, F.M., *Stephen Langton* (1928, 1965).

Raedts, Peter, *Richard Rufus of Cornwall and the Tradition of Oxford Theology* (1987).

Ramsey, Frances, 'Robert of Lewes, Bishop of Bath, 1136–1166: a Cluniac bishop in his diocese', in *Belief and Culture in the Middle Ages* (2001) 251–63.

Redfield, Robert, *Peasant Society and Culture* (Chicago, 1956), in *The Little Community and Peasant Society and Culture* (Chicago, 1960).

Reuter, Timothy, 'Symbolic Acts in the Becket Dispute', in his *Medieval Politics and Modern Mentalities*, ed. Janet Nelson (2006), 167–90.

Reynolds, Susan, *English Medieval Towns* (1977).

Reynolds, Susan, *Kingdoms and Communities in Western Europe, 900–1300* (1984).

Ridyard, Susan, 'Functions of a twelfth-century recluse revisited: the case of Godric of Finchale', *Belief and Culture* (2001), 236–50.

Rigg, A.G., *A History of Anglo-Norman Literature, 1066–1422* (1992).

Robinson, I.S., *Authority and Resistance in the Investiture Contest* (1978).

Robinson, I.S., *The Papacy, 1073–1198: Continuity and Innovation* (1990).

Robinson, J. Armitage, *Gilbert Crispin, Abbot of Westminster* (1911).

Roth, Cecil, *The Jews of Medieval Oxford* (1951).

Rubin, Miri, *Corpus Christi: The Eucharist in Late Medieval Culture* (1991).

Rubin, Miri, 'What did the Eucharist mean to thirteenth-century villagers?', *Thirteenth-Century England* 4 (1992), 47–55.

The St Alban's Psalter, eds Otto Pächt, C.R. Dodwell and Frances Wormald (1960).

Saltman, Avrom, *Theobald, Archbishop of Canterbury* (1956).

Sayers, Jane, *Innocent III* (1994).

Sharpe, Richard, *Norman Rule in Cumbria, 1092–1136* (2006).

Smalley, Beryl, *The Becket Conflict and the Schools: A Study of Intellectuals in Politics in the Twelfth Century* (1973).

Southern, R.W., *The Making of the Middle Ages* (1953, and many reprints since).

Southern, R.W., *St Anselm and His Biographer* (1963).

Southern, R.W., *Medieval Humanism and Other Studies* (1970).

Southern, R.W., *Western Society and the Church in the Middle Ages* (Pelican, 1970).

Southern, R.W., *Robert Grosseteste: The Growth of an English Mind in Medieval Europe* (1986).

Swanson, R.N., *The Twelfth-Century Renaissance* (1999).

Talbot, C.H. and Hammond, E.A., *The Medical Practitioners in Medieval England: A Biographical Register* (1965).

Thomas, Hugh, M., *Vassals, Heiresses, Crusaders and Thugs: The Gentry of Angevin Yorkshire, 1154–1216* (UPP, Philadelphia, 1993).

Thompson, Benjamin ed., *Monasteries and Society in Medieval Britain* (1999).

Thompson, Sally, *Women Religious: The Founding of English Nunneries after the Norman Conquest* (1991).

Thomson, Rodney, M., *Manuscripts from St Alban's Abbey, 1066–1235*, 2 vols (1982).

Thomson, Rodney, *William of Malmesbury* (1987).

Titow, J.Z., *English Rural Society 1200–1350* (1969).

Townley, Simon, 'Unbeneficed clergy in the thirteenth century', in *Studies in Clergy and Ministry*, ed. David Smith (York, 1991), 38–64.

Tyerman, Christopher, *England and the Crusades* (1988).

Tyerman, Christopher, *Who's Who in Early Medieval England* (1996).

Vaughan, Richard, *Matthew Paris* (1958).

Vincent, N.C., *Peter des Roches, Bishop of Winchester 1205–38: An Alien in English Politics* (1996).

Vincent, Nicholas, *The Holy Blood: King Henry III and the Westminster Blood Relic* (2001).

Vincent, Nicholas, 'The court of Henry II', in *Henry II: New Interpretations*, eds Christopher Harper-Bill and Nicholas Vincent (2007), 278–334.

Vincent, Nicholas, 'King Henry III and the Blessed Virgin Mary', *The Church and Mary*, ed. R.N. Swanson, *Studies in Church History* 39 (2004), 126–46.

Vincent, Nicholas, 'Stephen Langton, Archbishop of Canterbury', *Etienne Langton*, eds L.-J. Bataillon and others (Turnhout, 2010), 51–123.

Walker, David, *The Normans in Britain* (1995).

Ward, Benedicta, *Miracles and the Medieval Mind* (1982).

Warren, W.L., *Henry II* (1973).

Watkins, C.S., *History and the Supernatural in Medieval England* (2007).

Watt, D.E.R., *Medieval Church Councils in Scotland* (2000).

Webber, Teresa, *Scribes and Scholars at Salisbury Cathedral, c. 1075–1125* (1992).

Williams, Ann, *The English and the Norman Conquest* (1995).

Williams, David and Lewis, J.M., *The White Monks in Wales* (National Museum of Wales, Cardiff, 1976).

Wolf, Kenneth B., *The Poverty of Riches: St Francis of Assisi Re-considered* (2003).

Wormald, Patrick, 'Aethelwold' in *Bishop Aethelwold*, ed. Barbara Yorke (1988).

Yarrow, Simon, *Saints and their Communities: Miracle Stories in Twelfth-Century England* (2006).

Index

Abel 90
Aberdeen 7, 264
Abingdon Abbey 47
Acre 186
Adam, Abbot of Evesham 218
Adam Marsh 250–53
Adam of Dryburgh 192
Adam of Eynsham 162, 194–96
Adelard of Bath 208–10
Adelsheilige 20, 33
Adrian IV, Pope 81
adultery 246
advowsons, see patronage of churches
Aethelfryth, St, see Etheldreda
Aethelwold, Bishop of Winchester see
    Ethelwold
Ailnoth, engineer 15
Ailred, Abbot of Rievaulx 10, 73, 109,
    118, 126, 147, 152–54, 158,
    160–62, 213, 277
Aire, River 42
Alan of Richmond, Count 38, 180
Alberic of Ostia, Cardinal 71–72
Alcuin, Prior of Worcester 136
Aldhelm, St 138
Aldida of Sturminster 6
Alexander, Mr, Abbot of St Augustine's
    Canterbury 223
Alexander, Bishop of Lincoln 4, 120,
    158, 171, 206, 212, 241
Alexander I, King of Scotland 63, 65
Alexander II, King of Scotland 264
Alexander III, King of Scotland 264
Alexander II, Pope 28, 31
Alexander III, Pope 83, 185, 193, 201,
    230, 257

Alexander Nequam 226
Alexander of Ashby 116
al-Khwarizmi 208–10
Alnwick Castle 107
Alphege, St, Archbishop of Canterbury
    58, 82
Alphonse of Poitiers 249
Althoff, Gerd 163
Altmann, Bishop of Passau 166
amicitia, see friendship
Anacletus II, anti-pope 65
Angers 88
Anketill, goldsmith 136
Anno, Archbishop of Cologne 27
Anselm, Archbishop of Canterbury 9,
    20, 49–53, 57, 82, 88–89, 92–93,
    119–20, 193
Anselm, Bishop of Lucca 25–26
Anselm of St Saba, Abbot of Bury St
    Edmunds 134
Anselm, Richard I's Chaplain 159
Anthony of Padua, St 233–34, 246
Anthony the Hermit, St 131
appeals to Rome 35–36, 48–49,
    76–79, 92
Arabic 208–10
Arabic numerals 206
arblasters 15
archbishops 27–29, 34
archdeacons 8, 17–18, 54, 79, 91,
    96–97, 273
architecture 36, 66, 122, 150, 176–77,
    181, 192, 225–26
aristocracy, ideal of 196–97
Aristotle 248, 252–57, 265, 275
arithmetic 206–08

Arnulf, Bishop of Lisieux 108–09
Arthur, King 214–15
Ashby Priory 116
assarts 2
Assisi 229–30, 232–33
Assize of Arms (1181) 100
astrolabe 207–08
astronomy 207–10
Athelwold, Bishop of Carlisle 45, 54, 65, 69–72, 169
Atwick 175–76
Audoen, Bishop of Evreux 46
Augustine of Hippo 23, 32, 94, 166, 169, 191, 254, 270
Augustinian Canons 5, 20–21, 23, 28, 45–46, 55, 63–66, 89, 96, 116, 126, 149, 166–79, 191–92, 229, 241–43
Austin, David 165
Avalon, Burgundy 193
Axholme 107
Aymer de Lusignan 250

Baldwin, Abbot of Bury St Edmunds 10
Baldwin, Abbot of Ford, Bishop of Worcester, Archbishop of Canterbury 127, 186, 193, 199, 218
Baldwin de Gant 175
Baldwin de Redvers 213
Banbury 4, 203
Bangor, bishop of, see Cadwgan
Barcombe 272
Barking Abbey 33
Barlow, Frank 74, 85–86, 90
Barnstaple 11
Barrow, Geoffrey 70–71
Barrow, Julia 185
Bartholomew, Bishop of Exeter 55, 91–92, 115, 127, 241–43
Bartholomew of Farne 14
Bartlett, Robert xvi–vii, 10, 109, 121, 167, 231
Bath Abbey 34, 125
Bath, bishop of, see Robert of Lewes
Batley 126
Battle Abbey 220
Battle of the Standard (1138) 109
Beaulieu Abbey 162–65

Bec Abbey 28–30, 38, 40, 88
Bede 35–36, 56, 60, 117, 127, 138
Bedford 213
beer 139
Beguines 269
Bellencombre 47
Belmeis family 134
Benedict, Abbot of Stratford Langthorne 159
Benedict Kepherin 177
benefactors 175
benefices 261–63, 266–67
Berengar of Tours 37, 119
Berkhamstead, Castle 86
Berkshire, Rectors of 273
Bernard, Bishop of St David's 48–49, 134
Bernard of Clairvaux, St 26, 65, 124, 131, 134, 148, 152, 194, 216, 241, 265, 277
Berwick 10
Bessingby 170–71, 174
bibles 36
Biggleswade 12
Binski, Paul 225
bishoprics, vacant 106
Bisson, Thomas 68
Blair, John 99, 176
Boethius 206
Bologna 127, 185, 192, 201, 220, 235, 239
Bonaventure, St 235, 246, 254
Bond, James 171
Boniface, St 265
Boniface of Savoy, Archbishop-elect 263
books 121–22, 233–34
books, liturgical 133, 135
Boxgrove Priory 129
Boynton 170–71, 174
Bracton 252, 256
Brade, Rikward, Ralph and Nicholas 112
Bramham 169
Brechin 264
Brecon 225, 271
Brentano, Robert 268
Brett, Martin 45
Bridlington Priory 169–76, 182, 243, 267
Bridlington Dialogue 167, 169–70, 172–74
Brihtric 101, 123

Bristol 5, 162, 167, 209
    St Mark's Hospital 267
Britain 31–32
Brooke, Christopher 9, 54, 201
Brooke, Z.N. 34, 76, 87–88, 259
Brown, Peter 8, 108, 139, 142, 196
Brown, R.A. 107
Bruern Abbey 218
Bucklebury 115, 146–47
Buckton 170–72
bureaucracy 69
burgage tenures 4
Burton by Hornsea 175–76
Burton Fleming 175
Bury St Edmunds Abbey 3, 34, 67, 130,
    136–37, 143, 243
Bynum, Caroline Walker 19, 272

Cadwgan, Bishop of Bangor 242
Caen 29–30, 138
Caen, Philip, Abbot of 190
Caithness 264
Calixtus II, Pope 61–62
Cambridge 237
    Peterhouse 275–76
Cambridgeshire, landholders in 38
candles 13–14, 67
canon law 25–27, 32, 34–36
canonization 86, 147, 224, 235
Canossa 94
Canterbury 32, 34, 37, 48, 108, 127,
    140, 192
Canterbury, archbishops of, see Anselm,
    Baldwin, Boniface, Edmund,
    Hubert, Lanfranc, Ralph, Richard
    of Dover, Stephen Langton,
    Stigand, Theobald, Theodore,
    Thomas Becket, William of Corbeil
    Archdeacon of 62
    Cathedral Priory 55, 67, 81, 180
    rights of 81–84, 87, 89
    St Augustines Abbey 223, 243
Cardigan 165
careerism 16–18, 83
Carlisle 64, 69, 71–72
Carlisle, Cathedral Priory 170
Carnaby 170–71, 174
Carpenter, David xvi, 184
Carthusians 193–94, 203

carucage 16
Cassian 131, 237
Cassiodorus 93
Castle Acre Priory 78
castles 4–5, 15–16, 42, 107, 184
Cathar heretics 92
cathedral priories 37–38
cathedrals 8
Catto, Jeremy 253–54
Celestine III, Pope 173, 264
Cercamp Abbey 87
Chadwick, Henry 24
chalices 269
Chamber, King's 106
chancellorship, royal 75–76
chants 38, 133
chaplains 115–16, 174–75, 180–81,
    266–69
chapters of the black monks 274–75
Chartres Cathedral 213–14
Chartreuse, La Grande 193–94
cheese 20
Cheney, Christopher 80, 190, 192
Chester, Bishopric of 31–32
Chichester 124–25, 277–78
    Bishopric of 13
Chichester, bishop of, see Hilary, John,
    Richard Poore, Richard of Wych,
    Seffrid II
    Church of Holy Cross 96
    reliefs of 214
    St Mary's Hospital 11
childbirth 139
Chislehampton 171
chivalry 68, 248
Cholsey 70
Christina of Markyate 7, 18–21,
    180, 195
Chrodegang of Metz 166
Cicero 47, 73, 213
Cistercians 65, 148–65, 270–71, 274,
    276–78
Citeaux Abbey 148, 277
Clairvaux Abbey 131, 148
Clanchy, Michael 116
Clarendon
    Constitutions of 77–81, 83–84
    Council of, 1164 77, 83
Clares 106

class 142, 151, 158–59
clergy, vices of 124
clerical marriage 117–19
clericalism 119–24
Cleveland Charter 157
Clifton Hampden 171
Cluniacs 149
Coates, Alan 275
Colchester 11
Coleshill 177
Common Law, English 219
Concerning the Diverse Orders and Callings in the Church, c. 1130 167
concubines of priests 141, 178
confession 118, 138–40, 143, 167, 200, 231, 239–47, 251, 268, 270–71
confirmation 200
Conques Abbey 43
conscience 251
constipation 139
conversi, see lay-brothers
copes 19, 133
Cornwall 220
coronation 82
coroners 187
corporeality 272
Corpus Christi, feast of 269
Coss Peter 132
Coventry 164
Coventry, bishop of, see Hugh Nonant
Cowdrey, John 166
Cowley 99
Crafter, Timothy 160
criminal fugitives 190–91
criminous clerks 78–80, 83
cross, carrying of 86
crosses, processional 108
Crouch, David 216
Crowland, Abbot of 102
crowns 67
crown-wearings 67
crucifix, bleeding 112
crucifixes, flying 96–97
crusade 248
    First 241
    Second 108, 216, 241
    Third 155, 186–87, 198
    Fifth 226
    preaching of 226

Culross Abbey 151
Cumberland 64, 66, 69, 71–72
Cum Universi Christi 264
cures 142, 152–53, 178–79
Curia Regis Rolls 175
Cuthbert, St 58

Daimbert, Archbishop of Sens 51
David, King of Scotland 60, 64–65, 70–73, 212
Davies, Rees xix, 47, 165, 227
d'Avray, David 201, 223, 247
dead, masses for the 115
Denis, St 82
Denmark 7, 26, 136
devil 8–9
Dialogue of the Exchequer 185, 206–07
Dickinson, J.C. 173
Dictatus Papae (1075) 27–28
Dissolution of the Monasteries 171–72
doctors 12–13, 16
Domesday Book 38, 42, 70, 113
Dominic, St 233, 250, 277
Dominicans 229, 233, 244, 247, 250, 254, 269
Dorchester-on-Thames Abbey 171
dormitories, nuns' 181
dowries 182
draining 2–3
drains 150
Dublin, bishop of, see Patrick
duel, at York 175–76
Duffy, Eamon 221
Duggan, Anne 74
Dulcote 125
Dunblane 264
Dundee 7
Dunfermline Abbey 32
Dunkeld 264
Dunstable 16, 19
Dunstan, St 20, 58
Durham 13, 29, 34, 64, 126–27
    Bishopric 31
Durham, bishops of, see Hugh Puiset, Walcher, William of St Calais
    Cathedral Priory 14, 35–36, 114, 117, 274–75
    Hospital at 140

Eadmer 58, 60–63, 134
Earley 141
Eartham 125
East Anglia 107, 112
East Riding of Yorkshire 174–75
ecclesia anglicana 184–85
Eddington 177
Edmund, St 67, 148
Edmund of Abingdon, Archbishop of
    Canterbury 226, 263
Edmund of Eynsham 275
Edmund, son of Henry III 260, 268
Edward I, King 47
Edward of Westminster, 249
Edward the Confessor, St 86–87, 90,
    98, 147
eider ducks 14
Eilaf 126
Einhard 214
Eleanor, Queen of Henry III 250
Elias, Minister-General 234–35,
    238–39
Elias of Dereham 260, 262
Elizabeth of Schönau 154
Elkins, Sharon 180–81
Elkstone 122
Ellingham 117
Ely, Abbey 37–44, 138, 144, 275
    Bishopric of 38, 136
Ely, bishop of, see Hugh de Balsham,
    Nigel, William Longchamp
embroidery 19
Emelina 177
Emma, Queen 147
emotions 86
empiricism 209–10
engineers 15, 150
epilepsy 111
episcopal elections 53–56, 193, 195–96,
    262–63
Essex 206
estate surveys 16
Eston 218
Etheldreda, St 40–43, 58, 138, 144
Ethelelm, Abbot of Abingdon 38–39
Ethelred II, King 147
Ethelwold, Bishop of Winchester 20, 33, 37
ethnography 227–28
Eucharist 119, 127, 128, 140, 200, 269–70

Eugenius III, Pope 56, 118, 241
Eustace, Norwich moneyer 143
Evesham, Abbey 152, 274
    Battle of (1265) 252, 268
Exchequer 53, 68, 205–08
excommunications 81–82, 87, 196–97
exempla in sermons 224–27, 236–37
Exeter 124, 127, 216
Exeter, bishops of, see Bartholomew,
    William Warelwast
exile 90
Eynesford 80–81
Eynsham Abbey 195

Faith, St 43
Falaise 85, 197
falcons 86, 90
False Decretals, see Pseudo-Isidore
familiars 184
Faringdon 162
Faritius, Abbot of Abingdon 10, 209
Farne Island 14
feud 191
Filey 171, 174
Finchale 145
fisheries 4
Flamborough 170–71, 174, 242–43
Flanders 7, 89, 276
Flemish mercenaries 107, 112
Fliche, Augustin 24
Flint, Val 277
forbidden degrees of kinship 202
Ford Abbey 151
foreign favourites 253
foresters 197–98, 263
Forli 234
Fountains Abbey 152
France 84
Francis, St 122, 229–35, 238–39, 255
Franciscans c. 9, 260, 266, 268, 276
Frederick I, Barbarossa, Emperor 15, 75,
    83, 146
Frederick II, Emperor 239, 260, 262, 273
friendship 19–21, 47–49, 59–64, 71–73,
    85–86, 107, 161–62

Gameson, Richard 133
Ganton 172–74
Gascony 249, 251

Gebuin, Chanter of Troyes, Mr 88
Gedgrave 112
Gelasius II, Pope 60
Gem, Richard 65–66
gentry 131–32; see also knights
Geoffrey, Abbot of St Albans 18–21,
    134, 195
Geoffrey, Abbot of St Mary's York 152
Geoffrey, Archbishop of Rouen 46
Geoffrey Babion, Archbishop of
    Bordeaux 88
Geoffrey de Lardaria, Mr 218
Geoffrey de Mandeville 212
Geoffrey, Forester 197–98
Geoffrey of Coldingham 14
Geoffrey of Linby, cutler 139
Geoffrey of Monmouth 214–16
Geoffrey of Vinsauf 188
Gerald of Ostia 26
Gerald of Wales 49, 96–97, 101, 121,
    124, 160, 168, 224–28, 242,
    255, 271
Gerard, Archbishop of York 57
Germany 185
    cathedral canons in 126
Gervase of Cambridgeshire 37–44
Gervase of Chichester 123–24, 128–29,
    243
Gesta Henrici Secundi 107
Gesta Stephani 210–12
gestures 233
Gibson, Margaret 28
Gilbert, Bishop of London (1128–34)
    54, 134, 216
Gilbert, Bishop of Poitiers 93
Gilbert FitzRichard of Clare 48
Gilbert Foliot, Bishop of Hereford and
    London 55–56, 76, 77, 82–85, 92,
    101, 116, 118
Gilbert of Hoyland 277
Gilbert of Northampton, Mr 218
Gilbert of Sempringham 13, 102,
    110–11, 221–22, 227, 241
Gilbertines 180
Gilchrist, Roberta 181
Gillingham, John xix, 42, 54, 187
Glanvill 100–01, 104–06
Glasgow 264
Glasgow, bishops of, see John, Michael

glass 13
Glastonbury Abbey 2–3, 38, 275
Gloucester Abbey 114, 115–16, 274
Gloucester Candlestick 133
Godfrey, Bishop of Langres 108
Godfrey de Lucy 220
Godfrey of Lanthony, Mr 218
Godfrey, priest 117
Godric of Finchale 7–8, 13–14, 75, 140,
    144–45
Golding, Brian 180
goldsmiths 16, 136
Goscelin of St Bertin 138
gossip 110, 246
Grande Ordonnance (1254) 249
granges 150
Gratian's Decretum 220, 242
Great Rebellion of 1173–74 106,
    147, 185
Greenway, Diana xix
Gregorian Reform xv, 22–28, 36, 53, 59,
    98, 117, 119, 166–67, 200, 202,
    222, 262
Gregory I, the Great, Pope 17, 24–25,
    56, 60, 89, 90, 94, 127, 138, 159,
    194, 198–99, 224, 227, 251, 253,
    270
Gregory VII, Pope 22–28, 29, 31, 32,
    33–34, 50–51, 166
Gregory IX, Pope, and Cardinal
    Hugolino 234, 239, 262
Grestain Abbey 39
Grindale 170–71
Guala, Cardinal 259–60, 262
guilt 140, 152–53
Guisborough Priory 217–18
Guy of Étampes 46
Guy I, Prior of Chartreuse 194
Guy, Prior of Southwick 167, 242

Hackington 192
hagiography 138
Hallam, H.E. 3
Hand of St James, relic of 115, 141,
    146–47
Harbledon, Hospital of 141–42
Haselbury Plucknett 96, 110, 151, 159
Haseldine, Julian 72, 86
Haymo of Faversham 236, 239

healing, rituals of 139
Hellingly 112
Héloise 73, 213
Henry I, King 10, c. 3, 85, 126, 145–48,
    167, 174, 176, 179–80, 212–13
    dealings with the Welsh 47–48
    personality, 45–47, 71
Henry II, King 53, 73–90, 94, 130,
    146–47, 160, 165, 183–84, 187,
    197–98, 209, 214–15
    as Duke of Normandy 213
    legal reforms of 15–16, 100–07,
    156–57
Henry III, King 184, 248–51, 259–64,
    268, 273, 277
Henry III, Emperor 50–51
Henry IV, Emperor 33, 94
Henry V, Emperor 67, 146, 205
Henry VI, Emperor 155, 187
Henry, Abbot of Saltrey 159
Henry, Abbot of Sawtrey 271
Henry, master mason 249
Henry, Murdac, Archbishop of York 150
Henry of Blois, Bishop of Winchester
    135, 209
Henry of Huntingdon 56, 59, 212, 216
Henry, of Bindon 164
Henry, Prior of Canterbury 37
Henry, son of Henry II 82
Henry, son of Huddret 106
Herbert le Poore, Bishop of Salisbury 198
Herbert of Bosham 76, 90–94, 108–09,
    223
hereditary benefices 117–19
Hereford 127, 216
Hereford, bishops of, see Gilbert Foliot,
    Reinhelm, Robert of Bethune,
    Robert of Melun, William de Vere
Hereward the Wake 39
Herfast, Bishop of Thetford 34
Heribert, Archbishop of Cologne 25
hermits 145, 149
herring 5, 136, 151
Heslop, T.A. 135
Hexham 118, 126–27
Hilary, Bishop of Chichester 20–21, 81,
    92, 125, 243
Hilary of Poitiers 128
Hildebert, Bishop of Le Mans 46

Hildebrand of Norwich 144
Hildebrand, see Pope Gregory VII
Hildegard of Bingen 145
Hill, Bennett 158
Holme, prebend of 127
Holt, Sir James 160
Holy Commerce 244
honour, baronial 174
horoscopes 209
horses 162
hospitals 11–12, 20, 141–42
households, bishops' 54
Hubert, clergyman of St Paul's 77
Hubert Walter, Archbishop of
    Canterbury xviii, 15, 52, 114,
    162–63, 185–93, 196, 243, 266
Huddersfield 126
Hugh, Abbot of Beaulieu, Bishop of
    Carlisle 164, 259
Hugh, Abbot of Reading 134
Hugh Bigod, Justiciar 248
Hugh, Bishop of Lincoln, St 12, 52, 73,
    101, 163, 186, 192–204, 266
Hugh de Balsham, Bishop of Ely 275–76
Hugh de Die, Archbishop of Lyon 26, 51
Hugh de Digne 235
Hugh de Neville 159
Hugh de Pateshull 262
Hugh de Puiset, Bishop of Durham
    114, 117
Hugh Nonant, Bishop of Coventry
    54–55
Hugh of Buckland 206
Hugh of Fleury 51–52
Hugh of Kirkstall 152
Hugh of St Victor 159
Hugh the Chantor 30, 51, 53–54,
    57–61
humanism 213–14
'humiliation' of a saint 43
hunting 86, 197
Huntingdon 16, 18
Hurnard, Naomi 249
Hyams, Paul 191, 231

Ida, wife of Eustace, moneyer of
    Norwich 140
Iffley 96, 99, 122
Ilbert de Lacy 42

Ilkeston 170
'illiteracy' of clergy 225
inflation 156
Innocent II, Pope 65
Innocent III, Pope 164, 180, 188–89,
    202, 222–23, 226, 230, 259–61,
    263–65
insomnia 139, 178
Institutio Canonicorum 166
insults 87
Interdict, Papal 156, 223
investiture 49–56, 82, 266
Iorwerth ap Bleddyn of Powys 48
Ireland 5, 106
Isidore of Seville 97
Italy 260, 268, 276
itinerancy 69
itinerant justices 106–07
itinerary, royal 184
Ivo, Bishop of Chartres 51, 228, 242

James de Watsand 175–76
James of St Victor, Papal Legate 264
Jarrow Abbey 152
Jeremy, Archdeacon of Cleveland 122–23
Jerusalem 186, 248
Jerusalem, Kingdom of 16
Jews, 4–5, 7, 142–44, 177–78, 198
Jocelin, Archdeacon of Chichester 218
Jocelin, Bishop of Salisbury 82, 135
Jocelin of Brakelond 137, 148
John, King 54, 69, 148, 155–57, 162–64,
    188, 194, 196, 210, 223, 259
    as Count 162
John, Abbot of Ford 118, 151, 154–59,
    276
John, Bishop of Glasgow 63, 65, 72
John, Bishop of Wells 34
John, Dean and Bishop of Chichester
    129, 186, 218
John of Cornwall, Mr 218, 220–21, 226
John of Hexham 71
John of Parma 236
John of Plano Carpini 228
John of Salisbury 17–18, 91, 116, 120,
    227, 252, 255
John of Toledo, Cardinal 261–62
John of Tynemouth 221
John Parenti 234

Joinville, Jean de 248
Jolliffe, J.E.A. 107
Jordan de Breiset 180–81
Juliana of Cornillon 269
Jumièges Abbey 38
jurisdiction 40–41, 77–80

Kantorowicz, Ernst 222
Keen, Maurice 215
Keller, Hagen 279
Kennet, River 177
Kent 108–09
kingship, ideas about 32–33, 50–51,
    214–16
Kirklevington 218
knights 15–16, 38, 42, 68, 100–01, 105,
    111, 117, 131–32, 151–52,
    156–65, 174–76, 181, 184,
    190–91, 198
Knowles, David 73–74, 81–82, 89–90,
    213–14, 275–76

labour 3, 16, 113, 149–51
Lamb, David 237
Lambeth 190, 192
Lanfranc, Archbishop of Canterbury 17,
    25, 28–37, 52, 63, 119
Langbargh Wapentake 157
language 101–02, 122–23, 195–96, 220
Laon 127, 206, 208
    murdered Bishop of 179
Lateran archives 26
Lateran Council
    First (1123) 114
    Third (1179) 11, 185, 189, 192,
        203, 257
    Fourth (1215) 114, 192, 202–03, 224,
        226, 231, 243–44, 246, 258, 260,
        264, 273–74
Latin 116–17, 121, 124, 208–09, 243,
    267, 275
Lawrence, C.H. 260
Lawrence, Abbot of Westminster
    147, 152
Lawrence, nephew of a canon at Oxford
    178
lay-brothers 149–50, 175
Lay-Folks Mass Book 122–23
Le Goff, Jacques 159, 271

learning, monastic 274–75
Leicester, Abbey 243
Leicester, Castle 107
Lennard, Reginald 2, 113
Leo IX, Pope 22
lepers 11, 231–32
leprosy 141–42
Lewes, Battle of (1264) 252
Lewes Priory 135, 210, 272–73
Leyser, Henrietta 21, 120, 149, 168, 182
Leyser, Karl 67, 137, 203
libraries 128, 141, 194, 265
Lichfield, bishopric of 31
Liège 167, 206, 269
Lincoln 31, 39, 76, 124, 179, 198, 223
    Battle of (1141) 215
Lincoln, bishops of, see Alexander,
        Hugh, Robert de Chesney,
        Robert Grosseteste
    canons of 195–96
    Siege of (1141) 214
Lincolnshire 157–60
liturgy 133–36
Llandaff, bishops of, see Urban, William
Llanthony Priory 20, 168, 179
logic 25, 28, 37
London 11, 56, 127, 167, 179, 183–84,
        189–90, 231, 242, 256–57
London, bishops of, see Gilbert Foliot,
        Gilbert (1128–34), Maurice,
        Richard FitzNeal
    church of St Mary le Bow 189–90
    Clerkenwell Priory 180–82
    Haliwell, Shoreditch 181
    Hospital of St Bartholomew,
        Smithfield 11
    Hospital of St Giles, Holborn 11
    St Paul's Cathedral 134, 269
    Temple Church 203
Long Sutton 78
lordship 99–100
loss of face 72, 79, 85, 163
Lothingland 111
Louis VIII, King of France 194, 259, 262
Louis IX, King of France 248–50, 252,
        260
Louth Abbey 160
Lutton (Northants) 78
Lyon 238

Lyon, Poor Men of, see Waldensians
Lythe church 169

Mabel de Francheville 201
MacCulloch, Diarmaid 221–22
Maddicott, John 251–52
Magdeburg 37–38
magistri 12
Magna Carta 5–6, 68, 132, 155–57,
        160–62, 164–65, 187, 222–23,
        231, 242, 256–57, 259
majority principle 256–57
Malcolm, King of Scotland 180
Malger of Newark, Mr 117
Malmesbury Abbey 138
Manasses, Archbishop of Rheims 26
Marcham 47
Margaret, Queen of Scotland 32, 46
Margaret, d. of Henry III 264
Marinus of Eboli, Mr 261
marriage 18, 103, 161–62, 200–03, 221,
        247, 251
marriage, clerical 23, 59
Marrick Priory 181
martyrdom 90
marvels 97–98
Mary
    Assumption of 154
    cult of 249
    devotion to 277–78
    feast of Assumption of 233
    image on seal of 135
    Immaculate Conception of 9, 98,
        134, 154
    Miracles of 98
Master, title of 219
Matilda, daughter of Henry I, later
        'Empress' 67, 146, 205, 212
Matilda, Queen of Henry I 32, 46, 48,
        70, 180, 209
Matilda, Queen of Stephen 56
Matilda of Wareham 6–7, 13–14
Matthew, Donald 74, 77
Matthew, Mr 209
Matthew Paris 250, 273
Maurice, Bishop of London 33, 52
Maurice, Prior of Kirkham 6
Maurienne, Count of 194
medicine 12–13

Melbourne 65–72
memory 153, 209
Merton Priory 191–92
Michael, Bishop of Glasgow 64–65
Milan 22
Miles de Beauchamp 213
mill ponds 105
Milo, Abbot 159
Milsom, S.F.C. 105
minster churches 98–100, 176
miracles 10, 97–98, 101, 138–45,
    177–79
mitres 120–21, 133, 269
Molesmes Abbey 148
money-lenders 5, 143
Mongols 248
Montacute Priory 118
Moorman, J.R.H. 246
Moray 264
Morey and Brooke 116
Morris, Colin 22
Moses, Jew 4–5
Murray, Alexander 25, 97, 241, 246

nature 97–98, 149, 230
Newcastle-upon-Tyne 11
Newminster Abbey 276
Nicholas of Sigillo 17–18
Nicholl, Donald 6, 64
Nigel, Bishop of Ely, 7, 145, 206–07,
    212
Norfolk 186, 190–91
Normandy 52, 67–68, 104, 108, 155–56,
    183, 185, 198, 205–06
Northampton 5, 83, 146, 188, 216–17
Northampton, Council of (1164) 83,
    86–87, 91
Northaw 81
Northumberland 9, 64, 111
Norwich 11
Norwich, bishop of, see William
Norwich Cathedral Priory 13, 142–44,
    240
Nostell Priory 63–64, 71, 126, 169
novel disseisin 103–07
novices 153
novitiate 149
nunneries 179–82

obedience 24–25, 82
obedientiaries, monastic 137
Odard of Bamburgh, Sheriff of
    Northumberland 64
Odo, Abbot of Battle 116, 220
Odo, engineer 15
Odo of Bayeux 30, 35
Odolina of Crewkerne 6
Oldham 251
Olmütz 26
Orderic Vitalis 46–47, 58, 149, 216
Orkneys, bishop of the, see Ralph
Ormulum 116, 167
Osbern, priest 96, 118
Osbert Fitz Hervey 160
Osbert of Arundel, Mr 218
Osbert of Clare, Prior of Westminster
    134
Oseney Abbey 99, 132, 173, 177
Oswald, St 20
Otto, Bishop of Constance 23
Otto, Cardinal 264, 269
Otto I, Emperor 37–38
Ottringham 172, 174
Ouse, River 42, 182
Owain ap Cadwgan of Powys 48
Oxford 4–6, 13, 157, 176–79, 184, 199,
    216–21, 237–39, 251, 253–54,
    263, 265–66, 274–75
  churches in 176–77
  St Frideswide's Priory 145, 167,
    176–79, 241
  Merton College 255, 257–58, 275
  shoemakers guild at 5

Padua 239
pallium 33, 75
Panayotova, Stella 93, 223
Pandulf Masca, papal legate 164
papacy 58–59, 185
papal bureaucracy 261–62
papal judges-delegate 92, 219
papal legates 26, 59, 62–63, 82,
    259–64
papal provisions 261–62
papal tax collectors 262
papal taxation 273
'Paper Constitution' of 1244 268

Paris 91–92, 127, 188, 192, 199–200,
    202–03, 220, 225–26, 230,
    235–36, 239, 241–43, 247–49,
    253–54, 257, 271
  St Victor 242
  Ste Chapelle 249–50
  Treaty of (1259) 249
parish churches 112–19, 243
parish clergy 108–29, 143, 245–46,
    266–73
parishes 98–100
parliament 184
Pascal II, Pope 53, 60, 82
Patcham 272
Patrick, Bishop of Dublin 32
patronage of churches 78, 79–80,
    113–14, 117, 269–70
Paul, monk of Norwich 144
Pavia 28
peasants 43, 158–59, 167, 175
peasants, fighting 107, 109, 112
Peltzer, Jörg 185
penance 94
Penenden Heath, Trial of 30
penitential psalms, seven 43
penitentials 91
penitentiaries 241
Peter, Abbot of Gloucester 133
Peter Abelard 73, 93, 209, 213, 217, 228
Peter de Brus 157
Peter de Fribois 175–76
Peter de Melide, Mr 117
Peter des Roches, Bishop of Winchester
    268–69
Peter Lombard 92–94, 134, 243, 254
Peter of Celle 88
Peter of Cornwall 159
Peter of Savoy 250
Peter Peverell 144
Peter the Chanter 91, 188–89, 199–203,
    222–26, 242–43, 247–48, 258,
    260, 270
Peterborough Abbey 2, 38, 243, 275
Petrus Alphonsi 11, 209–10
Philip II, Augustus, King of France 155,
    162, 164, 187–88
Philip of Oxford, Mr 226
Philip of Wales, Brother 238

Philip, Prior of St Frideswide's, Oxford
    167, 177–79, 241
Pibo, Bishop of Toul 23–24
Picot of Cambridgeshire 38–44
Pietro Rosso 273
pigs 11, 16, 162
pilgrimage 139, 194, 240–41
Pipe Rolls 6–7, 79, 105–06, 188
Platonism 265
pleas of the crown 187
pluralists 71, 264–65, 267, 269
Poitou 156
policing 15–16
pollution, fear of 119–20
Pontefract 42
Pontigny Abbey 93
Poole, A.L. 87, 225
population, 1–3
portents, see marvels
Postan, M.M. 2
poverty 230–38, 244
Prague 26
prayer 153–54, 169–70
preaching 116, 167, 240–41, 246–47
Premonstratensian Canons of Otham 112
Prestbury (Glos) 20
primacy dispute 29–33, 56–65
prodigies, see marvels
production, of manuscripts 13
propaganda 70
proprietary church 99–100
Provisions of Oxford (1258) 250
Provisions of Westminster (1259) 132
psalms 93–94, 274
Psalter 223
Pseudo-Isidore 25, 34
purgatory 270–72, 279
pyxes 269

Quo Elongati, Bull 234

Raedts, Peter 255
Rainald Dassel, Archbishop of
    Cologne 75
Ralph, Abbot of St Alban's 135–36
Ralph, Archbishop of Canterbury 58–62
Ralph, Bishop of the Orkneys 31–32
Ralph Bocking 247

Ralph Gibuin 141
Ralph Haget xv
Ralph of Caugy 117
Ralph of Coggeshall 159–60, 162–63
Ralph of Diceto 76, 107
Ralph of Hadfield's wife 139
Ralph of Warenne 135
Ralph, priest of Norwich 121–22
Ralph the Physician, Mr 117
Ramsey, Frances 125
Ramsey Abbey 243
ransom 155, 187, 190
Ranulf Glanvill, Chief Justiciar 186
Ranulph of Chester, Earl 212
Raymund of Piacenza 232
Reading Abbey 70, 122, 141, 146–47,
    151–52, 274–75
recluses 6–7
Redfield, Robert 95–96
Reginald de Warenne 143
Reginald of Durham 7, 75, 144–45
Reimund Archdeacon of Leicester 199
Reinhelm, Bishop of Hereford 53
relics, see Hand of St James
reliquaries 146
revenants 9–10, 111
Revesby Abbey 158
Reynolds, Susan 4
Rheims
    Council of (1119) 61–62
    Council of (1148) 168
Rhys ap Gruffudd, Lord of Deheubarth
    165
Richard I, King 155, 159, 187–90, 196,
    198, 204
Richard, Abbot of St Albans 168
Richard de Ferrers 144
Richard de Lucy, Justiciar 220
Richard de Maton, Canon of Beverley
    127
Richard FitzNeal, Bishop of London 185,
    206–07
Richard of Anstey 201–02, 220
Richard of Devizes 186
Richard of Dover, Archbishop of
    Canterbury 193
Richard of Ilchester, Bishop of
    Winchester 55

Richard of Wych, Bishop of Chichester
    247, 263, 277
Richard Poore, Bishop of Chichester,
    Bishop of Salisbury 225–26, 244,
    260, 263–64, 267
Richard, Prior of Newburgh 218
Richard, Prior of St Mary's York, Abbot
    of Fountains 152
Richard Rufus of Cornwall 97, 209,
    254–57
Richard, son of Eilnold 140
Richmond (Yorks), lordship of 180
Ridyard, Susan 144–45
Rievaulx Abbey 150
ritual 133–36, 142, 163
Robert, brother of Bishop Hilary 125
Robert Courson, Cardinal 91
Robert de Beaumont, Earl of Leicester
    165
Robert de Bonville 125
Robert de Broc 81
Robert de Brun 64
Robert de Chesney, Bishop of Lincoln
    55–56, 78, 117, 120
Robert d'Oilly 4
Robert, Duke of Normandy 47, 52–53
Robert, Earl of Gloucester 5, 48,
    212, 215
Robert, Earl of Leicester 107, 112
Robert Fitz Harding 5
Robert Gresley 143
Robert Grosseteste, Bishop of Lincoln
    216, 238, 245, 247, 250–55,
    263–66, 268
Robert of Bedford, Mr 199
Robert of Bethune, Bishop of Hereford
    20, 45–46, 54, 168–69, 179
Robert of Cricklade 92
Robert of Flamborough 242
Robert of Knaresborough 7
Robert of Lewes, Bishop of Bath 125,
    210, 216
Robert of Melun, Bishop of Hereford
    91–92
Robert of Merton 192
Robert of Meulan, Count 61
Robert of Mortain, Count 39
Robert of St-Remy 99, 122

Robert of Sorbonne 257
Robert of Stanford 141
Robert of Valoines 81
Robert Passelewe, Archdeacon of Lewes 263, 265
Robert, Prior of Nostell and Bishop of St Andrews 63–64
Robert Pullen, Cardinal 54, 127, 217
Robert Tweng 262
Roger, Abbot of Reading 115, 146
Roger, Bishop of Salisbury 46, 53, 134, 179, 206–07, 209, 212
Roger, Bishop of Worcester 85, 92, 96, 195
Roger de Clare, Earl 80–81
Roger de Mowbray 107
Roger of Asterby 160
Roger of Howden 187–90
Roger of Pont l'Évêque, Archbishop of York 11, 82, 86, 109–10, 126, 218
Roger of Rolleston, Mr, Dean of Lincoln 199
Roger, priest of Stanway 96–97
Rome 23–24, 26–27, 33, 203, 260–61, 265, 273
Rome, Council at 49–50
Romsey Abbey 180
rosary 278
Ross 264
Rotuli de Dominabus 182
Rouen 39, 122
Rouergue, Counts of 43
Rule of St Benedict 149, 253, 274–76
rural deans 79, 115–16, 118, 273

sabbatarianism 139
sacrality in kingship 146, 204, 222
St Albans
    Abbey 13, 19–20, 76–77, 81, 133, 180
    Hospital of St Julien 20
    Psalter of 20
St Andrews, bishopric of 7, 63–64, 264
St Andrews, bishops of, see Eadmer, Robert
St David's Cathedral 165
St David's, bishop of, see Bernard
St Evroult Abbey 46, 58, 149

St Osyth's Priory 169
St Patrick's Vision of Purgatory 159, 270–71
Saint-Saens 47
Saladin 16
Salerno 27
Salisbury 127–28, 225–26, 261, 267–68
Salisbury, bishops of, see Herbert, Hubert Walter, Jocelin, Richard Poore, Roger
    canons of 46, 116
Sallust 211
salt cellar 182
Samson, Abbot of Bury St Edmunds 3, 16, 102, 130, 136–37
Samson, Bishop of Worcester 30
sanctuary 189–91
Sandwich 108
Sawley Abbey 276
Scarborough, burgess of 79
schools 16, 19
Schwarzrheindorf 66
science, experimental 254–55
Scone, Abbey 63
Scotland 7, 31–32, 49, 63–65, 69–72, 107, 151, 263–64
Scots 107, 109
seals 106, 120–21, 135–36
Seffrid II, Bishop of Chichester 11, 112–13, 129, 185–86
Segar, priest 151, 159
Sempringham, Order of 158
Seneca 225
Serlo, monk 152
Sexburga, St 40, 43
sexual fear 178
Shaftesbury Abbey 180
Shenstone 173
Sherborne Abbey 135
sheriffs 103
shires 132, 180
shoes 217
shrines 3, 43, 111, 137–48, 194, 249
Sicily 208
Siegfried, Archbishop of Mainz 26–27
silver 64, 69
Silvester, Archdeacon of Chichester, Mr 96–97

Simeon, Abbot of Ely 39–42
Simon de Montfort, Earl of Leicester 250–53, 266, 268
Simon Langton 260
Simon, the King's Dispenser 47
simony 23–24
skinners 144
Smalley, Beryl 88–89, 91, 211, 247–48
'society' 226–28
Soissons, shrine of St Drausius 87
sokemen 41
Solomon, Brother 237
Somerset 3–5
Song of Lewes 252–53, 256, 275
Song of Roland 96, 186
Southampton 5, 76, 217
Southern, R.W. 45, 134, 167, 213, 217–19, 279
Southwark 274
Spain 26
Spalding 102
Speeton 170–71
Sproatley 172, 174
Stanway 96
Stedham 272
Stenton, Doris 188
Stephen, King 19, 71–72, 146, 158, 210–16, 222
  'Anarchy' of reign of 79, 140, 190–91
Stephen Langton, Archbishop of Canterbury 91, 159, 164, 188, 222–23, 225–26, 260
Stephen of Sawley, Abbot of Fountains 276–79
Stigand, Archbishop of Canterbury 29
Stoughton 272
Strata Florida Abbey 151, 165
Strongbow, Richard of Clare 5, 106
Suetonius 214
Suffolk 143
Suger, Abbot of St-Denis 68
suicide, attempted 177
Sunning 267–68
Sussex 112, 272–73
Sutherland, D.W. 105
Swarkestone 69
Swithun, St 58
symbols 50–51, 54, 66, 68–69, 72, 135
synods, diocesan 268–69, 273

Taillefer 96
Talbot, C.H., and Hammond, E.A. 12
talk 157–62
Taxation of Pope Nicholas IV 174
Tellenbach, Gerd 24
Templars 16, 184
Thames, River 5–6, 70, 157, 171
Theobald, Archbishop of Canterbury 17, 55–56, 75–76, 81, 110
Theobald, priest 173
Theodore, Archbishop of Canterbury 29
Theodwine, Abbot of Ely 39
theology 36–37, 91–94, 128–29, 134, 159, 221–28, 233–34, 243
Thomas, Hugh 174–75
Thomas, Keith 140, 152
Thomas Aquinas 134, 213, 228, 252, 256
Thomas of Bayeux, Archbishop of York 29–32, 126
Thomas II, Archbishop of York 30, 59
Thomas, Archdeacon of Wells 218
Thomas Becket
  Archbishop of Canterbury 3, 27, 33, 54, 63, 73, c. 4, 96, 108–10, 120, 138–39, 145, 155, 191–92, 194, 196–97, 200, 219, 224
  blood of 116
  books of 94
Thomas Docking 251–53
Thomas Lebreton 248
Thomas of Celano 235
Thomas of Chobham 116, 242, 270–71
Thomas of Eccleston 236–39
Thomas of Monmouth 121, 143–44
Thomson, Rodney 98, 211
thuribles 136
Thurkill, exchequer clerk 206
Thurkill, peasant, Vision of 9, 160
Thurstan, Archbishop of York 54–65, 76, 85, 109, 126, 152, 169–70, 173, 182
Thurstan of Caen, Abbot of Peterborough 38
Tiller, Kate 171
Tilney (Norfolk) 3, 16
timber 81
tin 188

Tinchebrai, Battle of (1106) 47, 52, 206
Tiron Abbey 65
tithes 99–100, 109–11, 114, 272
titles to ordination 114–15, 267
Toledo 262
Tonbridge, castle of 80–81
tournaments 215–16
Tours 239
    Council of (1163) 75
Townley, Simon 115
towns 4–5, 22–23, 179, 182
Trent, River 69
Trinity, feast of Holy 93
Turold, Abbot of Peterborough 38
Twelfth-Century Renaissance xvi, 46

Udo, Archbishop of Trier 24
Ulian, son of Thurstan 106
Ulviva of Canterbury 141
Upmarden 272
Urban, Bishop of Llandaff 48–49, 65, 76
Urban II, Pope 49–50, 82

Varenne, River 47
Vézelay 87
vicarages 113–15, 117, 125–6, 129,
    173–74
Victorines 242
villages 95–101, 108–10, 113–15,
    158–59
Visigothic councils 35
visions 154, 159–60
visitation of monasteries 275
Vitalis, Vicar of Sunning 267
Vivian, chaplain 125
vocation 120, 149–50, 181

W de Meisam, Mr 173
Walcher, Bishop of Durham 36
Walcher, Prior of Malvern 207–08, 210
Waldensians 230
Waleran of Meulan, Count 215
Wales 15, 47–49, 114, 148, 151, 165,
    220, 225, 227–28, 242
Walkelin, Bishop of Winchester 39, 57
Walsingham, Our Lady of 249
Walter, Abbot of Evesham 138
Walter Cantilupe, Bishop of Worcester
    251, 268–69

Walter, crossbowman 15
Walter Daniel 10, 154, 158, 160, 165
Walter d'Espec 109, 165
Walter de Lucy, Abbot of Battle 57
Walter de Gant 175
Walter de Merton 257–58
Walter Map 9, 17, 111
Walter, monk of Glastonbury 121
Walter of Coutances, Archdeacon of
    Oxford 216, 220
Walter of Madeley, Brother 237–38
Waltham 130
Ward, Benedicta 97, 255
Watkins, Carl 97, 159
Wear, River 144
Webber, Teresa 46, 128
Wells Cathedral 125, 225
Wells, bishop of, see John
West Lavington 272
West Lydford 125
Westminster 77, 184
    Abbey 13, 46, 56, 134, 147,
        249–50
    Council of 1102 57
    Council of 1163 83
    Council of 1200 114, 116, 192,
        203, 233
    monk of 75
    the King's Bed-Chamber at 249
Westmorland 64
Westout 272
Wetmore 113
Wharram le Street 169
Whitby Abbey 152
Whithorn 264
Whitland 165
Wichermann 243
widows 198
Willerby 172–74
William I, The Conqueror, King 30–31,
    33, 39, 42, 58, 68, 76, 197, 214
    as Duke of Normandy 29
William II, King 35, 45, 70, 82
William the Lion, King of Scotland 107,
    162, 264
William of Corbeil, Archbishop of
    Canterbury 55, 63, 88–89, 169
William, Bishop of Llandaff 114
William, Bishop of Norwich 15, 243

William, Bishop of Syracuse 208
William, Chaplain of Sutton 78
William Clito 47, 52, 215–16
William de Blois, Bishop of Worcester 263
William de Braose 165
William de Montibus, Mr, Chancellor of Lincoln Cathedral 199–200, 223, 242–43
William de Roumara, Earl of Lincoln 102, 165
William de Vere, Bishop of Hereford 242
William, Earl of Warenne III 135
William FitzOsbert 189–91, 231
William FitzStephen 76, 80–81
William Giffard, Bishop of Winchester 53
William Longchamp, Bishop of Ely 189
William of Auvergne, Bishop of Paris 271
William of Canterbury 107
William of Eynesford 80–81
William of Malmesbury 39, 47, 98, 138, 211–12, 216
William of Newburgh 10, 107
William of Norwich, St 13–14, 111, 140–44
William of Rubruk 248
William of St Calais, Bishop of Durham 35–36, 52, 126
William of St John 129
William of Warenne 47
William of Wrotham 188
William of Wycombe, Prior of Llanthony 168
William, son of Henry I 52, 67
William the Poet, Master 12
William Warelwast, Bishop of Exeter 53, 61
William Waude, Dean of Salisbury 267
Williams, Ann 39
Williams, David 151
Wilmart, André 277
Wilton Abbey 180

Winchester 31, 34, 37, 127, 184, 245, 249
Winchester, bishops of, see Aymer de Lusignan, Ethelwold, Godfrey de Lucy, Henry of Blois, Peter des Roches, Richard of Ilchester, Walkelin, William Giffard
Treaty of (1153) 213
Windsor 31, 81
Winston, Anne 278
wit 196–98
Witham Priory 192, 194–95, 199
Withburga, St 40, 43
Wolf, Kenneth B. 232
women 7, 10–11, 103, 139–41, 143, 145, 154, 158, 161, 178, 179–82, 269
Woodstock 48, 197, 216
wool 5, 11, 131, 151, 162, 276
Worcester 31–34, 37, 135, 163
Worcester, bishops of, see Baldwin, Roger, Samson, Walter Cantilupe
Wormald, Patrick 37
writs, royal 78
Wulfric of Haselbury 3–7, 101, 118, 121, 127
Wulfstan II, Bishop of Worcester 38
Wye 220

Yarmouth 5, 136, 143
Yarrow, Simon 142–43
Yeo, River 4
York 6–7, 13, 42, 49, 124–27, 182, 219, 264
York, archbishops of, see Gerard, Henry Murdac, Roger of Pont l'Évêque, Thomas of Bayeux, Thomas II, Thurstan
canons of 60
Clementhorpe Priory 181–82
St Leonard's Hospital 11, 109–10
St Mary's Abbey 152
Yorkshire 158, 160–61, 169